THE STORY OF UTOPIAS

THE STORY OF UTOPIAS

BY

LEWIS MUMFORD

"A Map of the World that does not include Utopia is not worth even glancing at. . . ."

THE VIKING PRESS • NEW YORK

VIKING COMPASS EDITION
with a new introduction by the author
issued in 1962 by The Viking Press, Inc.
625 Madison Avenue, New York, N.Y. 10022

Distributed in Canada by
The Macmillan Company of Canada Limited

SBN 670-00112-0

Library of Congress catalog card number: 62-4429

Printed in the U.S.A. by The Murray Printing Company

Ninth printing April 1974

PREFACE

The word utopia stands in common usage for the ultimate in human folly or human hope—vain dreams of perfection in a Never-Never Land or rational efforts to remake man's environment and his institutions and even his own erring nature, so as to enrich the possibilities of the common life. Sir Thomas More, the coiner of this word, was aware of both implications. Lest anyone else should miss them, he elaborated his paradox in a quatrain which, unfortunately, has sometimes been omitted from English translations of his *Utopia*, the book that at last gave a name to a much earlier series of efforts to picture ideal commonwealths. More was a punster, in an age when the keenest minds delighted to play tricks with language, and when it was not always wise to speak too plainly. In his little verse he explained that utopia might refer either to the Greek "eutopia," which means the good place, or to "outopia," which means no place.

In conceiving *The Story of Utopias*, soon after the First World War, I was still living in the hopeful spirit of an earlier age, and yet was aware, like many other contemporaries, that the impetus of the great nineteenth century, with its fund of buoyant idealism and robust social enterprise, had come to an end. If we were to cope with the new age before us, whose grim outlines had long been visible to sensitive, probing minds, like those of a Jacob Burckhardt or a Henry Adams, we would have to overcome the massive aberrations that had in fact led to the debacle of the First World War. That calamitous miscarriage of human effort had suddenly reversed the currents of our life.

When I started to explore the historic utopias, I was seeking to discover what was missing, and to define what was still possible. Such virtues as this survey may have are not due to exhaustive scholarly investigation or the discovery of forgotten texts. In this respect it does not bear comparison with such a classic production as J. E. Spingarn's *Literary Criticism in the Renaissance,* also the work of a very young man. Whatever merits this *Story of Utopias* boasts, spring from two other sources, which continue to flow through all my work, and were already visible, at least as a promising trickle, in this book. One of them is a foreboding awareness of the problems and pressures of the contemporary world. That quality indeed marks most of the classic utopias from those of Plato down to Theodor Herzl's *Altneuland* or H. G. Wells's *A Modern Utopia.* Almost every utopia is an implicit criticism of the civilization that served as its background; likewise it is an attempt to uncover potentialities that the existing institutions either ignored or buried beneath an ancient crust of custom and habit.

The classic utopian writers, in attempting to extract the ideal element from the matrix of contemporary society, often by that very effort to achieve a purer form of community left out many necessary components which, like the baser elements in an alloy, fortify the precious metal and make it more serviceable. The workings of the natural environment and human history provide even the poorest community with a rich compost, far more favorable to life than the most rational ideal schemes would be if they lacked such a soil to grow in. But the utopian belief that life presents many latent, unused potentialities that could be cultivated and brought to perfection nevertheless seemed to me as a young man a salutary one; and I still retain this belief in the continued possibility of man's self-transformation and self-transcendence. In this I share fully the sense of my older contemporary, A. N. Whitehead, and my still older master, Emerson, that the human adventure has only begun—that was my second qualification.

The revolutionaries of the eighteenth century and their later followers often, it is true, exaggerated the malleability of society; and what is worse, they imagined that merely by discarding the past they had a key to a better future, wholly rational in design, and therefore, according to their lights, ideal. For them, following Locke, human society was a product of the human mind, and might be treated as a blank sheet of paper, on which each generation could, by erasing the past, leave its own ideal imprint. Thus they erred in overestimating both the quantity and the value of the creative mutations that occur in every generation; and they underestimated the importance of the "remnants" and "persistents" that have been deposited by every previous generation and that add unimaginably to the richness of human life, and indeed, like language itself, are essential to human survival. Even as a young man, I did not make that mistake.

Though I was looking for fresh ideals in this survey of utopias, as more than one reader had done before me,

I found them in an unexpected place; and I quickly discovered that far too large a number of classic utopias were based upon conceptions of authoritarian discipline that seemed to me, as a countryman of Emerson, Thoreau, and Whitman, far from ideal. Perhaps "quickly" is too generous a word; for I was still so deeply under the spell of Plato that I tended to gloze over the fact that he had set a bad precedent for all later utopian writers in this respect. Bertrand Russell, on an early visit to Soviet Russia, was to liken the communist system, not unfairly with respect to its more repressive aspects, to that one finds in *The Republic*, and the later developments of fascism made it easy for others, like R. H. Crossman, to see even more clearly that Plato, for all his genius, might be described as a proto-fascist, believing in the rulership of an élite, in autarchy, in using lies to facilitate government, in valuing military regimentation, and in many other unpleasant, indeed horrifying, respects.

But once beyond Plato, I was aware of the dictatorial tendencies of most classic utopias. They sought to impose a monolithic discipline upon all the varied activities and interplaying interests of human society, by creating an order too inflexible, and a system of government too centralized and absolute, to permit any change that would disturb the pattern or meet the new exigencies of life. In other words, each utopia was a closed society for the prevention of human growth: and the more the institutions of utopia succeeded in stamping the minds of its members, the less possibility existed of furthering creative and purposeful change. This static aspect of utopias went along with a static conception of life itself. As with the old Greek innkeeper

Procrustes, the utopians either stretched the human organism to the arbitrary dimensions of the utopian bed, or they lopped off its limbs. Even an essentially humane writer like Edward Bellamy came forth with such a grim mechanical ideal, and some of the worst features of the communist system in our time have the sanction of various supposedly beneficent passages in descriptions of ideal commonwealths. Though Marx and Engels mocked at utopian socialism, their followers, for lack of any better precedent, smuggled many utopian social inventions through the back door.

These rigid virtues, these frozen institutions, these static and self-limiting ideals did not attract me; and if that had been all I found in the utopian method of thought I might have dropped my investigation before I was half through with it. But from the beginning I was aware of another virtue that had been singularly overlooked: the classic utopian works had all treated society as a whole, and had, in imagination at least, done justice to the interaction of work, people, and place, and to the interrelationship of functions and institutions and human purposes. Our own society—indeed this ranks as the characteristic vice of all "higher" civilizations—had divided life into compartments: economics, politics, religion, war, education; and within these larger divisions efforts at reform and improvement, or at invention and creativity, went on in even smaller compartments, with all too little reference to the whole in which they played a part.

Utopian thinking, as I came to regard it, then, was the opposite of one-sidedness, partisanship, partiality, provinciality, specialism. He who practiced the utopian method must view life synoptically and see it as an interrelated whole: not as a random mixture, but as an organic and increasingly organizable union of parts, whose balance it was important to maintain—as in any living organism—in order to promote growth and transcendence.

Thanks to the example set by my earliest master, Patrick Geddes, this belief in balance and wholeness was already deeply implanted in me when I wrote the present book. I had renounced the rewards, if not the toil, of the specialist, and had consciously embarked on my career as a "generalist," one who was more interested in putting the fragments together in an ordered and significant pattern than in minutely investigating the separate parts—though from time to time I have done my small share in the specialist's kind of spadework.

In fine, though this book takes seriously the literature of utopias, it turns out in the end to be an anti-utopian tract: for in appreciating the positive contributions of utopian thought, which I will define in a moment, it also was one of the first to bring out, in a more understanding spirit than Macaulay's, the essential weakness of this tradition. More than once people have suggested to me that I should present my own utopia; and by that fact they betray that they do not in the least understand the nature of my work. One of the titles of a chapter in my book *Faith for Living* is: "Life is Better than Utopia," and that of another chapter in a later book is: "Regression to Utopia." Both these brief statements imply, if they do not fully express, my deepest convictions.

I have accordingly no private utopia: if I had one, it would have to include the private utopias of many other men, and the realized ideals of many other societies; for life has still too many potentialities to be encompassed by the projects of a single generation, by the hopes and beliefs of a single thinker. Unlike most utopian writers, I must find a place in any scheme for challenge and opposition and conflict, for evil and corruption, since they are visible in the natural history of all societies; and if I emphasize the sanifying virtues and point to more transcendental goals, it is because the negative moments of life take care of themselves, and need no encouragement. One does not have to plan chaos and dissolution, for this is what happens when the spirit ceases to be in command. My utopia is actual life, here or anywhere, pushed to the limits of its ideal possibilities. So to me the past is as much the source of utopias as the future; and the vivid interplay between all these aspects of existence, including many events that cannot be wholly formulated or grasped, constitutes for me a reality surpassing anything one can imagine or depict by the exercise of pure intelligence alone.

Two main positive ideas came from my survey of utopias and have been supported by further study and reflection. These ideas were a confirmation of the intuitions that had led me in the first place to undertake a systematic survey. One was the idea that every community possesses, in addition to its going institutions, a reservoir of potentialities, partly rooted in its past, still alive though hidden, and partly budding forth from new crossings and mutations, which open the way to further development. This points to the pragmatic function of ideals: for no society is fully awake either to its inherent nature or to its natural prospects, if it ignores the fact that there are many alternatives to the path it is actually following, and many conceivable and possible goals besides those which are immediately visible. The other positive idea derived from utopias is that of wholeness and balance, which biological science has demonstrated are essential attributes of all organisms. These attributes become conscious imperatives for man, precisely because his own balance, both in his personal and his communal life, is such a delicate one; and because his own wholeness has often been lamed, and his performance curtailed, by a perverse overemphasis upon some supposedly all-important ideology, institution, or mechanism.

Both these perceptions were salutary ones to counterbalance the preoccupations of our lopsided civilization; for this civilization, even whilst I was growing up, had passed from the Age of Confidence to the Age of Violence; and they have thus become even more vital to our well-being today, in this even more sinister age of nuclear, bacterial, and chemical mass-extermination.

The most simpleminded utopia that has yet been written still possesses notable human qualities that are entirely lacking in the plans of the scientific "supermen" and moral imbeciles who have devised the current Russo-American military strategy of total extermination. Utopian idealists who have overestimated the power of the ideal are plainly much more fully in possession of their senses and more closely linked to human realities than the scientific and military "realists" who have turned the use of absolute weapons into a compulsive ideal. These under-dimensioned minds are ready to mutilate or annihilate the human race rather than to abandon the arbitrary and irrational premises upon which their corrupt—and now bankrupt—strategy has been based. The leaders of science, technology, and military affairs who have most despised the function of ideals have actually turned the expansion of their equipment for destruction and extermination into an ultimate ideal. This is utopianism with a vengeance: the nihilistic perfection of nothingness.

Thus the original intuitions that underlay *The Story of Utopias* have been mainly confirmed, rather than undermined, by the experience of the past forty years. The need for understanding the multifold potentialities of life, for achieving balance and wholeness in every aspect of our existence, for pursuing perfection in other spheres besides technics, was never greater than today; and to the extent that *The Story of Utopias* helps support this need it may still serve a useful purpose.

Considered only as a personal document, *The Story of Utopias* foreshadows, I have no doubt, much of my later work: so much so that I slipped most of the section on the Country House into *The Condition of Man*, more than twenty years later, without anyone's noting either the borrowing or the continuity. From a literary standpoint, the book was a *tour de force*, but from a scholarly point of view, almost an affront to decency. At a distance of forty years, both facts leave me shocked and breathless, though not, I fear, sufficiently ashamed. For I conceived this book in February 1922, did the necessary reading for it by the end of March, and turned the final draft over to the publisher in June, in time to read the proofs before I sailed for Europe toward the end of July. By current standards even the publishing schedule is startling, not to say fantastic. Such untoward speed accounts for the incompleteness and superficiality of this survey; likewise for its happy brevity. If I sought to repair these weaknesses now I should have to write a new book. But this possibility does not tempt me; for it would remove the very quality that perhaps makes *The Story of Utopias* worth republishing today: the spirit of youthful audacity in which it was written.

In our terrified and discouraged age that spirit may serve as a tonic, to remind the reader of human attitudes and human hopes that once existed and flourished, and may burgeon again, since they are rooted, not merely in the sentiments of a particular generation, but in the defiant animal faith that each new baby brings back into the world with the very act of birth. With a little of this faith and audacity we may still disarm the castrated intelligences that now plan to cover up their political folly and impotence by sacrificing all life to their lunatic rituals and their Nuclear Gods. In that triumph, if it comes to pass, we will not seek for utopia on a distant historic horizon in future, still less on the moon or on a remote planet. We shall find it in our own souls, and in the earth beneath our feet, still ready to nourish the forces of life and love, and to renew in man himself the sense of his more-than-human potentialities.

LEWIS MUMFORD

New York, 1922
Amenia, 1962

THE STORY OF UTOPIAS

CHAPTER ONE

How the will-to-utopia causes men to live in two worlds, and how, therefore, we re-read the Story of Utopias—the other half of the Story of Mankind.

1

Utopia has long been another name for the unreal and the impossible. We have set utopia over against the world. As a matter of fact, it is our utopias that make the world tolerable to us: the cities and mansions that people dream of are those in which they finally live. The more that men react upon their environment and make it over after a human pattern, the more continuously do they live in utopia; but when there is a breach between the world of affairs and the overworld of utopia, we become conscious of the part that the will-to-utopia has played in our lives, and we see our utopia as a separate reality.

It is the separate reality of utopia that we are going to explore in the course of this book—Utopia as a world by itself, divided into ideal commonwealths, with all its communities clustered into proud cities, aiming bravely at the good life.

This discussion of ideal commonwealths gets its form and its color from the time in which it is written. Plato's Republic dates from the period of social disintegration which followed the Peloponnesian War; and some of its mordant courage is probably derived from the hopelessness of conditions that came under

Plato's eye. It was in the midst of a similar period of disorder and violence that Sir Thomas More laid the foundations for his imaginary commonwealth: Utopia was the bridge by which he sought to span the gap between the old order of the Middle Age, and the new interests and institutions of the Renascence.

In presenting this history and criticism of utopias we are perhaps being pulled by the same interests that led Plato and More onwards, for it is only after the storm that we dare to look for the rainbow. Our fall into a chasm of disillusion has stimulated us to discuss in a more thorough way the ultimate goods, the basic aims, the whole conception of the "good life" by which, in modern times, we have been guided. In the midst of the tepid and half-hearted discussions that continue to arise out of prohibition laws and strikes and "peace" conferences let us break in with the injunction to talk about fundamentals—consider Utopia!

2

Man walks with his feet on the ground and his head in the air; and the history of what has happened on earth—the history of cities and armies and of all the things that have had body and form—is only one-half the Story of Mankind.

In every age, the external scenery in which the human drama has been framed has remained pretty much the same. There have been fluctuations in climate and changes in terrain; and at times a great civilization, like that of the Mayas in Central America, has arisen where now only a thick net of jungle remains; but the hills around Jerusalem are the hills that David saw;

and during the historic period the drowning of a city in the Netherlands or the rise of a shifting bank of real estate along the coast of New Jersey is little more than the wearing off of the paint or a crack in the plaster. What we call the material world constantly changes, it goes without saying: mountains are stript of trees and become wastes, deserts are plowed with water and become gardens. The main outlines, however, hold their own remarkably well; and we could have travelled better in Roman days with a modern map than with the best chart Ptolemy could have offered us.

If the world in which men live were the world as it is known to the physical geographer, we should have a pretty simple time of it. We might follow Whitman's advice, and live as the animals, and stop whining for all time about our sins and imperfections.

What makes human history such an uncertain and fascinating story is that man lives in two worlds—the world within and the world without—and the world within men's heads has undergone transformations which have disintegrated material things with the power and rapidity of radium. I shall take the liberty of calling this inner world our idolum (ido'lum) or world of ideas. The word "ideas" is not used here precisely in the ordinary sense. I use it rather to stand for what the philosophers would call the subjective world, what the theologians would perhaps call the spiritual world; and I mean to include in it all the philosophies, fantasies, rationalizations, projections, images, and opinions in terms of which people pattern their behavior. This world of ideas, in the case of scientific truths, for example, sometimes has a rough correspondence with what people call the world; but it is important to note that it has contours of its own which are quite independent of the material environment.

Now the physical world is a definite, inescapable thing. Its limits are narrow and obvious. On occasion, if your impulse is sufficiently strong, you can leave the land for the sea, or go from a warm climate into a cool one; but you cannot cut yourself off from the physical environment without terminating your life. For good or ill, you must breathe air, eat food, drink water; and the penalties for refusing to meet these conditions are inexorable. Only a lunatic would refuse to recognize this physical environment; it is the substratum of our daily lives.

But if the physical environment is the earth, the world of ideas corresponds to the heavens. We sleep under the light of stars that have long since ceased to exist, and we pattern our behavior by ideas which have no reality as soon as we cease to credit them. Whilst it holds together this world of ideas—this idolum—is almost as sound, almost as real, almost as inescapable as the bricks of our houses or the asphalt beneath our feet. The "belief" that the world was flat was once upon a time more important than the "fact" that it was round; and that belief kept the sailors of the medieval world from wandering out of sight of land as effectively as would a string of gunboats or floating mines. An idea is a solid fact, a theory is a solid fact, a superstition is a solid fact as long as people continue to regulate their actions in terms of the idea, theory, or superstition; and it is none the less solid because it is conveyed as an image or a breath of sound.

3

This world of ideas serves many purposes. Two of them bear heavily upon our investigation of utopia. On one hand the pseudo-environment or idolum is a substitute for the external world; it is a sort of house of refuge to which we flee when our contacts with "hard facts" become too complicated to carry through or too rough to face. On the other hand, it is by means of the idolum that the facts of the everyday world are brought together and assorted and sifted, and a new sort of reality is projected back again upon the external world. One of these functions is escape or compensation; it seeks an immediate release from the difficulties or frustrations of our lot. The other attempts to provide a condition for our release in the future. The utopias that correspond to these two functions I shall call the utopias of escape and the utopias of reconstruction. The first leaves the external world the way it is; the second seeks to change it so that one may have intercourse with it on one's own terms. In one we build impossible castles in the air; in the other we consult a surveyor and an architect and a mason and proceed to build a house which meets our essential needs; as well as houses made of stone and mortar are capable of meeting them.

4

Why, however, should we find it necessary to talk about utopia and the world of ideas at all? Why should we not rest secure in the bosom of the material environment, without flying off into a region apparently beyond space and time? Well, the alternative before us is not whether we shall live in the real world or dream away our time in utopia; for men are so constituted that only by a deliberate discipline—such as that followed by a Hindu ascetic or an American business man—can one or the other world be abolished from consciousness. The genuine alternative for most of us is that between an aimless utopia of escape and a purposive utopia of reconstruction. One way or the other, it seems, in a world so full of frustrations as the "real" one, we must spend a good part of our mental lives in utopia.

Nevertheless this needs a qualification. It is plain that certain types of people have no need for private utopias and that certain communities seem to be without them. The savages of the Marquesas whom Hermann Melville described seem to have had such a jolly and complete adjustment to their environment that, except for the raids of hostile tribes—and this turned out to be chiefly sport which only whetted their appetites for the feast that followed—everything needed for a good life at the South Sea level could be obtained by direct attack. The Marquesans had no need to dream of a happier existence; they had only to grab it.

At times, during childhood perhaps, life has the same sort of completeness; and without doubt there are many mature people who have manufactured out of their limitations a pretty adequate response to a narrow environment; and have let it go at that. Such people feel no need for utopia. As long as they can keep their contacts restricted, only a deliberate raid from the outside world would create such a need. They are like the sick man in the parable of the Persian poet, whose only desire was that he might desire something;

and there is no particular reason to envy them. People who will not venture out into the open sea pay the penalty of never having looked into the bright eyes of danger; and at best they know but half of life. What such folk might call the good life is simply not good enough. We cannot be satisfied with a segment of existence, no matter how safely we may be adjusted to it, when with a little effort we can trace the complete circle.

But there have been few regions, few social orders, and few people in which the adjustment has not been incomplete. In the face of perpetual difficulties and obstructions—the wind and the weather and the impulses of other men and customs that have long outlived their use—there are three ways, roughly, in which a man may react. He may run away. He may try to hold his own. He may attack. Looking around at our contemporaries who have survived the war, it is fairly evident that most of them are in the first stage of panic and despair. In an interesting article on The Dénouement of Nihilism, Mr. Edward Townsend Booth characterized the generation born in the late eighties as suffering a complete paralysis of will, or else, "if any initiative remains to them, they emigrate to Europe or the South Sea Islands, or crawl off into some quiet corner of the United States—but most of them continue where they were stricken in a state of living death."

Speaking more generally, running away does not always mean a physical escape, nor does an "attack" necessarily mean doing something practical "on the spot." Let us use Dr. John Dewey's illustration and suppose that a man is denied intercourse with his friends at a distance. One kind of reaction is for him to "imagine" meeting his friends, and going through, in fantasy, a whole ritual of meeting, repartee, and discussion. The other kind of reaction, as Dr. Dewey says, is to see what conditions must be met in order to cement distant friends, and then invent the telephone. The so-called extrovert, the type of man who has no need for utopias, will satisfy his desire by talking to the nearest human being. ("He may try to hold his own.") But it is fairly plain that the extrovert, from the very weakness and inconstancy of his aims, is incapable of contributing anything but "good nature" to the good life of the community; and in his hands both art and invention would probably come to an end.

Now putting aside the extrovert, we find that the two remaining types of reaction have expressed themselves in all the historic utopias. It is perhaps well that we should see them first in their normal, everyday setting, before we set out to explore the ideal commonwealths of the past.

More or less, we have all had glimpses of the utopia of escape: it is raised and it collapses and it is built up again almost daily. In the midst of the clanking machinery of a paper factory I have come across a moving picture actress's portrait, stuck upon an inoperative part of the machine; and it was not hard to reconstruct the private utopia of the wretch who minded the levers, or to picture the world into which he had fled from the roar and throb and muck of the machinery about him. What man has not had this utopia from the dawn of adolescence onwards—the desire to possess and be possessed by a beautiful woman?

Perhaps for the great majority of men and women that small, private Utopia is the only one for which they feel a perpetual, warm interest; and ultimately every other utopia must be translatable to them in some such intimate terms. Their conduct would tell us as much if their words did not confess it. They leave their bleak office buildings and their grimy factories, and night after night they pour into the cinema theater in order that they may live for a while in a land populated by beautiful, flirtatious women and tender, lusty men. Small wonder that the great and powerful religion founded by Mahomet puts that utopia in the very foreground of the hereafter! In a sense, this is the most elementary of utopias; for, on the interpretation of the analytical psychologist, it carries with it the deep longing to return to and remain at rest in the mother's womb—the one perfect environment which all the machinery and legislation of an eager world has never been able to reproduce.

In its most elemental state, this utopia of escape calls for a complete breach with the butcher, the baker, the grocer, and the real, limited, imperfect people that flutter around us. In order to make it more perfect, we eliminate the butcher and baker and transport ourselves to a self-sufficient island in the South Seas. For the most part, of course, this is an idle dream, and if we do not grow out of it, we must at any rate thrust other conditions into it; but for a good many of us, idleness without a dream is the only alternative. Out of such fantasies of bliss and perfection, which do not endure in real life even when they occasionally bloom into existence, our art and literature have very largely grown. It is hard to conceive of a social order so complete and satisfactory that it would rob us of the necessity of having recourse, from time to time, to an imaginary world in which our sufferings could be purged or our delights heightened. Even in the great idyll painted by William Morris, women are fickle and lovers are disappointed; and when the "real" world becomes a little too hard and too sullen to face, we must take refuge, if we are to recover our balance, into another world which responds more perfectly to our deeper interests and desires—the world of literature.

Once we have weathered the storm, it is dangerous to remain in the utopia of escape; for it is an enchanted island, and to remain there is to lose one's capacity for dealing with things as they are. The girl who has felt Prince Charming's caresses too long will be repulsed by the clumsy embraces of the young man who takes her to the theater and wonders how the deuce he is going to pay the rent if they spend more than a week on their honeymoon. Moreover, life is too easy in the utopia of escape, and too blankly perfect—there is nothing to sharpen your teeth upon. It is not for this that men have gone into the jungle to hunt beasts and have cajoled the grasses and roots to be prolific, and have defied, in little open boats, the terror of the wind and sea. Our daily diet must have more roughage in it than these daydreams will give us if we are not to become debilitated.

In the course of our journey into utopia we shall remain a little while in these utopias of escape; but we shall not bide there long. There are plenty of them, and they dot the waters of our imaginary world as the islands that Ulysses visited dotted the Ægean Sea. These utopias however belong to the department of pure literature, and in that department they occupy but a minor place. We could dispense with the whole lot of them, bag and baggage, in exchange for another Anna Karenin or The Brothers Karamazov.

5

The second kind of utopia which we shall encounter is the utopia of reconstruction.

The first species represents, the analytical psychologist would tell us, a very primitive kind of thinking, in which we follow the direction of our desires without taking into account any of the limiting conditions which we should have to confront if we came back to earth and tried to realize our wishes in practical affairs. It is a vague and messy and logically inconsequent series of images which color up and fade, which excite us and leave us cold, and which—for the sake of the respect our neighbors have for our ability to add a ledger or plane a piece of wood—we had better confine to the strange box of records we call our brain.

The second type of utopia may likewise be colored by primitive desires and wishes; but these desires and wishes have come to reckon with the world in which they seek realization. The utopia of reconstruction is what its name implies: a vision of a reconstituted environment which is better adapted to the nature and aims of the human beings who dwell within it than the actual one; and not merely better adapted to their actual nature, but better fitted to their possible developments. If the first utopia leads backward into the utopian's ego, the second leads outward—outward into the world.

By a reconstructed environment I do not mean merely a physical thing. I mean, in addition, a new set of habits, a fresh scale of values, a different net of relationships and institutions, and possibly—for almost all utopias emphasize the factor of breeding—an alteration of the physical and mental characteristics of the people chosen, through education, biological selection, and so forth. The reconstructed environment which all the genuine utopians seek to contrive is a reconstruction of both the physical world and the idolum. It is in this that the utopian distinguishes himself from the practical inventor and the industrialist. Every attempt that has been made to domesticate animals, cultivate plants, dredge rivers, dig ditches, and in modern times, apply the energy of the sun to mechanical instruments, has been an effort to reconstruct the environment; and in many cases the human advantage has been plain. It is not for the utopian to despise Prometheus who brought the fire or Franklin who captured the lightning. As Anatole France says: "Without the Utopians of other times, men would still live in caves, miserable and naked. It was Utopians who traced the lines of the first city. . . . Out of generous dreams come beneficial realities. Utopia is the principle of all progress, and the essay into a better future."

Our physical reconstructions however have been limited; they have touched chiefly the surfaces of things. The result is that people live in a modern physical environment and carry in their minds an odd assortment of spiritual relics from almost every other age, from that of the primitive, taboo-ridden savage, to the energetic Victorian disciples of Gradgrind and Bounderby. As Mr. Hendrik van Loon pithily says: "A human being with the mind of a sixteenth century tradesman driving a 1921 Rolls-Royce is still a human being with the mind of a sixteenth century tradesman." The problem is fundamentally a human problem. The more completely man is in control of physical nature, the more urgently we must ask ourselves what under the heavens is to move and guide and keep in hand the controller. This problem of an ideal, a goal, an end—even if the aim persist in shifting as much as the magnetic north pole—is a fundamental one to the utopian.

Except in the writings of the utopians, and this is an important point to notice in our travels through utopia, the reconstruction of the material environment and the reconstitution of the mental framework of the creatures who inhabit it, have been kept in two different compartments. One compartment is supposed to belong to the practical man; the other to the idealist. The first was something whose aims could be realized in the Here and Now; the other was postponed very largely to the sweet by-and-bye. Neither the practical man nor the idealist has been willing to admit that he has been dealing with a single problem; that each has been treating the faces of a single thing as if they were separate.

Here is where the utopia of reconstruction wins hands down. It not merely pictures a whole world, but it faces every part of it at the same time. We shall not examine the classic utopias without becoming conscious of their weaknesses, their sometimes disturbing idiosyncrasies. It is important at present that we should realize their virtues; and should start on our journey without the feeling of disparagement which the word utopian usually calls up in minds that have been seduced by Macaulay's sneer that he would rather have an acre in Middlesex than a principality in utopia.

6

Finally, be convinced about the reality of utopia. All that has happened in what we call human history—unless it has left a building or a book or some other record of itself—is just as remote and in a sense just as mythical as the mysterious island which Raphael Hythloday, scholar and sailor, described to Sir Thomas More. A good part of human history is even more insubstantial: the Icarians who lived only in the mind of Étienne Cabet, or the Freelanders who dwelt within the imagination of a dry little Austrian economist, have had more influence upon the lives of our contemporaries than the Etruscan people who once dwelt in Italy, although the Etruscans belong to what we call the real world, and the Freelanders and Icarians inhabited—Nowhere.

Nowhere may be an imaginary country, but News from Nowhere is real news. The world of ideas, beliefs, fantasies, projections, is (I must emphasize again) just as real whilst it is acted upon as the post which Dr. Johnson kicked in order to demonstrate that it was solid. The man who wholly respects the rights of property is kept out of his neighbor's field perhaps even more effectively than the man who is merely forbidden entrance by a no-trespass sign. In sum, we cannot ignore our utopias. They exist in the same way that north and south exist; if we are not familiar with their classical statements we at least know them as they spring to life each day in our own minds. We can never reach the points of the compass; and so no doubt we shall never live in utopia; but without the magnetic needle we should not be able to travel intelligently at all. It is absurd to dispose of utopia by saying that it exists only on paper. The answer to this is: precisely the same thing may be said of the architect's plans for a house, and houses are none the worse for it.

We must lose our sense of remoteness and severity in setting out on this exploration of ideal commonwealths, as some of the fine minds of the past have pictured them. Our ideals are not something that we can set apart from the main facts of our existence, as our grandmothers sometimes set the cold, bleak, and usually moldy parlor apart from the living rooms of the house: on the contrary, the things we dream of tend consciously or unconsciously to work themselves out in the pattern of our daily lives. Our utopias are just as human and warm and jolly as the world out of which they are born. Looking out from the top of a high tenement, over the housetops of Manhattan, I can see a pale tower with its golden pinnacle gleaming through the soft morning haze; and for a moment all the harsh and ugly lines in the landscape have disappeared. So in looking at our utopias. We need not abandon the real world in order to enter these realizable worlds; for it is out of the first that the second are always coming.

Finally, an anticipation and a warning. In our journey through the utopias of the past we shall not rest content when we have traversed the whole territory between Plato and the latest modern writer. If the story of utopia throws any light upon the story of mankind it is this: our utopias have been pitifully weak and inadequate; and if they have not exercised enough practical influence upon the course of affairs, it is because, as Viola Paget says in Gospels of Anarchy, they were simply not good enough. We travel through utopia only in order to get beyond utopia: if we leave the domains of history when we enter the gates of Plato's Republic, we do so in order to re-enter more effectively the dusty midday traffic of the contemporary world. So our study of the classic utopias will be followed by an examination of certain social myths and partial utopias that have played an important part in the affairs of the Western World during the last few centuries. In the end, I promise, I shall make no attempt to present another utopia; it will be enough to survey the foundations upon which others may build.

In the meanwhile, our ship is about to set sail; and we shall not heave anchor again until we reach the coasts of Utopia.

CHAPTER TWO

How the Greeks lived in a New World, and utopia seemed just round the corner. How Plato, in the Republic, is chiefly concerned with what will hold the ideal city together.

CHAPTER TWO

1

BEFORE the great empires of Rome and Macedonia began to spread their camps through the length and breadth of the Mediterranean world, there was a time when the vision of an ideal city seems to have been uppermost in the minds of a good many men. Just as the wide expanse of unsettled territory in America caused the people of eighteenth century Europe to think of building a civilization in which the errors and vices and superstitions of the old world might be left behind, so the sparsely settled coasts of Italy, Sicily, and the Ægean Islands, and the shores of the Black Sea, must have given men the hope of being able to turn over a fresh page.

Those years between six hundred and three hundred B. C. were city-building years for the parent cities of Greece. The city of Miletus is supposed to have begotten some three hundred cities, and many of its fellows were possibly not less fruitful. Since new cities could be founded there was plenty of chance for variation and experiment; and those who dreamed of a more, generous social order could set their hands and wits to making a better start "from the bottom up."

Of all the plans and reconstruction programs that must have been put forward during these centuries, only a scant handful remains. Aristotle tells us about an ideal state designed by one, Phaleas, who believed like Mr. Bernard Shaw in a complete equality of property; and from Aristotle, too, we learn of another utopia which was described by the great architect, city planner, and sociologist—Hippodamus. Hippodamus was one of the first city planners known to history, and he achieved fame in the ancient world by designing cities on the somewhat monotonous checkerboard design we know so well in America. He realized, apparently, that a city was something more than a collection of houses, streets, markets, and temples; and so, whilst he was putting the physical town to rights, he concerned himself with the more basic problem of the social order. If it adds at all to our sense of reality in going through utopia, let me confess that it is ultimately through the inspiration and example of another Hippodamus—Patrick Geddes, the town planner for Jerusalem and many other cities—that this book about utopias came to be written. In many ways the distance between Geddes and Aristotle or Hippodamus seems much less than that which separates Geddes and Herbert Spencer.

When we look at the utopias that Phaleas and Hippodamus and Aristotle have left us, and compare them with the Republic of Plato, the differences between them melt into insignificance and their likenesses are apparent. It is for this reason that I shall confine our examination of the Greek utopia to that which Plato set forth in the Republic, and qualified and broadened in The Laws, The Statesman, and Critias.

2

Plato's Republic dates roughly from the time of that long and disastrous war which Athens fought with

Sparta. In the course of such a war, amid the bombast that patriotic citizens give way to, the people who keep their senses are bound to get pretty well acquainted with their enemy. If you will take the trouble to examine Plutarch's account of the Laws of Lycurgus and Mr. Alfred Zimmern's magnificent description of the Greek Commonwealth you will see how Sparta and Athens form the web and woof of the Republic—only it is an ideal Sparta and an ideal Athens that Plato has in mind.

It is well to remember that Plato wrote in the midst of defeat; a great part of his region, Attica, had been devastated and burned; and he must have felt that makeshift and reform were quite futile when a Peloponnesian war could make the bottom drop out of his world. To Plato an ill-designed ship of state required more than the science of navigation to pull it through stormy waters: if it was in danger of perpetually foundering, it seemed high time to go back to the shipyards and inquire into the principles upon which it had been put together. In such a mood, I suggest parenthetically, we today will turn again to fundamentals.

3

In describing his ideal community Plato, like a trained workman, begins with his physical foundations. So far from putting his utopia in a mythical island of Avilion, where falls not hail nor rain nor any snow, it is plain that Plato was referring repeatedly to the soil in which Athens was planted, and to the economic life which grew out of that soil. Since he was speaking to his own countrymen, he could let a good many things pass for common knowledge which we, as strangers, must look into more carefully in order to have a firmer sense of his utopian realities. Let it be understood that in discussing the physical side of the Republic, I am drawing from Aristotle as well as Plato, and from such modern Greek scholars as Messrs. Zimmern, Myres, and Murray.

Nowadays when we talk about a state we think of an expanse of territory, to begin with, so broad that we should in most cases be unable to see all its boundaries if we rose five miles above the ground on a clear day. Even if the country is a little one, like the Netherlands or Belgium, it is likely to have possessions that are thousands of miles away; and we think of these distant possessions and of the homeland as part and parcel of the state. There is scarcely any conceivable way in which a Dutchman in Rotterdam, let us say, possesses the Island of Java: he does not live on the island, he is not acquainted with the inhabitants, he does not share their ideas or customs. His interest in Java, if he have an interest at all, is an interest in sugar, coffee, taxes, or missions. His state is not a commonwealth in the sense that it is a common possession.

To the Greek of Plato's time, on the contrary, the commonwealth was something he actively shared with his fellow citizens. It was a definite parcel of land whose limits he could probably see from any convenient hilltop; and those who lived within those limits had common gods to worship, common theaters and gymnasia, and a multitude of common interests that could be satisfied only by their working together, playing together, thinking together. Plato could probably not have conceived of a community with civilized pretensions in which the population was distributed at the rate of ten per square mile; and if he visited such a territory he would surely have said that the people were barbarians—men whose way of living unfitted them for the graces and duties of citizenship.

Geographically speaking, then, the ideal commonwealth was a city-region; that is, a city which was surrounded by enough land to supply the greater part of the food needed by the inhabitants; and placed convenient to the sea.

Let us stand on a high hill and take a look at this city region; the sort of view that Plato himself might have obtained on some clear spring morning when he climbed to the top of the Acropolis and looked down on the sleeping city, with the green fields and sear upland pastures on one side, and the sun glinting on the distant waters of the sea a few miles away.

It is a mountainous region, this Greece, and within a short distance from mountain top to sea there was compressed as many different kinds of agricultural and industrial life as one could single out in going down the Hudson valley from the Adirondack Mountains to New York Harbor. As the basis for his ideal city, whether Plato knew it or not, he had an "ideal" section of land in his mind—what the geographer calls the "valley section." He could not have gotten the various groups which were to be combined in his city, had they been settled in the beginning on a section of land like the coastal plain of New Jersey. It was peculiarly in Greece that such a variety of occupations could come together within a small area, beginning at the summit of the valley section with the evergreen trees and the woodcutter, going down the slope to the herdsman and his flock of goats at pasture, along the valley bottom to the cultivator and his crops, until at length one reaches the river's mouth where the fisher pushes out to sea in his boat and the trader comes in with goods from other lands.

The great civilizations of the world have been nourished in such valley sections. We think of the river Nile and Alexandria; the Tiber and Rome, the Seine and Paris; and so on. It is interesting that our first great utopia should have had an "ideal" section of territory as its base.

4

In the economic foundations of the Republic, we look in vain for a recognition of the labor problem. Now the labor problem is a fundamental difficulty in our modern life; and it seems on the surface that Plato is a little highbrow and remote in the ease with which he gets over it. When we look more closely into the matter, however, and see the way in which men got their living in the "morning lands"—as the Germans call them—we shall find that the reason Plato does not offer a solution is that he was not, indeed, confronted by a problem.

Given a valley section which has not been ruthlessly stript of trees; given the arts of agriculture and herding; given a climate without dangerous extremes of heat and cold; given the opportunity to found new colonies when the old city-region is over-populated—and it is only by an exercise of ingenuity that a labor problem could be invented. A man might become a slave by military capture; he did not become a slave by being compelled, under threat of starvation, to tend a machine. The problem of getting a living was answered by nature as long as men were willing to put up with nature's conditions; and the groundwork of Plato's utopia, accordingly, is the simple agricultural life, the growing of wheat, barley, olives, and grapes, which had been fairly well mastered before he arrived on the scene. As long as the soil was not washed away and devitalized, the problem was not a hard one; and in order to solve it, Plato had only to provide that there should be enough territory to grow food on, and that the inhabitants must not let their wants exceed the bounties of nature.

Plato describes the foundations of his community with a few simple and masterly touches. Those who feel that there is something a little inhuman in his conception of the good life, when he is discussing the education and duties of the ruling classes, may well consider the picture that he paints for us here.

Plato's society arises out of the needs of mankind; because none of us is self-sufficing and all have many wants; and since there are many wants, many kinds of people must supply them. When all these helpers and partners and co-operators are gathered together in a city the body of inhabitants is termed a state; and so its members work and exchange goods with one another for their mutual advantage—the herdsman gets barley for his cheese and so on down to the complicated interchanges that occur in the city. What sort of physical life will arise out of this in the region that Plato describes?

Well, the people will "produce corn and wine and clothes and shoes and build houses for themselves. . . . They will work in summer commonly stript and barefoot, but in winter substantially clothed and shod. They will feed on barley and wheat, baking the wheat and kneading the flour, making noble puddings and loaves; these they will serve up on a mat of reeds or clean leaves; themselves reclining the while upon beds of yew or myrtle boughs. And they and their children will feast, drinking of the wine which they have made, wearing garlands on their heads, and having the praises of the gods on their lips, living in sweet society, and having a care that their families do not exceed their means; for they will have an eye to poverty or war."

So Socrates, in this dialogue on the Republic, describes to his hearers the essential physical elements of the good life. One of his hearers, Glaucon, asks him to elaborate it a little, for Socrates has limited himself to bare essentials. It is the same sort of objection, by the way, that M. Poincaré, the physicist, made to the philosophy of Tolstoy. Socrates answers that a good state would have the healthy constitution which he has just described; but that he has no objection to looking at an "inflamed constitution." What Socrates describes as an inflamed constitution is a mode of life which all the people of Western Europe and America at the present day—no matter what their religion, economic status, or political creed may be—believe in with almost a single mind; and so, although it is the opposite of Plato's ideal state, I go on to present it, for the light it throws on our own institutions and habits.

The unjust state comes into existence, says Plato through the mouth of Socrates, by the multiplication of wants and superfluities. As a result of increasing wants, we must enlarge our borders, for the original healthy state is too small. Now the city will fill up with a multitude of callings which go beyond those required by any natural want; there will be a host of parasites and "supers"; and our country, which was big enough to support the original inhabitants, will want a slice of our neighbor's land for pasture and tillage; and they will want a slice of ours if, like ourselves, they exceed the limits of necessity and give themselves up to the unlimited accumulation of wealth. "And then we shall go to war—that will be the next thing."

The sum of this criticism is that Plato saw clearly that an ideal community must have a common physical standard of living; and that boundless wealth or unlimited desires and gratifications had nothing to do with a good standard. The good was what was necessary; and what was necessary was not, essentially, many goods.

Like Aristotle, Plato wanted a mode of life which was neither impoverished nor luxurious: those who have read a little in Greek history will see that this Athenian ideal of the good life fell rather symbolically between Sparta and Corinth, between the cities which we associate respectively with a hard, military life and with a soft, super-sensuous æstheticism.

Should we moderate our wants or should we increase production? Plato had no difficulty in answering this question. He held that a reasonable man would moderate his wants; and that if he wished to live like a good farmer or a good philosopher he would not attempt to copy the expenditures of a vulgar gambler who has just made a corner in wheat, or a vulgar courtesan who has just made a conquest of the vulgar gambler who has made a corner in wheat. Wealth and poverty, said Plato, are the two causes of deterioration in the arts: both the workman and his works are likely to degenerate under the influence of either poverty or wealth, "for one is the parent of luxury and indolence, and the other of meanness and viciousness, and both of discontent."

Nor does Plato have one standard of living for his ruling classes and another for the common people. To each person he would give all the material things necessary for sustenance; and from each he would be prepared to strip all that was not essential. He realized that the possession of goods was not a means of getting happiness, but an effort to make up for a spiritually depauperate life: for Plato, happiness was what one could put into life and not what one could loot out of it: it was the happiness of the dancer rather than the happiness of the glutton. Plato pictured a community living a sane, continent, athletic, clear-eyed life; a community that would be always, so to say, within bounds. There is a horror of laxity and easy living in his Republic. His society was stripped for action. The fragrance that permeates his picture of the good life is not the heavy fragrance of rose-petals and incense falling upon languorous couches: it is the fragrance of the morning grass, and the scent of crushed mint or marjoram beneath the feet.

5

How big is Plato's community, how are the people divided, what are their relations? Now that we have discussed the lay out of the land, and have inquired into the physical basis of this utopia, we are ready to turn our attention to the people; for it is out of the interaction of folk, work, and place that every community—good or bad, real or fancied—exists and perpetuates itself.

6

It follows almost inevitably from what we have said of Plato's environment, that his ideal community was not to be unlimited in population. Quite the contrary. Plato said that "the city may increase to any size which is consistent with its unity; that is the limit." The modern political scientist, who lives within a national state of millions of people, and who thinks of the greatness of states largely in terms of their population, has scoffed without mercy at the fact that Plato limited his community to an arbitrary number, 5,040, about the number that can be conveniently addressed by a single orator. As a matter of fact there is nothing ridiculous in Plato's definition: he was not speaking of a horde of barbarians: he was laying down the foundations for an active polity of citizens: and it is plain enough in all conscience that when you increase the number of people in a community you decrease the number of things that they can share in common. Plato could not anticipate the wireless telephone and the daily newspaper; still less would he have been likely to exaggerate the difference which these instrumentalities have made in the matters that most intimately concern us; and when he set bounds to the population his city would contain, he was anticipating by more than two thousand years the verdict of modern town planners like Mr. Raymond Unwin.

People are not the members of a community because

they live under the same system of political government or dwell in the same country. They become genuine citizens to the extent that they share certain institutions and ways of life with similarly educated people. Plato was primarily concerned with providing conditions which would make a community hold together without being acted upon by any external force—as the national state is acted upon today by war or the threat of war. This concern seems to underlie every line of the Republic. In attacking his problem, the business of supplying the physical wants of the city seemed relatively unimportant; and even though Greece in the time of Plato traded widely with the whole Mediterranean region, Plato did not mistake commercial unity for civic unity. Hence in his scheme of things the work of the farmer and the merchant and the trader was subordinate. The important thing to consider was the general conditions under which all the individuals and groups in a community might live together harmoniously. This is a long cry from the utopias of the nineteenth century, which we will examine later; and that is why it is important to understand Plato's point of view and follow his argument.

7

To Plato, a good community was like a healthy body; a harmonious exercise of every function was the condition of its strength and vitality. Necessarily then a good community could not be simply a collection of individuals, each one of whom insists upon some private and particular happiness without respect to the welfare and interests of his fellows. Plato believed that goodness and happiness—for he would scarcely admit that there was any distinct line of cleavage between these qualities—consisted in living according to nature; that is to say, in knowing one's self, in finding one's bent, and in fulfilling the particular work which one had the capacity to perform. The secret of a good community, therefore, if we may translate Plato's language into modern political slang, is the principle of function.

Every kind of work, says Plato, requires a particular kind of aptitude and training. If we wish to have good shoes, our shoes must be made by a shoemaker and not by a weaver; and in like manner, every man has some particular calling to which his genius leads him, and he finds a happiness for himself and usefulness to his fellows when he is employed in that calling. The good life must result when each man has a function to perform, and when all the necessary functions are adjusted happily to each other. The state is like the physical body. "Health is the creation of a natural order and government in the parts of the body, and the creation of disease is the creation of a state of things in which they are at variance with the natural order." The supreme virtue in the commonwealth is justice; namely, the due apportionment of work or function under the rule of "a place for every man and every man in his place."

Has any such society ever come into existence? Do not too hastily answer No. The ideal in Plato's mind is carried out point for point in the organization of a modern symphony orchestra.

Now Plato was not unaware that there were other formulas for happiness. He expressly points out however that in founding the Republic he does not wish to make any single person or group happier beyond the rest; he desires rather that the whole city should be in the happiest condition. It would be easy enough "to array the husbandmen in rich and costly robes and to enjoin them to cultivate the ground only with a view to their pleasure," and so Plato might have conferred a spurious kind of felicity upon every individual. If this happened, however, there would be a brief period of ease and revelry before the whole works went to pot. In this Plato is a thoroughgoing realist: he is not looking for a short avenue of escape; he is ready to face the road with all its ups and downs, with its steep climbs as well as its wide vistas; and he does not think any the worse of life because he finds that its chief enjoyments rest in activity, and not, as the epicureans of all sorts have always believed, in a release from activity.

8

Plato arrives at his apportionment of functions by a method which is old-fashioned, and which anybody versed in modern psychology would regard as a "rationalization." Plato is trying to give a firm basis to the division of classes which he favored; and so he compares the community to a human being, possessed of the virtues of wisdom, valour, temperance, and justice. Each of these virtues Plato relates to a particular class of people.

Wisdom is appropriate to the rulers of the city. Thus arises the class of guardians.

Valour is the characteristic of the defenders of the city and hence a military class, called auxiliaries, appears.

Temperance, or agreement, is the virtue which relates to all classes.

Finally, there comes justice. "Justice is the ultimate cause and condition of all of them. . . . If a question should arise as to which of these four qualities contributed most by their presence to the excellence of the State whether the agreement of rulers and subjects or the preservation in the soldiers of the opinion which the law ordains about the true nature of dangers, or wisdom and watchfulness in the rulers would claim the palm, or whether this which I am about to mention," namely, "everyone doing his own work and not being a busybody—the question would not be easily determined." Nevertheless, it is plain that justice is the keystone of the Platonic utopia.

We must not misunderstand Plato's division of classes. Aristotle criticizes Plato in terms of a more simple system of democracy; but Plato did not mean to institute a fixed order; within his Republic the Napoleonic motto—*la carrière est ouverte aux talents*—was the guiding principle. What lay beneath Plato's argument was a belief which present-day studies in pyschology seem likely to confirm; a belief that children come into the world with a bent already well marked in their physical and mental constitutions. Plato advocated, it is true, an aristocracy or government by the best people; but he did not believe in fake aristocracies that are perpetuated through hereditary wealth and position. Having determined that his city was to contain three classes, rulers, warriors, and workers, his capital difficulty still remained to be faced; how was each individual to find his way to the right class, and under what conditions would he best fulfill his functions there?

The answers to these questions bring us to the boldest and most original sections of the Republic: the part that has provoked the greatest amount of antagonism and aversion, because of its drastic departure from the rut of many established institutions—in particular, individual marriages and individual property.

In order to perpetuate his ideal constitution Plato relies upon three methods: breeding, education, and a discipline for the daily life. Let us consider the effect of these methods upon each of the classes.

We may dismiss the class of artisans and husbandmen very briefly. It is not quite clear whether Plato meant his system of marriage to extend to the members of this class. As for education, it is clear that he saw nothing to find fault with in the system of apprenticeship whereby the smith or the potter or the farmer trained others to follow his calling; and so he had no reason for departing from methods which had proved, on the whole, very satisfactory. How satisfactory that system was, indeed, we have only to look at an Athenian ruin or vase or chalice to find out. Any improvements that might come about in these occupations would result from the Platonic rule of justice; and Plato followed his own injunction strictly enough to keep away from other people's business.

This of course seems an odd and hasty manner of treatment, as I said before, to those of us who live in a world where the affairs of industry and the tendencies of the labor movement are forever on the carpet. But Plato justifies his treatment by saying that "when shoemakers become bad, and are degenerate, and profess to be shoemakers when they are not, no great mischief happens to the state; but when the guardians of the law and the State are not so in reality, but only in appearance, you see how they entirely destroy the whole constitution, if they alone shall have the privilege of an affluent and happy life." Hence Plato concentrates his attack upon the point of greatest danger: while the shoemaker, as a rule, knows how to mind his own business, the statesman is for the most part unaware of the essential business which he has to mind; and tends to be negligent even when he has some dim notion as to what it may be—being all too ready to sacrifice it to golf or the favors of a beautiful woman. As we saw in Plato's original description of the State, the common folk would doubtless have a good many of the joys and delights traditional in the Greek cities; and doubtless, although Plato says nothing one way or the other, they would be permitted to own such property as might be needed for the conduct of their business or the enjoyment of their homes. The very fact that no definite rule was prescribed for them, makes us suspect that Plato was willing to let these things go on in the usual way.

The next class is known as the warriors, or auxiliaries. They are different in character from the guardians who rule the state; but frequently Plato refers to the guardians as a single class, including the auxiliaries; and it seems that they figured in his mind as the temporal arm of that class. At any rate, the auxiliaries as they are painted in the Critias, which was the dialogue in which Plato attempted to show his Republic in action, dwelt by themselves within a single enclosure; and had common meals and common temples of their own; and so we may surmise that their way of life was to be similar to that of the higher guardians, but that it was not capable of being pushed to the same pitch of development on the intellectual side. These warriors of Plato are, after all, not so very much unlike the regular or standing army in a modern State: they have a life of their own within the barracks, they are trained and drilled to great endurance, and they are taught to obey without question the Government. When you examine the naked business of the warriors and artisans, you discover that Plato is not, for all the difference in scale, so very far away from modern realities. Apart from the fact that women were permitted an equal place with men in the life of the camp and the gymnasium and the academy, the real difference comes in the matter of breeding and selection. At last we approach the Governors, or the Guardians.

How does the Guardian achieve his position and power? Plato is a little chary of answering this question; he hints that it can only happen at the beginning if a person with the brains of a philosopher happen to be born with the authority of a king. Let us pass this by. How are the Guardians born and bred? This is the manner.

For the well-being of the state the Guardians have the power to administer medicinal lies. One of these is to be told to the youth when their education has reached a point at which it becomes possible for the Guardians to determine their natural talents and aptitudes.

"Citizens, we shall say to them in our tale, you are brothers, yet God has framed you differently. Some of you have the power to command, and these he has composed of gold, wherefore also they have the greatest honor; others of silver, to be auxiliaries; others again who are to be husbandmen and craftsmen he has made of brass and iron; and the species will generally be preserved in the children. But as you are of the same original family, a golden parent will sometimes have a silver son, or a silver parent a golden son. And God proclaims to the rulers, as a first principle, that before all things they should watch over their offspring, and see what elements mingle in their nature, for if the son of a golden or silver parent has an admixture of brass and iron, then nature orders a transposition of the ranks; and the eye of the ruler must not be pitiful towards his child because he has to descend in the scale and will become a husbandman or artisan, just as there may be others sprung from the artisan class who are raised to honor, and become guardians and auxiliaries."

As the safeguard of this principle of natural selection of functions, Plato proposed a system of common marriage. "The wives of these guardians are to be common, and their children are also common, and no parent is to know his own child, nor any child his parent." Starting from the day of the hymeneal, the bridegroom who was then married will call all the male children who are born ten and seven months afterwards his sons, and the female children his daughters, and they will call him father. . . . And those who were born at the same time they will term brothers and sisters, and they are not to intermarry." One of the features of this system is that the best stocks—the strongest and wisest and most beautiful—are to be encouraged to reproduce themselves. But this is not worked out in detail. There is to be complete freedom of sexual selection among the guardians; and those who are most distinguished in their services are to have access to a great number of women; but beyond encouraging the guardians to be prolific, Plato did not apparently consider the possibilities of cross-breeding between the various classes.

On the whole, one may say that Plato puts it up to the Guardians to perpetuate themselves properly, and indicates that this is to be one of their main concerns. His good breeding was biological breeding, not social breeding. He recognized—as some of our modern eugenists have failed to—that good parents might throw poor stock, on occasion, and that abject parents might have remarkably good progeny. Even if the Guardians are to be encouraged to have good children, Plato provides that the children themselves must prove their goodness before they are in turn recognized as Guardians. As for the children of the baser sort—well, they were to be rigorously limited to the needs and resources of the community. Plato lived at a time when a great many children were born only to be murdered through "exposure" as it was called; and he had no qualms, apparently, about letting the Guardians send the children with a bad heredity into the discard. If his population could not grow properly in the sunlight without getting rid of the weeds, he was prepared to get rid of the weeds. People who were physically or spiritually too deformed to take part in the good life were to be eliminated. Plato, like a robust Athenian, was for killing or curing a disease; and he gave short shrift to the constitutional invalids.

9

But to breed Guardians is only one-half the problem. The other half comes under the heads of education and discipline; and when Plato discusses these things, he is not speaking, as a modern college president perhaps would, of book-learning alone; he is referring to all the activities that mold a person's life. He follows the older philosopher, Pythagoras, and anticipates the great organizer, Benedict, by laying down a rule of life for his guardians. He did not imagine that disinterested activities, spacious thoughts, and clear vision would arise in people who normally put their personal comfort and "happiness" above the necessities of their office.

Let us recognize the depth of Plato's insight. It is plain that he did not despise what a modern psychologist would call "the normal biological career." For the great majority of people happiness consisted in learning a definite trade or profession, in doing one's daily work, in mating, and when the tension of the day relaxed, in getting enjoyment and recreation in the simple sensualities of eating, drinking, singing, lovemaking, and what not. This normal biological career is associated with a home, and with the limited horizons of a home; and a host of small loyalties and jealousies and interests are woven into the very texture of that life.

Each home, each small circle of relatives and friends, tends to be a minature utopia; there is a limited community of goods, a tendency to adjust one's actions to the welfare of the little whole, and a habit of banding together against the world at large. But the good, contrary to the proverb, is frequently the enemy of the better; and the little utopia of the family is the enemy—indeed the principal enemy—of the beloved community. This fact is notorious. The picture of a trade union leader which Mr. John Galsworthy portrays in Strife, whose power to act firmly in behalf of his group is sapped by the demands made by family ties, could be matched in a thousand places. In order to have the freedom to act for the sake of a great institution, a person must be stript of a whole host of restraining ties and sentimentalities. Jesus commanded his followers to leave their families and abandon their worldly goods; and Plato, in order to preserve his ideal commonwealth, laid down a similar rule. For those who as guardians were to apply the science of government to public affairs, a private life, private duties, private interests, were all to be left behind.

As to the education of the Guardians, I have scarcely the space to treat the more formal part of it in detail; for among other things, as Jowett points out, the Republic is a treatise on education; and Plato presents a fairly elaborate plan. The two branches of Greek education, music and gymnastic, applied in the student's early years to the culture of the body and the culture of the mind; and both branches were to be followed in common by both sexes. Instruction during the early part of a child's life was to be communicated through play activities, as it is today in the City and Country School in New York; and only with manhood did the student approach his subjects in a more formal and systematic manner. In the course of this education the students were to be tested again and again with respect to their mental keenness and tenacity and fortitude;

and only those who came through the fire purified and strengthened were to be admitted to the class of guardians.

The daily life of the Guardians is a rigorous, military regime. They live in common barracks, and in order to avoid paying attention to private affairs, instead of minding the good of the whole community, no one is allowed to "possess any substance privately, unless there be a great necessity for it"; next, Plato continues, none shall have any dwelling or storehouse into which whoever inclines may not enter; and as for necessaries, they shall be only such as brave and temperate warriors may require, and as they are supported by other citizens, they shall receive such a reward of their guardianship as to have neither an overplus nor a deficit at the end of the year. They shall have public meals, as in encampments, and live in common. They are to refrain from using gold and silver, as all the gold and silver they require is in their souls.

All these regulations, of course, are for the purpose of keeping the Guardians disinterested. Plato believed that the majority of people did not know how to mind public business; for it seemed to him that the ordering of a community's life required a measure of science which the common man could not possibly possess. Indeed, in a city of a thousand men he did not see the possibility of getting as many as fifty men who would be sufficiently well versed in what we should today call sociology to deal intelligently with public affairs—for there would scarcely be that many first-rate draughts players. At the same time, if the government is to be entrusted to a few, the few must be genuinely disinterested. If they possessed lands and houses and money in a private way they would become landlords and farmers instead of Guardians; they would be hateful masters instead of allies of the citizens; and so "hating and being hated, plotting and being plotted against, more afraid of the enemies within than the enemies without, they would drag themselves and the rest of the state to speedy destruction."

It remains to take a glance at the manhood and later life of the Guardians.

As young men, the Guardians belong to the auxiliaries; and since they are not permitted to perform any of the manual arts—for skill in any of the trades tended to make a man warped and one-sided, like the symbolic blacksmith god, Hephæstos—their physical edge was maintained by the unceasing discipline of the gymnasium and "military" expeditions. I put military in quotation marks, because a greater part of the warriors' time is spent not in war but in preparation for war; and it is plain that Plato looked upon war as an unnecessary evil, for it arose out of the unjust state; and therefore he must have resorted to warlike discipline for the educational values he found in it. From thirty-five to fifty the potential Guardians undertake practical activities, commanding armies and gaining experience of life. After fifty, those who are qualified devote themselves to philosophy: out of their experience and their inner reflection they figure the essential nature of the good community; and on occasion each guardian abandons divine philosophy for a while, takes his turn at the helm of the state, and trains his successors.

10

What is the business of the Guardian? How does

Plato's ideal statesman differ from Julius Cæsar or Mr. Theodore Roosevelt?

The business of the Guardian is to manufacture liberty. The petty laws, regulations, and reforms with which the ordinary statesman occupies himself had nothing to do, in Plato's mind, with the essential business of the ruler. So Plato expressly foregoes making laws to regulate marketing, the affairs of industry, graft, bribery, theft, and so forth; and he leaves these matters with the curt indication that men can be left to themselves to devise on a voluntary basis the rules of the game for the different occupations; and that it is not the business of the Guardian to meddle in such matters. In a well-founded state, a great number of minor maladjustments would simply fall out of existence; whilst in any other state, all the tinkering and reforming in the world is quite powerless to amend its organic defects. Those make-believe statesmen who try their hand at legislation and "are always fancying that by reforming they will make an end of the dishonesties and rascalities of mankind," do not know that in reality they are trying to cut away the heads of a hydra.

The real concern of the Guardians is with the essential constitution of the state. The means that they employ to perfect this constitution are breeding, vocational selection, and education. "If once a republic is set a-going, it proceeds happily, increasing as a circle. And whilst good education and nurture are preserved, they produce good geniuses; and good geniuses, partaking of such education, produce still better than the former, as well in other respects, as with reference to propagation, as in the case of other animals." All the activities of the Republic are to be patterned after the utopia which the Guardians see with their inward eye. So gradually the community becomes a living unity; and it exhibits the health of that which is organically sound.

11

What do we miss when we look around this utopia of Plato's? Contacts with the outside world? We may take them for granted. Downy beds, Corinthian girls, luxurious furniture? We can well spare them. The opportunity for a satisfactory intellectual and physical life? No: both of these are here.

What Plato has left out are the poets, dramatists, and painters. Literature and music, in order to contribute to the noble education of the Guardians, are both severely restricted in theme and in treatment. Plato has his limitations; and here is the principal one: Plato distrusted the emotional life, and whilst he was prepared to do full homage to man's obvious sensualities, he feared the emotions as a tight-rope walker fears the wind; for they threatened his balance. In one significant passage he classifies "love" with disease and drunkenness, as a vulgar misfortune; and though he was ready to permit the active expression of the emotions, as in the dance or the sexual act, he treated the mere play upon the feelings, without active participation, as a form of intemperance. Hence a great deal of music and dramatic mimicry was taboo. Foreign as this doctrine sounds to the modern reader, there is perhaps more than a grain of sense in it: William James used to teach that no one should passively experience an emotion at a concert or a play without trying to express that emotion actively as soon as he could make the opportunity. At any rate, let us leave this problem which Plato opens up with a free mind; and note here in passing that in the utopia of William Morris novels drop naturally out of existence because life is too active an ectasy to be fed with the pathetic, the maudlin, and the diseased.

12

As we leave this little city of Plato's, nestling in the hills, and as the thin, didactic voice of Plato, who has been perpetually at our elbows, dies away from our ears—what impression do we finally carry away?

In the fields, men are perhaps plowing the land for the autumn sowing; on the terraces, a band of men, women, and children are plucking the olives carefully from the trees, one by one; in the gymnasium on the top of the Acropolis, men and youths are exercising, and as they practice with the javelin now and then it catches the sun and glints into our eye; apart from these groups, in a shaded walk that overlooks the city, a Guardian is pacing back and forth, talking in quick, earnest tones with his pupils.

These are occupations which, crudely or elaborately, men have always engaged in; and here in the Republic they engage in them still. What has changed? What has profoundly changed is not the things that men do, but the relations they bear to one another in doing them. In Plato's community, servitude and compulsion and avarice and indolence are gone. Men mind their business for the sake of living well, in just relations to the whole community of which they are a part. They live, in the strictest sense, according to nature; and because no one can enjoy a private privilege, each man can grow to his full stature and enter into every heritage of his citizenship. When Plato says no to the institutions and ways of life that men have blindly fostered, his eyes are open, and he is facing the light.

CHAPTER THREE

How something happened to utopia between Plato and Sir Thomas More; and how utopia was discovered again, along with the New World.

CHAPTER THREE

1

THERE is a span of nearly two thousand years between Plato and Sir Thomas More. During that time, in the Western World at any rate, utopia seems to disappear beyond the horizon. Plutarch's Life of Lycurgus looks back into a mythical past; Cicero's essay on the state is a negligible work; and St. Augustine's City of God is chiefly remarkable for a brilliant journalistic attack upon the old order of Rome which reminds one of the contemporary diatribes of Maximilian Harden. Except for these works there is, as far as I can discover, scarcely any other piece of writing which even hints at utopia except as utopia may refer to a dim golden age in the past when all men were virtuous and happy.

But while utopia dropt out of literature, it did not drop out of men's minds; and the utopia of the first fifteen hundred years after Christ is transplanted to the sky, and called the Kingdom of Heaven. It is distinctly a utopia of escape. The world as men find it is full of sin and trouble. Nothing can be done about it except to repent of the sin and find refuge from the trouble in the life after the grave. So the utopia of Christianity is fixed and settled: one can enter into the Kingdom of Heaven if a passport has been granted, but one can do nothing to create or mold this heaven. Change and struggle and ambition and amelioration belong to the wicked world, and bring no final satisfaction. Happiness lies not in the deed, but in having a secure credit in the final balance of accounts—happiness, in other words, lies in the ultimate compensation. This world of fading empires and dilapidated cities is no home except for the violent and the "worldly."

If the idea of utopia loses its practical hold during this period, the will-to-utopia remains; and the rise of the monastic system and the attempts of the great popes from Hildebrand onward to establish a universal empire under the shield of the church show that, as always, there was a breach between the ideas which people carried in their heads and the things which actual circumstances and going institutions compelled them to do. There is no need to consider these partial, institutional utopias until we get down to the nineteenth century. What concerns us now is that the Kingdom of Heaven, as a utopia of escape, ceased to hold men's allegiance when they discovered other channels and other possibilities.

The shift from a heavenly utopia to a worldly one came during that period of change and uneasiness which characterized the decline of the Middle Age. Its first expression is the "Utopia" of Sir Thomas More, the great chancellor who served under Henry VIII.

2

In the introduction to More's "Utopia" one gets a vivid impression of the forces that were stirring men's minds out of the sluggish routine into which they had settled. The man who is supposed to describe the commonwealth of Utopia is a Portuguese scholar, learned in Greek. He has left his family possessions with his kinsmen and has gone adventuring for other continents with Americus Vesputius. This Raphael Hythloday is the sort of sunburnt sailor one could probably have encountered in Bristol or Cadiz or Antwerp almost any day during the late part of the fifteenth century. He has abandoned Aristotle, whom the schoolmen had butchered and had made pemmican of, and through his conquest of Greek he has come into possession of that new learning which stems back to Plato; and his brain is teeming with the criticisms and suggestions of a strange, pagan philosophy. Moreover, he has been abroad to the Americas or the Indies, and he is ready to tell all who will listen of a strange land on the other side of the world, where, as Sterne said of France, "they do things better." No institution is too fantastic but that it might exist—on the other side of the world. No way of life is too reasonable but that a philosophical population might follow it—on the other side of the world. Conceive of the world of ideas which Greek literature had just opened up coming headlong against the new lands which the magnetic compass had given men the courage to explore, and utopia, as a fresh conception of the good life, becomes a throbbing possibility.

3

In setting out for Utopia Sir Thomas More left behind a scene which in its political violence and economic maladjustment looks queerly like our own. Indeed, there are a good many passages which need only have a few names altered and the language itself cast into modern English in order to serve as editorial comment for a radical weekly review.

Consider this man Raphael Hythloday, this errant member of the intelligentzia. Life as he knows it in the Europe of his day no longer has a hold upon him. The rich are fattening upon the poor; land is being gathered into big parcels, at least in England; and turned over into sheep runs. The people who used to cultivate the land are compelled to leave their few acres and are thrown on their own resources. Soldiers who have returned from the wars can find nothing to do; disabled veterans and people accustomed to live as pensioners on the more prosperous have become destitute. Extravagant luxury grows on one hand; misery on the other. Those who are poor, beg; those who are proud, steal; and for their pains the thieves and the vagrants are tried and sentenced to the gibbet, where by dozens they hang before the eyes of the market crowds.

Just as today, people complain that the laws are not strict enough or that they are not enforced; and everyone stubbornly refuses to look at the matter through Raphael Hythloday's eyes and to see that the robbery and violence which are abroad are not a cause of bad times but a result of them.

What can a man of intelligence do in such a world?

More's friend, Peter Giles, who is represented as the sponsor for Raphael, wonders why a man of Raphael's talent does not enter into the service of the king—in short, go in for politics. Raphael answers that he does not wish to be enslaved; and he cannot try to fetch happiness on terms so abhorrent to his disposition, for "most princes apply themselves more to the affairs of war than to the useful arts of peace, and are more set on acquiring new kingdoms right or wrong than on governing those they possess." There is no use trying to tell them about the wiser institutions of the Utopians: if they could not refute your arguments they would say that the old ways were good enough for their ancestors and are good enough for them, even though they have willingly let go of all the genuinely good things that might have been inherited from the past.

So much for the help an intelligent man might give on domestic problems. As for international affairs, it is a mess of chicane and intrigue and brigandage. While so many people of influence are advising preparedness and "how to carry on the war," what chance would a poor intellectual like Hythloday have if he stood up and said that the government should withdraw their armies from foreign parts and try to improve conditions at home, instead of oppressing the people with taxes and spilling their blood without bringing them a single blessed advantage, whilst their manners are being corrupted by a long war, and their laws fall into contempt, with robbery and murder on every hand.

More, through the tongue of Raphael Hythloday, is painting a picture of the life he sees about him; but in it we seem to see every feature of our own national countenance.

This unhonored and disoriented intellectual is the very emblem of some of our best spirits today. Rack and ruin have gone too far to admit of any sort of repair except that which proceeds from the bottom up; and so Hythloday freely admits that "as long as there is any property, and while money is the standard of all other things, I cannot think that a nation can be governed either justly or happily; not justly, because the best things will fall to the share of the worst men; nor happily, because all things will be divided among a few (and even these are not in all respects happy), the rest being left to be absolutely miserable." In short, says Hythloday, there is no salvation except through following the practices of the Utopians.

So the new world of exploration brings us within sight of a new world of ideas, and the beloved community, whose seed Plato had sought to implant in men's minds, springs up again, after a fallow period of almost two thousand years. What sort of country is it?

4

Geographically viewed, the island of Utopia exists only in More's imagination. All that we can say of it is that it is two hundred miles broad, shaped something like a crescent, with an entrance into its great bay which lends itself to defence. There are fifty-four cities in the island; the nearest is twenty-four miles from its neighbor, and the farthest is not more than a day's march distant. The chief town, Amaurot, is situated very nearly in the center; and each city has jurisdiction over the land for twenty miles around; so that here again we find the city-region as the unit of political life.

5

The economic base of this commonwealth is agriculture, and no one is ignorant of the art. Here and there over the countryside are great farm-houses, equipt for carrying on agricultural operations. While those who are well-adapted for rural life are free to live in the open country the whole year round, other workers are sent by turns from the city to take part in the farm-labor. Every farmstead or "family" holds no less than forty men and women. Each year twenty of this family come back to town after two years in the country; and in their place another twenty is sent out from the town, so that they may learn the country work from those who have had at least a year's experience.

Agricultural economics is so well advanced that the countryside knows exactly how much food is needed by the whole city-region; but the Utopians sow and breed more abundantly than they need, in order that their neighbors may have the overplus. Poultry-raising is also highly advanced. The Utopians "breed an infinite multitude of chickens in a very curious manner; for the hens do not sit and hatch them, but vast numbers of eggs are laid in a gentle and equal heat, in order to be hatched"—in short, they have discovered the incubator!

During the harvest season the country magistrates inform the city magistrates how many extra hands are needed for reaping; a draft of city workers is made, and the work is commonly done in short order.

While every man, woman, and child knows how to cultivate the soil, since each has learned partly in school and partly by practice, every person also has some "peculiar trade to which he applies himself, such as the manufacture of wool or flax, masonry, smith's work or carpenter's work"; and no trade is held in special esteem above the others. (That is a great jump from the Republic where the mechanic arts are considered base and servile in nature!) The same trade usually passes down from father to son, since each family follows its own special occupation; but a man whose genius lies another way may be adopted into a family which plies another trade; and if after he has learnt that trade, he wishes still to master another, this change is brought about in the same manner. "When he has learned both, he follows that which he likes best, unless the public has more occasion for the other."

The chief and almost the only business of the magistrates is to see that no one lives in idleness. This does not mean that the Utopians wear themselves out with "perpetual toil from morning to night, as if they were beasts of burden," for they appoint eight hours for sleep and six for work, and the rest of the day is left to each man's discretion. They are able to cut down the length of time needed for work, without our so-called labor saving machinery, by using the services of classes which in More's time were given for the most part to idleness—princes, rich men, healthy beggars, and the like. The only exception to this rule of labor is with the magistrates—who are not in the habit of taking advantage of it—and the students, who upon proving their ability are released from mechanical operations. If there is too great a surplus of labor, men are sent out to repair the highways; but when no public undertaking is to be performed, the hours of work are lessened.

6

So much for the daily industrial life of the Utopians. How are the goods distributed?

Between the city and the country there is a monthly exchange of goods. This occasion is made a festival, and the country people come into town and take back for themselves the goods which the townspeople have made; and the magistrates "take care to see it given to them." In back of this direct interchange of goods between town and country, between household and household, there are doubtless regulations; and it is simply our misfortune that Raphael Hythloday did not think it necessary to go into them. Within the cities, we must add, there are storehouses where a daily market takes place.

As with the business of production, the family is the unit of distribution; and the city is composed of these units, rather than of a multitude of isolated individuals. "Every city is divided into four equal parts, and in the middle of each there is a market-place; what is brought hither, and manufactured by the several families, is carried from thence to houses appointed for that purpose, in which all things of a sort are laid by themselves; and thither every father goes and takes whatever he or his family stand in need of, without either paying for it or leaving anything in exchange. There is no reason for giving denial to any person, since there is such plenty of everything among them; and there is no danger of a man's asking for more than he needs; they have no inducements to do this, since they are sure they shall always be supplied."

More goes on to explain this direct system of exchange, and to justify it. "It is the fear of want that makes any of the whole race of animals either greedy or ravenous, but besides fear, there is in man a pride that makes him fancy it a particular glory to excel others in pomp and excess. But by the laws of the Utopians there is no room for this. Near these markets are others for all sorts of provisions, where there are not only herbs, fruits, and bread, but also fish, fowl, and cattle. There are also, without their towns, places appointed near some running water for killing their beasts, and for washing away their filth."

In addition to the monthly apportionment of goods by the local magistrates, the great council which meets at Amaurot once a year undertakes to examine the production of each region, and those regions that suffer from a scarcity of goods are supplied out of the surplus of other regions, "so that indeed the whole island is, as it were, one family."

Taking it all together, there is pretty much the same standard of well-being that we found in the Republic. More recognizes the instinct for self-assertion and the exhibitionist element in man's makeup; but he does not pander to it. The precious metals are held in contempt: gold is used to make chamberpots and chains for slaves; pearls are given to children who glory in them and enjoy them while they are young and are as much ashamed to use them afterwards as they are of their puppets and other toys. Gaudy clothes and jewelry are likewise out of fashion in Utopia. The shopkeepers of Bond Street and Fifth Avenue would break their hearts here; for it is impossible to spend money or to spend other people's labor on articles which lend themselves solely to conspicuous display, and are otherwise neither useful nor beautiful. Contrast More's Utopia with St. John's vision of heaven, and the worldly Utopia seems quite naked and austere. Two hundred years later, in Penn's city of Philadelphia, we might have fancied that we were walking about the streets of Amaurot.

7

The town life of the Utopians, as I have explained, rests upon rural foundations; there is such a mixture of town and country as Peter Kropotkin sought to realize in his sketch of "Fields, Factories, and Workshops." Let us conjure up the town of Amaurot and see in what sort of environment the townspeople spend their days. Our Utopian city, alas! reminds us somewhat of its rivals in latter-day America; for Raphael tells us that he who knows one of their towns knows all of them.

Amaurot lies on the side of a hill; it is almost a square, two miles on each side; and it faces the river Anider which takes its rise eighty miles above the town, and gets lost in the ocean sixty miles below. The town is compassed by a high, thick wall; the streets are convenient for carriages and sheltered from the winds; and the houses are built in rows so that a whole side of the street looks like a single unit. (It was so that the great people built their houses in eighteenth century London and Edinburgh, as Belgrave Square, Charlotte Square, and the great Adelphi Mansion designed by the Brothers Adam show us.) The streets are twenty feet broad; and in back of the houses are gardens, which everyone has a hand in keeping up; and the people of the various blocks vie with each other in ordering their gardens, so that there is "nothing belonging to the whole town that is more useful and more pleasant."

In every street there are great halls, distinguished by particular names, and lying at an equal distance from each other. In each hall dwells the magistrates of a district, who rules over thirty families, fifteen living on one side and fifteen on another; and since a family consists of not more than sixteen and not less than ten people, this magistrate—or Philarch as he is called—is the "community leader" of some four hundred people.

In these halls everyone meets and takes his principal meal. The stewards go to the market place at a particular hour, and, according to the number of people in their halls, carry home provisions. The people who are in hospitals—which are built outside the walls and are so large they might pass for little towns—get the pick of the day's food. At the hours of dinner and supper the whole block is called together by a trumpet, and everybody joins company, except such as are sick or in hospital, just as the students and fellows to this day eat their principal meal in an Oxford college. The dressing of meat and the ordering of the tables belongs to the women; all those of every family taking their place by turns. In the same building there is a common nursery and chapel; and so the women who have children to care for labor under no inconvenience.

The midday meal is dispatched unceremoniously; but at the end of the day music always accompanies the meals, perfumes are burnt or sprinkled around, and they "want nothing that may cheer up their spirits." Bond Street and Fifth Avenue may weep about the absence of conspicuous waste in Utopia; but at supper time, at any rate, William Penn would be uncomfortable. There is the odor of an uncommonly good club in the description of the final meal of the day: the smell of the barracks or the poorhouse, which we should find later in Robert Owen's common halls, does not intrude for an instant. More, when you examine him closely, does not altogether forget the mean sensual man who dwells occasionally in all of us!

8

Now that we have laid the foundations of the material life, we must observe the limitations that are laid upon the daily activities of the Utopians. This brings us to the government.

The basis of the Utopian political state, as in the economic province, is the family. Every year thirty families choose a magistrate, known as a Philarch; and over every ten Philarchs, with the families subject to them, there is an Archphilarch. All the Philarchs, who are in number 200, choose the Prince out of a list of four, who are named by the people of the four divisions of the city. The Prince is elected for life, unless he be removed on suspicion of attempting to enslave the people. The Philarchs are chosen for a single year; but they are frequently re-elected. In order to keep their rulers from conspiring to upset the government, no matter of great importance can be set on foot without being sent to the Philarchs, "who, after they have communicated it to the families that belong to their divisions, and have considered it among themselves, make report to the senate; and upon great occasions the matter is referred to the council of the whole island."

Recollect that each household is an industrial as well as a domestic unit, as was usual in the Middle Age, and you will perceive that this is an astute combination of industrial and political democracy on a genuine basis of common interest.

The greater part of the business of the government relates to the economic life of the people. There are certain other matters, however, which remain over for them; and these affairs constitute a blot on More's conception of the ideal commonwealth. One of them is the regulation of travel; another is the treatment of crime; and a third is war.

It is interesting to note that on two subjects which More is mightily concerned to rectify in his own country—crime and war—he establishes conditions which are pretty far from being ideal or humane in his Utopia. A. E. has well said that a man becomes the image of the thing he hates. Everything that Raphael brings up against the government of England in the Introduction to Utopia could be brought with almost equal force, I believe, against the very country which is to serve as a standard.

While any man may travel if there is no particular occasion for him at home—whether he wishes to visit friends or see the rest of the country—it is necessary for him to carry a passport from the Prince. If he stay in any place longer than a night he must follow his proper occupation; and if anyone goes out of the city without leave or is found wandering around without a passport, he is punished as a fugitive, and upon committing the offense a second time is condemned to slavery. This is a plain example of unimaginative harshness; and it is hard to explain away; indeed, I have no intention to.

Apparently More could not conceive of a perfectly happy commonwealth for the majority of men if they still had to perform certain filthy daily tasks, like the slaughtering of beef; and so he attempts to kill two birds with one stone: he creates a class of slaves, and he fills this class by condemning to it people who have committed venial crimes. In doing this, he overlooks the final objection to slavery in all its forms; namely, that it tends to corrupt the master.

Since we are discussing the conditions that undermine More's commonwealth, we may remark that war, too, remains; the difference being that the Utopians attempt to do by strategy, corruption, and what we should now call propaganda what less intelligent people do by sheer force of arms. If the Utopian incubator anticipates the modern invention, their method of conducting war likewise anticipates our modern technique of undermining the enemy's morale: these Utopians, in the good and the bad, are our contemporaries! Among the just causes of war the Utopians count the seizure of territory, the oppression of foreign merchants, and the denial of access to land to nations capable of cultivating it. They take considerable pains to keep their "best sort of men for their own use at home, so they make use of the worst sort of men for the consumption of war." In other words, they regard war as a means, among other things, of weeding out undesirable elements in the community.

It is a relief to turn away from these residual iniquities to marriage and religion!

In marriage there is a curious mixture of the personal conception of sexual relations, which is the modern note, with a belief in certain formal specifications which was the distinctly mediæval quality. Thus on one hand the Utopians take care that the bride and the bridegroom are introduced to each other, in their nakedness, before the ceremony; and the grounds for divorce are adultery and insufferable perverseness. When two people cannot agree they are permitted to escape the bond by mutual agreement under approval granted by the Senate after strict inquiry. On the other hand, unchastity is sternly punished, and those who commit adultery are condemned to slavery and not given the privilege of a second marriage.

In religion there is complete toleration for all creeds, with this exception: that those who dispute violently about religion or attempt to use any other force than that of mild persuasion are punished for breaking the public peace.

9

There is not the space to follow the life of the Utopians in all its details. It is time to discuss the world of ideas by which these Utopians chart their daily activities. This exposition of the basic Utopian values has been so admirably put by Sir Thomas More himself that the greater part of our conclusion will inevitably fall within quotation marks.

The Utopians "define virtue thus: that it is a living according to Nature, and think that we are made by God for that end; they believe that a man then follows Nature when he pursues or avoids things according to the direction of reason. . . . Reason directs us to keep our minds as free from passion and as cheerful as we can, and that we should consider ourselves bound by the ties of good-nature and humanity to use our utmost endeavors to help forward the happiness of all other persons; for there never was any man such a morose and severe pursuer of virtue, such an enemy to pleasure, that though he set hard rules for men to undergo much pain, many watchings and other rigors, yet did not at the same time advise them to do all they could to relieve and ease the miserable, and who did not represent gentleness and good nature as amiable dispositions. . . . A life of pleasure is either a real evil, and in that case we ought not to assist others in their pursuit of it, but, on the contrary, to keep them from it all we can, as from that which is most hurtful and deadly; or if it is a good thing, so that we not only may but ought to help others to it, why then ought not a man to begin with himself? Since no man can be more bound to look after the good of another than after his own. . . .

"Thus as they define Virtue to be living according to Nature, so they imagine that Nature prompts all people to seek after pleasure, as the end of all they do. They also observe that in order to further our supporting the pleasures of life, Nature inclines us to enter into society; for there is no man so much raised above the rest of mankind as to be the only favorite of Nature, who, on the contrary, seems to have placed on a level all those that belong to the same species. Upon this they infer that no man ought to seek his own conveniences so eagerly as to prejudice others; and therefore they think that all agreements between private persons ought to be observed, but likewise that all those laws ought to be kept, which either a good prince has published in due form, to which a people that is neither oppressed with tyranny nor circumvented by fraud, has consented, for distributing these conveniences of life which afford us all our pleasures.

"They think it is an evidence of true wisdom for a man to pursue his own advantages, as far as the laws allow it. They account it piety to prefer public good to one's private concerns; but they think it unjust for a man to seek for pleasure by snatching another man's pleasures from him.

"Thus upon an inquiry into the whole matter, they reckon that all our actions, and even all our virtues, terminate in pleasure, as in our chief end and greatest happiness; and they call every motion or state, either of body or mind, in which Nature teaches us to delight, a pleasure. They cautiously limit pleasure only to those appetites to which Nature leads us; for they say that Nature leads us only to those delights to which reason as well as sense carries us, and by which we neither injure any other person nor lose the possession of greater pleasures, and of such as draw no troubles after them."

Thus the Utopians discriminate between natural pleasures and those which have some sting or bitterness concealed in them. The love of fine clothes is considered by Utopians as a pleasure of the latter sort; likewise is the desire of those who possess fine clothes to be kowtowed to by other people. Men who heap up wealth without using it are in the same class; and those who throw dice or hunt—for in Utopia hunting is turned over to the butchers, and the butchers are slaves.

Now Utopians "reckon up several sorts of pleasures which they call true ones; some belong to the body and others to the mind. The pleasures of the mind lie in knowledge, and in that delight which the contemplation of truth carries with it; to which they add the joyful reflections on a well-spent life; and the assured hopes of a future happiness. They divide the pleasures of the body into two sorts; the one is that which gives our senses some real delight, and is performed, either by recruiting nature, and supplying those parts which feed the internal heat of life by eating and drinking; or when nature is eased of any surcharge that oppresses it; when we are relieved from sudden pain, or that which arises from satisfying the appetite which Nature has wisely given for the propagation of the species. There is another kind of pleasure that arises neither from our receiving what the body requires, nor its being relieved when overcharged, and yet by a secret, unseen virtue affects the senses, raises the passions, and strikes the mind with generous impressions; this is the pleasure that arises from music. Another kind of bodily pleasure is that which arises from an undisturbed and vigorous constitution of body, when life and active spirits seem to actuate every part. This lively health, when entirely free from all mixture of pain, of itself gives an inward pleasure . . . and Utopians reckon it the foundation and basis of all the other joys of life, since this alone makes the state of life easy and desirable; and when this is wanting a man is really capable of no other pleasure." The crowning pleasure of the Utopian is the cultivation of the mind; and the leisure hours of the people, as well as the professional scholars, are spent in the lecture hall and the study.

10

Such are the goals for which the Utopians direct their social order. These values are, I need scarcely point out, rooted in the nature of man, and not in any set of external institutions. The aim of every Utopian institution is to help every man to help himself. When we put the matter in these bald phrases, what More brings forward seems weak and platitudinous. Behind it all, however, is a vital idea: namely, that our attempts to live the good life are constantly perverted by our efforts to gain a living; and that by juggling gains and advantages, by striving after power and riches and distinction, we miss the opportunity to live as whole men. People become the nursemaids of their furniture, their property, their titles, their position; and so they lose the direct satisfaction that furniture or property would give.

To cultivate the soil rather than simply to get away with a job; to take food and drink rather than to earn money; to think and dream and invent, rather than to increase one's reputation; in short, to grasp the living reality and spurn the shadow—this is the substance of the Utopian way of life. Power and wealth and dignity and fame are abstractions; and men cannot live by abstractions alone. In this Utopia of the New World every man has the opportunity to be a man because no one else has the opportunity to be a monster. Here, too, the chief end of man is that he should grow to the fullest stature of his species.

CHAPTER FOUR

How the new Humanism of the Renascence brings us within sight of Christianopolis; and how we have for the first time a glimpse of a modern utopia.

CHAPTER FOUR

1

A HUNDRED years pass, and the man who next conducts us into Utopia is a Humanist scholar. After the manner of his time, he answers to the latinized name, Johann Valentin Andreæ. He is a traveller, a social reformer, and above all things a preacher; and so the vision he imparts to us of Christianopolis seems occasionally to flicker into blackness whilst he moralizes for us and tells us to the point of tedium what his views are concerning the life of man, and in particular the conceptions of Christianity which his countrymen, the Germans, are debating about. Sometimes, when we are on the point of coming to grips with his utopia, he will annoy us by going off on a long tirade about the wickedness of the world and the necessity for fastening one's gaze upon the life hereafter—for Protestantism seems just as other-worldly as Catholicism. It is the Humanist Andreæ rather than the Lutheran Andreæ who paints the picture of a Christian city. While Andreæ sticks to Christianopolis his insight is deep, his views are sound, and his proposals are rational; and more than once he will amaze us by putting forward ideas which seem to leap three hundred years ahead of his time and environment.

It is impossible to get rid of the personal flavor of Andreæ: his fine intelligence and his candor make our contacts with Christianopolis quite different from the dreary guidebook sketches which some of the later utopians will inflict upon us. The two other utopians who wrote in the same half century as Andreæ—Francis Bacon and Tommaso Campanella—are quite second-rate in comparison; Bacon with his positively nauseating foppishness about details in dress and his superstitious regard for forms and ceremonials, and Campanella, the lonely monk whose City of the Sun seems a marriage of Plato's Republic and the Court of Montezuma. When Bacon talks about science, he talks like a court costumer who is in the habit of describing the stage properties for a masque; and it is hard to tell whether he is more interested in the experiments performed by the scientists of the New Atlantis or the sort of clothes they wear while engaged in them. There is nothing of the snob or the dilettante about Andreæ: His eye fastens itself upon essentials, and he never leaves them except when—for he is necessarily a man of his age—he turns his gaze piously to heaven.

This teeming, struggling European world that Andreæ turns his back upon he knows quite well; for he has lived in Herrenburg, Koenigsbrunn, Tuebingen, Strassburg, Heidelberg, Frankfurt, Geneva, Vaihingen, and Calw; and he is in correspondence with learned men abroad, in particular with Samuel Hartlib, who lives in England, and with John Amos Comenius. Like the Chancellor in Christianopolis, he longs for an "abode situated below the sky, but at the same time above the dregs of this known world." Quite simply, he finds himself wrecked on the shore of an island dominated by the city of Christianopolis. After being examined as to his ideas of life and morals, his person, and his culture, he is admitted to the community.

2

This island is a whole world in miniature. As in the Republic, the unit once more is the valley section, for the "island is rich in grain and pasture fields, watered with rivers and brooks, adorned with woods and vineyards, full of animals."

In outward appearance, Christianopolis does not differ very much from the pictures of the cities one finds in seventeenth century travel books, except for a unity and orderliness that these cities sometimes lack. "Its shape is a square whose side is 700 feet, well fortified with four towers and a wall. . . . It looks therefore towards the four quarters of the earth. Of buildings there are two rows, or if you count the seat of the government and the storehouses, four; there is only one public street, and only one marketplace, but this one is of a very high order." In the middle of the city there is a circular temple, a hundred feet in diameter; all the buildings are three stories; and public balconies lead to them. Provision against fire is made by building the houses of burnt stone and separating them by fireproof walls. In general, "things look much the same all around, not extravagant nor yet unclean; fresh air and ventilation are provided throughout. About four hundred citizens live here in religious faith and peace of the highest order." The whole city is divided into three parts, one to supply food, one for drill and exercise, and one for looks. The remainder of the island serves the purposes of agriculture, and for workshops.

3

When we look back upon the Republic, with its external organization so plainly modeled upon military

Sparta, we see the camp and the soldier giving the pattern to the life of the whole community. In Utopia, the fundamental unit was the farmstead and the family; and family discipline, which arises naturally enough in rural conditions, was transferred to the city. In Christianopolis, the workshop and the worker set the lines upon which the community is developed; and whatever else this society may be, it is a "republic of workers, living in equality, desiring peace, and renouncing riches." If Utopia exhibits the communism of the family, Christianopolis presents the communism of the guild.

Industrially speaking, there are three sections in Christianopolis. One of them is devoted to agriculture and animal husbandry. Each of these departments has appropriate buildings, and directly opposite them is a rather large tower which connects them with the city buildings; under the tower a broad vaulted entrance leads into the city, and a smaller one to the individual houses. The dome of this tower roofs what we should call a guildhall, and here the citizens of the quarter come together as often as required to "act on sacred as well as civil matters." It is plain that these workers are not sheep led by wise shepherds, as in the Republic, but the members of autonomous, self-regulating groups.

The next quarter contains the mills, bake-shops, meat-shops, and factories for making whatever is done with machinery apart from fire. As Christianopolis welcomes originality in invention, there are a variety of enterprises within this domain; among them, paper manufacturing plants, saw mills, and establishments for grinding and polishing arms and tools. There are common kitchens and wash houses, too; for, as we shall see presently, life in this ideal city corresponds to what we experience today in New York, London, and many another modern industrial city.

The third quarter is given over to the metallurgical industries, as well as to those like the glass, brick, and earthenware industries which require constant fire. It is necessary to point out that in planning the industrial quarters of Christianopolis, these seventeenth century Utopians have anticipated the best practice that has been worked out today, after a century of disorderly building. The separation of the city into zones, the distinction between "heavy" industries and "light" industries, the grouping of similar industrial establishments, the provision of an agricultural zone adjacent to the city—in all this our garden cities are but belated reproductions of Christianopolis.

Moreover, in Christianopolis, there is a conscious application of science to industrial processes; one might almost say that these artisans believed in efficiency engineering; for "here in truth you see a testing of nature herself. The men are not driven to a work with which they are unfamiliar, like pack-animals to their task, but they have been trained before in an accurate knowledge of scientific matters," on the theory that "unless you analyze matter by experiment, unless you improve the deficiencies of knowledge by more capable instruments, you are worthless." The dependence of industrial improvement upon deliberate scientific research may be a new discovery for the practical man, but it is an old story in Utopia.

4

What is the character of this artisan democracy?

The answer to this is summed up in one of those sayings that Andreæ, in the midst of his energetic exposition, drops by the way.

"To be wise and to work are not incompatible, if there is moderation."

So it follows that "their artisans are almost entirely educated men. For that which other people think is the proper characteristic of a few (and yet if you consider the stuffing of inexperience by learning, the characteristic of too many already) this, the inhabitants argue, should be attained by all individuals. They say that neither the substance of letters is such, nor yet the difficulty of work, that one man, if given enough time, cannot master both."

"Their work, or as they prefer to hear it called, 'the employment of their hands,' is conducted in a certain prescribed way, and all things are brought into a public booth. From here every workman receives out of the stock on hand whatever is necessary for the work of the coming week. For the whole city is, as it were, one single workshop, but of all different sorts and crafts. The ones in charge of these duties are stationed in the small towers at the corners of the wall; they know ahead of time what is to be made, in what quantity, and of what form, and they inform the mechanics of these items. If the supply of material in the work booth is sufficient, the workmen are permitted to indulge and give free play to their inventive genius. No one has any money, nor is there any use for any private money; yet the republic has its own treasury. And in this respect the inhabitants are especially blessed, because no one can be superior to the other in the amount of riches owned, since the advantage is rather one of power and genius, and the highest respect that of morals and piety. They have very few working hours, yet no less is accomplished than in other places, as it is considered disgraceful by all that one should take more rest and leisure time than is allowed."

In addition to the special trades, there are "public duties to which all citizens have obligation, such as watching, guarding, harvesting of grain and wine, working roads, erecting buildings, draining ground; also certain duties of assisting in the factories which are imposed upon all in turn according to age and sex, but not very often nor for a long time. For even though certain experienced men are put in charge of all the duties, yet when men are asked for, no one refuses the state his services and strength. For what we are in our homes, they are in their city, which they not undeservedly think a home. And for this reason it is no disgrace to perform any public function. . . . Hence all work, even that which is considered rather irksome, is accomplished in good time, and without much difficulty, since the promptness of the great number of workmen permits them easily to collect or distribute the great mass of things."

In this Christianopolis, as Mr. Bertrand Russell would put it, the creative rather than the possessive impulses are uppermost. Work is the main condition of existence, and this good community faces it. It is a pretty contrast to the attitude of the leisured classes who, as Andreæ says, with an entirely mistaken sense of delicacy shrink from touching earth, water, stones, coal, and things of that sort, but think it grand to have in their possession to delight them "horses, dogs, harlots and other similar creatures."

5

The place of commerce in this scheme of life is simple. It does not exist for the sake of individual gain. Hence no one engages in commerce on his own hook, for such matters are put in the hands of "those selected to attend to them," and the aim of commerce is not to gain money but to increase the variety of things at the disposal of the local community; so that—and again Andreæ steps in for emphasis—"we may see the peculiar production of each land, and so communicate with each other that we may seem to have the advantages of the universe in one place, as it were."

6

The constitution of the family in Christianopolis follows pretty definitely upon the lines dictated by urban occupations; for Andreæ is a city man, and since he does not despise the advantages city life can give, he does not shrink from their consequences. One of these consequences is, surely, the restriction of domesticity, or rather, the projection in the city at large of the functions that in a farmstead would be carried on within the bosom of the family.

When a lad is twenty-four and a lass is eighteen, they are permitted to marry, with the benefit of Christian rites and services, and a decorous avoidance of drunkenness and gluttony after the ceremony. Marriage is a simple matter. There are no dowries to consider, no professional anxieties to face, no housing shortage to keep one from finding a home, and above all, perhaps, no landlord to propitiate with money, since all houses are owned by the city and are granted and assigned to individuals for their use. Virtue and beauty are the only qualities that govern a marriage in Christianopolis. Furniture is provided with the house out of the public store. If in Utopia the families are grouped together in a patriarchal household, such as More himself maintained at Chelsea, in Christianopolis they consist of isolated couples, four, at most six people in all, a woman, a man, and such children as are not yet of school age.

Let us visit a young couple in Christianopolis. We reach the house by way of a street, twenty feet broad, faced by houses with a wide frontage on the street, some forty feet in length, and of from fifteen to twenty-five feet in depth. In our crowded towns, today, where people pay for land by the front foot, the frontage is narrow and the houses are deep; and as a result there is a dreadful insufficiency of light and air; but in Christianopolis, as in some of the older European towns, the houses are built to get a maximum of air and sunlight. If it is raining when we make our visit, a covered walk, five feet wide, supported by columns twelve feet high, will shelter us from the rain.

Our friends live, we shall say, in one of the average apartments; so they have three rooms, a bathroom, a sleeping apartment, and a kitchen. "The middle part within the tower has a little open space with a wide window, where wood and the heavier things are raised aloft by pulleys"—in short, a dumbwaiter. Looking out from the window in the rear, we face a well-kept garden; and if our host is inclined to give us wine, he may let us take our pick from among the cobwebs of a small private cellar in the basement, where such things are kept. If it is a cold day, the furnace is going; or if we happen to make our visit in the summer time, the awnings are drawn.

Our host makes apologies, perhaps, for a litter of wood and shavings that occupies a corner of the kitchen, for he has just been putting up a few shelves in his spare time, and has borrowed a kit of tools from the public supply house. (Since he is not a carpenter, he has no need for these tools the rest of the year; and other people can have their turn at them.) Coming from Utopia, one of the things that strikes us is the absence of domestic attendance; and when we ask our hostess about it, she tells us that she will not have anyone to wait upon her until she is confined.

"But isn't there a lot of work for you to do all by yourself?" we shall ask.

"Not for anybody with a college training," she will answer. "You see that our furnishings are quite simple; and since there are no gimcracks to be dusted, no polished tables to be oiled, no carpets to be swept, and nothing in our apartment that is just for show to prove that we can afford to live better than our neighbors, the work is scarcely more than enough to keep one in good health and temper. Of course, cooking meals is always something of a nuisance; and washing up is worse. But my husband and I share the work together, in everything but sewing and washing clothes, and you would be surprised how quickly everything gets done. Work is usually galling when somebody else is taking his ease while one is doing it; but where husband and wife share alike, as in Christianopolis, there is really nothing to it. If you'll stay to dinner, you'll find out how easily it goes. Since you haven't brought your rations, my husband will get some cooked meats in the public kitchen, and that will do for all of us."

"No one need be surprised at the rather cramped quarters," Andreæ hastens to interject. "People who house vanity . . . can never live spaciously enough. They burden others and are burdened themselves, and no one measures their necessities, nay even their comforts, easily otherwise than by an unbearable and unmovable mass. Oh, only those persons are rich who have all of which they have real need, who admit nothing else, merely because it is possible to have it in abundance."

Carried to its extreme, you will find this philosophy put once for all in Thoreau's Walden. We have got our bearings in Utopia, I believe, when we have determined what a life abundant consists of, and what will suffice for it.

7

Suppose that our friends have children. During the early years of their life they are in the care of their mother. When they have completed their sixth year, the children are given over to the care of the community, and both sexes continue in school through the stages of childhood, youth, and early maturity. "No parent gives closer or more careful attention to his children than is given here, for the most upright preceptors, men as well as women, are placed over them. Moreover," the parents "can visit their children, even unseen by them, as often as they have leisure. As this is an institution for the public good, it is managed agreeably as a common charge for all the citizens. They see to it that the food is appetizing and wholesome, that the couches and beds are clean and comfortable, and that the clothes and attire of the whole body are clean. . . . If diseases of the skin or body are contracted, the individuals are cared for in good time; and to avoid the spreading of infection, they are quarantined."

There is scarcely need to examine the program of study except in its broad outlines. It is enough to observe that "the young men have their study period in the morning, the girls in the afternoon, and matrons as well as learned men are their instructors. . . . The rest of their time is devoted to manual training and domestic art and science, as each one's occupation is assigned to his natural inclination. When they have vacant time they are permitted to engage in honorable physical exercises either in the open spaces of the town or in the field."

Two points, however, deserve our attention. The first is that the school is run as a miniature republic. The second is the calibre of the instructors. "The instructors," says our zealous humanist, "are not men from the dregs of human society nor such as are useless for other occupations, but the choice of all the citizens, persons whose standing in the Republic is known and who very often have access to the highest positions of the state."

The last phrase again transports me back to the modern world. I see this fine humanist ideal budding in another place. This time it is a summer school in the hills of New Hampshire, where the children govern themselves in the classroom, where there is no punishment except temporary exclusion from the group, and where, above all, each instructor is chosen because of his creative practice in the subject which he teaches: a highly gifted composer teaches music, an athlete teaches gymnastics, a poet teaches literature. Then I think of all the casual and wasted talents of people who for little more than the asking would share their love of the arts and sciences with little children, if only those who are in charge of little children were not too blind or too fearful to make use of them. Faraday's classic lectures on the physics of the candle, and Ruskin's addresses to a young ladies' boarding school on the function of literature—such things might be multiplied. It is not the creation of this utopian method that is difficult; for the thing has already been done: what we need is its extension. Then children might come to school as gaily as they do in Peterborough, N. H., on the lush summer mornings; and people would not turn their backs on learning any more than they would turn their backs on life. If anyone thinks that Johann Andreæ's prescription for a teaching staff is an impossible one, let him visit the Peterborough School, and examine its records and achievements.

It remains to record the further stages of learning. The halls of the central citadel are divided into twelve departments, and except for the armory, the archives, the printing establishment, and the treasury, these halls are devoted entirely to the arts and sciences.

There is, to begin with, a laboratory of physical science. "Here the properties of metals, minerals, and vegetables, and even the life of animals, are examined, purified, increased, and united for the use of the human race and in the interests of health. . . . Here men learn to regulate fire, make use of air, value the water, and test the earth."

Next to this laboratory is a Drug Supply House, where a pharmacy is scientifically developed, for the curing of physical disease, and adjoining this is a school of medicine, or as Andreæ reports, "a place given over to anatomy. . . . The value of ascertaining the location of the organs and of assisting the struggles of nature no one would deny, unless he be as ignorant of himself as are the barbarians. . . . The inhabitants of Christianopolis teach their youth the operations of life and the various organs, from the parts of the physical body."

We come now then to a Natural Science laboratory which is in effect a Museum of Natural History, an institution founded in Utopia a century and a half before a partial and inadequate substitute—a mere extension of the curio chamber of a Country House—was presented to an admiring world as the British Museum. "This," as Andreæ says, "cannot be too elegantly described," and I heartily agree with him; for he paints the picture of a museum which the American Museum at New York or South Kensington in London has only begun to realize within the last decade or two of their existence.

"Natural history is here seen painted on the walls in detail, and with greatest skill. The phenomena of the sky, views of the earth in different regions, the different races of men, representations of animals, the forms of growing things, classes of stones and gems, are not only on hand and named, but they even teach and make known their nature and qualities. . . . Truly is not recognition of things of the earth much easier of competent demonstration if illustrative materials are at hand and if there is some guide to the memory? For instruction enters altogether more easily through the eyes than through the ears, and much more pleasantly in the presence of refinement than among the base. They are deceived who think it is impossible to teach except in dark caves and with a gloomy brow. A liberal minded man is never so keen as when he has his instructors on confidential terms."

Going farther, we find a mathematics laboratory and a department of mathematical instruments. The first is "remarkable for its diagrams of the heavens, as the hall of physics for its diagrams of the earth. . . . A chart of the star-studded heavens and a reproduction of the whole shining host above were shown," . . . and also "different illustrations representing tools and machines, small models, figures of geometry; instruments of the mechanical arts, drawn, named, and explained." I cannot help expressing my admiration here for the concrete imagination of this remarkable scholar: he deliberately anticipated, not in the vague, allegorical form that Bacon does, but as lucidly as an architect or a museum curator, the sort of institute which South Kensington, with its Departments of Physical and Natural Science, or perhaps the Smithsonian in America, has just begun to resemble. If our museums had begun with the ideal Andreæ had in mind, instead of with the miscellaneous rubbish which was the nucleus of their collections—and still remains the nucleus in many of the less advanced institutions—the presentation of the sciences would be a more adequate thing than it is.

Does Andreæ leave the fine arts out of his picture? By no means. "Opposite the pharmacy is a very roomy shop for pictorial art, an art in which the city takes the greatest delight. For the city, besides being decorated all over with pictures representing the various phases of the earth, makes use of them especially in the instruction of youth and for rendering learning more easy. . . . Besides, pictures and statues of famous men are to be seen everywhere, an incentive of no mean value to the young for striving to imitate their virtue. . . . At the same time also, the beauty of forms is so pleasing to them that they embrace with a whole heart the inner beauty of virtue itself."

At the summit of art and science we naturally find in Christianopolis the temple of religion. Alas! the hand of Calvin has been busy in Christianopolis—recollect that Andreæ once lived in Geneva and admired its ordinances—and attendance at prayers is compulsory. In order to get an idea of this great circular temple, three hundred sixteen feet in circumference and seventy feet high, we must think of a colossal moving picture theater in a modern metropolis. The comparison is not essentially sacrilegious; and I believe that those who will take the trouble to look below the surface will find without difficulty the common denominator between the profane and the ecclesiastical institution. (Attendance at motion pictures, I must quickly add for the benefit of the future historian, has not yet been made compulsory in the modern metropolis.)

One-half of the temple is where the public gatherings take place; and the other is reserved for the distribution of the sacraments and for music. "At the same time, the sacred comedies, by which they set so much store, and are entertained every three months, are shown in the temple."

8

We have discussed folk, work, and place in Christianopolis; and we have dealt in an admittedly sketchy fashion with culture and art. We must now turn attention to the polity; and here we must note that Andreæ's description shifts for once to an allegorical plane, and departs not a little from the realism of his treatment of science and the arts.

At the bottom of the polity there are glimpses of a local industrial association, meeting in the common halls that are provided in the towers of each of the industrial quarters; and we gather that to represent the city at large twenty-four councilmen are chosen, while as the executive department there is a triumvirate consisting of a Minister, a Judge, and a Director of Learning, each of whom is married, for metaphorical point, to Conscience, Understanding, and Truth, respectively. "Each one of the leaders does his own duty, yet not without the knowledge of others; all consult together in matters that concern the safety of the state."

In the censorship of books, Christianopolis reminds us of the Republic; in the exclusion of lawyers it calls up nearly every other utopia; and in its attitude towards crime it has a temperance and leniency that is all its own, for "the judges of this Christian city observe this custom especially, that they punish most severely those misdeeds which are directed straight against God, less severely those which injure men, and lightest of all those who harm only property. As the Christian citizens are always chary of spilling blood, they do not willingly agree upon the death sentence as a form of punishment. . . . For anyone can destroy a man but only the best can reform."

How shall we sum up this government? Let Andreæ speak his own words; for he has reached the innermost shrine of Christianopolis and perceives the center of activity in the state.

"Here religion, justice, and learning have their abode, and theirs is the control of the city. . . I often wonder what people mean who separate and disjoint their best powers, the joining of which might render them blessed as far as may be on earth. There are those who would be considered religious, who throw off all things human; there are some who are pleased to rule, though without any religion at all; learning makes a great noise, flattering now this one, now that, yet applauding itself most. What finally may the tongue do except provoke God, confuse men, and destroy itself? So there would seem to be a need of co-operation which only Christianity can give—Christianity which conciliates God with men and unites men together, so that they have pious thoughts, do good deeds, know the truth, and finally die happily to live eternally."

There are some who might object to this statement on the ground that it smacked too heartily of supernatural religion; but it remains just as valid if we translate it into terms whose theological reactions have been neutralized. To have a sense of values, to know the world in which they are set, and to be able to distribute them—this is our modern version of Andreæ's conception of religion, learning, and justice. A little search might uncover another expression of the Humanist ideal as complete and magnificent as this; but I doubt if it would find a better one. In essence, this blunt and forthright German scholar is standing shoulder to shoulder with Plato: his Christianopolis is as enduring as the best nature of men.

CHAPTER FIVE

How Bacon and Campanella, who have a great reputation as utopians, are little better than echoes of the men who went before them.

CHAPTER FIVE

1

A Genoese sea-captain is the guest of a Grand Master of the Knights Hospitaller. This sea-captain tells him of a great country under the equator, dominated by the City of the Sun. The outward appearance of this country is a little strange—the city with its seven rings named after the seven planets, and its four gates that lead to the four quarters of the earth, and the hill that is topt by a grand temple, and the walls covered with laws and alphabets and paintings of natural phenomena, and the Rulers—Power, Wisdom, and Love—with the learned doctors, Astrologus, Cosmographus, Arithmeticus, and their like: it is an apparition such as never yet was seen on land or sea. Small wonder, for this City of the Sun existed only in the exotic brain of a Calabrian monk, Tommaso Campanella, whose Utopia existed in manuscript before Andreæ wrote his Christianopolis.

We shall not stay long in the City of the Sun. After we have become familiar with the outward color and form of the landscape, we discover, alas! that it is not a foreign country we are exploring, but a sort of picture puzzle put together out of fragments from Plato and More. As in the Republic, there is a complete community of property, a community of wives, and an equality of the sexes; as in Utopia, the younger people wait upon the elders; as in Christianopolis, science is imparted, or at least hinted at, by demonstration. When one subtracts what these other Utopian countries have contributed, very little indeed remains.

But we must not neglect to observe two significant passages. One of them is the recognition of the part that invention might play in the ideal commonwealth. The people of the City of the Sun have wagons that are driven by the wind, and boats "which go over the waters without rowers or the force of the wind, but by a marvelous contrivance." There is a very clear anticipation of the mechanical improvements which began to multiply so rapidly in the eighteenth century. At the tale end of the sea-captain's recital, the Grand Master exclaims: "Oh, if you knew what our astrologers say of the coming age, that has in it more history within a hundred years than all the world had in four thousand years before! Of the wonderful invention of printing and guns, and the use of the magnet. . . . " With the mechanical arts in full development, labor in the City of the Sun has become dignified: it is not the custom to keep slaves. Since everyone takes his part in the common work, there is not more than four hours' work to be done per day. "They are rich because they want nothing; poor because they possess nothing; and consequently they are not slaves to circumstances, but circumstances serve them."

The other point upon which Campanella's observation is remarkably keen is his explanation of the relation of private property and the private household to the commonwealth. Thus:

"They say that all private property is acquired and improved for the reason that each one of us by himself has his own home and wife and children. From this self-love springs. For when we raise a son to riches and dignities, and leave an heir to much wealth, we become either ready to grasp at the property of the state, if in any case fear should be removed from the power which belongs to riches and rank; or avaricious, crafty, and hypocritical, if any is of slender purse, little strength, and mean ancestry. But when we have taken away self-love, there remains only love for the state."

How shall the common Utopia keep from being neglected through each one's concern for his little private utopia?

This is the critical problem that our utopians have all to face; and Campanella loyally follows Plato in his solution. It is perhaps inevitable that each utopian's personal experience of life should enter into his solution, and overwhelmingly give it color; and here the limitations of our utopians are plain. More and Andreæ are married men, and they stand for the individual family. Plato and Campanella were bachelors, and they proposed that men should live like monks or soldiers. Perhaps these two camps are not so far away as they would seem. If we follow the exposition of that excellent anthropologist, Professor Edward Westermarck, we shall be fairly well convinced, I believe, that marriage is a biological institution, and thorough promiscuity is, to say the least, an unusual form of mating. Plato perhaps recognized this when he left us in doubt as to whether a community of wives would be practiced by his artisans and husbandmen. So he perhaps paves the way for a solution by which the normal life for the great majority of men would be marriage, with its individual concerns and loyalties, whilst for the active, creative elements in the community a less secluded form of mating would be practiced. The painter, Van Gogh, has given us a kernel to chew on when he says that the sexual life of the artist must be either that of the monk or the soldier, for otherwise he is distracted from his creative work.

We may leave this question in the air, as long as we realize that all our utopias rest upon our ability to discover some sort of a solution.

2

Francis Bacon's New Atlantis is not a utopia in the sense that I have explained our principle of selection in the preface to the bibliography. It is only a fragment, and not very good as fragments go; and it would drop out altogether from our survey were it not for the hugely over-rated reputation that Bacon has as a philosopher of natural science—indeed, as *the* philosopher after Aristotle.

The greater part of Bacon's ideas are anticipated and more amply expressed by Andreæ. When we have deleted Bacon's multitudinous prayers and exhortations, when we have disposed of his copious descriptions of jewels and velvets and satins and ceremonial regalia, we find that the core of his commonwealth is Salomon's House, sometimes known as the College of the Six Days' Works; which he describes as the noblest foundation that ever was upon earth, and the lantern of the kingdom.

The purpose of this foundation is the "knowledge of the causes and secret motions of things; and the enlarging of the bounds of human empire, to the effecting of all things possible." The material resources of this foundation are manifold. It has laboratories dug into the sides of hills, and observatories with towers half a mile high; it has great lakes of salt and fresh water which seem to anticipate the marine laboratories we know today; and it has engines for setting things in motion. Besides this, there are spacious houses where physical demonstrations are made, and sanatoria where various novel cures are attempted; there are experimental agricultural stations, too, where grafts and crosses are tried. Add to this pharmaceutical laboratories, industrial laboratories, and numerous houses devoted to such things as experiments with sounds, lights, perfumes, and tastes—which Bacon presents in a wild farrago without any regard to the essential sciences to which the work he describes is related—and one has a tally of the "riches of Salomon's House."

Twelve fellows of the college travel into foreign lands to bring back books and abstracts, and reports on experiments and inventions. Three make a digest of experiments. Three collect the experiments of all the mechanical arts, and also of practices which are not brought into the arts. Three try new experiments. Three devote themselves to classifications; and another three, known as dowry men or benefactors, look into the experiments of their fellows and cast about for means of applying them to human life and knowledge. Three fellows consult with the whole body of scientific workers and plan new channels of investigation; and three, who are called interpreters of nature, attempt to raise the results of particular investigations into general observations and axioms.

In telling all this, as in the rest of his New Atlantis,

Bacon is incredibly childish and incoherent: he gives such a description of Salomon's House as a six-year-old schoolboy might give of a visit to the Rockefeller Foundation. Beneath these maladroit interpretations, however, we see that Bacon had a grasp on some of the fundamentals of scientific research, and of the part that science might play in the "relief of man's estate." It is nothing more than a hint, this New Atlantis; but a word to the wise is enough; and as we look about the modern world we see that, in its material affairs at any rate, the great scientific institutes and foundations—the United States Bureau of Standards, for one—play a part not a little like that of the College of the Six Days' Works.

Campanella with his dream of powerful mechanical inventions, in which he had been anticipated by Leonardo, and Bacon with his sketch of scientific institutes—with these two utopians we stand at the entrance to the utopia of means; that is to say, the place in which all that materially contributes to the good life has been perfected. The earlier utopias were concerned to establish the things which men should aim for in life. The utopias of the later Renascence took these aims for granted and discussed how man's scope of action might be broadened. In this the utopians only reflected the temper of their time; and did not attempt to remold it. As a result of our preoccupation with the means, we in the Western World live in an inventor's paradise. Scientific knowledge and mechanical power we have to burn; more knowledge and more power than Bacon or Campanella could possibly have dreamed of. But to-day we face again the riddle that Plato, More, and

Andreæ sought to answer: what are men to do with their knowledge and power?

As we skip here and there through the Utopias of the next three centuries, this question gets more deeply impregnated in our minds.

CHAPTER SIX

How something happened in the eighteenth century which made men "furiously to think," and how a whole group of utopias sprang out of the upturned soil of industrialism.

CHAPTER SIX

1

There is a gap in the Utopian tradition between the seventeenth century and the nineteenth. Utopia, the place that must be built, faded into no-man's land, the spot to which one might escape; and the utopias of Denis Vayrasse and Simon Berington and the other romancers of this in-between period are in the line of Robinson Crusoe rather than the Republic.

One finds the clue to this lapse in Tiphaigne de la Roche's Giphantia, a sketch of what was and what is and what will be, and in particular, an inquiry into the "Babylonian" mode of life. The author of Giphantia tells a parable about Sophia, the incarnation of Wisdom, who rejects the offers of the spendthrift, the merchant, the soldier, and the student, and accepts the suit of a diffident fellow who had retired in solitude to the country, to spend his days like a cultivated gentleman. One remembers the way in which Montaigne spent his declining years; one remembers Voltaire; and one sees how deeply the ideal of Robinson Crusoe—a cultivated Robinson Crusoe, surrounded with books and beyond the reach of any king and court—colored the deepest aspirations of this period. Rousseau, writing about the corrupting influence of the arts and sciences, and Chateaubriand, seeking the noble savage in the American wilderness and finding him in his own bosom—these men struck the dominating note of the eighteenth century. In a society that was already painfully artificial and "arranged" the institutes of Lycurgus and Utopus must have seemed as repressive as those of Louis XIV. So almost two centuries pass before we find any fresh regions to explore in Utopia.

2

The Utopia of Sir Thomas More, and those of the later men of the Renascence, arose, as I have pointed out, from the contrast between the possibilities that lay open beyond the sea and the dismal conditions that attended the breakdown of the town economy of the Middle Age. Like Plato's Republic, it attempted to face the difficult problem of transition.

In the course of the next three centuries the adventure of exploring and ransacking strange countries loses its hold upon men's imagination; and a new type of activity becomes the center of interest. The conquest of alien countries and the lure of gold do not indeed die out with this new interest; but they are subordinated to another type of conquest—that which man seeks to effect over nature. Here and there, particularly in Great Britain, untrained men "with a practical turn" begin to busy themselves with improving the mechanical appartus by which the day's labor is done. A retired barber, named Arkwright, invents a spinning frame, a Scotchman named MacAdam discovers a new method of laying roads; and out of a hundred such inventions during the late eighteenth and early nineteenth centuries a new world comes into existence—a world in which energy derived from coal and running water takes the place of human energy; in which goods manipulated by machinery take the place of goods woven or sawed or hammered by hand. Within a hundred years the actual world and the idola were transformed.

In this new world of falling water, burning coal, and whirring machinery, utopia was born again. It is easy to see why this should have happened, and why about two-thirds of our utopias should have been written in the nineteenth century. The world was being visibly made over; and it was possible to conceive of a different order of things without escaping to the other side of the earth. There were political changes, and the monarchic state was tempered by republicanism; there were industrial changes, and two hungry mouths were born where one could feed before; and there were social changes—the strata of society shifted and "faulted," and men who in an earlier period would have been doomed to a dull and ignominious round, perhaps, took a place alongside those whom inheritance had given all the privileges of riches and breeding.

In contrast to all these fresh possibilities were the dismal realities which were easily enough perceived by people who stood outside this new order, or who by temperament revolted against the indignities and repressions and vilenesses that accompanied it. It is not my particular business here to deal with the facts of history; but unless one understands the facts of history, the utopias which I am about to present lose a good part of their meaning. Those machines whose output was so great that all men might be clothed; those new methods of agriculture and new agricultural implements, which promised crops so big that all men might be fed—the very instruments that were to give the whole community the physical basis of a good life turned out, for the vast majority of people who possessed neither capital nor land, to be nothing short of instruments of torture.

I do not speak too harshly of the early industrial age; it is impossible to speak too harshly. Take the trouble to read Robert Owen's "Essay on the Formation of Character" (Manchester: 1837) and learn what conditions were like in a model factory run by an enlightened employer: it is a picture of unmitigated brutality. One must go back to the blackest periods of ancient slavery for a parallel, if indeed one would find it, for the Pyramids that were built under the lash have a certain grandeur and permanence which justify their existence, whilst the goods which were produced in Yorkshire through the maimed bodies of pauper children proved to be as impermanent as the lives that were sacrificed in making them.

Those who were inside this new order—the Gradgrinds and Bounderbys whom Dickens pictures in "Hard Times"—sought to realize their utopia of the Iron Age on earth. When we are through with the genuine utopians we shall examine the idola by which all the "practical" men of the nineteenth century, Marx as well as Macaulay, patterned their behavior. Those who stood out against this new order were not so much opposed to the new methods as to the purposes for which they were being used: they felt that an orderly conquest of Nature had turned into a wild scramble for loot, and that all the goods industrialism promised were being lost, for the benefit of a few aggressive and unsocialized individuals. With the host of critics and interpreters and reformers that arose in the nineteenth century we shall have a little reckoning to make presently: those who concern us here however belong to the stock of Plato, More, and Andreæ, in that they attempted to see society as a whole, and to protect a new order which would be basically sound as well as superficially improved. Yet with the exception of the utopias which revolted against industrialism these nineteenth century essays are partial and one-sided; for they tend to magnify the importance of the industrial order as much as Gradgrind and Bounderby did, and in doing this they lose sight of the whole life of man. These industrial utopias are no longer concerned with values but with means; they are all instrumentalist. I doubt whether an intelligent peasant in India or China would get out of the whole batch of these utopias a single idea which would have any bearing on the life that he has experienced—so little of human significance remains when the problems of mechanical and political organization have been disposed of!

One symptom of this lack of individuality, this lack of what, in the old-fashioned sense used to be called a philosophy, is the fact that we can treat all these industrial utopias in groups. The first of these group-utopias I shall call, perhaps somewhat arbitrarily, the Associationists.

3

Among the Associationists, the most influential utopian is Charles François Marie Fourier. He was a prolific and incoherent writer, and his Utopia, if the truth be told, exists as disjecta membra rather than as a single work; but in his case I make an exception to the criterion of selection; because in every other respect he has a claim upon our attention. This Fourier was a dry little French commercial traveller, whose personal fortune was lost in the French revolution and whose hopes for founding a real eutopia were blasted by the July revolution of 1830. Again and again he transferred himself from one line of goods to another in order to increase the area of the territory he covered and learn more of the workings of society; and so in his writings a wealth of concrete detail goes hand in hand with personal crotchets and the opinionativeness which arises almost inevitably out of an undisciplined solitude. What follows is a distillation of Fourier's thought, with the lees and orts left in the bottom of the flask.

Fourier differs largely from the early utopians in that he is concerned first of all not with modifying human nature but with finding out what it actually is. His utopia is to be based upon an understanding of man's actual physical and mental makeup, and its institutions are to be such as will permit man's original nature to function freely. The motive which draws his community together is attraction; the power which sets his institutions going is "the passions." Under the head of passions—the original biological equipment—Fourier gives a list of tendencies which corresponds roughly with the modern psychologist's list of instincts.

Fourier takes these passions as "given"; his utopia is not designed to "effect any change in our passions . . . their direction will be changed without changing their nature." As Brisbane says in his Introduction to Fourier's philosophy, social institutions are to these passional forces what machinery is to material forces. A good community, according to

Fourier, is one which will bring all these passions into play, in their complex actions and interactions.

As in the Republic, the ideal behind Fourier's utopia is harmony; for man has a threefold destiny; namely, "an industrial destiny, to harmonize the material world; a social destiny, to harmonize the passional or moral world; and an intellectual destiny, to discover the laws of universal order and harmony." What was at fault with modern civilized societies was that they were incomplete, and in their functioning they created a social dissonance. To overcome this, says Fourier, men must unite into harmonious associations which will give play to all their activities, and which, by erecting common institutions, will do away with the waste arising in the individual's attempts to do for himself all the things which would be done by a complete community.

For this perfect association Fourier provides minute plans and tables; but the general plan can be outlined with brevity.

First of all, Fourier, too, goes back to the valley section. The initial nucleus of his utopia is to consist of a company of 1,500 or 1,600 persons, owning a good stretch of land comprising at least a square league. Since this experimental phalanx, as Fourier called it, would have to stand alone, and without the support of neighboring phalanxes, there will in consequence of this isolation be many gaps in "attraction," and "many passional calms to dread in its workings." To overcome this, Fourier insists that it is necessary to locate the phalanx on soil fit for a variety of functions. "A flat country, such as Antwerp, Leipsic, Orleans, would be totally unsuitable . . . owing to the uniformity of land surface. It will therefore be necessary to select a diversified region, like the surroundings of Lausanne, or at the very least, a fine valley, provided with a stream of water and a forest, like the valley of Brussel or of Halle."

This domain would be laid out in fields, orchards, vineyards, and so forth, according to the nature of the soil and industrial requirements. By devotion to horticulture and arboriculture, Fourier figures, an intensive development would supply abundantly the needs of the colony. The main economic occupation of the phalanx would be agricultural—this is perhaps the great distinction between Fourier and later Utopians—but all the arts would be practiced within the phalanstery, since otherwise the association would be incomplete.

The principle of the association is concretely embodied in a vast edifice in the center of the domain: "a palace complete in all its appointments serving as the residence of the associates. In this palace there are three wings, corresponding to the Material, the Social, and the Intellectual domains. In one wing are the workshops and halls of industry. In another are the library, the scientific collections, museums, artists' studios, and the like. In the center, devoted to the social element, are banquet halls, a hall of reception, and grand salons. At one end of the palace is a Temple of the Material Harmonies, devoted to singing, music, poetry, dancing, gymnastics, painting, and so forth. At the other end is the Temple of Unityism, to celebrate with appropriate rites man's unity with the universe. On the summit there is an observatory with telegraph and signal tower, for communication with other phalanxes.

The phalanx men are associationists; but it follows

from Fourier's theory of the passions that they have private interests as well as public ones; and these private interests are permitted to flourish as long as they do not interfere with social solidarity. Thus they avoid the waste inherent in private housekeeping by having public kitchens, where, incidentally, the children are trained from an early age at cooking, as they are today in one or two experimental schools: nevertheless it is possible to dine in solitude as well as in company. By the same token, every member of the phalanx is guaranteed a minimum of food, clothing, lodging, and even amusements without respect to work; at the same time, private property is sanctioned, and each member extracts from the common store a dividend in proportion to the amount of stock he holds in the association. This dividend, it must be qualified, is considerably reduced by the fact that a system of profit sharing replaces the pure wage system. There is thus a sort of balance between private self-seeking and the maintenance of the public good.

In order to manufacture goods economically, large scale production is introduced wherever possible, and the division of labor is forced to its ultimate limits. Fourier takes account of the resulting monotony, however, and suggests that the monotony be corrected by having recourse to changing tasks and occupations from time to time. In commercial exchange, the phalanx acts as a unit; it constitutes a great self-governing body which traffics in surplus goods with similar associations, without any middleman, in something of the manner, perhaps, that the Co-operative Wholesale Societies do today.

By abolishing the individual household, the phalanx

gives a new freedom to women; and Fourier does not see how it is possible to maintain the system of monogamic proprietorship once women have a free choice of mates. So the women of the phalanx are not intellectual nonentities; and since they no longer preside over the individual home, they help run the whole community. Is it necessary to add the common nurseries, the common schools, the informal education of the children, and the number of other things which follow from this emancipation?

Perhaps one of the most remarkable characteristics of this utopia is its utilization of a moral equivalent for war, long before Professor William James invented the phrase. One of the great functions of the phalanx is the assemblage of productive armies even as "civilization" assembles destructive ones. There is a fine passage in which Fourier pictures an industrial army of golden youths and maidens, "instead of devastating thirty provinces in a campaign, these armies will have spanned thirty rivers with bridges, re-wooded thirty barren mountains, dug thirty trenches for irrigation, and drained thirty marshes." It is for lack of such industrial armies, says Fourier, that civilization is unable to produce anything great.

4

What strikes us when we put together the fragments of Fourier's utopia—as one might put together a jigsaw puzzle—is the fact that he faces the variety and inequality of human nature. Instead of erecting a standard for men to live up to, and rejecting mankind as unfit for utopia because the standard is far beyond its height, the standard itself is founded upon the utmost capacity which a community might be able to exhibit. Fourier meets human nature half-way: he endeavors to project a society which will give regular channels to all its divergent impulses, and prevent them from spilling unsocially all over the landscape. In his statement of this aim there are plenty of weaknesses and absurdities; and I confess that it is hard to take this pathetic little man seriously; but when one has grappled with Fourier's thought one discovers that there is something to take.

Fourier died without persuading anyone to give a trial to his scheme of association; and yet his work was not without its practical influence. The Brook Farm experiment in America was a fumbling attempt to plant a phalanstery without paying any attention to the conditions which Fourier would have rigorously imposed; and the "familistere" of the great steel works of Godin at Guise, in France, is another direct result of Fourier's inspiration. He remains, I believe, the first man who had a plan for colonizing the wilderness of industrial barbarism that existed at the beginning of the nineteenth century, and redeeming that wilderness to civilization.

5

The name of Robert Owen is usually associated with utopianism; but his work belongs more to the "real" world than to the idola of utopia; and I pass over him with the briefest mention, for his projects for a model industrial town have more of the flavor of a poor colony than that of a productive human society. Let us grant him good intentions, organizing ability, and moral fervor: without doubt he is a noble figure, even when his attitude is strained and his tone strident. The series of essays he wrote on love and marriage are marked by fine sympathy and common sense; and it is to be regretted that they are not as widely known as his plans for a new moral world. If this little note can repair the neglect, I have done Owen ample justice: as an active figure in English and American public life he is properly a subject for the social historian. With Owen I must also dismiss John Ruskin, who began in the last quarter of the nineteenth century to develop plans for a "Guild of St. George." This guild was to form a little island of honest labor and sound education in the midst of the turbid sea of industrialism; but it did not embrace the whole of society, and it was utopian only in the sense that the Oneida Community, let us say, was utopian. While they are full of pregnant suggestions, the plans for the Guild are as fragmentary as the New Atlantis.

6

One of the neglected utopias of the mid-nineteenth century is that of James Buckingham.

James Buckingham was one of those erratic men of affairs which the fertile soil of British individualism produces, and which hard British common sense persistently ignores. Like Owen, Buckingham was acquainted with industrial and commercial affairs from the inside: he travelled widely and wrote upon various matters with that copious, amateurish dogmatism and spirit which marks him, perhaps, as the philistine counterpart of John Ruskin. If the utopias of the past express the ideals of the soldier, the farmer, and the artisan, the community which Buckingham projected represents the ideal of the bourgeoisie. Buckingham's Victoria is the ideal aspect of that Coketown which in a later chapter we shall attempt to describe.

We talk loosely of the individualism of the nineteenth century; but in reality it was a period that was thriving with associations. The scope of joint stock companies and philanthropic societies had immeasurably widened. Along with the Mudfog Association, "for the advancement of everything," which Dickens satirized, there sprang up a hundred different societies for performing some special function in the industrial system or realizing some particular purpose in society. Buckingham gives us a picture of his contemporaries which is also a criticism:

"We have the government of the country itself, passing acts of parliament for the better drainage of towns, and a more ample supply of water and air for ventilation. . . . Hence, too, arise associations of noblemen and others for building model lodging houses for the labouring classes; associations for improving the dwellings of the poor; societies for providing baths and bath houses for families unable to procure such conveniences for themselves; associations for establishing suburban villages for the working classes, and to get them at night at least out of the crowded haunts and vicious atmosphere of the towns. And hence we have Temperance Societies, Tract Societies, Home Missions, Asylums for Repentant Magdalens, Homes for Seaman out of Employ, and Houses of Refuge for the Destitute, with soup kitchens and other modes of temporary relief. . . ."

What does this all come to? Let Buckingham answer:

"They are, after all, mere palliatives, and do not reach the seat of the disease. . . . This can only be done by uniting the disjointed efforts of all these well-meaning but partially curative bodies into one, in order to achieve, by their union of means, influence, and example, the erection of a "Model Society," with its model farms, model pastures, model mines, model manufactures, model town, model schools, model workshops, model kitchens, model libraries, and places of recreation, enjoyment, and instruction; all of which could be united in one new Association."

Without inquiring too closely into what a model pasture may be, we may admit that the notion behind Buckingham's proposal was not unsound. The industrial society of his day was in an inchoate, indeed in a chaotic state. In order to sift out the necessary institutions and put them on a firm basis, it was the better part of wisdom to start anew on a fresh area of land and attempt to plan the development of the community as a whole. It is true that in this proposal of Buckingham's there is none of Fourier's brilliant intuitions of a true social order, and none of Ruskin's critical inquiry into what composed a good life: Buckingham took contemporary values for granted. What he sought to do was to realize these values completely, and in orderly fashion. Here are the elements of his proposal.

There is to be formed a model town association, with a limited liability, for the purpose of building a new town called Victoria. The town is to contain every improvement in "position, plan, drainage, ventilation, architecture, supply of water, light, and every other elegance and convenience." Its size is to be about a mile square and the number of inhabitants is not to exceed 10,000. A suitable variety of manufactures and handicraft trades is to be established near the edge of the town; and the town itself is to be surrounded by farm land 10,000 acres broad. All of the lands, houses, factories, and materials are to be the property of the company, and not of any individual; and this property is to be held for the benefit of all in proportion as their shares entitle them. No person is to be a member of the company or an inhabitant of the town except one who is a bona fide shareholder to the extent of at least twenty pounds, and who is ready to subscribe to a drastic series of blue laws which, while permitting freedom in religious worship and preventing child labor, do away with liquor, drugs, and even tobacco.

In addition to these provisions there are to be common laundries, kitchens, refectories, and nurseries; and medical advice is to be given free, at home or in the hospital, as in the army and navy. Education is to be undertaken by the community. Justice, it should be noted by those who are acquainted with an experiment which has recently been started in New York, is to be administered by competent arbitrators under a written code of laws, without the expense, delay, and uncertainty of ordinary legal proceedings. All members are to sign declarations accepting arbitration and waiving other legal proceedings against members of the company.

All these affairs, especially the manner in which the town is to be built, are worked out in considerable detail; thus the size and character of the houses are set forth on the plan, and it is provided that each workingman is to occupy at least one entire and separate room for himself; whilst each married couple without children gets two rooms, and each family in which there are children is to occupy at least three rooms for domestic purposes. I have set down all these details baldly because the plan itself is a bald one; and no amount of fine writing will embellish it. Buckingham's society is not based upon a thoroughgoing criticism of human institutions: the ends for which this society exists are doubtless those which were held good and proper by the Macaulays and the Martineaus. What is interesting in Buckingham's utopia is the definite plans and specifications, accompanied by drawings; for this is surely one of the first attempts to put a problem in social engineering on a basis from which an engineer or an architect could work.

Buckingham thought that, given a successful model town, the rest of England might in time be colonized by the surplus population, and thus the old centers of black industry would be wiped out. Nor was Buckingham altogether deceived. His utopia was a limited one, but out of his limitations has come success. In 1848 this utopia was a chimera; in 1898, Mr. Ebenezer Howard reconstructed it and set it forth in a persuasive little book called Tomorrow, and as a direct result of the plans advocated by Mr. Howard, a flourishing garden city called Letchworth has come into existence; which in turn has propagated another garden city, called Welwyn; and at the same time has, by example, paved the way for numerous garden villages and garden suburbs in various parts of Europe and in America.

With this mid-Victorian theorist, we pass over from a pre-scientific method of thinking to one which sacrifices the artistic imagination to a realistic grasp of the facts; and in this passage something is gained and something is lost. Buckingham gains by confining his proposals to what is immediately practicable. He loses by not having the imaginative energy to criticize the ways, means, and ends that are sanctioned by current practise. If utopia begins with Plato's glorious dream of an organic community, the image of the just man made perfect, it cannot end with Buckingham's invention of a shell. Nevertheless, through the nineteenth century the superficial utopians, the shell-builders, are dominant; and we must continue to examine them.

CHAPTER SEVEN

How some utopians have thought that a good community rested at bottom on the right division and use of land; and what sort of communities these land-animals projected.

CHAPTER SEVEN

1

Before the Industrial Revolution upset the balance of social power, there were little villages in England where, on a limited scale and to no very grand purpose, a quiet and placid and fairly jolly existence must have been the rule of things. These villages were those in which the land was either held in freehold by small proprietors, or where there still remained for the use of each inhabitant certain common pastures and wastes. Under this regime there was a fair degree of prosperity with which only the wind and the weather and war could interfere. Something of the savor of this life Mr. W. H. Hudson finely conveys in his A Traveller in Little Things; and a century ago Cobbett made a series of excellent snapshots in his Rural Rides.

When the mediæval order broke down the great proprietors began to seize this common land; and during the eighteenth century, under the incentive of big-scale scientific agriculture, the seizure went on at a merry pace. The peasant without land was forced to migrate to the new towns, as the Hammonds have pictured in their graphic work on the Town Laborer; and the labor of the peasant and his family fed the machines which the Watts and Arkwrights were developing in the eighteenth century. Industrial progress and social poverty went hand in hand. The period before the

Industrial Revolution seemed in comparison a real utopia; and the key to this utopia was the land.

The importance of land in the constitution of civil society was emphasized by the Diggers of Cromwell's time; one of them, Gerard Winstanley, wrote a minor utopia to prove that the land should be held in common; and this view was reinforced—without the communism—in a purely political utopia called Oceana by James Harrington, who lived during the same period. Harrington advocated such a distribution of land that the landed gentry should be the leaders, and the commonalty should have the preponderance of power.

Out of all the modern utopias with which we have to reckon there are two, in particular, in which the common possession of land is the foundation of every other institution. These are Spensonia and A Visit to Freeland.

2

The early part of the nineteenth century is remarkable for the fact that men of common stock, usually self-educated, began to apply their wits to improving the conditions of the class to which they belonged; and in particular there was in London a peasant named William Cobbett, a tailor named Francis Place, and a stationer named Thomas Spence who devoted a good part of what remained over from their working days to plans for bettering man's estate.

Thomas Spence had a shop in High Holborn from which he published little pamphlets of rough philosophy, called Pig's Meat; in 1795 he issued A Description of Spensonia, which was followed in 1801 by The

Constitution of Spensonia: A Country in Fairyland situated between Utopia and Oceana; brought from thence by Captain Swallow. Spence's title to have written a complete utopia rests upon the fact that he proposes a return to an environment which had once been, in its fashion, complete.

Spensonia begins with a parable about a father who had a number of sons, who built them a ship for traffic, and who provided that the profits of the enterprise were to be shared in common. This ship is wrecked upon an island; and the sons quickly awake to the conclusion that if "they did not apply the Marine Constitution given them by their father to their landed property, they would soon experience inexpressible inconveniences. They therefore declared the property of the island to be the property of them all collectively, in the same manner as the ship had been, and that they ought to share the profits thereof in the same way. The island they named Spensonia, after the ship which their father had given them. They next chose officers to mark out such portions of the land, as every person or family desired to occupy, for which they were to receive for the use of the public a certain rent according to its value. This rent was applied to public uses or divided among themselves as they thought proper. But in order to keep up the remembrance of their rights, they decreed that they should never fail to share at rent-time, an equal dividend, though ever so small, and though the public demands should be ever so urgent. . . . As they had determined, when seeing that every ship they should build and man, should . . . be the property of the crew, so, in conformity therewith, they decreed that every district or parish which they should people, should be the property of the inhabitants, and the rent and police of the same at their disposal. . . . A National Assembly or Congress consisting of delegates from all the parishes takes care of the national concerns, and defrays the expenses of the state and matters of common utility, by a pound rate from each parish without any other tax."

What is a parish and what is its work? Look around the English countryside and see.

A parish, to begin with, is a "compact portion of the country, designedly not too large that it may the more easily be managed by the inhabitants with respect to its revenues and the police."

"The parishes build and repair houses, make roads, plant hedges and trees, and in a word do all the business of a landlord. . . . A parish has many heads to contrive what ought to be done. Instead of debating about mending the state, . . . (for ours needs no mending) we employ our ingenuity nearer home, and the result of the debates are in every parish, how we shall work such a mine, make such a river navigable, drain such a fen, or improve such a waste. These things we are all immediately interested in, and have each a vote in executing."

There is a rough, homespun quality about this utopia, and it needs a visit to the English villages of the New Forest or the Chiltern Hills, where some of the common lands have been kept, to see what a rural utopia would be like if it could keep itself free from invaders who sought to live off the fat of the land without contributing their labor. Spence was not altogether blind to the necessity of keeping watch over this constitution of equality; and he places his utopia in the care of two guardian angels—Voting by Ballot and the Universal Use of Arms—two angels which look less formidable and potent in the twentieth century than they did in the first decade of the nineteenth, when the first had still to be tried, and when the second was not complicated by the invention of machine guns and poison gases.

At the bottom of Spence's Utopia, however, lies the conviction which he shares with Plato and all the other genuine utopians; namely, that in Thoreau's words less is accomplished by the thousands who are hacking at the branches of evil than by one who is striking at the root. Spence, it must be remembered, wrote in the thick of the agitation for parliamentary reform which was the keynote of so much nineteenth century activity —the chartist movement, parliamentary socialism, and the like, being so many rainbows in the bubble of political effort which burst with such a bang when the Great War broke out. Spence saw the futility of these superficial demands. He said:

"Thousands of abortive schemes are daily proposed for redressing grievances and mending the constitution, whereas, the shoes were so ill-made at first, and so worn, rotten, and patched already, that they are not worth the trouble or expense, but ought to be thrown to the dunghill; and a new pair should be made, neat, tight, and easy as for the foot of one that loves freedom and ease. Then would your controversies about this and the other way of cobbling, that continually agitate you, be done away; and you would walk along the rugged and dirty path of life easy and dry-shod."

3

The next utopia, Freeland, marks a transition between the utopia in which the land alone is held by the community and that in which land and capital and all the machinery of production belong to a national state.

The writer of this utopia was an Austrian economist, Theodor Hertzka; and he first published his view in considerable detail, with reference to current economic doctrines, in a book called Freeland: A Social Anticipation. He condensed these doctrines in another book called A Visit to Freeland, or the new Paradise Regained, an attempt to picture his freeman's commonwealth in action.

These books formed the center of a whirlwind of agitation; a magazine sprang up; societies were organized in various cities in Europe and America; and a definite attempt was made to colonize a certain section of Africa, selected by Hertzka; an attempt which, alas! met with speedy failure as a result of the obtuseness and international jealousy of various colonial officials. The first book was published in 1889; and all this happened in the early nineties. Perhaps the only practical effect of it was—and this is mere conjecture—to turn the thoughts of certain Zionists, like Israel Zangwill, from establishing Zion in Jerusalem to building it up again in some more suitable region in the heart of Africa.

Freeland may be described as an individualist Utopia on a social foundation. Hertzka was filled with sympathy and admiration for the doctrines that Adam Smith set forth in The Wealth of Nations; and he desired to realize a society in which the maximum amount of individual freedom and initiative would prevail, especially in industrial enterprises. This leads to a paradox; namely, that in order to ensure freedom it is impossible to practise laissez faire; for the effect of laissez faire is to permit accidental aggregations of wealth and power to threaten the freedom that less fortunate individuals seek to enjoy. So far from being an anarchist utopia, Freeland is a co-operative commonwealth in which the State acts as an interested party in the production and distribution of goods. This differs from socialism in name; and it differed from the practical socialist agitation of the time in that it relied, not upon turning over established institutions in Europe, but in turning over a new leaf in the Kenia Highlands of Africa; but Hertzka's "individualism" comes to almost the same thing.

4

A visit to Freeland teaches us little about the arts of social life or the constitution of a good society. What we can learn is one of the methods by which—on hypothesis anyway—the industrial mechanism might be controlled.

In Freeland there are five fundamental laws; and of these the first is the most important; namely, that:

Every inhabitant has an equal right to the common land and to the means of production which are furnished by the state.

The other fundamental laws have to do with the support of women and children, old men, and those otherwise unfit to work, all of whom have the right of maintenance, corresponding to the amount of credit belonging to the state; with the provision of universal suffrage for all above twenty-five years of age; and with the establishment of independent legislative and executive branches of the government.

Let us follow the visitor to Freeland as he makes his first explorations in Edendale, its principal city, and learns how affairs are conducted. If this is an individualist utopia it is not by any means free from the services of a bureaucracy; for first of all the visitor turns to the Central Statistical Office, where records are kept of the occupations that are open and the amount of pay offered by each. "Every inhabitant of Freeland," our visitor finds, "has the right to become a member of any business he pleases. One has only to present oneself for this purpose; for the managers only decide upon the manner in which the members are to be employed, and not on the membership itself." In practice, the number of individuals with private businesses and partnerships seems to be limited, for big companies not merely operate factories but provide restaurant service, build houses, and even supply domestic service to private individuals and households.

(The visitor has his boots blacked by one of these associated menials, and his hostess explains how the services of a caterer and a valet may be obtained by calling up a central distributing agency.)

The sole condition upon which a person or company is allowed to engage in business is that the public be kept informed of all business transactions. "The companies are therefore obliged to conduct their bookkeeping openly. The prices at which goods are bought and sold, the net profits and the number of workmen, must be communicated at intervals which are fixed according to the judgment of the central office."

Observe that Hertzka reckons with the fact that in an industrial society, access to machinery is just as important as access to the land, since, in a manner of speaking, all our modern activities, even agriculture, are parasitic upon machinery. Hence the collection and distribution of capital is managed in the interests of the whole community; the first being taken care of by a yearly tax, which obviates the need—and perhaps the possibility—of individual savings, whilst the capital is distributed without interest to the companies that make application for it. The community pays for the plant through the added charge which is laid on consumers; the credit advanced is cancelled out through production. This arrangement does away with the standing charge for capital which is maintained under present day production for profit even after the original capital has been paid off in dividends; and above all, it does away with the practice of capitalizing increased returns in such a way as to enlarge the amount of the standing charge for capital. The social use of capital to advance production, rather than to provide fixed incomes for a rentier class, is recognized in Freeland.

Since our visitor is an engineer, he turns to a plant devoted to the manufacture of railway equipment; and notes that it is run under the following statutes.

1. Everyone is free to join the first Edendale Engine and Railway Manufacturing Co., even if he also belongs to other companies. Everyone is also permitted to leave the company whenever he chooses. The board of management decides in what branch of the works the members shall be employed.

2. Every member is entitled to an amount of the net proceeds of the company corresponding to the quantity of work which is done.

3. The amount of work is calculated according to the number of hours, to which two per cent. is added to that of the older members, and ten per cent. to foremen, and ten per cent. for night work.

4. The engineers are paid as if working from ten to fifteen hours, according to ability. The value of the manager is estimated in the general assembly.

5. Out of the company's profits a deduction is first made towards repayment of capital, and after this the tax to the state is deducted. The remainder is divided among members.

6. If the company is dissolved or liquidated, the members are responsible in proportion to the amount of profit which they get from revenues of the company, and this responsibility for the amount which is still pledged is proportionately laid upon new members. When a member leaves the company, his responsibility for debt which has already been contracted is not extinguished. In case of dissolution, liquidation, or sale, this responsibility corresponds to the claim of the responsible member to the means of the company which are in hand, or to his share in what is sold.

7. The principal judicial body of the company is the general assembly in which every member has the same right to speak and exercise the same active and passive right of choice. The general assembly makes its determination by simply counting the majority of votes. A majority of three quarters is necessary for changing the statutes and for a dissolution or liquidation of the company.

8. The general assembly practises its right either directly or by means of chosen officials, who are answerable to it for their actions.

9. The business of the society is managed by a directorate of three members who hold office at the will of the general assembly. The subordinate functionaries are chosen by the managers.

10. The general assembly selects every year a committee of inspection which consists of five members. This body has to control and make a report upon the books and the manner in which the company is conducted.

Now, as a member of the company, our visitor would have the amount he has earned credited to him at a Central Bank, which keeps his accounts and sends him an abstract every week; and through this bank he would make the larger part of his disbursements. The products of the company, moreover, are valued, stored, and sold by a Central Warehouse, in much the same fashion that under the present regime a manufacturer's whole output may be disposed of through a big department store or a mail order house.

Let us now sum this up. The collection and disposition of capital belongs to the community; and the total capital available for further production each year is based directly upon the productive capacities of the community, without the waste and leakage that arises in present-day society though what Mr. Thorstein Veblen calls the conspicuous waste—the futile expenditures—of the leisured classes. That this collection of a capital tax upon income would be any more difficult than the present corporation tax or private income tax, which is now dissipated to the extent of some 90 per cent. or so upon armies and navies, is seriously to be doubted. In addition to this, the process of open book-keeping enables the Central Bank and the Central Warehouse to have an accurate knowledge of potential production, and thus there exists an accurate basis for apportioning credit. At the same time the value of commodities comes by this means to have a direct relation to the costs of production rather than to what the traffic will bear.

On all these heads the trained economist will doubtless have many points to contest; but in their broad outlines there is no abrupt departure from current practise in any of these items, and not much reason, perhaps, why they should not be more thoroughly instituted.

With the various ramifications of Edendale industry and corporate finance it is not my business to deal; we have gone far enough to see that very little indeed remains when the question of means has been gone into.

The chief good that Freeland seems to offer is freedom in industrial enterprise. An association of men can get land and capital on demand, and devote themselves to either agriculture or manufacturing industry; and the risk of failure is minimized by a complete knowledge of the probable demand and probable supply calculated by the statistical bureau. Failing an outlet for industry through association, there remains the land itself, for individual cultivation. "Every family in Freeland dwells in its own house, and every house is surrounded by its great garden, a thousand square meters in extent. These houses are the private property of the inhabitants, and serve, like the gardens, for private use. The inhabitants of Freeland do not, as a rule, recognize any kind of ownership of land; they rather go upon the principle that the land must be put in everyone's hands to do with what he chooses. This, in the most literal and wide sense of the word, means that every inhabitant of Freeland can cultivate every piece of land whenever he pleases. But this only relates to the land which is set apart for cultivation, and not that set apart for living upon. . . . The inhabitants of Freeland have agreed, with regard to the size and disposition of the land, serving for the creation of a dwelling house, to form regulations, and a kind of building court . . . which has to determine what ground is and what is not to be built upon, parcels out the land for building, sees to the laying out of streets, canals, and the like, and especially takes care that not more than one building is erected upon one building allotment."

5

What sort of life arises out of this kind of industrial association, these provisions for the common use of machinery and land? It is all rather dry and colorless, a sort of picture postcard view of the Promised Land.

We are told that there are a great number of public buildings in Edendale—an administrative palace, the Central bank, the University, the Academy of Arts, three Public Libraries, four Theaters, the grand central goods warehouse, a great number of schools and other buildings. In addition, extraordinary means are taken to provide for public cleanliness, and the aqueducts in Edendale—we seem to be reading a Chamber of Commerce report!—are "almost without any equal in the world," moreover, "they are being extended daily." The refuse is cleaned away by a system of pneumatic sucking apparatus. The streets are entirely macadamized. Electric tramways cross them in every direction and bind the suburbs to the town. Such glimpses as we get of Edendale remind us, in fact, of a go-ahead city in California or South Africa. The utopia of Freeland is progressive enough in all conscience; for many of these mechanical devices were only vague anticipations in 1889; but it is progressive in a mechanical sense; and when we examine it carefully, people seem to live the same sort of life here as they do in a "modern" European or American city.

There are differences, of course; and I do not seek to minimize their importance: the slum proletariat has been abolished; everyone belongs to the middle class and enjoys the felicities of a high-grade clerk or an engineer or minor official. This is the peculiarity of our nineteenth century utopians: they do not so much criticize the goods of their times as demand more of them! Buckingham and Hertzka, though they differ in details, wish to extend middle class values throughout society—comfort and security and a plenitude of soap and sanitation. Even when the means they propose are revolutionary, the institutions they would erect are conceived very much in the image of current use and wont, and are unspeakably tame.

As we pass from Hertzka to Bellamy these facts glare insistently at us. The slight air of tedium that I have not been able to disguise in dealing with these utopias arises, I believe, from our excessive familiarity with their contents. Our nineteenth century utopias, if we except those of Fourier and Spence and a few more distinguished ones which we shall presently come to, do not dream of a renovated world: they keep on adding inventions to the present one. These utopias become vast reticulations of steel and redtape, until we feel that we are caught in the Nightmare of the Age of Machinery; and shall never escape. If this characterization seem unjust, I beg the reader to compare the utopias before Bacon with the utopias after Fourier, and find out how little human significance remains in the post-eighteenth century utopia when the machinery for supporting the good life is blotted out. These utopias are all machinery: the means has become the end, and the genuine problem of ends has been forgotten.

CHAPTER EIGHT

How Étienne Cabet dreamed of a new Napoleon called Icar, and a new France called Icaria; and how his utopia, with that which Edward Bellamy shows us in Looking Backward, gives us a hint of what machinery might bring us to if the industrial organization were nationalized.

CHAPTER EIGHT

1

ÉTIENNE CABET opened his eyes upon the year that preceded the meeting of the National Assembly in 1788, and closed them upon the Empire of Napoleon III.

It would be foolish to give an account of Cabet's Voyage en Icarie without noting these facts; for the reason that Cabet's most impressionable years were drenched with the flamboyant light of the Napoleonic conquests and the Napoleonic tradition which remained as an afterglow when the conquests themselves had fallen below the horizon. The spectacle of a nationalized church and a nationalized system of education, extending their ministrations to the smallest commune through a vast system of bureaucracy, must have given a solidity to his dreams which the interruption of the first Napoleon's personal downfall could only have reinforced.

To understand why the Journey to Icaria, as we may call it, should have been one of the best sellers among workingmen in 1845, and to see why Louis Blanc should have attempted to set up an organization of National Workshops in 1848, one must realize the historic momentum of Napoleon's dictatorship. Cabet consciously or unconsciously idealized the Napoleonic tradition; and in Icaria he consummated it. That Cabet's futile will-to-power should have led him, under the inspiration of Owen, to the swamps of Missouri as the leader of a little band of communist pioneers is an ironic twist of circumstance: his Icaria was a national state, with all its pomp and dignity and splendor, and not a squalid collection of huts in the midst of a dreary prairie. Cabet died in America, as much perhaps from an outraged sense of dignity as from any physical disease, and nothing came of his utopia until Edward Bellamy gave it a fresh outline in Looking Backward.

2

With the romantic element in the Journey to Icaria —the English lord and the Icarian family he visits, and the various friendships and love affairs that are outlined in its pages—I purpose to have nothing to do. These things add an element of complication to Cabet's picture without doing very much to illuminate it.

Icaria is a country divided into a hundred provinces almost equal in extent and almost the same in population. These provinces are in turn divided into ten communes, which are likewise almost equal, and the provincial capital is in the center of the province, whilst each communal city is the center of the commune. The elegance and precision of the decimal system has overlaid the facts of geography and as one looks over the map of the imaginary country one recalls the way in which the French revolution divided France into arbitrary administrative areas called departments, upsetting those ancient regional groupings which corresponded, roughly, with the natural units of soil, climate, population, and historic continuity.

In the midst of Icaria is the city of Icara. Icara is a reconstructed Paris, built on a reconstructed Seine.

It is almost circular, cut into two equal parts by a river whose banks have been straightened and enclosed in two straight walls; and the bed has been deepened to receive ocean vessels. In the middle of the city the river divides into two arms, which form a rather big circular island—though the islands formed naturally by the division of a river are inevitably not circular!—and here is the civic center, planted with trees, in the midst of which stands a palace. There is a superb garden elevated on a terrace; in the center, a vast column surmounted by a colossal statue that dominates all the buildings. On each side of the river is a big quay, bordered by public offices. The effect is indubitably metropolitan.

The city is divided into quarters: Icara has sixty communes of almost equal size. In each quarter is a school, a hospital, a temple, shops, public places, and monuments. The streets are straight and wide, the city being traversed by fifty avenues parallel to the river and fifty perpendicular to it. How it is possible to reconcile this street plan with a circular city I have no notion; and Cabet apparently did not take the trouble to cast his verbal specifications into a definite picture or plan. Each block has fifteen houses on each side, with a public building in the middle, and one at each end; and between the rows of houses are gardens which the inhabitants of Icaria, like those of Utopia, have a great pride in keeping up. The blocks are arranged around squares, very much like those of Belgravia and Mayfair in London; but the gardens are public ones and are cared for by the inhabitants.

The Icarian villages are almost as metropolitan as the principal city itself. One notes a great preoccupation with hygienic conveniences and sanitary regulations. There are dust collectors of special model; the sidewalks are covered with glass against rain; and the stations for omnibuses are also covered. The streets are well-lighted and paved. Stables, slaughter houses, and hospitals are on the outskirts of the village. The factories and warehouses are on the railway lines and canals, and half the streets are closed to all traffic except dog-carts.

In sum, Icaria enjoys a highly sophisticated and metropolitan form of life. Everything has been "arranged," everything has been "attended to." There are no upsetting complications and diversities. Even the weather has been disposed of. Nothing short of a very powerful and persistent organization could have accomplished these things. What is this organization?

3

In the beginning was Icar, the dictator who established the government of Icaria, and out of Icar there sprang a number of bureaux, departments, and committees. Let us follow a typical Icarian through his day, and examine the institutions he comes in contact with.

Our Icarian is an early riser by necessity, for at 6 A. M. breakfast is served in a restaurant or factory. It is not a capricious breakfast; it is such a breakfast, perhaps, as the guardians of Battle Creek, Michigan, dream of. The food that is served in Icaria is regulated by a committee of scientists; and while everybody has all that is good for him, precisely what is good and in what amounts, someone else has decided in advance.

So it is at present in our armies and navies, and to some extent in our cheap lunchrooms, the difference being that there remains, outside Icaria, the possibility of breaking away from the routine and following caprice and appetite without respect for the committee of dietitians.

When our Icarian has breakfasted, he goes to his work, seven hours in summer, six in winter. He works the same number of hours as every other Icarian, and whether he works in the field or the workshop, the products of his industry are deposited in public stores. Who is his employer? The State. Who owns all the instruments of production and service, down to the horses and carriages? The State. Who organizes the workers? The State. Who constructs the stores and factories, attends to the cultivation of the ground, has houses built, and makes all the things necessary for clothing, lodging, and transport? The same. In theory, the public is the sole proprietor and director of industry; in practice—Cabet doesn't tell us otherwise and it necessarily follows in a system of national industry—a body of engineers and officials have taken over the dictatorship of Icar and are running the affairs of the community.

How familiar this Icaria seems to us. Utopia—*c'est la guerre!*

When he is through with his work, our Icarian possibly changes his clothes. Exactly what clothes are necessary, and what are permissible has already been prescribed by a committee on clothes; which comes to saying that every Icarian's dress is a uniform, even as every Icarian is an official of the State. Eating, working, dressing, sleeping—there is no getting away from

State regulations. The uniformity that irks us in modern life and that makes people who have some remnant of free initiative in their makeup chafe in the civil service, to say nothing of the army, is extended to the last degree in Icaria. Napoleon's conception of a nation in arms is dominant; only now it is a nation in overalls.

Our Icarian's father and mother were married after a six-month interval of courtship. Since they took advantage of the institution at the earliest moment permitted by law, he was twenty and she was eighteen. By education, they had been taught to look upon conjugal fidelity as a desideratum; and they realized that concubinage and adultery would be looked upon as crimes by public opinion, even if these crimes were not punished by law. Before our Icarian was born his mother received public instruction on maternity.

Up to the age of five our Icarian's education was domestic; but from the fifth to the seventeenth or eighteenth year, domestic instruction was combined with intellectual and moral education, under a program laid down by a committee which had consulted all systems of education, ancient and modern. His general or elementary education was the same as that of every other Icarian; but at seventeen for girls and eighteen for men, his professional education began.

The only industries or professions open to our Icarians were those recognized and sanctioned by the State; and every year a list is published telling the number of workers needed in each profession. The number of workers, in turn, is determined by a committee on industry, which plans the amount of goods that must be produced during the coming year. Our

Icarian begins work at eighteen, his sister at seventeen; and he is exempt from work at sixty-five, while she would be exempt at fifty. The republic, I may note parenthetically, asks from each commune the sort of industrial and agricultural production which goes best with its natural resources; delivering its surplus production to other communes and giving it, in turn, what it may lack.

Cabet describes all these institutions in the minutest fashion, down to the noiseless window with which each Icarian's house is equipt; but the broad outlines of the industrial and social system are contained in this picture. What we see is a National State, abundantly organized for war, and remaining on that footing in the midst of its peace-time activities. What is not of national importance, in this scheme of things, is of no importance; and the people who decide what is or is not of national importance are the officeholders—I find it difficult to discover a utopian equivalent for this word or to fancy any great improvement in utopia—in the capital.

The political activities that regulate these Icarian institutions do not greatly reassure us. From each of the thousand communes two deputies are chosen to hold office for two years: this constitutes the national representation. The basis of this system is the communal assembly; and from this communal assembly the provincial representatives are drawn. The national executive consists of sixteen members, each with a special department; and it is plain that here is the seat of power; for exactly what business remains in the hands of the two thousand legislators when the food committee has determined the amount and variety of food, the industrial committee the quantity and kind of manufactured products, and the educational committee the methods, subjects, and aims of education, it is a little hard to determine.

There are no newspapers and no means of organized criticism, except the right of submitting propositions to the popular assemblies. The only thing resembling public opinion is the collective opinion of these assemblies. The newspapers are published by the government, one for the nation, one for the province, and one for the commune; and they are devoted solely to the presentation of news, divorced from opinion. For this kind of political system, and for all the power that it might presume to wield, there is a word in philosophy which has no substitute—epiphenomenon. The popular system of representation in Icaria is but a shadow of that dictatorial power which was first wielded by Icar and was in turn transmitted to the committees and bureaux.

If I have been criticizing Icaria in terms of the last century of political experience, I can only plead that it is because Icaria is so little like Utopia and so much like the actual order of things. It must be prepared to stand fire as a *fait accompli:* indeed, in the early days of the second Russian revolution it came near to being a *fait accompli*—there was more of Cabet than of Marx perhaps in embryonic Soviet Russia! Icaria is essentially not an ideal but an idealization; and it is in order to keep the two from being confused that I have emphasized its little weaknesses. What is good in Icaria is what is good in the institution of an army; what is bad is what is bad in the execution of a war. If the good life could be perpetrated by a junta of busybodies, as Plato would call them, Icaria would be a model community.

4

Looking backward into the future: that was the paradox by which a young New England romancer, Edward Bellamy, concerned like Thoreau and Emerson and the rest of the great Concord school with the well-being of his community, descended from literature to sociology; and stirred the minds of thousands of people in America in much the same fashion that Theodor Hertzka, writing at the same time, stirred his European contemporaries. Having begun to romanticize about reality, Bellamy during the decade that followed the publication of Looking Backward, devoted himself to realizing his romance. In a later work, Equality, he set forth his picture of the New Society of the year 2000 in much greater detail; just as if the popularity of his first work committed him to take up seriously the tasks of the economist and the statesman.

The chief pleasure, nowadays, in both of these books is the familiar one of recognition; for if Bellamy did not portray a better future he at any rate, like Mr. H. G. Wells, in his early romances, outlined many parts of a future that has for us, in the twentieth century, become an actuality; a fact which makes us realize very poignantly the limitations of his utopia. In spite of a thin-lipped style, Bellamy handles his story in a neat, workmanlike way, with a certain plausibility and familiarity which doubtless explains the fact that it can still be found, without any difficulty, on the fiction shelves of our circulating public libraries.

The preface to Looking Backward is dated: "Historical Section Shawmut College, Boston, December 26, 2000." In that preface the work is presented as an avowed romance which will enable the readers of 2000 to realize the gaps that separate them from their ancestors, and to value the prodigious "moral and material" transformation that has taken place in a few generations. Julius West is a person whom our Shawmut historian invents, to bridge the gap between the two eras, Julius West, a young man of wealth, sensitive to the ignominy of his position, and feeling that, as a "rich man living among the poor, an educated man among the uneducated," he "was like one living in isolation among a jealous and alien race." In order to overcome his insomnia West sleeps in a vaulted room in the foundations of his house, and gets put to sleep by a hypnotist; and so by a dramatic oversight he hibernates for 113 years, and awakens among strange faces. Needless to say, West has a love affair in the old world which is carried on in the new, through a descendant of the girl he meant to marry; and it is equally needless to observe that he reawakens to the world of 1887 as soon as the institutions of 2000 have been described and the love affair has been resolved.

Let us take West's muzziness, his amazement, and his sense of isolation for granted, and follow him as he explores his new environment.

5

If Plato cavalierly disposes of the labor problem of the Republic by permitting things to remain pretty much as they were, Bellamy makes the solution of labor organization and the distribution of wealth the key to every other institution in his utopia.

In the United States of 1887 the growing organization of labor and the aggregation of capital into trusts were the two chief economic factors: Dr. Leete, Julius West's host, pictures how this aggregation and combination were continued until, by a mere shift of gears, "the epoch of trusts had ended in The Great Trust." In a word, "the people of the United States concluded to assume the conduct of their own business, just as one hundred years before they had assumed the conduct of their own government, organizing now for industrial purposes on precisely the same grounds that they had organized for political purposes." Was there any violence in this transition? Ah no! everything had been prepared beforehand by public opinion, the great corporations had gradually trained everybody into an acceptance of large-scale organization, and the final step of merging all the big corporations into a national corporation occurred without a jar. With the assumption by the nation of the mills, machinery, railroads, farms, mines, and capital in general, all the difficulties of labor vanished, for every citizen became by virtue of his citizenship an employee of the government, and was distributed according to the needs of industry.

In 2000 "the labor army" is not a figure of speech: it is an army indeed, for the nation is a single industrial unit, and the principle upon which the working force is recruited is universal compulsory industrial service. After a man's education has been completed in the common school system, which extends straight through college, he must first serve a term of three years in an unclassified labor army, which performs all the rough and menial tasks of the community. When this period is over, he is permitted to offer himself as a recruit in any of the trades or professions which may be declared open by the government, and can train for his calling up to the age of thirty, in the national schools and institutes. In order to attract people into occupations where they are needed, the hours are reduced and, for the dangerous trades, volunteers are called for. There are however no discriminations in pay. Every person is credited with a sum of four thousand dollars per annum at the National Bank, a sum which he receives because of his needs as a man and not because of his capacity as a worker. Instead of being rewarded for giving the full measure of his energies and abilities, a man is penalized if he fails to do so. It is possible to shift from one branch of the service to another, under certain restrictions, even as in the navy one can change one's rating and apply for service on a different ship or station, but except for the possibility of retiring on a half-income at the age of thirty-three, everyone must remain at work until he is forty-five.

To this rule there is one exception; and we may note ironically that it is made in favor of the writer's guild. If a man produces a book he may name his own royalties, and live as long from this income as the sale will allow; and if he wishes to start a newspaper or a magazine, and can get credit from a sufficient number of other people to support his enterprise, there is nothing to prevent him from remitting service to the amount his guarantors are ready to deduct from their personal income. In other words, a man must "either by literary, artistic, or inventive productiveness indemnify the nation for the loss of his services, or must get a sufficient number of people to contribute to such an indemnity." This is the one open hole in our militarized, industrial utopia; and I think it is the most acceptable feature in the whole system. A community organized as a single unit, directed by a general staff at Washington, and perpetually exhibiting a herd complex which every institution would naturally reinforce, might not be a very genial shelter for the soul of an artist; but if it were, this means of support would doubtless be fair and excellent for the encouragement of the arts.

To go back to our army. The entire field of production and distribution is divided into ten great departments, each representing a group of allied industries; and each particular industry is in turn represented by a subordinate bureau, which has a complete record of the plant and the force under its control, of the present product, and of the means of increasing it. The estimates of the distributive department, after adoption by the administration, are sent as mandates to the ten great departments, which allot them to the subordinate bureaux, representing the particular industries, and these set the men at work. . . . "After the necessary contingents have been detailed for the various industries, the amount of labor left for other employment is expended in creating fixed capital, such as buildings, machinery, engineering works, and so forth."

In order to safeguard the consumer from the caprices of the administration, a new article must be produced as soon as a certain guaranteed demand for it has been established by popular petition, whilst an old article must be continued to be produced as long as there are customers for it, provision being made that the price rise in accordance with the greater cost of production per unit.

Now the general of this industrial army is the president of the United States. He is chosen from among the corps commanders; and it is provided that every officer in the army, from the president down to the sergeant, must work his way up from the grade of common laborer. The chief peculiarity of this system consists in the way in which the voting is done. The voters are all honorary members of the guild to which they belong; that is, men who are over forty-five years old; this applies not merely to the ten lieutenant generals, but to the commander-in-chief, who is not eligible for the presidency until he has been a certain number of years out of office. The president is elected by vote of all the men of the nation who are not connected with the industrial army; for any other method, Bellamy thinks, would be prejudicial to discipline. There are various names for this practice: one of them is gerontocracy, or government by the aged; and another, more familiar, is "alumni control." When we recollect that the hardships of military service look rather mild and pleasant to the man who has been mustered out, I doubt if the youngsters in the industrial army would stand much chance of having their lot improved if the initiative for a change had to come from the alumni. Yet we know what even the formation of a worker's shop committee would be in an industrial army: it would be mutiny. As for criticism of the administration, that would be treason; admiration for the practices of another country would be disloyalty; and advocacy of a change in the method of industry would be sedition.

True: corruption and bribe-taking and all the dirty scandals that we associate today with a financial oligarchy would be wiped out in utopia; but this merely means that the defects of the old order would disappear along with its virtues. What would remain would be the defects that arise when a nation is in arms, and when there is no escape, by travel or mental withdrawal, from its institutions; in short, the defects of a state of war. To call this a peaceful community is absurd: one might as well call a battleship a pleasure-craft because a modern one possesses a band and shows motion pictures to the crew. The organization of this utopia is an organization for war; and the one rule that such a community would not tolerate is "live and let live." If this is the peace that "industrial preparedness" ensures it is scarcely worth having. Any community that liked this state of life would scarcely need the constant exhortation of the recruiting sergeant or the final compulsion of a conscription act.

6

The great part of Looking Backward is a discussion of this perfected form of industrial organization; the manner in which it is worked; and the effects of complete economic equality in doing away with the necessity for the greater part of the legal machinery of the present day, since crimes with an economic motive would almost, according to Bellamy, be unthinkable. Here and there however we have glimpses of the social life of this new age.

First of all, there floats before our eyes the picture of a vast body of superannuated persons, who for the most part spend their time in a sort of country-club existence. They can travel, because the other countries in the world are likewise nationalized, and by a simple system of book-keeping foreign credit for goods and personal services can be transferred from one country to another; and they can take up special vocations and hobbies during their superannuated years; but it is equally plain that their work has not done very much to foster intellectual or emotional maturity, since in relation to the citizens the state exists as a "Great White Father"; and there is good reason perhaps for the great interest in sport which characterizes Bellamy's utopia. Games are organized, apparently, upon lines of industrial guild rivalry; just as one has sports nowadays between rival battleship squadrons perhaps; for "if bread is the first necessity of life, recreation is a second, and the nation caters for both." The demand for bread and circuses, our guide explains, is recognized in the year 2000 as a wholly reasonable one. Both work and play are external to the citizen's inner trends and interests; and we should not be surprised if an infantile element predominated in the character of this happy republic.

This externalism, this impersonality, seems to characterize the whole scene. We follow Julius West and his new love, Edith, into a modern shop, where everything is displayed by sample, and an order for goods is sent to a central warehouse, and along with undoubted economies of space and time, we note that there is an almost complete absence of personal contacts or relationships: more than ever the worker has become a cog in the machine, more than ever he deals with a thin, barren, abstract world of paper notations, more than ever his desire for social contacts is dammed up; and so, more than ever, there must be occasion in this new age for stimulants and socialities beside which the roller coasters of Coney Island and the promiscuities of a modern dance hall would be insipid things. Bellamy does not show us what these compensatory institutions would be: but he has invented a high-powered engine of repression, and he does not fool us when he conceals the safety-valve. Unless there is a safety-valve his universal army, under a rigorous discipline for twenty-four years, is bound to blow up the works. We can guess when we read the cheap illustrated papers, when we go to the movies, when we watch the behavior of the crowds on Broadway, what this twenty-first century Utopia would be like—it would be all that a modern city is, exaggerated. In The New Society, Dr. Walter Rathenau drew a picture of a socialized modern society, moving along its present path without any change in its aims and ideals; and that nightmare of his must be added to Bellamy's dream in order to define it.

It is the same with every other institution. There is a big communal restaurant in which each family of the neighborhood has a private room; this is the place where the principal meal is ordered by the family, and served by young conscript waiters. Am I at fault if I point out that this universal hostelry is a little too elaborate and mechanical; that there is more promise of a genuine utopia in Plato's olives and cheese and beans, simply served, than in the "perfection of catering and cooking" which the new age boasts. So one could go down the line and enumerate the mechanical marvels which take the place of a fully humanized life; marvels like the telephone concerts and sermons which astoundingly anticipate by thirty-odd years the radio broadcasting service which is now a prevalent mania in America. Are these things, as Aristotle would have said, the material bases of the good life, or are they substitutes for the good life? There may have been some doubt as to the answer in Bellamy's time; but I think there need not be any at present. In so far as these instruments are consonant with humanized purposes they are good; in so far as they are irrelevant they are so much rubbish—idiotic rubbish. A free public library is a good thing; but a free public library devoted exclusively to distributing the novels of Gene Stratton Porter and the uplift books of Mr. Orison Swett Marden would not contribute so much as a useful platitude towards a vivid and stimulating society.

There is no escaping the problem of ends and the problem of ends, if I may be permitted a pun, belongs at the beginning. Subordinate to humanized ends, machinery and organization—yes, complicated machinery and organization—have undoubtedly a useful contribution to make towards a good community; unsubordinated, or subordinated only to the engineer's conceptions of an efficient industrial equipment and personnel, the most innocent machine may be as humanly devastating as a Lewis gun. All this Bellamy overlooked in Looking Backward, and yet—something remains.

What remains in Looking Backward is the honest passion that inspired the man; the play of generous impulses; the insistence that there is no fun for an ordinarily imaginative person in dining with Dives whilst Lazarus hangs around the table. Bellamy wanted everyone to be equally educated, so that everyone might be his companion; he wanted everyone to be decently fed and sheltered; he wanted to take his share in the dirty work and to see that accidents of wealth did not keep other people from taking theirs. He wanted private life to be simple and public life to be splendid. He wanted men and women to mate with each other without permitting this relationship to be compromised by obligations to a father, a mother, or the butcher, the baker, and the grocer. He wanted the generous, the just, and the tender-hearted to be as well endowed as the cold-hearted, the greedy, and the self-seeking. He pleaded for an absence of artificiality and restraint in the relations of the sexes; for such a candor as has perhaps come into fashion again—thank heaven!—today, a candor which permits women physical freedom in dress, and a spiritual freedom in exhibiting their love, and giving it freely. All this is to the good. I do not question Bellamy's fine motives; I question only the outlets he imagined for them. There is a breach between Bellamy's conception of the good life and the structure he erected to shelter it. This breach is due, I believe, to an over-emphasis of the part that wholesale mechanical organization, directed by a handful of people, would play in such a reconstruction. If Bellamy sometimes exaggerated the bad in modern society, with its muddle of competitive privileges, he likewise overestimated the good that it contained; and he was more than fair to the present order of things when he made the future so closely in its image.

CHAPTER NINE

How William Morris and W. H. Hudson renew the classic tradition of utopias; and how, finally, Mr. H. G. Wells sums up and clarifies the utopias of the past, and brings them into contact with the world of the present.

CHAPTER NINE

1

It would be a pretty sad thing if the Utopias of the nineteenth century were all of a piece with those of Buckingham and Bellamy. In general we may say that all the utopias of reconstruction had a deadly sameness of purpose and a depressing singleness of interest; and although they saw society whole, they saw the problem of reconstructing society as a simple problem of industrial reorganization. Fortunately, the utopias of escape have something to contribute which the utopias of reconstruction lack; and if William Morris, for example, seems too remote from Manchester and Minneapolis to be of any use, he is by that token a little nearer the essential human realities: he knows that the chief dignity of man lies not in what he consumes but in what he creates, and that the Manchester ideal is—devastatingly consumptive.

Before I go into these utopias of escape, I wish to point out the strange way in which the three utopias we shall examine return as it were upon their classic models, each of the returns being, it is fairly plain, without the consciousness of the writer. Mr. W. H. Hudson returns upon More; and in A Crystal Age the farmstead and the family is the ultimate unit of social life. In News from Nowhere the city of workers, such as Andreæ dreamed of, comes again into being; and in A Modern Utopia, with its order of Samurai, we are ruled once more by a highly disciplined class of Platonic guardians. Mr. Hudson is a naturalist with a deep sympathy for the rural life of England; William Morris was a craftsman who knew what the English town was like before it had been blighted by industrialism; and with both of these men we feel close to the essential life of man and the essential occupations.

2

As the clouded vision of the traveller to the Crystal Age clears, he finds himself received in a great Country House, which is inhabited by a large group of men and women who till the land and perform the simple operations of weaving and stonecutting and the like. All over the world, one gathers, these great country houses dot the landscape. Each of them is no week-end center of social life but a permanent home; indeed their permanence is almost past believing; for in each house traditions are carried back thousands of years. The great cities and the complicated metropolitan customs that they produced have long been wiped away, as one might wipe away mold. The world has been stabilized; the itch for getting and spending has disappeared. Our traveller must bind himself to work for a whole year in order to pay for the garments his house-mates weave for him, garments whose texture and cut have a classic turn.

This household, I say, is the social unit of the Crystal Age: the house-father administers the laws and customs, and he dispenses the punishment of seclusion when the visitor trespasses upon the code of the house. The house-mates work together, eat together, play together, and listen together to the music of a mechanical instrument called the musical sphere. At night they sleep in separate little cubicles which can be opened to the night air. The horses and dogs of the Crystal Age have a degree of intelligence which our common breeds do not possess, so that the horses all but harness themselves to the plow, and the dog teaches the traveller when to leave off working the animals. Each household has not merely its laws and traditions: it has its literature; its written history; and the very girl with whom the traveller falls in love bears a resemblance to the sculptured face of an unhappy house-mother who lived and suffered in the immemorial past. These houses, these families, these social relations are built for endurance. What is the secret of their strength?

The secret of our Crystal Age Utopia is the secret of the beehive: a queen bee. The Crystallites have done away with the difficulties of mating by appointing one woman, in every house, to be the house-mother, the woman whose capital duty is to carry on the family: the entire burden of each generation falls upon her shoulders, and in return for the sacrifice she is treated with the respect due to divinity, like the young man who was chosen in the Kingdom of Montezuma, as the tales have it, to represent the chief deity until at the end of a year he was disembowelled. The wish of a house-mother is a command; the word of the house-mother is law. For a year before her retirement as mother she is put into communion with the sacred books of the house, and has at her command a store of knowledge which the rest of the hive are not permitted to share. It is she who keeps burning the fires of life.

For all except the house-mother sex is a matter of

purely physical appearance. The Crystallites, if we may speak irreverently, are "content with a vegetable love—which would certainly not suit me" nor, it appears, did it suit our traveller to the Crystal Age, when he discovers that his passion could never be reciprocated by his beloved, even if she so far transgressed the laws of the household as to give way to him. Against the appearance of passion and all the mortal griefs that it carries with it, the house-mother possesses a remedy. When in the murk of despair our traveller turns to her for advice and consolation, she gives him a phial of liquid. He drinks it in the belief that it will make him as free from passion as his house-mates; and he is not deceived; for—he dies.

The social life of the household is not to be wrecked by the storms and stresses of the individual's passions. The engines of life are no longer dangerous: the fuel has been taken away! A "chill moonlight felicity" is all that remains.

3

There are times when one may look upon the whole adventure of civilized life as a sort of Odyssey of domestication; and in this mood the Crystal Age marks a terminus upon that particular aspect of the adventure. To the objection that this sort of utopia requires that we change human nature, the answer, in terms of modern biology, is that there is no apparent scientific reason why certain elements in human nature should not be selected and brought to the front, or why certain others should not be reduced in importance and eliminated. So, for all practical purposes, there is no apparent reason why human nature should not be changed, or why we should not be prepared to believe that in times past it has been changed—communities which selectively bred for pugnacity and aggression committing suicide and opening the way for communities which socially selected other traits that made for survival. It is possible that in times past man has done a great deal to domesticate himself and fit himself for harmonious social life; and a utopia which rests upon the notion that there should be a certain direction in our breeding is not altogether luny; indeed, is nowadays less so than ever before, for the reason that it is possible to separate romantic love from physical procreation without, as the Athenians did, resorting to homosexuality.

If A Crystal Age opens our minds to these possibilities it is not to be counted purely as a romance; in spite of the fact that as a romance it has passages that rival Green Mansions. Between the individual households and common marriages, the utopia of the beehive is a third alternative which possibly remains to be explored.

4

There are regions in the world—I am thinking perhaps of the table land of South Africa and the Mississippi Valley—where if one dreamed about utopia the apparatus to support it would be a gigantic network of steel, and huge communities of people would naturally flow together and coalesce in complicated patterns, somewhat after the fashion of those which Mr. H. G. Wells describes in When the Sleeper Awakens. It would be almost impossible, I fancy, to dream of a simple life and of handfuls of people in those parts of the earth: the simplicity would be barrenness, and a handful of people would be lost.

It is different with the valley of the Thames, that little stream which begins a short way above Oxford and meanders between banks of lush grass and bending willows, down through Marlow, where musty ales have long been made, past Windsor between the Great Park and the Chiltern Hills, through Richmond and so down to Hammersmith where one might perhaps ford the river at low tide if an iron bridge did not carry one across, till below the city of London the estuary becomes a wide tide of water and expands proudly to meet the sea. Nature has carved this valley to the human scale: the houses are not dwarfed by the landscape; and except for the huge warren of London—for which nature is not responsible—there is a fitness between the actor and the scene which, without offering any great Olympian moments, gives the naïve and jolly and wholehearted effect that one finds in a good English hunting print or, let us say, in Pickwick Papers. In such an atmosphere, particularly as one thinks of it on a day late in June, human nature bubbles naturally into good nature, and whatever harshness remains, a tankard of ale will drain away.

It is in this valley of the Thames that William Morris awoke to find his utopia, after returning to his home in Hammersmith, the last really urban borough of London as one goes upstream. From that landscape, sweetened and freshened and ridden of cockney landmarks, Morris evokes the spirit of the River God, as Socrates and Phædrus, by the banks of the Ilyssus, call forth the spirit of Pan.

With all the grime and tedium of the dull 'eighties

lying upon his soul, Morris finds himself transported to a world which has been cleansed by a revolution of a greater part of the nineteenth century landmarks. In the meanwhile, grass has laid a decent blanket over many irretrievable ruins. The house in which he has gone to bed is now a Guest House; and he is first received into this refurbished world by a boatman who takes him for a morning swim on the Thames, and knows about the value of money only as a collector of copper curios might. At breakfast, he finds himself among a group of friendly people, who call him "Guest"; and he is taken firmly and sweetly and quite serenely in hand by the comely young women who preside over the house. These women, like everyone else in the new Thames valley, are healthy, full-blooded, athletic, sane, and free from the puling maladies which idleness or overwork gave to the women of the nineteenth century. The other guests are a weaver who has come down from the north to take a turn at the boatman's job while the latter goes up towards Oxford to help gather in the hay, and a loquacious dustman in marvellous greens and golds.

In this new England, work has become what one would call in the kindergarten "busy work": in the simplification of the standard of living and the release from the pressure of artificially stimulated wants, the main business of getting a living is easily performed, and the chief concern of everyone is to do his work under the pleasantest conditions possible—a demand which brings back many of the handicrafts, and places a great premium on manual skill. Although the mechanical arts have been improved in certain directions, for in his trip up the Thames our guest meets with a barge driven by some internal engine, let us say by electricity, a good many devices have been allowed to fall into disuse, because, although the output in goods might be greater, the work itself and the way of life it promotes are not so beneficial as the simple methods of hand labor. In every direction, simplicity and direct action and the immediate supply and interchange of goods out of local produce, has taken the place of the monstrously complicated system of traffic that prevailed in the earlier imperialistic world. Work is given freely, and the proceeds of work exchanged freely, as a man might give of his goods and services nowadays when he welcomes a friend within his own house. A great part of the energy of this new community has gone into building; and architecture, sculpture, and painting flourish in the townhalls and common dining halls of which each village boasts.

It follows from this that the big cities have disappeared. London is again a congeries of villages, mingled in great woodlands and meadows where in the summer children roam about and camp and pick up the simple occupations of rural life. Of all the proud monuments of London that the nineteenth century left, only the Houses of Parliament remain, as a storage-place for dung. There are shops, where one takes for the asking, and there are common halls where people eat and have conversation, as they do now in restaurants—only these new hostels are beautiful, spacious, and well-served.

Since economic pressure is absent, the people of the Thames valley seem to live a life of leisure; but this life of leisure is not the aimless leisure of the country house, with its artificial stimulants, its artificial exercises, and the like: the life of dignified leisure is a life of work; in short, the life of the artist. If other people have talked of the necessity for labor, the dignity of labor, the heroism of labor, these simple Englishmen have discovered the beauty of leisurely work—the simple grace that follows when even the practical arts are pursued as if they were liberal arts. In this utopia the instinct of workmanship, the creative impulse, has free play; and since the majority of people are neither scholars nor scientists, as Sir Thomas More would have had them, they find their fulfillment in adding beauty to all the necessities of their daily toil. Where the work itself leads purely to some useful end, as in the growing of wheat or grass, the joy of work arises out of the comradeship and good-feeling that bind together those who perform it, and the comparative lightness of the tasks that find many hands eager almost to the point of competition to perform them.

One looks at the faces of these people, and the effects of their life are visible. Their women are ten or fifteen years older than we should judge by their appearance; and on every face is written the healthy serenity that follows when people do good work, with a good spirit, in a good place. There is a candor, a plainness, a wholesomeness, an absence of furtive repressions in their every gesture; and as far as men can be satisfied and happy in a good environment, this community is satisfied and happy. There are grumblers, it goes without saying. One of them is a crusty old fellow who has read ancient history and who sighs for the cutthroat practices of the competitive era; and there is another who complains of the tameness of Utopian literature, as compared with that which dealt with the miseries and warped passion of an earlier age.

The only wretchedness in this utopia comes out of the essential human tragedy—the disparity between one's aims and one's attainments, between one's desires and the circumstances that clog their fulfillment. How can unhappiness be altogether wiped out as long as maids are fickle and sexual passion strong? The boatman, for example, has been mated with a beautiful girl who leaves him for another man; but she tires of her new love, and under the eyes of the Guest her uncle brings the pair together, and the drama of courtship and mating goes on all over again; for there are no laws to bind people together when every fibre of their being drives them apart; and in a civilization that deals kindly even with its adults there is no difficulty about giving the children all the care they need. For the most part, those who suffer in love bear their burdens manfully, without wailing over imaginary wrongs which are associated with the worship of impossible chastities and reticences; and they turn their balked impulses into the channels of work and poetry as completely as they know how.

Is this the arcadian age of innocence all over again? Are brutality and lust forever wiped out? Not at all. In sudden passion even murders occur, no matter how good and helpful the social order; but instead of compounding murder with an additional murder, the guilty person is left to his own remorse. Use and wont are more powerful than law, and the whole guild that earns its living from the frictions and dissidences of our social life has dropt into limbo. By the same token, the game of the ins and the outs, which we call political government, has disappeared; for the only matters in which our community is interested are as to whether a new field is to be laid under the plow or a bridge thrown over a stream or a townhall built; and about such things the local community is competent to decide, without lining up in a purely fictitious antagonism.

5

Sanity and health and good-will and tolerance—as one sculls along the Thames, above Richmond, on a Sunday morning, between boatloads of gay picnickers and sauntering people, it is not impossible to imagine a new social order developing on simple lines and bringing these things into existence. With five million people in England, and perhaps half a million in the Thames valley, the thing would not be impossible. Then the whole countryside would be dressed again in green; then buildings would arise in the landscape like flowers out of the ground; then the kindliness and spontaneous cooperation of a happy holiday would be prolonged into the workaday week. We should know how to spend our time and with what to occupy our heads and hands, if the great wen of London were removed from the Thames valley, and all the cheap cockney things that London has conjured into existence were to be blasted away. We should know all these things, because William Morris has told us about them; and we should do all these things, because in our heart of hearts we realize that they would satisfy.

6

The utopia that remains for consideration is the last important one in point of time; and it is, curiously enough, the quintessential utopia, for it is written with a free and critical gesture, and with a succinct familiarity towards the more important books that came before it. Mr. H. G. Wells, it is true, has made more than one excursion into an imaginary commonwealth: The Time Machine is his earliest and The World Set Free may possibly be considered as his latest. A Modern Utopia combines the vivid fantasy of the first picture with the more strict regard for present realities that marks the second; and it is, altogether, a fine and lucid product of the imagination.

The assumption upon which Mr. Wells gains entrance into his utopia differs from those shipwrecks and somnambulisms in which our modern utopias have been stereotyped. He conceives of a modern man, a little thickset and protuberant, seated at a desk and brooding over the possibilities of man's future; and gradually this image comes to life and defines his views, and his voice rises into narrative in something like the fashion of a lecturer, throwing from time to time his illustrations of a New World upon the screen. He enters utopia by hypothesis; that is, without any other subterfuge than an act of the imagination; and in the thickening realities of a utopian community, first discovered in an Alpine pass, he finds himself in the company of a sentimental botanist, who is sick with a love affair and is maudlin about dogs, and who again and again wrecks this exploration of utopia by dragging into the midst of the scene some petty complication—about his sweetheart or his doggie—that he has acquired on earth!

Where and what is this modern utopia? By hypothesis, it is a globe identical with the one on which we live; it has the same oceans and continents, the same rivers and minor land-masses, the same animals and plants; yes, even the same people, so that each one of us has his utopian counterpart. Conveniently, this new earth is located beyond Sirius; and for the most part its history is parallel to ours; except that it had a critical turn for the better at a not too remote period; so that, while mechanical invention and science and all that sort of thing is exactly on the same level as ours, the scale and order is entirely different.

The scale and order of things is indeed different. Utopia is a world community; it is a single civilization whose net of monorails and posts, whose identification bureaux, whose rules of law and order are the same in England as in Switzerland; and presumably the same in Asia and Africa as in Europe. In every sense it is a modern utopia. Machinery plays an important part, and the absence of menial service is conspicuous from the very first contacts in which our travellers get the hospitality of an inn, and find that interior decoration has verged towards the style of the modern lunch-room and subway station, so that the whole room can be redded, after use, by the guest himself. There is no harking back to the past in industry, in architecture, or in the mode of living. All that machinery has to offer has been accepted and humanized: there is a cleanliness, an absence of squalor and confusion, in this world-community, which indicates that utopia has not been purchased by evasion.

The price of this order and spaciousness is not as heavy as that which Bellamy was willing to pay in Looking Backward. The land and its natural resources are owned by the community and are in the custody of regional authorities; and the means of communication and travel are in the hands of one common administrative body. There are great socialized enterprises such as the railways, with planetary ramifications; there are regional industries, and there are a good many minor affairs which are still undertaken by private individuals and companies. Farms are worked by a co-operative association of tenant farmers, upon lines suggested by Dr. Hertzka in Freeland. Perhaps the most remarkable feature of utopian organization is the registration of every individual, with his name, numeral, finger-print, changes of residence and changes in life; all of which is filed in a huge central filing office, to become part of a permanent file upon the individual's death. Utopian registration gets our travellers into hot water, for they are naturally mistaken for their utopian doubles; but outside of its use in the story this little device seems strangely beside the point, and it arose, I believe, out of Mr. Wells' temperamental regard for tidiness—tidiness on a planetary scale—the tagging and labelling of a well-conducted shop. . . .

The people of our Modern Utopia are roughly divided into four classes: the kinetic, the poietic, the base, and the dull. The kinetic are the active and organizing elements in the community: as active kinetics they are the managers, the enterprisers, the great administrators, as passive kinetics they are the minor officials, the innkeepers, the shoptenders, farmers, and the like. The poietic are the creative elements in the community; the "intellectuals" we should perhaps call them. This follows in general the lines laid down by Comte—chiefs, people, intellectuals, and emotionals, and perhaps something of the same classification was outlined by More in his Philarchs, people, priests, and scholars. This division of classes is a very ancient one. In that old Indian script, the Bhagavad Gita, we find that the population is divided into Brahmans, Kshatriyas, Vaisryas, and Sudras, and that their duties are "determined by the modes that prevail in their separate natures." The residual classes of the base and the dull correspond to the Sudras; they are, of course, the slag of the community; and the active elements in this class, the criminals, the habitual drunkards, and the like are exported to various islands in the Atlantic where they have organized a community of their own in which they may practice fraud, chicane, and violence to their hearts' content.

Like Plato, Mr. Wells is concerned to provide for the education, discipline, and maintenance of people who will be sufficiently disinterested and intelligent to keep this vast organization a going concern—no ordinary politician or captain of industry will do. Hence there arises a class of Samurai. These Samurai are selected by rigorous mental and physical tests out of youth who are past twenty-five, up to which time they may be foolish and unsettled and may sow their wild oats. These Samurai have a high intellectual standard of achievement. They live a simple life. They are under strict moral discipline, and follow a minute regimentation of dress and minor details of conduct. They cannot marry out of their class. Once a year they are sent out into the forests, the mountains, or the waste places to shift for themselves; they go "bookless and weaponless, without pen or paper, or money"; and they come back again with a new hardness and fineness and fortification of spirit. It is such an organization as might have been evolved at the time of the Reformation had the Order of Jesuits been able to effect a dictatorship of Christendom. I say this without disparagement of either the Jesuits or the Samurai, in order to point out that these guardians of A Modern Utopia are plausible historic characters. All the important economic and political enterprises of the state, and important vocations like that of the physician, are in the hands of Samurai. They are as necessary to the social organization of A Modern Utopia as the research laboratories, which are provided by charter with each factory, are necessary to its industrial organization.

7

The glimpses that one gets of this utopia are full of color and light and movement; there are finely contained cities, surrounded by wide suburban territories, cities that are not built of paper and alabaster. Lovers pass arm in arm through the streets in the twilight; and there is a soft dignity in the women, with their gay, sexually unemphatic dresses, that charms. There are electric trains weaving silently on rails over the landscape of Europe, crossing under the English Channel by tube, and emerging in London with none of the bustle, the grinding, or the dirt of a modern railway ride. There are well-cultivated fields and adequate inns. There are no obstreperous patriotisms, as one suspects in Looking Backward; there is none of the shirking one might fear in News from Nowhere. (While our travellers are waiting to be identified they stay for a while in a residential quadrangle at Lucerne, and are given employment in a toy workshop.) There is less dogmatism about creeds than in Christianopolis, and an entire absence of menialism which contrasts with More's Utopia.

This modern utopia brings together, compares, and criticizes important points that all the other utopias have raised; and it does all this with a deftness and a turn of humor that speaks for Mr. Wells at his best. Above all, A Modern Utopia strikes a new note, the note of reality, the note of the daily world from which we endeavor in vain to escape. More or less, all the other utopias assume that a change has come over the population; that it has been diminished; that the blind, the lame, and the deaf have been cured; that the mean sensual man has been converted and is ready to flap his wings and sing Hallelujah! There is a minimum of these assumptions in A Modern Utopia. It is above all other things an accounting and a criticism; and so it forms a fitting prelude to the remainder of this book.

CHAPTER TEN

How the Country House and Coketown became the utopias of the Modern Age; and how they made the world over in their image.

CHAPTER TEN

1

Now that we have ransacked the literature of ideal commonwealths for examples of the utopian vision and the utopian method, there remains another class of utopias which has still to be reckoned with, in order to make our tally complete.

All the utopias that we have dealt with so far have been filtered through an individual mind, and whereas, like any other piece of literature, they grew out of a certain age and tradition of thought, it is dangerous to overrate their importance either as mirrors of the existing order or as projectors of a new order. While again and again the dream of a utopian in one age has become the reality of the next, as O'Shaughnessy sings in his famous verses, the exact connection between the two can only be guessed at, and rarely, I suppose, can it be traced. It would be a little foolish to attempt to prove that the inventor of the modern incubator was a student of Sir Thomas More.

Up to the present the idola which have exercised the most considerable influence upon the actual life of the community are such as have been partly expressed in a hundred works and never perhaps fully expressed in one. In order to distinguish these idola from those that have occupied us till now, we should perhaps call them collective utopias or social myths. There is a considerable literature that relates to these myths in French, one of the best known works being M. George Sorel's Reflections on Violence; and in practice it is sometimes rather hard to tell where the Utopia leaves off and the social myth begins.

The history of mankind's social myths has still in the main to be written. There is a partial attempt at this over a limited period in Mr. Henry Osborn Taylor's The Mediæval Mind; but this is only a beginning, and other ages are almost untouched. The type of myth that concerns us here is not the pure action myth which M. Sorel has analyzed; we are rather interested in those myths which are, as it were, the ideal content of the existing order of things, myths which, by being consciously formulated and worked out in thought, tend to perpetuate and perfect that order. This type of social myth approaches very closely to the classic utopia, and we could divide it, similarly, into myths of escape and myths of reconstruction. Thus the myth of political freedom, for example, as formulated by the writers of the American revolution, frequently serves as an excellent refuge for disturbed consciences when the Department of Justice or the Immigration Bureau has been a little too assiduous in its harassment of political agitators.

Unfortunately, it has become a habit to look upon our idola as particularly fine and exalted, and as representing the better side of human nature. As a matter of fact, the myths which are created in a community under religious, political, or economic influences cannot be characterized as either good or bad: their nature is defined by their capacity to help men to react creatively upon their environment and to develop a humane life. We have still to recognize that a belief in these idola is not by itself a creditable attitude. Even quite base and stupid people are frequently governed by ideals; indeed, it is the ideals that are in many cases responsible for their baseness and stupidity. Neither is the habit of responding to idola any evidence of rational thought. People respond to "ideas"—that is, to word-patterns—as they respond to the stimulus of light or heat, because they are human beings and not because they are philosophers, and they respond to projections, to idola, for the same reason, and not because they are saints. Our myths may be the outcome of rational thought and practice or not; but the response to these myths is not perhaps more than ten times in a hundred the result of following the processes of reason from beginning to end.

We must think of our idola as a sort of diffused environment or atmosphere, which differs in "chemical content" and in extension with each individual. Some of these idola have so uniformly taken possession of men's minds in a particular age that they are as much a part of the environment a baby is born into as the furniture of his house. The sociologists who follow Emile Durkheim have called a certain part of these idola collective representations but they are wrong, I believe, when they limit these "representations" to savage or ignorant groups for they are an important part of every civilized person's luggage. Parallel with The Story of Mankind and with The Story of Utopias, which I have just told, it would be amusing to write The Story of Mankind's Myths. This work, however, would require the scholarship and industry of another Leibniz, and all that I wish to do here is to put together the chief social myths that have played a part in Western Europe and America during the modern period, to contrast these idola with the utopias of the past and the partial remedies for the present, and to suggest the bearing of all this upon any new departures we may be ready to make.

In selecting these idola—The Country House, Coketown, the Megalopolis—I have been forced to gauge their strength and test their quality very largely by their actual results in the workaday world, and it is a little hard to purify them from the various institutions, old and new, in which they are mixt. Yet with all this taint of actuality, these idola are scarcely as credible as the Republic and it will help matters a little to realize that we are still within the province of utopia, and may exercise all the utopian privileges.

2

To understand the utopia of the Country House we must jump back a few centuries in history.

Anyone who has ranged through the European castles that were built before the fourteenth century will realize that they were no more built for comfort than is a modern battleship. They were essentially garrisons of armed men whose main occupation was theft, violence, and murder; and every feature of their environment reflected the necessities of their life. These castles would be found beetling a cliff or a steep hill; their walls and their buttresses would be made of huge, rough hewn stones; their living arrangements would resemble those of a barracks with an almost complete lack of what we now regard as the normal decencies and privacies, except possibly for the lord and his lady;

and the life of these feudal bands was necessarily a crude and limited one.

Up to the fourteenth century in Western Europe the little fortified town, or the unfortified town that lay beneath the protection of a garrison on a hill, was the only other social unit that competed with the even more limited horizons of the peasant's village, or with the spacious claims for the Here and the Hereafter which were put forward by the Roman Church. To dream of huge metropolises and farflung armies and food brought from the ends of the earth would have been wilder in those days than anything More pictured in his Utopia.

During the fifteenth century in England, and in other parts of Europe the same thing seems to have happened sooner or later, this life of agriculture and warfare and petty trade was upset: the feudal power of the reigning nobles was concentrated in the hands of a supreme lord, the King; and the King and his archives and his court settled in the National Capital, instead of moving about from place to place in the troubled realm. The territories of the feudal lords ceased to be dispersed; their possessions were confined more and more within what were called national boundaries; and instead of remaining in their castles the great lords gave up their crude, barbaric ways, and went up to the capital to be civilized. In the course of time money took the place of direct tribute; instead of receiving wheat and eggs and labor, the lord came into possession of a rent which could be figured in pence and pounds; a rent which could be transferred to the new trading cities for the goods which the rest of the world had for sale. There is a fascinating picture of this change in W. J. Ashley's Economic History; and the old life itself is outlined, with a wealth of significant detail, in J. S. Fletcher's Memorials of a Yorkshire Parish.

At the same time that this change was taking place in the physical life of Western Europe, a corresponding change was taking place in the domain of culture. Digging about the ruins of Rome and other cities, the men of the late Middle Age discovered the remains of a great and opulent civilization; and exploring the manuscripts and printed books which were getting into general circulation, they found themselves face to face with strange conceptions of life, with habits of refinement, ease, and sensuous luxury which the hard life of the camp and the castle had never really permitted. There followed a reaction against their old life which was little less than a revulsion; and in that reaction two great institutions fell out of fashion. Men ceased to build castles to protect themselves against physical dangers; and they left off entering monasteries in order to fortify their souls for the Hereafter. Both the spiritual and the temporal life began to shift to a new institution, the Country House. The idolum of the Country House drew together and coalesced; and as a familiar symbol of this change the colleges at Oxford which date from the Renascence can scarcely be distinguished in architectural detail from the palaces which the aristocracy were building in the same period; while our banks and our political edifices to this day bear almost universally the stamp of that Roman and Grecian litter which men discovered on the outskirts of the mediæval city.

3

We do not know the Country House until we realize, to begin with, what its physical characteristics are like. There are a great many descriptions which the reader may consult if he does not happen to live in the neighborhood of a great Country House: but perhaps instead of examining the contemporary Country House it will be well to go back to its beginnings, and see how it was pictured in all its encrusted splendor at the first movement of the Renascence—in the setting which François Rabelais, in one of the few downright serious passages in his great work, Gargantua, sought to provide for the good life.

Gargantua purposes to build a new Abbey which he calls the Abbey of Theleme. This Abbey is to be in every respect what the mediæval Abbey was not. Hence to begin with, the Abbey, unlike the castle, is to lie in the midst of the open country; and unlike the monastery, it is to have no walls. Every member is to be furnished with a generous apartment, consisting of a principal room, a withdrawing room, a handsome closet, a wardrobe, and an oratory; and the house itself is to contain not merely libraries in every language, but fair and spacious galleries of paintings. Besides these lodgings there is to be a tilt-yard, a riding court, a theatre, or public playhouse, and a natatory or place to swim. By the river, for the Abbey is to be situated on the Loire, there is to be a Garden of Pleasure, and between two of the six towers of the hexagon, in which form the building is arranged, there are courts for tennis and other games. Add to this orchards full of fruit trees, parks abounding with venison, and an archery range, fill all the halls and chambers with rich tapestries, cover all the pavements and floors with green cloth—and the furnishing of the Abbey of Theleme is complete.

The costumes of the inmates are equally splendid and elaborate. In order to have the accoutrements of the ladies' and gentlemen's toilets more convenient, there was to be "about the wood of Theleme a row of houses to the extent of half a league, very neat and cleanly, wherein dwelt the goldsmiths, lapidaries, jewellers, embroiderers, tailors, gold drawers, velvet weavers, tapestry makers, and upholsterers. . . ." They were to be "furnished with matter and stuff from the hands of Lord Nausiclete, who every year brought them seven ships from the Perlas and Cannibal Islands, laden with ingots of gold, with raw silk, with pearls and precious stones."

The women who are admitted to Theleme must be fair, well-featured, and of sweet disposition; the men must be comely and well-conditioned. Everyone is to be admitted freely and allowed to depart freely; and instead of attempting to practice poverty, chastity, and obedience, the inmates may be honorably married, may be rich, and may live at liberty.

The liberty of Theleme is indeed complete; it is such a liberty as one enjoys at a Country House to this day, under the care of a tactful hostess; for everyone does nothing except follow his own free will and pleasure, rising out of his bed whenever he thinks good, and eating, drinking, and laboring when he has a mind to it. In all their rule and strictest tie of their order, as Rabelais puts it, there is but one clause to be observed—

"Do what you please."

4

When we turn our attention from Rabelais' conceit of an anti-monastic order, we discover that he has given us an excellent picture of the Country House, and of what I shall take the liberty of calling Country House culture. We see pretty much the same outlines in the introduction to Boccaccio's Decameron; it is elaborately described in terms of that most complete of Country Houses, Hampton Court, in Pope's Rape of the Lock; it is vividly pictured by Meredith in his portrait of The Egoist; and it is analyzed in Mr. H. G. Wells' cruel description of Bladesover in Tono-Bungay, as well as by Mr. Bernard Shaw in Heartbreak House. Whether Mr. W. H. Mallock holds the pattern of Country House culture up to us in The New Republic or Anton Chekhov penetrates its aimlessness and futility in The Cherry Orchard, The Country House is one of the recurrent themes of literature.

This renascence idolum of the Country House, then, is powerful and complete: I know no other pattern which has imposed its standards and its practices with such complete success upon the greater part of European civilization. While the Country House was in the beginning an aristocratic institution, it has penetrated now to every stratum of society; and although we may not immediately see the connection, it is responsible, I believe, for the particular go and direction which the industrial revolution has taken. The Country House standards of consumption are responsible for our Acquisitive Society.

5

Perhaps the shortest way to suggest the character

of Country House institutions is to say that they are the precise opposite of everything that Plato looked upon as desirable in a good community.

The Country House is concerned not with the happiness of the whole community but with the felicity of the governors. The conditions which underly this limited and partial good life are political power and economic wealth; and in order for the life to flourish, both of these must be obtained in almost limitless quantities. The chief principles that characterize this society are possession and passive enjoyment.

Now, in the Country House possession is based upon privilege and not upon work. The title to land which was historically obtained for the most part through force and fraud is the economic foundation of the Country House existence. In order to keep the artisans and laborers who surround the Country House at their work, it is necessary to keep them from having access to the land on their own account, provision always being made that the usufruct of the land shall go to the owner and not to the worker. This emphasis upon passive ownership points to the fact that in the Country House there is no active communion between the people and their environment. Such activities as remain in the Country House—the pursuit of game, for instance—rest upon imitating in play activities which once had a vital use or prepared for some vital function, as a child's playing with a doll is a preparation for motherhood. The Country House ideal is that of a completely functionless existence; or at best, an existence in which all the functions that properly belong to a civilized man shall be carried on by functionaries. Since this ideal cannot be realized in the actual world, for the reason that it is completely at odds with man's biological inheritance, it is necessary in the Country House utopia to fill in by play and sport an otherwise desirable vacuity.

In the Country House literature and the fine arts undoubtedly flourish: but they flourish as the objects of appreciation rather than as the active, creative elements in the community's life; they flourish particularly in the fashion that Plato looked upon as a corrupting influence in the community. In the arts, a gourmandizing habit of mind—the habit of receiving things and being played upon by them—prevails; so that instead of the ability to share creative ecstasy, the chief canon of judgment is "taste," a certain capacity to discriminate among sensory stimuli, a capacity which is essentially just as hospitable to a decomposing cheese as to the very staff of life. The effect of this gourmandism in the arts can be detected in every element of the Country House from cellar to roof; for the result has been to emphasize the collection of good things rather than their creation, and there is an aspect in which the Country House is little better than a robber's hoard or a hunter's cache—a miniature anticipation of the modern museums of natural history and art.

Observe the architecture of our Country House. If it has been built in England during the last three hundred years, the style is probably that bastard Greek or Roman which we call Renascence architecture; if the Country House was built in America during the last thirty years, it is as likely as not a Tudor residence with traces of castle fortification left here and there on the façade. On the walls there will be plenty of paintings; indeed a whole gallery may be devoted to them. In all probability, however, the paintings have been created in other times by men long since dead, and in other countries: there may be a portrait by Rembrandt, a Persian miniature, a print by Hokusai. Some very fine element in the structure, a fireplace or a bit of panelling, may have been removed piece by piece from the original Country House in England, Italy, or France; even as many features of the original Country House were quarried, perhaps, from some mediæval abbey. The very china that we use upon our tables nowadays is a Country House importation which took the place of pewter and earthenware; and wall paper is another importation. From feature to feature everything is derivative; everything, in the last analysis, has either been stolen or purchased from the original makers; and what has not been stolen or purchased has been basely copied.

The insatiability of the Country House to possess art is only equalled by its inability to create it. In the Country House, the arts are not married to the community, but are kept for its pleasure.

Let there be no confusion as to either the facts or the ideal we are examining. There is a vast difference between that fine mingling of traditions which is the very breath of the arts, as the lover of classic Greek statuary knows, and the rapacious imperialistic habit of looting the physical objects of art which has been the essence of the Country House method in modern times, even as it seems to have been a couple of thousand years ago in the Roman villa. A genuine culture will borrow steadily from other cultures; but it will go to them as the bee goes to the flower for pollen, and not as the beekeeper goes to the hive for honey. There is a creative borrowing and a possessive borrowing; and the Country House has in the main limited itself to possessive borrowing. The Country House ideal, in fact, is limitless possession: so the great Country House masters have five or six houses, perhaps, in their name, although they need but a single one to cover their heads.

Now the Country House idolum involves a dissociation between the Country House and the community in which it is placed. If you will take the trouble to examine mediæval conditions, you will find that differences of rank and wealth did not make a very great difference between the life of the lord in his castle, and his retainers: if the common man could not claim to be as good as his lord, it is plain that the lord shared most of the common man's disabilities, and was, for all the exaggerations of chivalry, just as ignorant, just as illiterate, just as coarse. In the cities, too, the lowest workman in the guild shared the institutions of his masters: the churches, the guild pageants, and the morality plays were all part and parcel of the same culture.

The Country House changed this condition. Culture came to mean not a participation in the creative activities of one's own community, but the acquisition of the products of other communities; and it scarcely matters much whether these acquisitions were within the spiritual or the material domain. There had of course been the beginnings of such a split in mediæval literature, with its vulgar Rabelaisian tales and its refined romances of the court; but with the integration of the Country House idolum, this divorcement was accentuated in every other activity of the community. One of the results of this split was that popular institutions were deprived of their contacts with the general world of culture, and languished away; or they were transformed, as the public schools of England were transformed into restricted upper class institutions. Far more important than this, perhaps, was the fact that each separate Country House was forced to obtain for its limited circle all the elements that were necessary to the good life in a whole community such as Plato described. We shall deal with the effects of this presently.

6

Let us admit what is valid in the utopia of the Country House. Enjoyment is a necessary element in achievement, and by its regard for the decent graces of life, for such things as an ease in manners and a fine flow of conversation and the clash of wits and a sensitiveness to beautiful things, the Country House was by all odds a humanizing influence. In so far as the Country House fostered a belief in contemplation and a desire for the arts apart from any uses that might be made of them by way of civic advertisement; in so far as it urged that all our pragmatic activities must be realized in things that are worth having or doing for themselves, the Country House was right, eminently right. It was no snobbery on the part of Russian soviet officialism when it opened up some of its Country Houses as rest houses for the peasants and workers, and then insisted that some of the airs of the Country House should be acquired there, to replace the rough usages of the stable, the dungpile, and the field. Ruskin and Samuel Butler were possibly right when they insisted that the perfect gentleman was a finer product than the perfect peasant or artisan: he is a finer product because he is essentially more alive. Even by its emphasis upon appreciation the Country House did no mean service; for it called attention to the fact that there were more permanent standards—standards which were common to the arts of Greece and China—than those which were looked upon as sufficient in the local region. In sum, the Country House emphasized a human best, which was the sum of a dozen partial perfections; and so all that was crude and inadequate in the old regional cultures was brought to light and criticized. All these virtues I admit; and they hold just as good today as they ever did.

The fatal weakness of Country House culture comes out all the plainer for this admission. The Country House did not see that enjoyment rested upon achievement, and was indeed inseparable from achievement. The Country House strove to put achievement in one compartment and enjoyment in another; with the result that the craftsman who no longer had the capacity to enjoy the fine arts no longer had the ability to create them. The effect of an isolated routine of enjoyment is equally debilitating; for enjoyment, to the masters of the Country House came too easily, with a mere snap of the fingers, as it were, and the tendency of connoisseurship was to set novelty above intrinsic worth. Hence the succession of styles by which Country House decoration has become a thing for mockery: Chinese in one age, Indian in another, Persian in the next, with Egyptian, Middle African, and heaven knows what else destined to follow in due order. There is nothing to settle to, because there is no task to be done, and no problem to work out; and as soon as the first taste for a style gets exhausted it is speedily supplanted by another.

It would be impossible to calculate the extent to which the Country House has degraded our taste but I have little doubts as to the source of the degradation. The stylicism which has perverted the arts and has kept a congruent modern style from developing has been the work of Country House culture. I remember well the contempt with which a furniture manufacturer in the Chiltern Hills told me about the way in which he produced an original Sheraton: his knowledge of sound furniture design was subordinated to some other person's knowledge of "style" and the miscarriage of the man's innate craftsmanship made him so mordant on the subject that it seemed as though he had been reading Thorstein Veblen's Theory of the Leisure Class. It is the same through all the arts. A visit to the industrial sections of the Metropolitan Museum in New York will show how dismally the taste for novelty, which led the Sheratons and Chippendales to find "classic motifs" in one age, causes the designers of the present day to seek the motifs of Sheraton and Chippendale. So much for what happened to the arts when enjoyment and achievement are separated.

7

The industrial bearing of the Renascence ideal is of capital importance.

During the Middle Age the emphasis in industry was upon the production of tangible goods; the craft guilds set high standards in design and workmanship; and the aim of the worker, in most of the trades, was to get a living from his work, and not simply to get enough money to free himself from the necessity of working. This is a broad generalization, I need scarcely emphasize, and there is plenty of evidence of pecuniary interests under the best of conditions; but it seems fair to say that the dominant ideals of the older industrial order were industrial rather than commercial. In the trading ventures that the Country House promoted under its Drakes and Raleighs, ventures which were needed to bring them "Ships from the Perlas and Cannibal Islands," the emphasis shifted from workmanship to sale; and the notion of working and gambling to acquire multifarious goods took the place of that earlier ideal which Henry Adams so sympathetically described in Mt. St. Michel and Chartres. Thus the good life, as I have said elsewhere, was the Goods Life: it could be purchased. If the whole community no longer offered the conditions for this life, one might filch what one wanted from the general store, and try to monopolize for self or family all that was needed for a good life in the community.

What is the chief economic outcome of this ideal? The chief outcome, I think, is to exaggerate the demand for goods, and to cause an enormously wasteful duplication of the apparatus of consumption. If the limit to one's possessions should be simply the extent of one's purse; if happiness is to be acquired through obtaining the comforts and luxuries of life; if a man who possesses a single house is considered fortunate, and a man who possesses five houses five times as fortunate; if there are no standards of living other than the insatiable one that has been set up in the Country House —well, then there is really no limit to the business of getting and spending, and our lives become the mean handiwork of coachman, cook, and groom. Our Country House will not merely be a house: there will be a chapel, an art gallery, a theater, a gymnasium, as François Rabelais imagined. As the common possessions of the community dwindle, the private possessions of individuals are multiplied; and at last, there remains no other community than a multitude of anarchic individuals, each of whom is doing his best to create for himself a Country House, notwithstanding the fact that the net result of his endeavors—this is the drab tragedy and the final thing to be said against it—is perhaps nothing better than six inadequate rooms at the end of nowhere in a Philadelphia suburb.

The Country House, then, is the chief pattern by means of which the mediæval order was transformed into the modern order. It does not matter very much whether the Country House is an estate on Long Island or a cottage in Montclair; whether it is a house in Golder's Green or a family manor in Devonshire: these are essentially affairs of scale, and the underlying identity is plain enough. The idolum of the Country House prevails even when quarters are taken up in the midst of the metropolis. More than ever the Country House today tries to make up by an abundance of physical goods for all that has been lost through its divorce from the underlying community; more than ever it attempts to be self-sufficient within the limits of suburbia. The automobile, the phonograph, and the radio-telephone have only served to increase this self-sufficiency; and I need not show at length how these instrumentalities have deepened the elements of acquisitiveness and passive, uncreative, mechanical enjoyment.

The Country House's passionate demand for physical goods has given rise to another institution, Coketown; and it is the idolum of Coketown, the industrial age's contribution to the Country House, that we have now to consider.

8

The chief difference between the individual utopias of the nineteenth century and the "collective representation" of Coketown is that these individual utopias were concerned to repair certain points where Manchester, Newark, Pittsburgh, and Elberfeld-Barmen fell short of the ideal. In repairing these points, Bellamy and Hertzka were ready to alter the conventional arrangements by which property and land were held, and capital was accumulated. The final end however was the same; and the differences are therefore more apparent than real.

If the illustrative example of the Country House is in the Abbey of Theleme, that of Coketown is in the sharp picture of industrialism which Charles Dickens presents in Hard Times.

Coketown, as Dickens sees it, is the quintessence of the industrial age. It is perhaps one of the few idola of the modern world which has no parallel in any earlier civilization that we have been able to explore. In order to understand what Coketown brought into the world, we must realize that before Coketown came into existence the center of every important European city consisted of a marketplace, shadowed over by a Cathedral, a Market Court, and a Guildhall; and frequently there would be an adjacent university. This was the typical formation. The various quarters of the city were subordinated to these central institutions, and the work which was carried on within the city's walls was more or less concretely realized in the local community.

Coketown, on the other hand, was the outcome of other conditions and necessities. The center of Coketown's activity was the mill, set at first in the open country near falling water, and then as coal was applied to steam engines, removed to areas more accessible to the coal fields. The factory became the new social unity; in fact it became the only social unit; and, as Dickens sharply put it, "the jail looked like the town hall, and the town hall like the infirmary"—and all of them looked like the factory, a gaunt building of murky brick that once was red or yellow. The sole object of the factory is to produce goods for sale; and every other institution is encouraged in Coketown only to the extent that it does not seriously interfere with this aim.

What are the outward physical aspects of Coketown? To begin with, the city is laid out by an engineer; it is laid out with a mathematical correctness and with a complete disregard for the amenities. If there are hills where Coketown ought to stand, the hills are leveled; if there are swamps, the swamps are filled; if there are lakes, the lakes are drained away. The pattern to which Coketown's activities are fitted is that of the gridiron; there are no deviations and no allowances in the working out of this plan; never will a street swerve as much as a hair's breadth to save a stand of trees or open up a vista. In the matter of transportation and intercourse, the aim of Coketown is to "get somewhere"; and it fancies that by laying down straight lines and joining them in rectangles this aim is expedited; despite the demonstration in every city of older growth that a radial system of intercommunication is much more economical than the gridiron. As a result, there is no terminus to any of the avenues of Coketown; for they begin on a draughting board and end in infinity. It is impossible to approach from the front the jails, hospitals, and sanatoria of which Coketown boasts; the tendency is to run past them. So much for the physical layout of the industrial city; what remains is obscured by smoke.

The factory is the center of Coketown's social life; and it is here that the greater part of the population spend their days. At its purest, that is to say, during the first half of the nineteenth century, and in a great many centers to this day, the factory is the only institution that provides anything like a social life, in spite of the fact that the unremitting toil which accompanies its routine reduces the graces of social intercourse to such a minimum that drunkenness and copulation are the only amusements which the inhabitants can engage in as a relief from their noble duty of providing the rest of the world with necessities, comforts, luxuries, and nullities.

The Coketown idolum has been disintegrating a little during the last two decades, under the influence of the garden cities movement, and I am aware that in certain departments I am celebrating a lost cause and an abandoned idealism; but there still remain in acres and acres of workingmen's dwellings, such as one finds in Battersea and Philadelphia, and in old-fashioned railway stations, and in buildings like the Mechanics Halls of

Pittsburgh and Boston, a notion of what Coketown stood for when Coketown, the Frankenstein which had been created by the Country House, had not been repudiated by its master.

Coketown is devoted to the production of material goods; and there is no good in Coketown that does not derive from this aim. The only enjoyment which those who are inured to the Coketown routine can participate in is mechanical achievement; that is to say, activity along industrial and commercial lines; and the only result of this achievement is—more achievement. It follows that all the standards of Coketown are of a quantitative kind; so many score of machines, so many tons of gew-gaws, so many miles of piping, so many dollars of profit. The opportunities for self-assertion and constructiveness in such a community are practically boundless; and I can never confront the mechanical felicities of a printing plant without realizing how fascinating these opportunities are, and how deeply they satisfy certain elements in our nature. The unfortunate thing about Coketown, however, is that these are the only sort of opportunities that are available; and work whose standards are of a qualitative sort, the work of scholars and artists and scientists, is either frozen out of the community by deliberate ostracism, or is hitched to the machine; the artist, for example, being compelled to sing the praises of Coketown's goods or to paint the portrait of Coketown's supreme esthetic achievement—the Self-Made Man.

In its pristine state, Coketown is not a complete community. So it is natural that the idolum should have provided certain additions. In the first place, the activities of Coketown, whether they are beneficial or wasteful, satisfy only certain elements in the human makeup; and although much may be done by compulsory education to discipline the younger generation to the machine, and to show them the necessity of doing nothing which would interfere with the continued activity of the machine—for work in Coketown, as Samuel Butler fearfully predicted in Erewhon, is in the main simply attendance upon machinery—here and there the igneous instincts of the workers will break through the solidified layer of habit which the school and the factory have produced, and the arcane energies of the population will flow either into the Country House or into that other simulacrum of the civic life, Broadway.

Coketown for the workaday week, the Country House for the weekend, is the compromise that has been practically countenanced; although the country houses of the working classes may be nothing more than a diminutive extension of the urban slum near sea or mountain. But it must be admitted that there is a permanent Country House and a permanent Coketown population in the more ideal aspects of the order. Mr. Wells in the Time Machine has given a picture of Coketown which is perhaps a little exuberant in some of its details—the picture of a happy and careless Country House population, living on the surface of the earth, mid all the graces of a jolly weekend, and that of the factory population, the Morlocks, living in the bowels of the earth and performing the necessary industrial functions. Mr. Wells' presentation is a little exaggerated, however, and we must be content here with such a plain and outright description as Messrs. Bounderby and Gradgrind would approve of.

In the Coketown scheme of things, all that does not contribute to the physical necessities of life is called a comfort; and all that does not contribute either to comforts or necessities is called a luxury. These three grades of good correspond to the three classes of the population: the necessities are for the lower order of manual workers, together with such accessory members as clerks, teachers, and minor officials; the comforts are for the comfortable classes, that is, the small order of merchants, bankers, and industrialists; while the luxuries are for the aristocracy, if there is such an hereditary group, and for such as are able to lift themselves out of the two previous orders. Chief among the luxuries, it goes without saying, are art and literature and any of the other permanent interests of a humane life.

Let us note what an improvement the three classes of Coketown are upon the three classes in Plato's Republic. The custom of limiting the earnings of the working classes to the margin of subsistence is singularly effective in keeping them occupied with the business of production—as long as there is no overplus in the market to throw them out of work—and it is thus a safeguard of efficiency and industry which Plato, who was deplorably obtuse in these matters, did not provide. It is likewise obvious that the life of a middle class citizen, with plenty to eat and drink, with his life protected by the policeman, his pocketbook protected by the insurance company, his spiritual happiness protected by the church, his human sympathies protected by the charity organization society, his intelligence protected by the newspaper, and his economic privileges protected by the State—this middle class citizen is, after all, a much more fortunate and happy individual than those Platonic warriors whose life was a perpetual effort to keep the edge on their bodies and minds. As for the Guardians of the State, it is plain that Plato did not offer them any inducement to do their work which would attract a normal commercial man: anyone who was worth a hundred thousand dollars a year would have thought twice before assuming leadership in Plato's impoverished commonwealth, whereas in Coketown he would find that his simple ability to make money would be taken as sufficient proof of his education, his insight, and his wisdom in every department of life. More than that, Coketown, when all is said and done, welcomes the artist with a cordiality that puts Plato to shame: Coketown can afford its luxuries since, when you look at the matter squarely, a rare painting might be worth as much as a rare postage stamp; and it is accordingly an acceptable addition to the Coketown milieu.

Coketown has, in fact, only one question for the arts to answer: What are they good for? If the answer can be expressed in money, the art in question is taken to be almost as satisfactory as a device to save labor, to increase speed, or to multiply the output.

9

There is one phenomenon still to be accounted for in the economy of Coketown; one monumental instrument without which the wheels of Coketown would become clogged and the very breath of Coketown be extinguished.

I refer to the rubbish heaps.

The aim of production in Coketown is naturally more

production, and it is only by making things sufficiently shoddy to go to pieces quickly, or by changing the fashion sufficiently often, that the machinery of Coketown can for the most part be kept running. The rage and fury of Coketown's production has to be balanced off by an equal rage and fury of consumption—continence would be fatal. As a result, nothing in Coketown is finished or permanent or settled: these qualities are another name for death. Coketown makes china to be broken, clothes to be worn out, and houses to be torn down; and if something remains over from an earlier age which made things more soundly, it is either incarcerated in a museum, and derided as the monument of a non-progressive age, or it is demolished as a nuisance. So powerful is the idolum of Coketown that in the workaday world building after building continues to meet with irreparable ruin at the hands of barbarians from Coketown: why, I have even seen innocent little half-timbered fifteenth century cottages whose fronts were obliterated by a nineteenth century plasterer, in the name of progress.

The status of every family in Coketown can be told by the size of its rubbish heap. In fact, to "make a pile" in the markets of Coketown is ultimately to make another pile—of dust and junk and litter—on the edge of the town where the factory district dribbles off into the open country. So in Coketown consumption is not merely a necessity: it is a social duty, a means of keeping "the wheels of civilization turning." At times there appears to be a possibility that this utopia may defeat its purposes by producing goods at such a pace that the rubbish heaps will fall behind the demands of the market; and while this mars the theoretic perfection of the Coketown social organization, it is offset by periods of war, when the market is practically inexhaustible, and Coketown's prosperity increases to a point at which the working classes are on the point of becoming the comfortable classes without having had sufficient previous training to make their contribution to the rubbish heap—a serious pass, amidst which confusion the working classes of Coketown might take to reducing their working days and enjoying their leisure without sufficient consumptive effort.

This, then, is the idolum of Coketown. There are certain features in it which need to be noticed. The first is that there is a certain solid reality in Coketown that remains when all its pretensions and idiocies have been incinerated. An environment that is devoted solely to the production of material goods is obviously no sort of environment for a good community, for life is more than a matter of finding what we shall eat and wherewithal we shall be clothed: it is an interaction with a whole world of landscapes, living creatures and ideas, in comparison with which Coketown is a mere blister on the earth's surface. Nevertheless, with respect to the business of melting steel and building roads and performing certain essential industrial operations, the aims of Coketown are, up to a certain point, relevant: we have already encountered them in Andreæ's Christianopolis. There is no need to dismiss the good that lies inside of industrialism because it does not embrace the good that lies beyond it.

Up to a certain point, then, using mechanical power rather than human power is good; so is large-scale production, so is the division of labor and division of operation; so is rapid transportation; so is the accurate methodology of the engineer; and so are various other features in the modern industrial world. One might even say a word for efficiency, as against "doing things rather more or less." Coketown made the horrid mistake of believing that all these things were good in themselves. New factories, for example, drew a bigger population into the city: Coketown did not perceive that, as Plato pointed out, beyond a certain point the city as a social unit would cease to exist. Bigger and better was Coketown's motto; and it resolutely refused to see that there was no necessary connection between these adjectives. The whole case for and against Coketown rests upon our admission of the phrase "up to a certain point." Up to a certain point, industrialism is good, especially in its modern, neotechnic, electrical phase: Coketown, on the other hand, believes that there is no limit to the usefulness of industrialism.

Up to a certain point—but what point? The answer is, up to the point at which the cultivation of a humane life in a community of humane people becomes difficult or impossible.

Men come together, says Aristotle, to live; they remain together in order to live the good life. This determination of the good life is the only check and balance that we can have upon Coketown; and it is perhaps because we have been so little concerned with it that the practical effect of the Coketown idolum has been so devastating. "Invention and organization," as Mr. George Santayana admirably points out, "which ought to have increased leisure by producing the necessaries of life with little labor, have only increased the population, degraded labor, and diffused luxury." William Morris conceived that men in the future might discard many complicated machines because they could live more happily, aye, work more happily without them. Whether indeed a good part of modern organization and machinery could be scrapt is perhaps a debatable question: but the possibility of scrapping it is at least conceivable once we become more interested in the actual result of industrialism upon the life and happiness of the people who are part of the organization than we are in the profits which pile up upon paper, and are finally realized in an ever-growing rubbish heap.

10

By what means can the Country House keep Coketown working for it? The idolum of the Country House, which was built up during the Renascence, and the idolum of Coketown, which was formed in the early part of the nineteenth century, are obviously two separate worlds; and in order that each might be realized in our daily life, it was necessary that some connecting tissue be manufactured to keep them together. This tissue was the social myth, the collective utopia, of the National State.

There is a sense in which we may look upon the National State as a fact; but that great philosopher of the National State, Mazzini, realized that the National State had continually to be willed; and its existence lies plainly, therefore, on a different plane from the existence of a bit of territory, a building, or a city. In fact, it is only by the persistent projection of this utopia for the last three or four hundred years that its existence has become credible; for all the minute descriptions which the political historian gives to the

National State, its origins and its institutions and its people, read a good deal like that fine story which Hans Andersen told about the king who walked the streets naked because two rascally tailors had persuaded him that they had woven and cut up for him a beautiful outfit of clothes.

It will help us to appreciate this beautiful fabrication of the National State if we turn aside for a moment and glance at the actual world as it is known to the geographer and the anthropologist. Here are the physical facts in defiance of which the utopia of nationalism has been clapped together.

11

The earth that the geographer surveys is divided into five great land masses. These land masses in turn can be broken up into a number of natural regions, each of which has within its rough and approximate frontiers a certain complex of soil, climate, vegetation, and, arising out of these, certain primitive occupations which the inhabitants of the region originally practiced and later, through the advance of trade and invention, elaborated. Between these natural regions there are occasionally frontiers, such as the barrier of the Pyrenees which separates "France" from "Spain"; but these barriers have never altogether prevented movements of population from one area to another. In order to have a more faithful knowledge of regional groupings in certain important areas, the reader might with profit consult Professor Fleure's Human Geography in Western Europe. (London: Williams and Norgate.)

These natural regions are the groundwork of human regions; that is, the non-political grouping of population with respect to soil, climate, vegetation, animal life, industry and historic tradition. In each of these human regions we find that the population does not consist of a multitude of atomic individuals: on the contrary, when the geographer plots houses and buildings on a topographic map, he finds that people and houses cohere together in groups of more or less limited size, called cities, towns, villages, hamlets. Normally, a vast amount of intercourse takes place between these groupings; and in the Middle Age, before the utopia of the National State had been created, the pilgrim and the wandering scholar and the journeyman and the strolling player could have been met with on all the highways of Europe. Under the dispensation of the National State, however, the population, as the German economist Buecher points out, tends to be more settled, and we transport goods rather than people. It is important to realize that, so far as the geographer can discover, this trade and intercourse between local groups has been a part of Western European civilization since Neolithic times, at least: it takes place continually between individuals and corporate groups in one place and another, and as far as geographical facts are concerned might more easily exist between Dover and Calais, let us say, than between Calais and Paris.

Now the interesting thing about the utopia of the National State is that it has only the most casual relation to the facts of geography. Wherever it suits the purposes of the Guardians of the State, the facts are ignored, and an artificial relation is *willed* into existence. The human communities which the regional sociologist recognizes do not always coincide with those which the statesman wishes to incorporate as "national territory," and when this conflict occurs, the idea rather than the reality triumphs, if necessary by brute force.

In the utopia of the National State there are no natural regions; and the equally natural grouping of people in towns, villages and cities, which, as Aristotle points out, is perhaps the chief distinction between man and the other animals, is tolerated only upon the fiction that the State hands over to these groups a portion of its omnipotent authority, or "sovereignty" as it is called, and permits them to exercise a corporate life. Unfortunately for this beautiful myth, which generations of lawyers and statesmen have labored to build up, cities existed long before states—there was a Rome on the Tiber long before there was a Roman Imperium—and the gracious permission of the state is simply a perfunctory seal upon the accomplished fact.

Instead of recognizing natural regions and natural groups of people, the utopia of nationalism establishes, by the surveyor's line, a certain realm called national territory, and makes all the inhabitants of this territory the members of a single, indivisible group, the nation, which is supposed to be prior in claim and superior in power to all other groups. This is the only social formation that is officially recognized within the national utopia. What is common to all the inhabitants of this territory is thought to be of far greater importance than any of the things that bind men together in particular civic or industrial groups.

Let us look at this world of national utopias. The contrast between the politician's map and the geographer's would be little less than amazing were our eyes not used to it, and were we not taught in modern times to look upon it as inevitable. Instead of the natural grouping of land masses and regions, one finds a multitude of quite arbitrary lines: boundaries like those that separate Canada and the United States or Belgium and the Netherlands are just as frequent as the natural frontier of sea that surrounds England. Sometimes these national territories are big, and sometimes they are little; but the bigness of empires like those of France, England, or the United States is not due to any essential identity of interests between the sundry communities of these empires, but to the fact that they are forcibly held together by a political government. National lines, in other words, continue to exist only as long as the inhabitants continue to act in terms of them; are ready to pay their taxes to support customs bureaux, immigration offices, frontier patrols, and educational systems; and are prepared, in the last extremity, to lay down their lives to prevent other groups from crossing these imaginary lines without permission.

The chief concern of the national utopia is the support of the central government, for the government is the guardian of territory and privilege. The principal business of that government is to keep the territory properly defined, and to increase its limits, when possible, so as to make the taxable area larger. By stressing the importance of these concerns, and constantly playing up the dangers of rivalry from other national utopias, the State builds a bridge between the Country House and Coketown, and persuades the workers in Coketown that they have more in common with the classes that exploit them than they have in common with other groups within a more limited community. It would seem that this reconciliation of Coketown and the Country House is little less than miraculous, even as an ideal; and perhaps it would be interesting to examine a little more carefully the apparatus by which this is effected.

12

The chief instrument of the National State is Megalopolis, its biggest city, the place where the idolum of the National Utopia was first created, and where it is perpetually willed into existence.

In order to grasp the quintessential character of Megalopolis we must shut our eyes to the palpable earth, with its mantle of vegetation and its tent of clouds, and conceive what might be made of the human landscape if it could be entirely fabricated out of paper; for the ultimate aim of the Megalopolis is to conduct the whole of human life and intercourse through the medium of paper.

The early life of a young citizen in Megalopolis is spent in acquiring the tools by which paper may be used. The names of these tools are writing, reading, and arithmetic; and once upon a time these constituted the main elements in every Megalopolitan's education. There was, however, a good deal of dissatisfaction, on paper, against this somewhat barren curriculum, and so at a fairly early date in the history of Megalopolis, various other subjects, such as literature, science, gymnastics, and manual training were added to the curriculum—on paper. It is indeed possible for a Megalopolitan student to know the atomic formula of clay without ever having seen it in the raw earth, to handle pine wood in the workshop without having walked through a pine forest, and to go through the masterpieces of poetic literature without having experienced a single emotion which would prepare him to appreciate anything different from one of the influential Megalopolitan magazines, "Smutty Stories", but as long as his hours of attendance can be recorded on paper, and as long as he can give a satisfactory account of his studies on an examination paper, his preparation for life is practically complete; and so he is graduated with a paper certificate of education into the industries of Coketown, or into the multitudinous bureaus of Megalopolis itself.

The end of this period of paper tutelage is but a prelude to its continuation in another form; for the religious care of paper is the Megalopolitan's life work. The daily newspaper, the ledger, the card index are the means by which he now makes contact with life, whilst the fiction magazine and the illustrated paper are the means by which he escapes from it. Through the translucent form of paper known as celluloid, it has been possible to do away on the stage with flesh-and-blood people; and therefore the drama of life, as the Megalopolitan story writers tell it, can be enacted at one remove from actuality. Instead of his travelling, the world moves before the Megalopolitan, on paper; instead of his venturing forth on the highways of the world, adventure comes to him, on paper; instead of his getting him a mate, his bliss may be all but consummated—on paper. In fact, so accustomed does the Megalopolitan become to experiencing all his emotions on paper that he can be entertained by the representation of a static bowl of flowers on a moving picture screen; while his cockney ignorance of nature is so vast that a certain vaudeville performer, seeking to amuse him by imitating the calls of birds and beasts, finds it wise to have moving pictures taken of the rooster, the dog, and the cat, in order to give his mimicries reality in minds destitute of any personal image.

The notion of direct action, direct intercourse, direct association, is a foreign one to Megalopolis. If any action is to be taken by the whole community, or by any group in it, it is necessary to carry it through the Megalopolitan parliament, and have it established on paper, after innumerable people, who have no genuine concern in the matter, have committed their views about it to paper. If any intercourse is to be carried on, it must be largely conducted on paper; and if that medium is not directly available, subsidiary instruments, like the telephone, are used. The chief form of association in Megalopolis is that by political party, and it is through the political party that the Megalopolitan expresses his views, on paper, as to what is necessary to amend the paper constitution or promote the welfare of the paper community; albeit he realizes that the promises made by political parties are written on what Megalopolitans in their more cynical moments call "non-negotiable" paper, and will probably never pass into currency.

By its traffic in Coketown's multifarious goods and by its command over certain kinds of paper known as mortgages or securities, Megalopolis ensures a supply of real foods and real staples from the countryside. Through incessant production of books, magazines, newspapers, boilerplate features, and syndicated matter, Megalopolis ensures that the idolum of the National Utopia shall be kept alive in the minds of the underlying inhabitants of the country. Finally, by the devices of "national education" and "national advertising" all the inhabitants of the National Utopia are persuaded that the good life is that which is lived, on paper, in the capital city; and that an approximation to this life can be achieved only by eating the food, dressing in the clothes, holding the opinions, and purchasing the goods which are offered for sale by Megalopolis. So the chief aim of every other city in the National Utopia is to become like Megalopolis; its chief hope is to grow as big as Megalopolis; its boast is that it is another Megalopolis. When the denizens of Megalopolis dream of a better world, it is only a paper perfection of that National Utopia which Edward Bellamy looked forward to in Looking Backward.

Working in connection with the Machine Process of Coketown, the Megalopolis erects a standard of life which can be expressed in commercial terms, on paper, even if it does not offer any tangible satisfaction in goods and services and perfections. The chief boast of this standard is its uniformity; that is, its equal applicability to every person in the community without respect to his history, his circumstances, his needs, his actual rewards. Hence such goods as Megalopolis creates in profusion are for the most part in the line of plumbing and sanitary devices which, if they do not exactly heighten the joy of living, at any rate make the routine of Megalopolitan life a little less formidable.

The total result of these standards and uniformities is that what was originally a fiction in time becomes a fact. Whereas the inhabitants of the national utopia may originally have been as diverse as the trees in a forest, they tend to become, under the influence of education and propaganda, as similar as telegraph poles along a road. It is not a little to the credit of Megalopolis that the National Utopia has pragmatically justified itself. It has created the sort of mental environment on paper which is necessary to a smooth adjustment of Coketown and the Country House. What is Megalopolis, in fact, but a paper purgatory which serves as a medium through which the fallen sons of Coketown, the producer's hell, may finally attain the high bliss of the Country House, the consumer's Heaven?

13

It should be plain that in describing the National Utopia and Megalopolis I have been trying to outline what Plato would call the pure form. It is equally clear, I trust, that the pure form is an idolum to which any existing national state or metropolis approximates only so far as the idolum does not conflict too grossly with the real men and women, the real communities, the real regions, the real workaday occupations which continue, despite the reign of these idola, to exist, and to occupy our main attention. Formal education has not altogether taken the place of vital education; loyalty to the state has not altogether succeeded as a substitute for deeper allegiances and affiliations: occasionally, here and there, people meet each other face to face, they eat real food, dig in real earth, smell real flowers instead of coal tar perfumes that arise from paper bouquets, and embark quite madly on real love affairs. It is true that these realities are a disturbing influence: they are always threatening to undermine the idola which the politicians and journalists and academic handymen unite so valiantly to build up; but there they are—and even the most stubborn idealist cannot help himself from occasionally confronting the world that he denies!

If you and I were perfect citizens of Megalopolis, we should never let anything come between us and our loyalty to the State: when the State called for our taxes, we should never think regretfully of the amusements we must forego in order to pay them; when the State demanded that we go to war, nothing like the claims of a family or an occupation or a moral conviction would ever step between us and our national duty. By the same token, we should never eat any other food than that which had been nationally advertized, and never buy anything direct from the producer when we might buy it from a third person in Megalopolis; we should never read any literature that is not produced in our own country, never desire any other climate than our own country can boast, and never seek to find in any other culture, remote in space or time, the things which we seem to miss in our own environment. If only this utopia of nationalism could be realized completely it would be self-sufficient; and there would be nothing on earth, in heaven, or in the waters over the earth which did not bear the authentic trademark of Megalopolis.

14

The picture of the National Utopia that I have drawn is perhaps a little too black to stand out clearly; and I must now add a few high lights for definition.

As in Coketown, there was a point up to which efficiency in mechanical production was a good thing, so in the national utopia there is a point up to which uniformity is a good thing. The National State seems historically to have arisen in some part through the relief which the people of the Middle Age experienced in being able to travel under the protection of the King's law along the King's highway, and their discovery that common laws and customs, common weights and measures, were on the whole an advantage over a multitude of senseless irregularities which continued to exist in particular neighborhoods. It was a distinct triumph for the good life when the men of London and the men of Edinburgh, let us say, realized that they had something in common as citizens of a single country, and emphasized the likenesses which bound them as men rather than the antagonisms that separated them as cities. If the National State erected barriers of trade against other countries, it at any rate broke down barriers that had long existed in even more limited regions, and that have long continued to exist in certain cities in Italy and France. So much is to the good.

But uniformity is not a good in itself. It is a good only in so far as it promotes association and social intercourse. In breaking down minor barriers, the State created major ones, and it created national uniformities in regions where they were meaningless. Moreover, nationalism is inimical to cultural unity, and it perpetuates irrelevant conflicts in the Kingdom of the Spirit where there should be neither slave nor free, neither white nor black, neither citizen nor outlander. As a matter of fact, the two great international cultural vehicles of the Middle Age—the Latin Language and the Roman Church—were broken down by the propagation of a National Language, that spoken at the National Capital, and a National Church, that which was subservient to the State; and nothing that nationalism has done since has repaired this loss. On one hand, the idolum of the National State is too narrow, because the world of culture is man's common inheritance, and not the mere segment of it which is called "national literature" or "national science." And on the other hand, the idolum is too big, for the reason that there is no bond except a paper one between men who are as far apart as Bermondsey and Bombay, or New York and San Francisco. The temporal community, as Auguste Comte finely pointed out, is local, restricted, and multiform; this is its essential nature and limitation. The spiritual community is universal. It was a great cultural misdemeanor when the National Utopia, in its extension as imperialism, sought to make the spiritual community restricted and the temporal community universal; and it is this heresy to the good life which makes all the pretensions of the national utopia so shabby and insincere.

15

If Coketown and the Country House and the National Utopia had remained on paper, they would doubtless be entertaining and edifying contributions to our literature. Unfortunately, these social myths have been potent; they have given a pattern to our lives; and they are the source of a great many evils that threaten, like stinking weeds, to choke the good life in our communities. It is not because these myths are utopias that I have been criticizing them so assiduously; it is rather because they continue to work such wholesale damage. Hence it has seemed worth while to point out that they are on pretty much the same level of reality as the Republic or Christianopolis. We may perhaps approach our social institutions a little more courageously when we realize how completely we ourselves have created them; and how, without our perpetual "will to believe" they would vanish like smoke in the wind.

CHAPTER ELEVEN

How we reckon up accounts with the one-sided utopias of the partisans.

CHAPTER ELEVEN

1

There have been many periods when men did not think it possible to make life in the community reach much higher levels than it had attained, without working a change upon human nature. The working of this change has been one of the chief preoccupations of religion; but no one can pretend that it has met, during the historic period, with any overwhelming success. In the eighteenth century men became impatient with the ministrations of institutional religion, and sought to effect an improvement in the common life by a different method—by improving the political, economic, and social mechanisms of society.

Up to this time the only method that had seemed feasible for improving the technique of social organization was the mandate of law. Although Aristotle, for instance, predicted that slavery would come to an end on the condition that the shuttle should weave by itself and the lyre play without human hand, no one in the Greek community of his time saw very much likelihood of improvement through mechanical inventions or wholesale innovations in agriculture; and no one, apparently, concerned himself seriously with the mechanical side of affairs.

It was the same during the Middle Age. If the men of that time were not exuberantly happy over their civilization, they had the dogmatic conviction that nothing very satisfactory could come of a race that had inherited the curse of Adam—a race whose only salvation could come when its individuals were purged one by one of sin, and delivered, by the intercession of the saints and the grace of God, into a more benignly constituted afterworld. One might relieve the pressure a little if the shoe pinched, perhaps, but scarcely anyone dreamed of travelling in seven-league boots, or of establishing an Arcadia in which boots could be dispensed with. It was foolish to look for a more perfect society in a world that was rife with imperfect men.

The Renascence, as we have seen, changed all this. Presently a school of philosophers followed on the heels of the utopians who devoted themselves to preparing fairly minute plans and specifications for the social order. In the beginning, these plans were devoted to politics and criminal reform, like those of Rousseau, Beccaria, Bentham, Jefferson, Godwin, and the eighteenth century reformers generally; in the nineteenth century the main accent was economic, and a number of movements arose which could be traced back to the semi-scientific investigations of Adam Smith, Ricardo, Proudhon, Malthus, Marx, and perhaps half a dozen other thinkers of outstanding importance, among whom we should perhaps include such latter day figures as Mill, Spencer, and Henry George.

All of these thinkers have in one way or another influenced our thoughts and deflected our actions; and if one adds to this galaxy the reforming elements which remained in the churches and the missionary brotherhoods and the philanthropic organizations, we can observe, growing up in the nineteenth century, a multitude of partisan organizations and movements, each of which is strenuously bent on realizing its private and partisan utopia. It is these private and partisan utopias that I purpose to make a slight reckoning with in the present chapter; but the field is such a huge and formidable one that I shall limit my criticism in the main to those that attempted to effect a change in the economic order.

2

For all the activities that men engage in we have separate words. This is a great misfortune; for in using these words we tend to believe that each action takes place in a separate compartment. Instead of beginning with a whole man interacting in a whole community, we are likely to consider only a partial man in a partial community, and by a mental sleight of hand, before we know it, we have let the part stand for the whole. It is this sort of abstraction, I believe, that has been responsible for a good deal of fallacious thinking with regard to the place of industry in the community. The economists seem to have made the error first by talking of a creature whom they called the Economic Man, a creature who had no instincts but those of construction and acquisition, no habits but of working and saving, and no other ultimate purpose than to become such a captain of industry as would make him a candidate for the biographic sketches of Mr. Samuel Smiles, and his present successors in the newspapers and popular magazines.

Now this Economic Man was the embodiment of honest labor and rapacious greed. Out of the better quality, Karl Marx painted the picture of the faithful laborer in Coketown whose masters swindled him out of the "surplus value" he produced; out of the worse quality classical economists like Ricardo painted an equally entrancing picture of the beneficent capitalist, through whose foresight, organizing ability, and boldness business could be conducted on a scale a simpler age had scarcely dreamed of. It was out of these conceptions, as they were elaborated and rationalized in books like Porter's Progress of the Nineteenth Century and Marx's Capital, that there grew up the notion that the only fundamental problem in the modern world was the labor problem—the problem as to who should control industry, who should profit by its advances, and who should own the complicated instruments by which it was conducted.

Our business here is not to examine the various programs that were offered during the last century in answer to these problems; merely to catalog them with the barest explanation of their purpose would be an imposing task, were it not for the fact that it has been neatly done for us by Mr. Savel Zimand. It is enough to see here the common element in capitalism, copartnery, State Socialism, Guild Socialism, Co-operation, Communism, Syndicalism, the One Big Union, Trades Unionism, and the like; whether these movements represent actual facts, like capitalism, copartnery, or trades unionism, or whether they are simply projections, like Syndicalism and the One Big Union.

If our excursion through the classic utopias has been of any use, it must have shown us how pathetic is this notion that the key to a good society rests simply on the ownership and control of the industrial plant of the community. Is it any less absurd when we confess that most of the movements which were founded upon this assumption were actuated by generous and humane motives, and that Francis Place, the tailor of Charing Cross, who believed in a radical application of laissez faire principles, was just as sincere a believer in the common weal as Karl Marx, who predicted a dictatorship of the proletariat? If a great many of these programs have had the notion that industrial machinery, under socialism or guildism or co-operation was to be used for the common benefit, what was lacking was any common notion as to what the common benefit was.

All that was common to these partisan utopias was a desire to get rid of positive evils such as overwork or starvation or irregularity of employment. In their rejection of the existing order of Coketown, with its rubbish heaps for the disposal of material waste, and its jails, hospitals, sanatoria, doss houses, Salvation Army Headquarters, and charitable organizations for the disposal of the human excrement of industrialism—in turning their backs upon these things and asserting the simple elements of human dignity, all our radical programs were right and inevitable. To reject what industrial society had to offer its members in the filthy factory districts and wretched slums of Coketown was obviously to reject barbarism and degradation of the worst sort: the incredible thing about the industrial revolution, indeed, is not that there were a few riots here and there against the use of machinery, but that the industrial population has not been in a state of continual insurrection, and that the industrial towns have not been looted and razed again and again. It is nothing less than a tribute to the fundamental good nature and sweetness of human beings that the strikes by which the workers have expressed their sense of grievance have not demolished the material hovels that today stand upright in the valleys of York-Riding, in the valleys of the Ohio and its tributaries, or in that terrible slum which stretches in back of the Jersey meadows from Elizabeth into Patterson. There are many districts in these areas which are scarcely worth the respect of orderly demolition. To give a grim rejection to the society that produced them only mildly meets the situation. They should be destroyed by trumpets and God's wrath—like Jericho!

So much for what is sound and valid in the various one-sided programs for reform. But if their attitude towards the past performances of industrialism was sound, their gesture towards the future, and their attitude towards the whole milieu, was little less than indifferent. There were to be certain gains in money wages, in political control, in the distribution of products, and so forth; but the realization of these gains was never projected in any very vivid way—a vague fellowship in peace and plenty under gay red banners was all that was left over when the current efforts to "educate the masses," "revise the constitution," or "organize the revolution" were taken for granted.

In his Socialism: Utopian and Scientific, Friedrich Engels made a plea for a realistic method of thought, which limited itself to a here and now, as against what he derided as the utopian method, the attempt on the part of a single thinker to give a detailed picture of the society of the future. Yet at the present time it is easy to see that if the utopian socialism of Owen has been ineffective, the realistic socialism of Marx has been equally ineffective; for while Owen's kind of socialism has been partly fulfilled in the co-operative movement, the dictatorship of the proletariat rests upon very shaky foundations, and such success as it has had is due perhaps as much to Marx's literary picture of what it would be like as to anything else. I do not doubt that the partisan movements have achieved many specific gains; consumer's co-operation alone has in England measurably lightened the physical burden of existence for a great many people. Their weakness consists in the fact that they have not altered the contents of the modern social order, even when they have altered the method of distribution; and in addition, a good many of these partisan utopias, for lack of any definite and coherent scheme of values, crumble away as soon as they meet the opposition of such powerful collective utopias as Coketown or the Country House. In America, particularly, the labor movement is paralyzed by this perpetual movement into the bourgeoisie—concretely speaking, into Suburbia and the Country House—and in Great Britain much the same sort of dereliction can be observed within the narrower group from which the leaders of the trades unions and the Labor Party are drawn.

Hence also the less interesting problem of the Tired Radical, which Mr. Walter Weyl suggestively outlined. There is indeed a pertinent criticism of the paper environment of Megalopolis, in the tenacious way in which people continue to cling to abstract programs and to movements which never approach perceptibly nearer their fulfillment. The marvel is that the concrete utopia of the Country House has not exercised a more potent influence than it actually does. When one compares the vast amount of agitation during the last century—the Chartist Movement, the Socialist Movement, the International Peace Movement—with the actual results in the reconstruction of work, place, and people, or with the actual effects any reconstruction has had upon our polity, our culture, our art—it is surprising that these movements have had any effective claim upon our allegiance. Men will indeed work for an idea—the notion that they will not is a superstition—but sooner or later the spirit must be made manifest in the flesh, and if it never comes to birth, or at best is an abortion, the idea is bound to wither away.

How long would the parliamentary clatter of socialism have mechanically kept on—had it not been for the dislocation of war? How long could its abstract programs have remained in the air, before coming down to specifications? I obviously cannot answer these questions; but it seems plain enough that our radical programs have had simply a sentimental interest: they moved people without giving them a specific task, they stirred them emotionally without giving them an outlet, and so, at best, they are but partial utopias of escape, using the powers of organization, collective meetings, and pronunciamentos to take the place of the emotional stimuli which the avowed utopia of escape, like News from Nowhere, supplies by introducing a beautiful girl. In this aspect, the Socialist Party, with its revolutionary demands, did not differ in its psychological performance from the Republican Party, which specialized in the rhetorical device of the full dinner pail; nor did it differ in any fundamental way from the defunct Progressive Party, which for a time believed in a new heaven and earth to follow the initiative, referendum, and recall with an intensity of moral conviction beside which the social revolutionist was positively tame.

Who doubts the honesty and sincerity of most of the members of these parties? Who doubts their devotion to revolution or "uplift"? It is all beside the point. A machine which doesn't work because it is badly constructed is just as useless as one that doesn't work because its maker is a deliberate fraud; and all the sincerity and good will and honesty doesn't make any one a smile the happier. It is about time that we faced the facts and realized that in all our sundry mechanisms of reform "there is a screw loose somewhere." This pregnant metaphor of the industrial age is usually applied to neurotic disorder; and I am using it in the present context with fell intentions. I mean that the utopia of the partisan is, psychologically speaking, a fetish; that is to say, it is an attempt to substitute the part for the whole, and to pour into the part all the emotional content that belongs to the whole. When a man gets hold of a lady's handkerchief or garter, and behaves towards that object with as much intensity and interest as he would towards its flesh and blood owner, the handkerchief or garter is said to be a fetish. I hazard the judgment that Socialism, Prohibition, Proportional Representation, and the various other abstract "isms" are the fetishes of the partisan: they are attempts to make some particular instrument or function of the community stand for the whole. It is doubtless much easier to filch a handkerchief than to win a girl. By the same token, it is easier to concentrate on the use of liquor or the ownership of machinery and land than upon the totality of a community's activities. It is easier indeed; but it is fatal; for the result of this fetishism is perhaps that the girl remains unmated, and the society fails to undergo any fundamental change. Moreover, the reforming elements in society become incapacitated by their practice of fetishism to take a normal part in the community's activities; and remain so much waste material—at best, they wander between two worlds, "one dead, the other powerless to be born."

We know these disoriented reformers, these disillusioned revolutionaries, these tired radicals; we could mention names if it were not so needless and so cruel. Apart from anything else, their original mistake was to keep their problem within the compartment of politics and economics, instead of venting it to the wide world. They forgot that the adjustment of some single activity or institution, without respect to the rest, begged the very difficulty they were trying to overcome. If they were anti-militarists, they saw the world simply as an armed camp; if they were socialists, they saw it as a gigantic mechanism of exploitation; and alas! they saw only so much of the world as would conveniently fit within these diagrams. The world is perhaps an armed camp and a mechanism of exploitation; it is all that and much more; but any attempt to deal with it on a wholesale plan by eliminating all the qualifying elements in the problem is bound to encounter the brute nature of things; and if the nature of things is essentially antagonistic, the reform itself will fail.

To say all this is to emphasize the obvious. If any further emphasis were needed it would be necessary only to compare the doctrines of Marx, as expounded by Lenin at the beginning of the Russian Revolution, and the doctrines of Lenin, as tempered by experience and circumstance a few years later.

3

There was still another weakness that characterized all the partisan utopias of the nineteenth century. That weakness was their externalism.

If the mediæval thinkers were convinced that, on the whole, nothing could be done to rectify men's institutions, while men themselves were so easily bitten by corruption, their successors in the nineteenth century committed the opposite kind of error and absurdity: they believed that human nature was unsocial and obstreperous only because the church, the state, or the institution of property perverted every human impulse. Men like Rousseau, Bentham, Godwin, Fourier, and Owen might be miles apart from one another in their criticism of society, but there was an underlying consensus in their belief in human nature. They looked upon human institutions as altogether external to men; these were so many straitjackets that cunning rulers had thrown over the community to make sane and kindly people behave like madmen; and they could conceive of changing the institutions without changing the habits and redirecting the impulses of the people by whom and for whom they had been created. If one devised neat political constitutions, with plenty of checks and balances, or laid out pauper colonies and invited the countryside to make use of them—well, all would be to the good.

There was, it is true, one great exception to this notion that institutions might be reformed without, in that process, making over men. I refer to the belief in education which accompanied these classic criticisms of human institutions; for this seems to point to a perception that men needed a special training and discipline before they could enter freely into the life of a reconstituted community. But upon examination, this exception melts away. The emphasis in the new programs of education was upon the formal, institutional acquirement of the apparatus of knowledge; and they, too, began with the clean slate of a new generation, whereas the critical difficulty was that of getting the adult community sufficiently educated, in a realistic sense, to be able to make over its educational institutions; and in this respect the reformers were just as much in Cuckooland as—well, Campanella. So it follows that the Country House and Coketown shared honors in building up the new educational organizations; and the outcome of the sort of education that the public school and college provided was to make these redoubtable utopias practically unassailable.

Besides, there were the adults: consider Robert Owen!

Robert Owen, one of the most sanguine advocates of popular education, was himself a living example of the need for a different kind of discipline than his narrow and homiletic mind, with its childish interpretation of religious belief and its equally childish rationalism, was capable of framing. No one ever frustrated so many good ideas, from the plan of garden cities down to the project for co-operative production than this same Owen, whose bumptiousness, arrogance, and conceit were bound to provoke reactions in other people which would have defeated the plans of Omnipotence itself. The capital difficulty was to get any sort of social improvement in a world that was full of refractory Owens. A locomotive may, in a sense, be a more perfect thing than the man who made it; but no social order can be better than the human beings who take part in it; for whereas the locomotive can stand apart from its operatives and perform all its functions effectively even if the workers themselves are deficient in every other respect than mechanics, with a social order the product and the producer continue to be one.

Not merely does a community need a Buddha, let us say, before it can produce Buddhism; it needs a whole succession of Buddhas if the religion itself is not to fritter away into the hideous ecclesiastical grind it became in Thibet. This principle has a general application. The social critics of the last century confused the mechanical problem of transforming an institution or of creating a new organization with the personal and social problem of spurring people to effect the transformation and see it through. Their tactics were those of a general who would go into battle without training his army; their strategy was that of the demagogue who talks of a million armed men springing up overnight. The personal problem, the problem of education, was as easy as that!

If we are to account for the poverty of our achievements in renovating the community, in contrast with the enormous amount of quite justifiable economic and political agitation, research, and criticism, it is perhaps not altogether fair to put the entire burden of failure upon the partisan's lop-sided utopia. The plans of our reformers have indeed been weak and jerrybuilt in themselves; but that is not all. What has perhaps been even more conspicuously lacking has been people who are accessible to the existing knowledge, people whose minds have been trained to play freely with the facts, people who have learned the fine and exacting art of co-operating with their fellows; people who are as critical of their own mental processes and habits of behavior as they are of the institutions they wish to alter. As Viola Paget says: "The bulk of thinking and feeling intended to help on human improvement has not really been good enough for the purpose. Not good enough in the sense of not sufficiently impersonal and disciplined."

Between our programs, our utopias, and their fulfillment there has usually dropt a thick veil of personalities; and were the plan itself the collaborate product of the best minds of the race; as Mr. H. G. Wells satirically pictured in Boon, it would still have to take its chances with the wild asses of the devil that human weakness, apathy, greed, lust for power, might release. Walt Whitman said of Carlyle that behind the tally of his work and genius stood the stomach, and gave a sort of casting vote. So one may say of every social movement, that behind the tally of its theoretic background and its concrete programs stand human beings—hale and sick, neurotic and stable, well-intentioned and malicious—and give the casting vote.

Anyone who has read an important book, and then met the author, who has respected an apparently significant social movement, and then met the leaders behind the scenes, will realize how frequent is the difficulty of reconciling theoretic agreement with the inaccessibilities and prejudices and repugnances of particular personalities. No one can join the work of even the most trivial sort of committee—be it a delegation to shake hands with the Congressman or a body designated to revise the rules of a tennis club—without discovering how the work in hand is perpetually being balked and diverted by the play of personalities.

It is not a little significant that popular speech gives the word "personalities" a derogatory meaning. Again and again the success or failure in large collaborations hinges upon human factors that have no bearing on the question at issue. Pope's satiric words about wretches hanging that jurymen may dine touches the point neatly. Our programs for reconstruction that have not reckoned with the perpetual cussedness of human nature and have no method for exorcising it are as shallow as those older theologies which sought to make men live in grace without altering the social order in which they functioned. Perhaps they could learn something from the story of that ancient agitator who cured the blind, the maimed, the sick, and the halt before he bade them enter into the Kingdom of Heaven. Emerson well said in his essay on Man the Reformer that it was stupid to expect any real or permanent change from any social program which was unable to regenerate or convert—these are religious phases for a common psychological phenomenon—the people who are to engineer it and carry it through.

It would be so easy, this business of making over the world, if it were only a matter of creating machinery. There has probably never been lacking the sort of energy and talent that is needed for this sort of work; and at any rate, during the last three centuries, with the growth of technology, the mechanical services at the command of our engineers and organizers are huge and adequate. Unfortunately, we are still in the same ditch that Carlyle mordantly pointed out in his essay on Characteristics: Given a world of knaves, we are trying by various cunning devices to produce an honesty from their united action. I do not share Carlyle's contempt for human nature in the raw, but he is quite right, I believe, in making fun of the superficiality of our partisan utopias. These utopias were so concerned to alter the shell of the community's institutions that they neglected to pay attention to the habits of the creature itself—or its habitat. That is why mechanical devices play such an important part, perhaps, in all these utopias, from Jeremy Bentham, with his Panopticon method of reforming criminals, down to the hideous cog-and-wheel utopia of Edward Bellamy.

The conceptions of human life that our reforming groups have had have been pretty thin and unsatisfying. Any adequate conception of a new social order would, it seems to me, include the scenery, the actors, and the play. It is a mark of our immaturity that we never seem able to get beyond the scene shifting. Our social theorists, in so far as they consider the actors at all, are inclined to treat them as mechanical puppets. As for the play itself—the universal drama of courtship and trial and adventure and contest and achievement, in which every human being is potentially the hero or heroine—the play itself has hardly entered into their consciousness. Their values have not been human values: they have been such values as have been authenticated by commerce and industry, values such as efficiency, fair wages, and what not. These, at any rate, have been the immediate objects of effort, and if human values hung vaguely in the background, they were to be realized in a distant and unascertainable future. So one often feels that no matter how base and deteriorated the modern community is, it nevertheless retains in its totality a greater measure of human values than many of the groups that have attacked its inadequacy have to offer.

All this comes out pretty plainly in the attitude of the labor groups towards the current situation. Whether they are organized for political action or for industrial warfare, their aims are curiously similar. In the very act of contending against the present order, they have accepted the ends for which that order stands and have been content to demand simply that they be universalized. This perhaps accounts for the essential uncreativeness of the labor movement. By a revolution they do not mean a transvaluation of values: they mean a dilution and spreading out of established practices and institutions. There may indeed be plenty of excuse for this attitude in any particular situation—a group of unorganized and semi-destitute workers such as those in many American steel plants—but the worst of it is that this attitude characterizes the more advanced and economically secure groups, and creeps into such ultimate programs as one can deduce from attempts to create workers' educational institutions—as if a change in ownership or the balance of power would alter the face of Coketown so that its fires would no longer burn and its cinders no longer smut.

I have emphasized what is the weakness, as it seems to me, of the labor movement; not because I am necessarily out of sympathy with any particular measure that might be proposed, but because it illustrates upon an enormous scale the point which I desire to make. The prohibition movement, or the charity organization movement—towards both of which I feel, on the contrary, a cordial antipathy—would serve just as well for illustration; for they all have this common distinction: they lack any explicit, consciously projected humane ends which would make any particular measure that they might offer justified.

4

Let me now anticipate the answer which this criticism will probably meet. To some people it will seem that the current movements for reform are inevitably secular; that they have no business to concern themselves with the ultimate faith of men; that they inevitably deal with a limited here and now, a dollar more of wages, a drop less of liquor, a touch more of uniformity, and so forth. In short, our partial utopias need not concern themselves with any of the questions that have to do with the life of the spirit.

The simple answer to this crude philosophy is—so much the worse for them. The breach between the institutions that deal with the material life and those that deal with the ideal life results either in a complete dissociation, by which each set of institutions becomes paralytic and imbecile; or, as so often happens, in a capitulation of the spiritual power to the temporal, and its complete engrossment in temporal ends. I am aware that these phrases, "spiritual" and "temporal," have a certain old-fashioned smell; but they precisely express my meaning: it is plain that every community contains the corresponding institutions—one group being devoted to values and the other to means. When our reforms are not touched by a sense of values, the result is that purely temporal ends are taken as ultimate, and we have such notions as efficiency or organization regarded as the very touchstone of social improvement. This is scarcely an improvement over the old order of things, with which we are now so dismally familiar—the state in which our values were not fertilized by any intercourse with the concrete and actual world about us, and so remained remote and sterile. In short, unless our reformers concern themselves with the ultimate values of men, with what constitutes a good life, they are bound to pander to such immediate faiths and superstitions as the National State, Efficiency, or the White Man's Burden.

5

There is a final criticism of the partial utopias: our one-sided reforms have had this fatal defect—they are one-sided. This partisanship was expressed by their relation to the facts upon which their programs were based, and in their attitude towards the people who were to be affected by them.

The mood of partisanship has been that of a lawyer who is getting up an argument and is looking for such facts as will bolster up his case. That mood is inimical to free and intelligent thought: its object is rhetorical triumph. Now it happens that in all the matters which intimately concern a community, a person's attitude towards the facts not merely seems more important than the facts themselves, but seems so deucedly important that the facts are ignored. The attitude of a group of Southern whites who will lynch a negro on the report that he has raped a white woman before they investigate the truth of the assertion is a bestial exaggeration of a very natural human tendency. Men are built for action rather than thought; or rather, since thought, on the psychologist's interpretation, is inhibited action, the business of inhibition naturally comes a little hard to us; and when we are in a place where we have the rough choice of pushing through the obstacle, under a strong impulse of resentment (instinct of pugnacity) or may quietly withdraw from the obstacle, survey it, and frame a plan of action to circumvent it, our fundamental impulse is to follow the first mode.

It is easy to see, for example, how the hideous human suffering which accompanied the growth of the capitalist organization—and still exists!—caused the socialists to concentrate attention upon the subjects of ownership and profits, and long blinded them to the specific problems of organization, distribution, and control within the industries that might be affected by the program of socialization. This concentration upon the particular aspect of a problem, like the concentration upon a particular aspect of the solution, has the weakness of ignoring the total situation, and it too crudely simplifies the difficulties. In their haste to arrive at solutions and remedies—for the life of man is short and the needs of the moment are pressing—the partisans neglect to make a complete tally of the facts; and they are too ready to let "common knowledge" take the place of a thorough investigation of the data.

This weakness arises out of an almost instinctive tendency towards partisanship; and it is one of the reasons that partisanship continues. If nothing else prevents groups from getting together, their failure to agree about the facts, and their lack of a method for getting at the facts and focussing them, is responsible. If an examination of the facts did nothing else, it might show at least the impossibility of drawing any conclusion from them, and it might warn the partisan to step warily. Thus the testimony that was offered for and against Prohibition came from fairly high authorities on both sides; and if there had been anything like right reason in the strategically stronger camp, it would have convinced those who were interested in the welfare of the community that nothing could be wisely done while the very basis for judgment—scientific knowledge as to the place of alcoholic stimuli in the life of the human organism—had not been established.

It is of course conceivable that men will quarrel and split when they are fully apprised of the facts: we may well remember the story of the British ambassador who confessed to his French colleague that the reason he did not get on very well with the Americans was that both countries unfortunately spoke the same language; but it is inconceivable that they should ever reach an intelligent agreement before they are in common possession of the facts. By ignoring the necessity for substantiating his claims and assertions the partisan frequently not merely fails to see his whole problem in all its implications, but also prevents any one else from seeing it. Even when the partisan is not intentionally blind, he lacks the discipline which is essential to an open-eyed judgment of the case. What that discipline may be I shall attempt to discuss in the next chapter.

The second weakness of partisanship is that it breaks the community into vertical divisions, and promotes fictitious antagonisms and kinships which run against the horizontal affiliations and loyalties of a man's life. This tendency was nicely illustrated in a play by Mr. St. John Ervine, called Mixed Marriage, which dealt with the love affair of a young girl and a young man who were separated by the religions that had been handed down by their parents. In Mr. Ervine's wretched little Ulster community, these religions served as an excuse to keep people from being friendly and decent to their neighbors. Now it is obvious that mating, and making friends with those who have common interests and sentiments, and mixing freely within the whole community, are highly important horizontal interests; they tend to unite people in a common bond which is fundamental for the reason that these interests and activities are essentially human. The antagonism between two Christian sects, on the other hand, undermines the good life as a whole, because it insists that there is no other good than a religious good—a good embodied in a pope, or in the practice of scoffing at a pope—while it is obvious to anyone who has possession of his senses that kissing a pretty girl is good, and having a friendly pipe with one's neighbor is good, and that institutions which prevent one from doing these things at appropriate times are perverted and anti-social. It is true that people who emphasize religious interests take "high ground," as the saying is, and that those who value the friendly pipe seem by implication to take low ground: but what the partisans fail to see is that there is a good human case for low ground, and that, for the great majority of people it may prove to be not merely the only practicable ground, but in its own right a good and sufficient one.

Now for Catholic and Protestant in Mr. St. John Ervine's play one may substitute Democrat and Republican, White Guard and Red Guard, Socialist and Financier, Prohibitionist and anti-Prohibitionist and the results will be just as deplorably the same. There are any number of interests in a well-wrought life which lie altogether beyond these categories, and it is the chief misdemeanor of partisanism, as opposed to utopianism, that it tends to slight these general interests, and either bring them into the service of the "ism" or urge that they be neglected in devotion to the "cause." The first method has been used by the apostles of nationalism. The National State, recognizing that art and culture and science could not be altogether engrossed in the strategy of political warfare, promptly put these goods in the pigeon hole labelled national resources. The partisans of the State talked about American science as opposed to German science, of Italian art as opposed to French art; and thus emphasized the things which men in America had with other Americans in order to mark off more clearly the things they had apart from men of similar interests in other countries. The same thing happened in the Russian communist state, with its attempt to set aside the common cultural heritage of mankind at large and define a purely proletarian culture. The results in every case are, I believe, incurably mischievous; and those who would promote the good life must cease this infantile practice of asserting vainly that "my father knows more than your father," "my mother is more beautiful than your mother"—and so on.

For the most part the second method has been indefatigably used. In the political state the partisans make a great show of the gulf which separates the political party in power from that which is outside, and every other interest in life is supposed to be secondary to this abysmal cleavage. In relatively crude communities, like the United States and Ireland, these differences seem to be taken by the great mass of people at their face value; whereas in England, which at least has the virtues of disillusion, it is the great tradition of Parliament that all the animosities of the floor are ignored in the bar of the House of Commons, while all the congenialities and convivialities that bind men together are emphasized. Lest I be accused of prejudice where none exists, let me add that in the most substantial reconstruction movement that Ireland possesses—I refer to agricultural co-operation as promoted by Sir Horace Plunkett and A. E.—the horizontal interests which bind men together as farmers and members of a local community are successfully emphasized to the exclusion of irrelevant vertical differences, at least in matters touching the organization and conduct of the Irish Agricultural Organization Society; and that, as far as I can see, this single organization has done more to promote the good life in Ireland than any other institution, with the possible exception of the equally non-partisan literary association which grew up in Dublin under the leadership of A. E., William Butler Yeats, Lady Gregory, and the rest of that fine and glorious crew.

Obviously, it is not altogether for nothing that men have joined together in vertical organizations which are as broad as a continent, let us say, or the European world. There is a sense in which the Christians of Jerusalem have more in common with the Christians of Rome than they have with the Jews and Mohammedans of their local region. In the same way, I find myself more deeply drawn to certain friends of mine in Bombay and London than I am towards my next door neighbor, with whom the only recognizable bond is our common animus against a rapacious landlord. So long as the vertical affiliation with people of the same views in politics or religion or philosophy is a spiritual affiliation a great deal of good may come out of it. When, however, the things that draw people together as members of a vertical group are used as a means of inflicting similar opinions or practices upon the local community, without respect to its regional qualities, the results are little less than disastrous. The rain falls on the just and the unjust; more than that, the food that we grow, the houses that we build, the roads that we lay down, the thoughts that we think, belong to us as members of the human species who have inherited the earth and the fullness thereof; and it is absurd to let differences in our idola prevent us from participating equally in this common heritage.

At long last, the things that unite human beings as human beings, the social inheritance that enables them to realize their stature as human beings, are more important than any particular element that the partisan may lay hold of. Whether our partisanism consists in being first and foremost an American or first and foremost a Theosophist, it tends to limit the world with which we may have commerce and so impoverishes the personality. The person who insists upon being a hundred per cent. American has by that very emphasis become something less than half a man. By fastening attention upon a segment of the world, the partisan creates a segment of a personality. It is these segments or sects that any movement which aims at a general good in the community must contend against. So long as work for the common welfare meets with irrelevant partisanisms, so long will we lack the means of creating whole men and women; and so long will the main concerns of civilization be side-tracked:

6

What a vision these partisan utopias present! They are like the scattered bones that the prophet saw in the terrible valley, and one doubts whether even the breath of the Lord could knit them together again into real bodies. . . .

One of these partisan utopias issues from a bundle of red-tape; everything is filed and ticketed and labelled there; and anything in life that cannot be treated in this fashion does not exist. Another is a mechanical contraption; somehow it seems to litter little mechanical contraptions; and its aim is, it would seem, to do away with vegetation and reproduction, so that everything under the sun might be performed with the sterile accuracy of the machine. A third utopia of the partisan calls human beings, with all their color and thickness, "individuals," and makes the good life a matter of legal relationships without any regard to their necessities in time and space; such a utopia could almost be carried in one's pocket, so much is it a matter of verbal statement. We need not go down the line. Singly, it is plain that not one of these utopias would create a happy community; while if all of these partisanisms could be realized the result could scarcely be anything else than discord—such a discord as now exists and every day becomes more raucous.

It would seem that we are at an impasse. Even if I have absurdly exaggerated the futility of the reformers and revolutionaries, their lack of any fundamental program and their inability to conceive an essential reorientation in modern society, come out pretty plainly. If our analysis did not prove this, the atmosphere of disillusion which we breathe today, and which permeates every branch of literature, would tell as much. In so far as we have accepted the modern social order we are in ruin; and the next war that now threatens will, if it actually comes to pass, only carry the ruin a little further. In so far as we have pinned our hopes to current movements for reconstruction or revolution, our plans are sickly and debilitated. In fact, the only genuine signs of life seem to be in regions like Ireland, Denmark, India, and China, which have stood outside the movement of industrial civilization and have retained the values of an order which elsewhere has been undermined and almost destroyed. It is not a pretty situation to face; and small wonder that we are so slow and so reluctant to face it. Whichever way we look, bankruptcy seems to threaten us.

It is time we endeavored to cash in the paper roubles of the partisan. If our civilization is to hold together we must place its intellectual currency on a new basis; we must exchange our abstract idealisms, our abstract programs, our paperized pursuit of happiness for some of the golden coinage of life, even though we cannot have our gold without mixing it with baser metals.

CHAPTER TWELVE

How the half-worlds go, and how eutopia may come; and what we need before we can build Jerusalem in any green and pleasant land.

CHAPTER TWELVE

1

THE sort of thinking that has created our utopias has placed desire above reality; and so their chief fulfillment has been in the realm of fantasy. This is true of the classic utopias that we have surveyed, and it is true—though not perhaps quite so apparent—of the partial utopias that were formulated by the various reconstruction movements during the last century.

While the classic utopias have so far been nearer to reality that they have projected a whole community, living and working and mating and spanning the gamut of man's activity, their projections have nevertheless been literally up in the air, since they did not usually arise out of any real environment or attempt to meet the conditions that this environment presented. This defect has been suggested by the very name of Utopia, for as Professor Patrick Geddes points out, Sir Thomas More was an inveterate punster, and Utopia is a mock-name for either Outopia, which means no-place, or Eutopia—the good place.

It is time to bring our utopian idola and our everyday world into contact; indeed, it is high time, for the idola that have so far served us are now disintegrating so rapidly that our mental world will soon be as empty of useful furniture as a deserted house, while wholesale dilapidation and ruin threaten the institutions that once seemed permanent. Unless we can weave a new pattern for our lives the outlook for our civilization is almost as dismal as Herr Spengler finds it in Der Untergang des Abendlandes. Our choice is not between eutopia and the world as it is, but between eutopia and nothing—or rather, nothingness. Other civilizations have proved inimical to the good life and have failed and past away; and there is nothing but our own will-to-eutopia to prevent us from following them.

If this dissipation of Western Civilization is to cease, the first step in reconstruction is to make over our inner world, and to give our knowledge and our projections a new foundation. The problem of realizing the potential powers of the community—which is the fundamental problem of eutopian reconstruction—is not simply a matter of economics or eugenics or ethics as the various specialist thinkers and their political followers have emphasized. Max Beer, in his History of British Socialism, points out that Bacon looked for the happiness of mankind chiefly in the application of science and industry. But by now it is plain that if this alone were sufficient, we could all live in heaven tomorrow. Beer points out that More, on the other hand, looked to social reform and religious ethics to transform society; and it is equally plain that if the souls of men could be transformed without altering their material and institutional activities, Christianity, Mohammedanism, and Buddhism might have created an earthly paradise almost any time this last two thousand years. The truth is, as Beer sees, that these two conceptions are still at war with each other: idealism and science continue to function in separate compartments;

and yet "the happiness of man on earth" depends upon their combination.

If we are to build up genuine eutopias, instead of permitting ourselves to pattern our behavior in terms of fake utopias like Coketown, the Country House, the National State, and all the other partial and inadequate myths to which we have given allegiance, we must examine anew the idola which will assist us in reconstituting our environment. So we are forced to consider the place of science and art in our social life, and to discuss what must be done in order to make them bear more concretely upon "the improvement of man's estate."

2

There was a time when the world of knowledge and the world of dreams were not separated; when the artist and the scientist, for all practical purposes, saw the "outside world" through the same kind of spectacles.

What we call "science" today was in its primitive state part and parcel of that common stock of knowledge and belief which makes up a community's literature, or, as Dr. Beattie Crozier would have said, its "Bible." The departure of science from this main body of literature begins for the Western World, probably, with the death of Plato and the institution of Aristotle's collections in natural history; and from that point onwards the separate sciences, increasingly isolate themselves from the general body of knowledge, and utilize methods which had been unknown to the earlier philosophers and sages; so that by the time the twentieth century dawns the process of differentiation has been completed, and philosophy, once the compendium of the sciences, has disappeared except as a sort of impalpable, viscous residue.

When Aristotle divided his writing into the exoteric and esoteric groups, into the popular and the scientific, he definitely recognized the existence of two separate branches of literature, two different ways of taking account of the world, two disparate methods of approaching its problems. The first branch was that of the philosophers, the prophets, the poets, and the plain people. Its background was the generality of human experience: its methods were those of discussion and conference: its criteria were those of formal dialectics: its interests were specifically those of the community, and nothing human was foreign to it. With the petrification of Greek thought that followed the collapse of the Alexandrian school, the second branch was slow in coming into its own. As late as the eighteenth century its adherents were called natural philosophers, to distinguish them from the more humane variety; and it is only with the nineteenth century that the subject became universally known as science and its practitioners as scientists.

In the Phædrus Socrates had expressed the humanist outlook of literature by saying: "Trees and fields, you know, cannot teach me anything, but men in the city can." The shortest way of describing the attitude of science is to say that it resolutely turned its back on men in the city and devoted itself to the trees and fields and stars and the rest of brute nature. If it paid attention to men at all it saw them—if we may abuse an old quotation—as trees walking. Socrates had said: Know thyself. The scientist said: Know the world that lies outside man's dominion. As science progressed these attitudes became more rigid, unfortunately, and a conflict grew up between literature and science, between the humanities and natural philosophy, which has given both art and science the peculiar twist we shall presently examine.

Now the developments in modern science go back, through the Arabic thinkers, to ancient Greece; but the great advances that have been made date back scarcely three centuries. On the basis of the precise knowledge of physical relations which became available in mathematics, physics, mechanics, and chemistry the startling changes which have been crudely labelled the "industrial revolution" were carried through. If the essential relationship between the world of ideas and the world of action were ever in doubt, the industrial revolution, especially in its later phases, would be a final demonstration; for beneath the ostensible skyscrapers, subways, factories, telephone lines, and sewers of the modern industrial city lie the immaterial foundations of western physical science, laid down stone by stone in the remote, theoretic researches of Boyle, Faraday, Kelvin, Leibniz, and the rest of that great galaxy. With the far reaching effect of the idola of physical science it is hardly necessary to deal. Everyone realizes how dependent the advance in technology has been upon theoretic science, even though the scientist himself, as Kropotkin pointed out, is sometimes slow in admitting the debt of science itself to practical invention. The actual world of machinery is at present, it seems fair to say, a parasite upon this body of knowledge, and it would speedily starve to death if the host were annihilated.

Science has provided the factual data by means of

which the industrialist, the inventor, and the engineer have transformed the physical world; and without doubt the physical world has been transformed. Unfortunately, when science has furnished the data its work is at an end: whether one uses the knowledge of chemicals to cure a patient or to poison one's grandmother is, from the standpoint of science, an extraneous and uninteresting question. So it follows that while science has given us the means of making over the world, the ends to which the world has been made over have had, essentially, nothing to do with science. Accordingly, as I have suggested, the idola of the Country House and Coketown and the National State, which were built up by literature and art, have given the effective direction to these transformations. So far, science has not been used by people who regarded man and his institutions scientifically. The application of the scientific method to man and his institutions has hardly been attempted.

Even when one qualifies this last generalization, its outline remains pretty sharp. The development of what are called the social sciences was dimly outlined in Bacon's Novum Organon; but it was not till the eighteenth century, with Quesnay and Montesquieu, that the movement gained any real headway, and down to this day a large part of what is called science in Economics, Politics, and Sociology is only disguised literature—work in which the jargon of science is accepted as a substitute for the scientific method of arriving at factual truth, and in which the effort to mold conduct overwhelms the attempt to reach correct conclusions. Indeed, among the economists and sociologists there has been a persistent dribble of discussion as to whether or not their subjects entitled them to the august designation of scientists.

It is not without reason that the social and human sciences have been distrusted by the devotees of physical science, so that, for example, the British Association has long had a single section devoted to the social sciences in which Sociology, the mother of them all, is permitted to enter as a subclassification of Anthropology! The nearer the investigator gets to man, the more easily he is overwhelmed with the complexity of his subject; and the more tempted he is to adopt the swift and easy partisan methods of the novelist, the poet, the prophet. The mere concealment of this act of seduction under the rough, grey cover of scientific jargon means frequently that the social scientist has added to the offense of not being a good scientist by not even being a good literary man.

Hence there is a great gap between the more external part of the world which has been affected by science, and that part, nearer to man and man's institutions, which has yet for the greater part to be conquered. While the physical equipment of New York compares with that of fourth century Athens as Athens itself would compare with an Aurignacian cave, the life of men in the city is perhaps more disordered and futile and incomplete than the author of the Republic found it. The moral of this contrast need hardly be pointed in so many words. The idolum of science is incomplete; for it chiefly touches life in its physical sector; and it remains to complete the span so that every activity and condition may be described, measured, and grasped in scientific terms. With the vast modern improvement in our physical arrangements in view, it must occur to almost anyone that a permanent advance in social life depends upon a much more thorough and realistic acquaintance with the facts than the social sciences have yet been able to provide. Before an army moves over the land it is well for it to have moved in someone's mind over a topographic map. Lacking such maps, all our day to day improvements have been wasteful sallies into eutopia, proceeding without order, without a sufficient equipment, and without any general plan.

3

There is a point up to which each science may well be left to cultivate its field for its own sake, without any regard for the fruits. Mr. Thorstein Veblen, in The Place of Science in Civilization, has well pointed out the way in which science arises out of idle curiosity; and science, studied and advanced for its own sake, is surely one of the great playthings of the race. In this aspect, while science seeks a quite different path to the contemplative life than art takes, its end is the same—the dominant interest is an esthetic one, the joy of pure perception. Science is thus a sort of world in itself, and it is self-sufficient: there is no need for it to make contact with the real world in which we fight and love and earn our daily bread. In its own world, science is no better and no worse than theosophy or astrology or fables about deity.

But the divorce of science from the daily life of the community is not altogether an advantage. If it fosters a whole-hearted cultivation of science for its own values, it tends to lose sight of realities without which its values are meaningless. It is hard perhaps to locate the point at which science, divorced from every day realities, ceases to have any social relevance; but it seems to me that such a point exists; and when the sciences remain disparate and unrelated one to the other, they tend to pass over from a public world to the private world of the specialist; and the knowledge which obtains in that world can with difficulty be brought out again to irrigate the common life of the community; or if it is brought out, as bacteriology is brought out in relation to the treatment of disease, it is divorced from a consideration of the total situation in a way that makes so many specialist advances in medicine, for example, the stamping ground for the fanatic.

This loss of contact, I believe, is highly dangerous; for it lessens the effect of scientific discipline upon daily affairs quite as much as a cloistered religion, by erecting impossible sanctions, opens the way for much unalloyed slackness and baseness, and by demanding that Pistol and Falstaff live like Christ prevents these biological rapscallions from achieving so much as the level of Robin Hood. The upshot of this dissociation of science and social life is that superstition takes the place of science among the common run of men, as a more easily apprehended version of reality.

Today the whole corpus of knowledge is in an anarchic state, and it lacks order precisely because it lacks any definite relations to the community which creates it, and for which it, in turn, provides the spectacles through which the world is seen. Against the gains that have come from the increasing specialization of the sciences, we have to set off the losses which the community suffers from the development of crude forms of science, and from quackeries like astrology and spiritualism which succeed in giving a complete account of man's place in the universe in terms that are fairly intelligible to the lay mind. It seems to me, then, that in the cultivation of the sciences a definite hierarchy of values must be established which shall have some relation to the essential needs of the community. The independence of science from human values is a gross superstition: the desire for order, for security, for esthetically satisfactory patterns—along with the desire for fame or the favor of princes—have all played their parts in the development of science. Though the logic of science may discount the human factor as far as possible in its internal operations, it is because men have placed a certain value upon disinterested intellectual operations that these activities are pursued in modern communities to the exclusion of other interests and claims.

Let us put the problem concretely. A community which cultivates chemical science to the point at which it is able to wipe out a whole city by a few explosions of poisonous gas is in a pretty treacherous situation. If the science that it possesses has not helped to found a eutopia, it has at any rate provided the foundations for a kakotopia, or bad place: in short, for a hell. Indeed scientific knowledge has not merely heightened the possibilities of life in the modern world: it has lowered the depths. When science is not touched by a sense of values it works—as it fairly consistently has worked during the past century—towards a complete dehumanization of the social order. The plea that each of the sciences must be permitted to go its own way without control should be immediately rebutted by pointing out that they obviously need a little guidance when their applications in war and industry are so plainly disastrous.

We must be prepared to recognize that "truths" do not stand together on a high and lofty pedestal: some are important and some are trivial, some are innocent and some are dangerous, and while the pursuit of truth is a good in itself—*and complete freedom in that pursuit is a* sine qua non *of a good social life*—certain departments of investigation may need to be offset and corrected by work in other fields. In a modern Western European community, a sociological insight into the causes and conditions of war and peace is a needed corrective to the crudities of applied physical science and without such correction the mere increase of scientific knowledge, of which we boast so vacuously, may be highly inimical to the practice of the good life in the community.

4

If the sciences are to be cultivated anew with respect for a definite hierarchy of human values, it seems to me that the sciences must be focussed again upon particular local communities, and the problems which they offer for solution. Just as geometry in Egypt arose out of the need for annually surveying the boundaries that the Nile wiped out, and as astronomy developed in Chaldea in order to determine the shift of the seasons for the planting of crops, as geology in modern times developed out of the questions that a practical stone mason, like Hugh Miller, found himself confronted with—so may the sciences which are today incomplete and partial develop along the necessary lines by a survey of existing conditions and intellectual resources in a particular community.

On one hand, science must be in contact with the whole idolum of scientific thought—with that vast over-world of scientific effort which is the product of no single place or people or time. On the other hand, it must be related to the definite local community, limited in time and in space, in which its researches and its speculations will be realized and applied. Out of these surveys of existing conditions we should find, I believe, that in social psychology, in anthropology, in economics there are a vast number of facts and relations which remain to be described; and that, similarly, certain departments like craniology and jurisprudence and folklore have been vastly overcultivated in proportion to any genuine importance that their researches may have upon our control over the community's development. Such an investigation would bring out, above all, the weakness of contemporary sociological thought, with its diabetic flatulence of special sociologies, and its lack of any general agreement as to the field which is to be cultivated.

Apart from its great function as a plaything, science is valuable only to the extent that its researches can be brought to bear upon the conditions in a particular community, in a definite region. The difference between science as a plaything and science as an instrument for enabling us to establish more effective relations with other men and with the rest of our environment, is the difference between firing a shot at a target and firing at a buck for provender. The practice one gets in firing at a target is great fun, and incidentally it improves one's marksmanship; such idle sport is perhaps one of the stigmata of a civilized community. Nevertheless, unless one's skill can be definitely brought home it remains a personal achievement; and the community as a whole is not a pound of meat the better for it. If science is to play the significant part that Bacon and Andreæ and Plato and the other great humanists desired it to, it must be definitely brought home and realized in our here and now.

The need for this humanization of science has already been perceived in Great Britain. During the last decade a movement has gathered headway in the schools and extended itself to associations outside the schools. The title of this movement is "Regional Survey," and its point of origin is, I believe, the Outlook Tower in Edinburgh which was well described more than two decades ago as the "world's first sociological laboratory."

The aim of the Regional Survey is to take a geographic region and explore it in every aspect. It differs from the social survey with which we are acquainted in America in that it is not chiefly a survey of evils; it is, rather, a survey of the existing conditions in all their aspects; and it emphasizes to a much greater extent than the social survey the natural characteristics of the environment, as they are discovered by the geologist, the zoologist, the ecologist—in addition to the development of natural and human conditions in the historic past, as presented by the anthropologist, the archæologist, and the historian. In short, the regional survey attempts a local synthesis of all the specialist "knowledges."

Such a survey has been conducted in the Southeastern counties of England under the auspices of various local scientific societies; and the result of it is a complete description of the community's foundations, its past, its manner of working and living, its institutions, its regional peculiarities, and its utilization of physical, vital, and social resources. Each of the sciences draws upon its general body of knowledge to illuminate the points under observation; and when problems arise which point definitely to the lack of scientific or scholarly data, new trails are opened and new territory defined.

In looking at the community through the Regional Survey, the investigator is dealing with a real thing and not with an arbitrary idolum. In so far as the local community has certain elements in common with similar regions in other countries, or has absorbed elements from other civilizations, these things will be given their full value, instead of being disregarded because they weaken the identity of the local community with that precious myth, the National State. The greater part of the data that is thus brought to light may be plotted on a map, graphically presented in a chart, or photographed. In Saffron Walden, England, there is an admirable little museum devoted to such an exhibition of its region; and in the Outlook Tower, at Edingburgh, there used to be a library and an apparatus of exhibition by which one could begin at the point where one was standing and work outwards, in thought, to embrace the whole wide world. Knowledge that is presented in this fashion is available so that whoever runs may read; it has every feature, therefore, of popular science as it is purveyed in the cheap newspaper and magazine, whilst it remains real science and is not presented as something that verges from a miracle to a superstition.

The knowledge embodied in the Regional Survey has a coherence and pithiness which no isolated study of science can possibly possess. It is presented in such a form that it can be assimilated by every member of the community who has the rudiments of an education, and it thus differs from the isolated discipline which necessarily remains the heritage of the specialist. Above all, this knowledge is not that of "subjects," taken as so many water tight and unrelated compartments: it is a knowledge of a whole region, seen in all its aspects; so that the relations between the work aspect and the soil aspect, between the play aspect and the work aspect, become fairly simple and intelligible. This common tissue of definite, verifiable, localized knowledge is what all our partisan utopias and reconstruction programs have lacked; and lacking it, have been one-sided and ignorant and abstract—devising paper programs for the reconstruction of a paper world.

Regional survey, then, is the bridge by which the specialist whose face is turned towards the library and the laboratory, and the active worker in the field, whose face is turned towards the city and region in which he lives, may come into contact; and out of this contact our plans and our eutopias may be founded on such a permanent foundation of facts as the scientist can build for us, while the sciences themselves will be cultivated with some regard for the human values and standards, as embodied in the needs and the ideals of the local community. This is the first step out of the present impasse: we must return to the real world, and face it, and survey it in its complicated totality. Our castles-in-air must have their foundations in solid ground.

5

The needed reorientation of science is important; but by itself it is not enough. Knowledge is a tool rather than a motor; and if we know the world without being able to react upon it, we are guilty of that aimless pragmatism which consists of devising all sorts of ingenious machines and being quite incapable of subordinating them to any coherent and attractive pattern.

Now, men are moved by their instinctive impulses and by such emotionally colored pattern-ideas or idola as the dreamer is capable of projecting. When we create these pattern-ideas, we enlarge the environment, so that our behavior is guided by the conditions which we seek to establish and enjoy in an imaginary world. However crude the Marxian analysis of society may have been, it at least had the merit of presenting a great dream—the dream of a titanic struggle between the possessors and the dispossessed in which every worker had a definite part to play. Without these dreams, the advances in social science will be just as disorderly and fusty as the applications of physical science have been in our material affairs, where in the absence of any genuine scale of values, a patent collar button is regarded as equally important as a tungsten filament if the button happens to bring the inventor as great a financial reward.

6

Up to about the middle of the seventeenth century, before modern physical science had rigorously defined its field, the breach between literature and science, which Aristotle had made, was not altogether complete;

and while the humanist ideal was intact both literature and science were regarded as coeval phases of man's intellectual activity. The two dominating figures of the Renascence, Leonardo da Vinci and Michael Angelo, were artists, technicians, and men of science; and in a comparison between a translation of Michael Angelo's sonnets and a photograph of St. Peter's the sonnets come off rather well.

The great contribution of the Renascence was the ideal of fully energized human beings, able to span life in all its manifestations, as artists, scientists, technicians, philosophers, and what not. This ideal exercised a powerful influence on lesser figures, like the Admirable Crichton and Sir Walter Raleigh, and even down to the time of Descartes it contributed to that exuberance of the intellectual life which was the Renascence at its best. When John Amos Comenius wrote his remarkable little book called The Labyrinth of the World and the Paradise of the Heart in 1623, he combined the outlooks of science and art in a remarkable synthesis; for the first part of this work is a picturesque survey of the actual world as Comenius found it, and the second a picture of the transition to the heavenly world promised in the Christian religion. The idea behind Comenius' Labyrinth was the same that inspired Andreæ; and were it not for the complete otherworldliness of this theological utopia, the Paradise of the Heart, Comenius' discourse would take a high place in the history of utopian thought.

There is no genuine logical basis, as far as I can see, in the dissociation of science and art, of knowing and dreaming, of intellectual activities and emotional activities. The division between the two is simply one of convenience; for both these activities are simply different modes in which human beings create order out of the chaos in which they find themselves. Such is the humanist view. As an instance of this, when the Royal Society was projected in England in the middle of the seventeenth century, Johann Andreæ advised his friend Samuel Hartlib, then in London, not to neglect the humanities while furthering the pursuit of the physical sciences. Unfortunately, the men who gathered together to form the Royal Society were specialists in physical science; and in the lapse of the humanist tradition through the religious acerbities of the time, they had lost some of their desire for a complete life. As a result, the original charter of the society confined its work to the physical sciences.

Insignificant as it now appears in the annals of science, this decision seems to me to mark a definite turning point in human thought. Henceforth the scientist was to be one sort of person and the artist another; henceforth the idolum of science and the idolum of art were not to be cemented together in a single personality; henceforth, in fact, the dehumanization of art and science begins. It is interesting to note that with the divorce of the humanities from science, art and science entered upon separate careers which, for all their diversities, are curiously similar. Both art and science, for example, ceased to be the common property of the community; and each of them split up into a multiplying host of specialisms. In this process, art and science made many notable advances; so that this period is usually spoken of as a period of enlightenment or progress; but the result on the community was what we discovered in our examination of Coketown and the Country House.

7

We must now consider the development of the arts in the modern community. At the height of the Middle Age, as in fifth century Athens, the arts formed together a living unity. A citizen did not go into a concert hall to hear music, to a church to say his prayers, to a theatre to see a play, to a picture gallery to view pictures: it was a mean town, indeed, that could not boast a cathedral and a couple of churches; and in these buildings, drama and music and architecture and painting and sculpture were united for the purpose of ringing changes on the emotional nature of men and converting them to accept the theological vision of otherworldly utopia.

The splitting up of these arts into a number of separate boxes was part of that movement towards individualism and protestantism whose effects most people are familiar with in the field of religion alone. Henceforward, music, drama, painting, and the other arts developed largely in isolation; and each of them was forced to build up a separate world. The greater part of the gains that were made in these worlds was not carried over into the community at large, but remained the possession of the artists themselves or their private patrons and critics in the Country House. With such exceptions as the Italian and Japanese woodcuts of the eighteenth century, and the few survivals of ballad and drama that slipt over from the Middle Age, popular art became another name for all that was coarse and stunted and depressed. The popular architecture of the nineteenth century is the sordid little redbrick rabbit hutch: popular religion is embodied in the stunted sheet-iron or brick chapel (as it is called in England) of the Baptists and Methodists: popular music is the latest barrel organ lilt: popular painting is the calendar lithograph: and popular literature is the dime novel.

The divorce of the art of the cultivated classes from that of the whole community tended to deprive it of any other standards than the artist himself was content to erect. Here again the comparison with science is curiously pertinent. The world of art is in a sense a separate world, and it can be cultivated for a time without reference to the desires and emotions of the community out of which it has sprung. But the motto "Art for art's sake" turns out in practice to be something quite different—namely, art for the artist's sake; and art which is produced in this manner, without any external standard of performance, is frequently just an instrument for overcoming a neurosis or enabling the artist to restore his personal equilibrium. Divorced from his community, the artist was driven back upon himself: instead of seeking to create a beauty which all men might share, he devoted himself to projecting a poignant angle of his personal vision—an angle which I shall call the picturesque. The cause of this divorce I have already pointed out in the chapter on the Country House; it is with the effects of this divorce, for which the artist was not greatly to blame, that we are here concerned.

This conflict between "beauty" and the "picturesque" is perhaps common to all the arts, and with sufficient factual detail I might be able to trace its effects on literature and music. For the sake of clearness and simplicity I shall confine myself to painting and sculpture, with the proviso that our conclusions will apply, by and large, to the whole field.

Let me emphasize, before going any further, that I am using the terms "beauty" and the "picturesque" in quite different senses from the vague ones that are usually attached to them; and that I use them without any preliminary judgment as to their place and value in the good life. The picturesque, in the quite arbitrary sense in which the word is used here, is an abstract quality of vision, sound, or meaning which creates what we might call pure esthetic experience. In painting, the picturesque probably arose with the discovery, on the part of the leisured classes in the Country House, that it was possible to achieve rapture, a sort of esthetic trance, a complete state of beatitude, by the more or less prolonged contemplation of a pictorial subject. Up to the time of this discovery, painting was simply a branch of interior decoration; the great paintings of the Christian World served, for the public, as illustrations to that outline of history which mediæval theology provided: they had a habitat, a social destination.

With the splitting off of the picturesque from the main body of ecclesiastical art, painting came into its own as an end in itself, apart from any place that it might have in the scheme of the community's affairs. The symptom of this change is the rise of landscape painting: in the search for pure esthetic experience the painter began to look for themes which were divorced from any human interest but that of pure contemplation. During the last century this split between painting as a form of social art and painting as a means of achieving contemplative ecstasy has become deeper: even those academic painters who followed the methods of the older artists no longer have the same field to work in, whilst the revolutionist—the impressionists of one period, the cubists of another, and the post-impressionists or expressionists of a third—are forced by the general irrelevance of art in Coketown to produce work which only the more or less initiate will appreciate.

Now, I would not for worlds underrate the gains which have been achieved by the divorce of art from the whole life of the community. In their isolation from the social group that produced them the modern artists have been able to pursue their solitary way to limits which the common man is probably incapable of reaching: they have widened the field of esthetic delight and have introduced new values into the world of painting, values which will remain even though the disease which created them disappears, just as one can salvage a pearl from an oyster whose sickness is healed. The view from the mountain top is none the worse because many people are afflicted with dizziness and nausea before they have reached the summit; and, like the pursuit of truth, the pursuit of esthetic values is a good in itself apart from any values which may be realized in the community. On these terms, Cézanne and Van Gogh and Ryder, to mention a few of the dead, will hold their own, and keep the boundaries of art from ever shrinking again, I trust, to its academic limits.

Nevertheless, the effects of focussing on the picturesque can no more be overlooked in art than the dangers of specialization in science. It is almost a banality to point out how, historically, as the picturesque developed in art, beauty has tended to disappear from life. Whilst the cultivated few have become gloriously alive to more exquisite sensations than their ancestors had probably ever experienced, the "mutilated many" have been forced to live in great cities and in abject country towns of a blackness and ugliness such as the world, if we are to judge by the records that exist, has never seen before. In other words, we have become more sensitive to experiences—to the contents of our inner worlds—only to become more callous to things, to the brash surfaces of the world without. In our preoccupation with the inner worlds we have to a large extent lost our hold upon beauty, which, in the limiting sense in which the word is used here, is the quality by which anything, from a torso to a building, shows its adaptation to an end and its sensitiveness to esthetic values—values which are abstracted and intensified in the pure picturesque—that are involved in such an adaptation. In this sense, the beautiful, as Emerson said, rests on the foundations of the necessary: it is the outward token of an inward grace; its appearance is the manifestation of a humanized life; and its existence and development constitute, in fact, a sort of index to a community's vitality.

The divorce of the artist from the community, and the turning away of his energies from beauty, in which the picturesque might be fulfilled, to the picturesque itself, separate from any practical needs, has scarcely been compensated by the advances that have been made in the separate world of art. The result has been that work which should have been done by artists of great capacity has been done by people of minor or degraded ability. Anonymous jerrybuilders have erected the greater number of our houses, absurd engineers have laid out our towns with no thought for anything but sewers and paving contracts; rapacious and illiterate men who have achieved success in business discourse to the multitude on what constitutes the good life—and so on. There is really no end to the number of things which we do badly in the modern community, for want of the artist to do them at all.

This generalization applies to the whole range of the arts. The greater part of the creative dreaming and planning which constitutes literature and art has had very little bearing upon the community in which we live, and has done little to equip us with patterns, with images and ideals, by means of which we might react creatively upon our environment. Yet it should be obvious that if the inspiration for the good life is to come from anywhere, it must come from no other people than the great artists. An intense social life, as Gabriel Tarde pointed out in his fine utopian fantasy, Underground Man, has "for its indispensable condition the esthetic life and the universal propagation of the religion of truth and beauty." The common man, when he is in love, has a little glimpse of the way in which the drudgery of the daily world may be transmuted through emotional stimulus; it is the business of the artist to make the transmutation permanent, for the only difference between the artist and the common man is that the artist is, so to say, in love all the while. It is out of the vivid patterns of the artist's ecstasy that he draws men together and gives them the vision to shape their lives and the destiny of their community anew.

8

No matter how the modern artist may use or fritter away his abilities, it is plain that he has an enormous reservoir of power at his disposal. What, for instance, has made America so wholly devoted to the conquest of material things? Why are we so given over to collecting those vast miscellanies of goods which are temptingly displayed in the advertising sections of our illustrated weeklies and monthly magazines? The necessity for ameliorating the hard, crude life of the pioneer has indeed been an important influence; but the traditions of this life in turn produced all the minor "artists" or "artlings" who write and draw for the popular papers, who create the plots of plays and motion picture scenarios; and since most of these poor wretches have never been educated in the humanist sense to any degree—since they know no other environment than New York or Los Angeles or Gopher Prairie, since they are acquainted with the achievements of no other age than their own, they have devoted themselves wholeheartedly to idealizing a great many of the things that are crude or ugly or stupid in their beloved community. So the idola of business have been perpetuated by "artlings" who themselves know only the standards of the business man.

Because of the limited horizons of the American artist, therefore, the rising generation aspires after the things that Messrs. Jack London, Rupert Hughes, Scott Fitzgerald, and heaven knows who else have thought good and fine; the younger generation talks like the heroes and heroines of a melodrama by Mr. Samuel Shipman, when they do not attain the higher level of comic cuts; the younger generation thrills to the type of beauty which Mr. Penryhn Stanlaws sets before its gaze. The notion that the common man despises art is absurd. The common man worships art and lives by it; and when good art is not available he takes the second best or the tenth best or the hundredth best. The success of Mr. Eugene O'Neil, one of the few playwrights of any girth who has contributed to the American stage, proves that the only way that people can be kept away from good art is by not providing it. The younger generation might just as well have had its idea-patterns shaped by Sophocles, Praxiteles, and Plato, if our genuine artists were not so aloof to their responsibilities, and if they were intellectually mature enough to accept the full burden of their vocation. It is a sign of a terrific neurosis—and no mark at all of esthetic aptitude—that our genuine art is so completely disoriented and so thoroughly out of touch with the community. We must turn to a man of such uneven parts as Mr. Nicholas Vachel Lindsay before we have anything like a recognition of the classic rôle of the artist.

Art for the artist's sake is largely a symptom of that neurotic individualism which drives the artist out of a public world which baffles him into a private world where he may reign in solitude as an unruly demiurge. Art for the public's sake, on the other hand, substitutes the vices of the extrovert for the vices of the introvert. When I say that art must have some vital contact with the community I do not mean, let me emphasize, that the artist must cater to public whim or demand. Art in its social setting is neither a personal cathartic for the artist, nor a salve to quiet the itching vanity of the community: it is essentially a means by which people who have had a strange diversity of experiences have their activities emotionally canalized into patterns and molds which they are able to share pretty completely with each other. Pure art is inevitably propaganda. I mean by this that it is meant to be propagated, and that in so far as it fails to impregnate the community in which it exists with its ideas and images, in so far as the community is not changed for better or worse by its existence, its claims are spurious. Propagandist art, on the other hand, is inevitably impure since instead of bringing people together on a common emotional plane, as men, it tends to accentuate their differences, and to void emotions which are proper to art into a realm where the emotions of the missionary's tent or the soapboxer's platform hold exclusive sway. It is just because the "artist" in America has been impure in motive—a propagandist for Pollyanna in the face of Euripides, a propagandist for "just folks" in the face of Swift, a propagandist for niceness in the face of Rabelais—that he has failed miserably as an artist, and has left our communities to stew so completely in their own savorless juice.

9

For examples of what the artist might be, and what his proper relation to the community might be when he was mature enough to recognize it and discipline himself to it, let us look at Mr. William Butler Yeats or A.E. There are doubtless a good many other examples that might be offered in Europe; but these are particularly good; for the reason that with A.E. one can see in his The National Being how the conceptions of art enter into the tissues of all his plans for renovating life in the Irish Countryside. In the work of these artists and their fellows we have a clue to one of the most promising attempts to establish a concrete eutopia which shall rise out of the real facts of the everyday environment and, at the same time, turn upon them and mold them creatively a little nearer the heart's desire.

In the account of Four Years which Mr. Yeats published in The Dial he explains his attitude towards the literature and social life of Ireland; and I recommend that account to all the forlorn revolutionaries and reformers who wonder why the dry bones of their doctrines remain dry bones, instead of knitting themselves together and becoming alive. This passage in particular, defines the relation of the artist both to the tradition of his art and to the community in which he must find a root:

"The Huxley, Tyndall, Carolus Duran, Bastien-Lepage coven, asserted that an artist or a poet must paint or write in the style of his own day, and this with the Fairy Queen and the Lyrical Ballads and Blake's early poems in its ears, and plain to the eyes, in book and gallery, those great masterpieces of later Egypt, founded upon that work of the ancient kingdom already further in time from Later Egypt than Later Egypt is from us." He dismisses this claim with the just assertion that the artist is free to choose any style that suits his mood and subject; for in the world of art time and space are irrelevant; and he goes on to say, "We had in

Ireland imaginative stories, which the uneducated classes knew and even sang, and might we not make those stories current among the educated classes, rediscovering, for the work's sake, what I have called 'the applied arts of literature,' the association of literature, that is, with music, speech, and dance; and at last, it might be, so deepen the political passion of the nation that all, artist and poet, craftsman and day laborer, would accept a common design. Perhaps even these images, once created and associated with river and mountain, might move of themselves and with some powerful, even turbulent life, like those painted horses that trample the rice-fields of Japan."

By citing Mr. Yeats' conceptions I do not mean to limit the artist to a single function—that of patterning the good life. It is quite plain that pure esthetic experience is a good in itself; and when the artist has rendered this experience in a picture, a poem, a novel, a philosophy, he has performed a unique and indispensable piece of work. Could italics keep this passage from being ignored I should employ them.

What I have called the picturesque is in reality just as self-sustaining and delightful as the radiant good health which Sir Thomas More rated so highly in his Utopia. If the community went to the dogs, it would still be exuberantly self-sustaining, whilst anyone had the time or the capacity to enjoy it. What I protest against is the way in which the field of the genuine artist, during these last three hundred years, has been whittled away, so that it has become more and more a mark of the artist to concern himself solely with the narrow province of pure esthetic experience, and to protest his complete aloofness from anything that lies outside this realm. Such an attitude would have struck Euripides or Milton or Goethe or Wagner as undignified and stupid, I am sure, because art is as large as life, and it does not gain in vigor or intensity by reducing its scope to that of the puppet stage. The point is that there is an artistic function to be performed in the community, for the community, as well as in the world of art, for those who are lifted up to art.

"Nations, races, and individual men," as Mr. Yeats says again, "are unified by an image, or a bundle of related images, symbolical and provocative of the state of mind that is of all states of mind not impossible, the most difficult to that man, race, or nation because only the greatest obstacle that can be contemplated without despair rouses the will to full intensity."

Whether these images shall be provided by patrioteers, hack editors, politicians, advertising men and commercialized "artists" or whether they shall be created by genuine playwrights and poets and philosophers is an important question. The function of creating these images is an artistic one, and the artist who evades his responsibility is making life for himself and his kind more difficult, since in the long run a community whose sacred literature is written by Colonel Diver and Scadder and Jefferson Brick—the great heroes of Civilization as the star of empire westward makes its way—will make even the most solitary cultivation of the arts a thorny and difficult task.

In the good life, the purely esthetic element has a prominent place; but unless the artist is capable of moving men to the good life, the esthetic element is bound to be driven farther and farther away from the common realities, until the world of the artist will scarcely be distinguishable from the phantasia of dementia præcox. Already, the symptoms of this corrosive futility have appeared in literature and painting in Western Europe and America; and such light as comes forth from this art is but the phosphorescence of decay. If the arts are not to disintegrate utterly, must they not focus more and more upon eutopia?

10

It comes to this then: our plans for a new social order have been as dull as mud because, in the first place, they have been abstract and cockney, and have not taken into account the immense diversity and complexity of man's environment; and in the second place, they have not created any vivid patterns that would move men to great things. They have not been "informed by science and ennobled by the arts."

Through the paralysis of the arts and sciences our contemporary programs for revolution and reform have done very little to lift our heads over the disorderly and bedraggled environments in which we conduct our daily business. This failure to create a common pattern for the good life in each region has made such excellent efforts as the garden city movement seem weak and ineffectual when we place them alongside the towns that mediæval civilization, which had such a common pattern, created. Without the common background of eutopian idola, all our efforts at rehabilitation—the new architecture, the garden city movement, the electrification of industry, the organization of great industrial guilds such as the Building Trades have achieved in England and the garment workers seem on the point of effecting in America—without these common idola, I say, all our practical efforts are spotty and inconsecutive and incomplete. It was not, let us remember, by any legislative device that the cities of the industrial age were monotonously patterned in the image of Coketown. It was rather because everyone within these horrid centers accepted the same values and pursued the same ends—as they were projected by economists like Ricardo, industrialists like Stephenson, and lyric poets like Samuel Smiles—that the plans of the jerrybuilder and the engineer expressed to perfection the brutality and social disharmony of the community. The same process that gave us Coketown can, when our world of ideas is transformed, give us something better than Coketown.

The chief use of the classic utopias that we have surveyed is to suggest that the same methods which are used by the utopian thinkers to project an ideal community on paper may be employed, in a practical way, to develop a better community on earth. The weakness of the utopian thinkers consisted in the assumption that the dreams and projects of any single man might be realized in society at large. From the bitter frustration of Fourier, Cabet, Hertzka, and even John Ruskin those who are in search of the beloved community may well take a warning. Where the critics of the utopian method were, I believe, wrong was in holding that the business of projecting prouder worlds was a futile and footling pastime. These anti-utopian critics overlooked the fact that one of the main factors that condition any future are the attitudes and beliefs which people have in relation to that future—that, as Mr. John Dewey would say, in any judgment of practise one's belief in a hypothesis is one of the things that affect its realization.

When we have projected the pattern of an ideal community and tend to warp our conduct in conformity with that pattern, we overcome the momentum of actual institutions. In feeling free to project new patterns, in holding that human beings can will a change in their institutions and habits of life, the utopians were, I believe, on solid ground; and the utopian philosophies were a great improvement over the more nebulous religious and ethical systems of the past in that they saw the necessity for giving their ideals form and life. In fact, it has been in the pictures of ideal commonwealths such as Plato's that the "ideal" and the "actual" have met.

It is true that the pure utopians have overlooked the fact that every institution has a momentum of its own: its speed may be quickened or reduced, it may be switched on another track, as the Roman Church during the Reformation was switched from the main line of civilization to a subsidiary route; and at times, in the catastrophe of war or revolution, an institution may jump the track altogether and be wrecked. The critical problem for the eutopian, the problem of the transition from one set of institutions to another, from one way of life to another, was overlooked. Plato's Republic, for example, was a fairly attractive place; but one wonders in what Greek city in the Fourth Century B.C. the transition could have taken place. A transition implies not merely a goal but a starting point: if we are to move the world, as Archimedes threatened to with his lever, we must have some ground to stand on. It is only by paying attention to the limitations of each region, and by allowing for the driving force of history, that we can make the earth come to terms with man's idola. This is perhaps the most difficult lesson that the eutopian must learn.

11

What, then, is the first step out of the present disorder? The first step, it seems to me, is to ignore all the fake utopias and social myths that have proved either so sterile or so disastrous during the last few centuries. There is perhaps no logical reason why the myth of the national state should not be preserved; but it is a myth which has done very little, on the whole, to promote the good life, and has on the contrary done a great deal to make the good life impossible; and to continue to cling to it in the face of perpetual wars, pestilences, and spiritual devastations is the sort of fanaticism which will probably seem as blind and cruel to future generations as persecutions for Christian heresy do to the present one. On the same grounds, there are a number of other social myths, like the proletarian myth, which run so badly against the grain of reality that they cannot be preserved without ignoring a great many values which are essential to a humane existence; and on pragmatic grounds it would be fine and beneficial to drop them quickly into limbo. There is no reason to think that there will be a quick conversion from these myths: the holocaust of war has only intensified the myth of the National State; and our experience with religious myths suggests on the contrary that the forms at any rate will be preserved long after the last shred of reality has disappeared. But the sooner those who are capable of intellectual criticism abandon these particular myths, the sooner will these idola fall into the state which has been happily described as "innocuous desuetude."

If our knowledge of human behavior counts for anything, however, we cannot put aside old myths without creating new ones. The eighteenth century agnostics very wisely realized that if they wished to maintain the values which had been created by Deism, they could not abandon God without inventing him all over again. In turning away from obsolete and disastrous social myths I do not suggest that we give up the habit of making myths; for that habit, for good or bad, seems to be ingrained in the human psyche. The nearest we can get to rationality is not to efface our myths but to attempt to infuse them with right reason, and to alter them or exchange them for other myths when they appear to work badly.

Here is where we reap the full benefit of the great utopian tradition. In turning away from the social myths that hamper us, we do not jump blindly into a blankness: we rather ally ourselves with a different order of social myth which has always been vivified and enriched by the arts and sciences.

The idolum of eutopia which we may seek to project in this or that region is not a *carte blanche* which any one may fill in at his will and caprice; certain lines have already been fixed; certain spaces have already been filled. There is a consensus among all utopian writers, to begin with, that the land and natural resources belong undividedly to the community; and even when it is worked by separate people or associations, as in Utopia and Freeland the increment of the land—the economic rent—belongs to the community as a whole.

There is also a pretty common notion among the utopians that, as land is a common possession, so is work a common function; and no one is let off from some sort of labor of body or mind because of any inherited privileges or dignities that he can point to. Finally, there is the almost equally common notion, among the utopians, that the perpetuation of the species leaves plenty of room for improvement, and that, as far as human knowledge and foresight are worth anything, it should be applied to propagation; so that the most reckless and ill-bred shall not burden the community with the support of their offspring while those of finer capacity are neglected or overwhelmed in numbers.

Besides these general conditions for the good life which the utopians unite to emphasize, there are certain other points in the utopian tradition of which one writer or another has given the classic statement.

With Plato we see the enormous importance of birth and education; we recognize the part good breeding, in every sense of the word, must play in the good community. Sir Thomas More makes us aware of the fact that a community becomes a community to the extent that it has shared possessions, and he suggests that the local group might develop such a common life as the old colleges of Oxford have enjoyed. When we turn to Christianopolis, we are reminded that the daily life and work of the community must be infused with the spirit of science, and that an acute practical intelligence such as we find today among the engineers need not be divorced from the practice of the humanities. Even the nineteenth century utopias have a contribution to make. They remind us by their overemphasis that all the proud and mighty idealisms in the world are so many shadows unless they are supported by the whole economic fabric—so that "eutopia" is not merely a matter of spiritual conversion, as the ancient religions taught, but of economic and geotechnic reconstruction. Finally, from James Buckingham and Ebenezer Howard we can learn the importance of converting the idolum of eutopia into plans and layouts and detailed projections, such as a townplanner might utilize; and we may suspect that a eutopia which cannot be converted into such specific plans will continue, as the saying is, to remain up in the air.

Taken together, there is a powerful impulse towards creating a good environment for the good life in the classic utopias we have examined: from one or another utopia we may draw elements which will enrich every part of the community's life. By following the utopian tradition we shall not merely escape from the fake utopias that have dominated us: we shall return to reality. More than that, we shall return upon reality and perhaps—who can tell?—we shall re-create it!

12

In discussing the foundations of Eutopia I am conscious of a certain abstractness in my method of argument; conscious that I have not been a good utopian in dealing with these proud idola that we may project in every region. Let us come down to earth now and realize what all this amounts to when we turn away from the library and mingle again on the highways that lead past our door.

First of all, I conceive that we shall not attempt to envisage a single utopia for a single unit called humanity; that is the sort of thin and tepid abstraction which the discipline of the Regional Survey will tend to kill off even in people who are now inured by education to dealing only in verbal things. All the human beings on the planet are a unity only for the sake of talking about them; and as far as that goes, there is very little profitable conversation that can apply to a Greenlander, a Parisian, and a Chinaman, except the mere observation that they are all on the same little boat of a planet and would probably be much happier if they minded their own business and were not too insistent about inflicting their institutions and their idola upon their neighbors.

We shall have to dismiss, as equally futile, the notion of a single stratification of mankind, such as the working class, serving as the foundation for our Eutopia: the notion that the working class consists simply of urban workers is a cockney imbecility, and as soon as one rectifies it and includes the agricultural population, we have "humanity" pretty much all over again. Finally, if we are to give eutopia a local habitation it will not be founded upon the National State, for the National State is a myth which sane people will no more sacrifice their lives to than they would hand their children into the furnace of some tribal Moloch; and a good idolum cannot be founded on the basis of a bad one.

As far as extent or character of territory goes, we will remember that the planet is not as smooth as a billiard ball, and that the limits of any genuine community rest within fairly ascertainable geographic regions in which a certain complex of soil, climate, industry, institutional life and historic heritage has prevailed. We shall not attempt to legislate for all these communities at one stroke; for we shall respect William Blake's dictum that one law for the lion and the ox is tyranny. There are some 15,000,000 local communities in the world, the Postal Directory tells us; and our eutopia will necessarily take root in one of these real communities, and include within its co-operations as many other communities, as have similar interests and identities. It may be that our eutopia will embrace a population as great as that in the Metropolis of London or New York; but it is needless to say that the land which lies beyond the limits of the metropolis will no longer be regarded as a sort of subterranean factory for the production of agricultural goods. In sum, as Patrick Geddes has finely said, in the Kingdom of Eutopia—the world Eutopia—there will be many mansions.

The inhabitants of our eutopias will have a familiarity with their local environment and its resources, and a sense of historic continuity, which those who dwell within the paper world of Megalopolis and who touch their environment mainly through the newspaper and the printed book, have completely lost. The people of Newcastle will no longer go to London for coals, as the people in the provinces have in a sense been doing this last century and more: there will be a more direct utilization of local resources than would have seemed profitable or seemly to the metropolitan world which now has command of the market. In these varied eutopias, it is safe to say, there will be a new realization of the fact that a cultivated life is essentially a settled life: their citizens will have discovered that the great privilege of travelling from Brooklyn to Bermondsey, and from Bermondsey to Bombay is scarcely worth the trouble when the institutions of Brooklyn, Bermondsey, and Bombay, and every other purely industrial center, are identical—sanitary drinking devices and canned goods and moving pictures being the same wherever mechanical duplication of goods for a world market has taken the place of direct adaptation to local needs.

It should not surprise us therefore if the foundations of eutopia were established in ruined countries; that is, in countries where metropolitan civilization has collapsed and where all its paper prestige is no longer accepted at its paper value. There was the beginning of a genuine eutopian movement in Denmark after the war with Germany in the 'sixties: under the leadership of Bishop Gruntwig came a revival of folk traditions in literature and a renascence of education which has renewed the life of the Danish countryside and made an intelligent farmer and an educated man out of the boor. It would not be altogether without precedent if such a eutopian renascence took place in Germany, in Austria, in Russia; and perhaps on another scale in India and China and Palestine; for all these regions are now face to face with realities which the "prosperous" paperism of our metropolitan civilization has largely neglected.

If the inhabitants of our Eutopias will conduct their daily affairs in a possibly more limited environment than that of the great metropolitan centers, their mental environment will not be localized or nationalized. For the first time perhaps in the history of the planet our advance in science and invention has made it possible for every age and every community to contribute to the spiritual heritage of the local group; and the citizen of eutopia will not stultify himself by being, let us say, a hundred per cent Frenchman when Greece, China, England, Scandinavia and Russia can give sustenance to his spiritual life. Our eutopians will necessarily draw from this wider environment whatever can be assimilated by the local community; and they will thus add any elements that may be lacking in the natural situation.

The chief business of eutopians was summed up by Voltaire in the final injunction of Candide: Let us cultivate our garden. The aim of the real eutopian is the culture of his environment, most distinctly not the culture, and above all not the exploitation, of some other person's environment. Hence the size of our Eutopia may be big or little; it may begin in a single village; it may embrace a whole region. A little leaven will leaven the whole loaf; and if a genuine pattern for the eutopian life plants itself in any particular locality it may ramify over a whole continent as easily as Coketown duplicated itself throughout the Western World. The notion that no effective change can be brought about in society until millions of people have deliberated upon it and willed it is one of the rationalizations which are dear to the lazy and the ineffectual. Since the first step towards eutopia is the reconstruction of our idola, the foundations for eutopia can be laid, wherever we are, without further ado.

Our most important task at the present moment is to build castles in the air. We need not fear, as Thoreau reminds us, that the work will be lost. If our eutopias spring out of the realities of our environment, it will be easy enough to place foundations under them. Without a common design, without a grand design, all our little bricks of reconstruction might just as well remain in the brickyard; for a disharmony between men's minds betokens, in the end, the speedy dilapidation of whatever they may build. Our final word is a counsel of perfection. When that which is perfect has come, that which is imperfect will pass away.

BIBLIOGRAPHY

For the benefit of the reader who wishes to travel further along the trails opened up in this survey of utopias, I am giving a list of the principal books on the subject. This list includes all the important utopias that are accessible in English, as well as a few that are not; but it is not exhaustive, for the region of Utopia has its swamps and arid places as well as its fertile and cultivated land; and no one but a scholarly explorer need attempt to enter the more forbidding parts of the country.

Needless to say, in dealing with our historic utopias I had a rough criterion of selection. I set out to treat such plans for the improvement of the human community as had been embodied in complete pictures of an ideal commonwealth: this excluded important essays in politics like Hobbes' Leviathan and Harrington's Oceana; and it ruled out any treatment of abstract idealisms which, however important, did not exemplify the essential utopian method. Next, I resolved to deal at length only with those utopias which have exercised some influence on thought and life, particularly in the Western European world. Third, I sought to emphasize what was common in the methods and ends of the classic utopias; making plain their relations within the world of utopias and their relevance in the present day, rather than attempting to show in any detail the social milieu in which each utopian wrote. In dealing with the nineteenth century my criterion became a little shaky; and I frankly chose the nineteenth century utopias on the basis of their association with temporal movements like state socialism, the single tax, and syndicalism, rather than because of their conformity to standards which served to weed out irrelevant utopias in the earlier centuries. In devoting a little space to Fourier and Spence and giving short shrift to Owen I have tried to restore these interesting and significant figures to the place that they deserve. There will doubtless be disagreements over my selections and the amount of space I have allotted to various writers; but at least, where there has been madness there has also been method.

Certain parts of the argument are not covered by this list of utopias. The best introductions to utopian literature in general are in German; see R. Blueher's excellent pamphlet on Moderne Utopien; Ein Beitrag zur Geschichte des Sozialismus, Bonn: 1920. While Mr. Van Wyck Brooks put me independently on the trail of Rabelais' Abbey of Theleme I must acknowledge, with as much grace as possible, that Herr Blueher anticipated me in grasping this clue to Renascence culture; and if any credit is due, he deserves it. The most exhaustive catalogue of pre-nineteenth century utopias is contained in Kautsky's Vorläufer des Modernen Sozialismus. Max Beer's History of British Socialism has an excellent discussion of the relation of the utopians to socialism. See also Moritz Kaufmann's Utopias; or Schemes of Social Improvement, from Sir Thomas More to Karl Marx, London: 1879. In the excellent History of Utopian Thought, by Dr. J. O. Hertzler (Macmillan: 1923), the phantasists are sympathetically treated.

The chapter on the Country House might well be prefaced by Mr. Thorstein Veblen's Theory of the Leisure Class, a satire which seems to me unique in scholarship and originality. The importance of our social myths and our collective representations has been noted by a whole school of French sociologists who follow Émile Durkheim; and the dynamic force of ideas has been treated by Alfred Fouillée. On both these topics there is a whole literature;

and it would give a sense of false simplicity to single out any particular essay. There is a fairly popular discussion of the place of myths and ideals in the George Sorel's Reflexions on Violence, and Benjamin Kidd's Science of Power (especially Chapter V.).

As a loose illustration of the general method and outlook embodied in this book I refer to the Making of the Future Series, edited by Messrs. Patrick Geddes and Victor Branford and published by Williams & Norgate, London. There is an able exposition of the regionalist movement and of the fundamental realities upon which this movement is based in two books published in that series; namely, Professor Fleure's Human Geography in Western Europe and C. B. Fawcett's The Provinces of England. Two works by the editors, The Coming Polity and Our Social Inheritance are likewise suggestive. Professor Geddes is the outstanding exponent of the Eutopian method both in thought and in practical activity; and the reader should consult his City Development (1904) and his Town-Planning towards City Development: a Report to the Durbar of Indore, 2 vols. Indore, 1918. Both of these books are mines from which all sorts of precious thoughts can be quarried. Remaindered copies of the first can be obtained from John Grant, Bookseller, Edinburgh; while the second is sold by Botsford, High Holborn, London. Professor Geddes' work exemplifies concretely a good part of what I have sought to explain and define in not altogether adequate prose.

UTOPIAS

Plato (427 B. C.-347 B. C.). The Republic. Translated with notes and essays by Benjamin Jowett. Oxford: 1894. See also Plato's Critias and Statesman in the same edition. The Laws, which is a more detailed attempt to work out the details of a good polity, is so lacking in Plato's original inspiration that, but for Aristotle's allusion to it, one would promptly take it for the work of another hand.

More, Sir Thomas (1478-1535). Utopia. Published originally in Latin in 1516. There are numerous modern editions. See Ideal Commonwealths, edited by Henry Morley.

Andreæ, Johann Valentin (1586-1654). Christianopolis. Published in 1619 and translated in 1916 by Felix Emil Held under the title of Christianopolis: An Ideal State of the 17th Century. Oxford University Press. Mr. Held's introduction contains an account of Andreæ's life.

Bacon, Francis (1561-1626). The New Atlantis. Published in 1627. Bacon contemplated writing a second part which would deal with the laws of his ideal commonwealth. See Ideal Commonwealths.

Campanella, Tomasso (1568-1639). The City of the Sun. Published in 1637 as Civitas Solis Poetica: Idea Reipublicæ Philosophiæ. See Ideal Commonwealths.

Allais, Denis Vairasse d' (—). L'Histoire des Sevarambes. Written in 1672 and translated into English as The History of the Sevarites, written by one Captain Siden, London: 1675. In Kautsky's Vorläufer des Modernen Sozialismus this utopia is given high praise and is ranked as the French parallel of More's Utopia; but I feel that this is a sad error in judgment which perhaps arose out of the bare fact that the first law of the great dictator Sevarias was to put all private property in the hands of the state, to be disposed of absolutely by its authority, and to do away with distinctions of rank and hereditary dignity. There is little that is fresh or imaginative in Vairasse's treatment, however, and there is nothing like More's detailed effort to guard against usurpation of power by the ruling classes. As simple fiction, the History of the Sevarites is, however, readable. See also L'Histoire des Galligènes, by Tiphaigne de la Roche; likewise the excellent satire, Giphantia. The description of Salentum, under Mentor, in Fénélon's Telemachus should not be neglected. The Abbé Morelly's Basiliade is little more than a definition of his Code de la Nature.

Mercier, Louis Sebastien (1740-1814). Memoirs of the Year 2500. Published in French in 1772 and translated into English, Liverpool: 1802.

Spence, Thomas (1750-1814). Description of Spensonia. Constitution of Spensonia. London: 1795. Privately printed at the Courier Press; Leamington Spa: 1917.

Fourier, Charles François Marie (1772-1837). Traité de l'Association domestique agricole. 2 vols. 1822. Le Nouveau Monde Industriel. 2 vols. 1829. See also Albert Brisbane in his General Introduction to the Social Sciences (Fourier's "Social Destinies"), and Selections from the Works of Fourier, translated by Julia Franklin, with an introduction by Charles Gide, London: 1901.

Cabet, Étienne (1788-1856). Voyage en Icarie. Published in 1845 and numerous editions followed during the next five years; see that of the Bureau du Populaie, Paris: 1848.

Buckingham, James Silk (1786-1855). National Evils and Practical Remedies, with a plan for a model town. London: 1848.

Bulwer-Lytton, E. (1803-1873). The Coming Race; or the New Utopia. London: 185—. A fantastic romance about a people who live underground, possess detachable wings, and command a potency known as "vril." It is perhaps not altogether without significance that this new hierarchy of industrial angels was conceived by Lytton in the same decade that saw the building of the Crystal Palace.

Pemberton, Robert (—). The Happy Colony. London: 1854. This is an appeal to the working class, somewhat similar in temper and method to Buckingham's appeal to the middle class. Pemberton had an individual system of psychology which he desired to apply in education. This utopia has now only a limited historical significance.

Bellamy, Edward (1850-1898). Looking Backward; Boston: 1888. Equality; Boston: 1897.

Hertzka, Theodor (1845-?). Freeland: A Social Anticipation. First edition published in German, 1889; English translation published by the British Freeland Association in 1891. A Visit to Freeland, or the New Paradise Regained. Translation published by the above Association, London: 1894. The first work lays the foundations for the utopia; the second is the ideal commonwealth in action.

Morris, William (1834-1896). News from Nowhere. London: 1890. There have been numerous editions.

HOWARD, EBENEZER (1850-?). Garden Cities of Tomorrow. London: 1902. First published as Tomorrow in 1898. Unique among utopian books in that its eutopia has been partly realized. See numerous descriptions of Letchworth, the first Garden City.

HUDSON, W. H. (—). A Crystal Age. London: 1906.

THIRION, EMILE (1825-?). Neustria: Utopie Individualiste. Paris: 1901. This is one of the rare, deliberately individualistic utopias, founded on work, liberty, and property. It assumes that a colony of Girondists were able to establish themselves in South America.

HERZL, THEODOR (1860–1904). Altneuland. Leipzig: 1903.

TARDE, GABRIEL (1843-1904). Underground Man. London: 1905. A deft and well-conceived fantasy, full of excellent criticism. Towards the past it is a utopia of reconstruction, towards the future—but herein lies much of its charm!—it is one of escape.

WELLS, H. G. (1866-?). A Modern Utopia. New York: 1905.

CRAM, RALPH ADAMS (1863-?). Walled Towns. Boston: 1919. Dr. Cram does not classify this work as a utopia; but the honest critic cannot help giving it that label. Dr. Cram sees no basis for eutopia without the system of values and the sanctions perpetuated by the Christian Church; since this leaves the greater part of humanity in Darkness, I cannot agree with him. Dr. Cram, however, is a fine scholar and a stimulating critic; and if one could only grant his assumptions his conclusions would be magnificent.

MORLEY, HENRY. Ideal Commonwealths; Plutarch's Lycurgus, More's Utopia, Bacon's New Atlantis, Campanella's City of the Sun, and a Fragment of Hall's Mundus Alter et Idem, with an introduction by Henry Morley. London: G. Routledge, 1886.

The Adventures of Tom Sawyer

MARK TWAIN

In his preface to *Tom Sawyer*, Mark Twain states that Tom "is a combination of the characteristics of three boys whom I knew." But as we read this delightful novel, we wonder if this statement, perhaps motivated by modesty, was not a deliberate attempt by the author to conceal the presence of his own image in the person of Tom. We clearly see in Tom the perceptive and sympathetic Twain who never lost his appreciation for the excitement and wonder of a boy's life. We see as well his own independence and love of adventure. It is said that at times Twain, in deference to his wife, a gentle woman with a high sense of propriety, softened the tone of his writings. But so sympathetic and compatible is the spirit of this novel with its natural, lovable characters that considerations of this nature could not have been of even the slightest concern to Twain when writing *Tom Sawyer*.

Mark Twain—Samuel Langhorne Clemens—was born in Florida, Missouri, in 1835. When he was four years old his family moved to Hannibal, Missouri, the Mississippi River town Twain was to re-create so effectively as the colorful setting of several of his novels.

Two experiences relatively early in his life had an important effect on Mark Twain's writings. The first was his work as a printer, the second, sailing the Mississippi as a riverboat pilot. As a printer, Twain was exposed, at an impressionable age, to the humorous stories and ancedotes popular in publications of the time, and he assimilated the various techniques of this kind of writing, developing his own talents in this vein. It was his humor that was to bring Twain his initial fame as a writer. As a riverboat pilot—and he himself marked the significance—Twain was to come in contact with a heterogeneous parade of people. Merchants and minstrels, slave owners and slaves sailed the river, and observing and listening, Twain attained the broad understanding of human nature that was to enrich his writings. And from this period in his life, Twain took his pen name. In riverboat language "Mark Twain" meant two fathoms deep and safe water. These two words have become the best known pseudonym in American literature.

Twain first won recognition with the rollickingly funny story, *The Celebrated Jumping Frog of Calaveras County.* Not long after its publication he found himself in demand as a lecturer, and it was a natural outgrowth of both his Mississippi River days and his lecture tours that he turned his hand to travel writing. But it was in 1876, with the publication of *The Adventures of Tom Sawyer,* that unforgettable excursion into the private province of the very young, that Twain attained the stature of greatness. Lively, touching, penetrating—the whitewashing incident is one of literature's wittiest dramatizations of applied psychology—*Tom Sawyer* is one of those rare novels that become more endearing with each reading. Its beloved sequel, *The Adventures of Huckleberry Finn,* published in 1884, is immortal.

In 1870 Twain had married Olivia Langdon. Although personal tragedies—the deaths of two of their children and severe financial reversals—punctuated their life together, their union was a happy one.

Twain died in 1910, at the age of seventy-five, leaving to the world a rich legacy of novels, short stories and other writings.

To my Wife
this book is affectionately dedicated

PREFACE

Most of the adventures recorded in this book really occurred; one or two were experiences of my own, the rest those of boys who were schoolmates of mine. Huck Finn is drawn from life; Tom Sawyer also, but not from an individual—he is a combination of the characteristics of three boys whom I knew, and therefore belongs to the composite order of architecture.

The old superstitions touched upon were all prevalent among children and slaves in the West at the period of this story—that is to say, thirty or forty years ago.

Although my book is intended mainly for the entertainment of boys and girls, I hope it will not be shunned by men and women on that account, for part of my plan has been to try to pleasantly remind adults of what they once were themselves, and of how they felt and thought and talked, and what queer enterprises they sometimes engaged in.

The Author

Hartford, 1876

CONTENTS

THE ADVENTURES OF TOM SAWYER

1 *Y-o-u-u Tom—Aunt Polly Decides Upon Her Duty —Tom Practices Music—The Challenge—A Private Entrance*

"Tom!"

No answer.

"Tom!"

No answer.

"What's wrong with that boy, I wonder? You TOM!"

No answer.

The old lady pulled her spectacles down and looked over them about the room; then she put them up and looked out under them. She seldom or never looked *through* them for so small a thing as a boy; they were her state pair, the pride of her heart, and were built for "style," not service—she could have seen through a pair of stove lids just as well. She looked perplexed for a moment, and then said, not fiercely, but still loud enough for the furniture to hear:

"Well, I lay if I get hold of you I'll——"

She did not finish, for by this time she was bending down and punching under the bed with the broom, and so she needed breath to punctuate the punches with. She resurrected nothing but the cat.

"I never did see the beat of that boy!"

She went to the open door and stood in it and looked out among the tomato vines and "jimpson" weeds that constituted the garden. No Tom. So she lifted up her voice at an angle calculated for distance and shouted:

"Y-o-u. *Tom*!'

There was a slight noise behind her and she turned just in time to seize a small boy by the slack of his roundabout and arrest his flight.

"There! I might 'a' thought of that closet. What you been doing in there?"

"Nothing."

"Nothing! Look at your hands. And look at your mouth. What *is* that truck?"

"*I* don't know, aunt."

"Well, *I* know. It's jam—that's what it is. Forty times I've said if you didn't let that jam alone I'd skin you. Hand me that switch."

The switch hovered in the air—the peril was desperate—

"My! Look behind you, aunt!"

The old lady whirled round, and snatched her skirts out of danger. The lad fled, on the instant, scrambled up the high board fence, and disappeared over it.

His Aunt Polly stood surprised a moment, and then broke into a gentle laugh.

"Hang the boy, can't I never learn anything? Ain't he played me tricks enough like that for me to be looking out for him by this time? But old fools is the biggest fools there is. Can't learn an old dog new tricks, as the saying is. But my goodness, he never plays them alike, two days, and how is a body to know what's coming? He 'pears to know just how long he can torment me before I get my dander up, and he knows if he can make out to put me off for a minute or make me laugh, it's all down again and I can't hit him a lick. I ain't doing my duty by that boy, and that's the Lord's truth, goodness knows. Spare the rod and spile the child, as the Good Book says. I'm a-laying up sin and suffering for us both, *I* know. He's full of the Old Scratch, but laws-a-me! he's my own dead sister's boy, poor thing, and I ain't got the heart to lash him, somehow. Every time I let him off, my conscience does hurt me so, and every time I hit him my old heart most breaks. Well-a-well, man that is born of woman is of few days and full of trouble, as the Scripture says, and I reckon it's so. He'll play hooky this evening,[1] and I'll just be obleeged to make him work, to-

[1] Southwestern for "afternoon."

morrow, to punish him. It's mighty hard to make him work Saturdays, when all the boys is having holiday, but he hates work more than he hates anything else, and I've *got* to do some of my duty by him, or I'll be the ruination of the child."

Tom did play hooky, and he had a very good time. He got back home barely in season to help Jim, the small colored boy, saw next day's wood and split the kindlings before supper—at least he was there in time to tell his adventures to Jim while Jim did three-fourths of the work. Tom's younger brother (or rather half brother) Sid was already through with his part of the work (picking up chips), for he was a quiet boy, and had no adventurous, troublesome ways.

While Tom was eating his supper, and stealing sugar as opportunity offered, Aunt Polly asked him questions that were full of guile, and very deep—for she wanted to trap him into damaging revealments. Like many other simple-hearted souls, it was her pet vanity to believe she was endowed with a talent for dark and mysterious diplomacy, and she loved to contemplate her most transparent devices as marvels of low cunning. Said she:

"Tom, it was middling warm in school, warn't it?"

"Yes'm."

"Powerful warm, warn't it?"

"Yes'm."

"Didn't you want to go in a-swimming, Tom?"

A bit of a scare shot through Tom—a touch of uncomfortable suspicion. He searched Aunt Polly's face, but it told him nothing. So he said:

"No'm—well, not very much."

The old lady reached out her hand and felt Tom's shirt, and said:

"But you ain't too warm now, though." And it flattered her to reflect that she had discovered that the shirt was dry without anybody knowing that that was what she had in her mind. But in spite of her, Tom knew where the wind lay, now. So he forestalled what might be the next move:

"Some of us pumped on our heads—mine's damp yet. See?"

Aunt Polly was vexed to think she had overlooked that bit of circumstantial evidence, and missed a trick. Then she had a new inspiration:

"Tom, you didn't have to undo your shirt collar where I sewed it, to pump on your head, did you? Unbutton your jacket!"

The trouble vanished out of Tom's face. He opened his jacket. His shirt collar was securely sewed.

"Bother! Well, go 'long with you. I'd made sure you'd played hooky and been a-swimming. But I forgive ye, Tom. I reckon you're a kind of a singed cat, as the saying is—better'n you look. *This* time."

She was half sorry her sagacity had miscarried, and half glad that Tom had stumbled into obedient conduct for once.

But Sidney said:

"Well, now, if I didn't think you sewed his collar with white thread, but it's black."

"Why, I did sew it with white! Tom!"

But Tom did not wait for the rest. As he went out at the door he said:

"Siddy, I'll lick you for that."

In a safe place Tom examined two large needles which were thrust into the lapels of his jacket, and had thread bound about them—one needle carried white thread and the other black. He said:

"She'd never noticed if it hadn't been for Sid. Confound it! sometimes she sews it with white, and sometimes she sews it with black. I wish to geeminy she'd stick to one or t'other—*I* can't keep the run of 'em. But I bet you I'll lam Sid for that. I'll learn him!"

He was not the Model Boy of the village. He knew the model boy very well though—and loathed him.

Within two minutes, or even less, he had forgotten all his troubles. Not because his troubles were one whit less heavy and bitter to him than a man's are to a man, but because a new and powerful interest bore them down and drove them out of his mind for the time—just as men's misfortunes are forgotten in the excitement of new enterprises. This new interest was a valued novelty in whistling, which he had just acquired from a Negro, and he was suffering to practice it undisturbed. It consisted in a peculiar birdlike turn, a sort of liquid warble, produced by touching the tongue to the roof of the mouth at short intervals in the midst of the music—the reader probably remembers how to do it, if he has ever been a boy. Diligence and attention soon gave him the knack of it, and he strode down the street with his mouth full of harmony and his soul full of gratitude. He felt much as an astronomer feels who has discovered a new planet—no doubt, as far as strong, deep, unalloyed pleasure is concerned, the advantage was with the boy, not the astronomer.

The summer evenings were long. It was not dark, yet. Presently Tom checked his whistle. A stranger was before him—a boy a shade larger than himself. A newcomer of any age or either sex was an impressive curiosity in the poor little shabby village of St. Petersburg. This boy was well dressed, too—well dressed on a weekday. This was simply astounding. His cap was a dainty thing, his close-buttoned blue cloth roundabout was new and natty, and so were his pantaloons. He had shoes on—and it was only Friday. He even wore a necktie, a bright bit of ribbon. He had a citified air about him that ate into Tom's vitals. The more Tom stared at the splendid marvel, the higher he turned up his nose at his finery and the shabbier and shabbier his own outfit seemed to him to grow. Neither boy spoke. If one moved, the other moved—but only sidewise, in a circle; they kept face to face and eye to eye all the time. Finally Tom said:

"I can lick you!"

"I'd like to see you try it."

"Well, I can do it."

"No you can't, either."

"Yes I can."

"No you can't."

"I can."

"You can't."

"Can!"

"Can't!"

An uncomfortable pause. Then Tom said:

"What's your name?"

" 'Tisn't any of your business, maybe."

"Well I 'low I'll *make* it my business."

"Well why don't you?"

"If you say much, I will."

"Much—much—*much*. There now."

"Oh, you think you're mighty smart, *don't* you? I could lick you with one hand tied behind me, if I wanted to."

"Well why don't you *do* it? You *say* you can do it."

"Well I *will*, if you fool with me."

"Oh yes—I've seen whole families in the same fix."

"Smarty! You think you're *some*, now, *don't* you? Oh, what a hat!"

"You can lump that hat if you don't like it. I dare you to knock it off—and anybody that'll take a dare will suck eggs."

"You're a liar!"

"You're another."

"You're a fighting liar and dasn't take it up."

"Aw—take a walk!"

"Say—if you give me much more of your sass I'll take and bounce a rock off'n your head."

"Oh, of *course* you will."

"Well I *will*."

"Well why don't you *do* it then? What do you keep *saying* you will for? Why don't you *do* it? It's because you're afraid."

"I *ain't* afraid."

"You are."

"I ain't."

"You are."

Another pause, and more eyeing and sidling around each other. Presently they were shoulder to shoulder. Tom said:

"Get away from here!"

"Go away yourself!"

"I won't."

"*I* won't either."

So they stood, each with a foot placed at an angle as a brace, and both shoving with might and main, and glowering at each other with hate. But neither could get an advantage. After struggling till both were hot and flushed, each relaxed his strain with watchful caution, and Tom said:

"You're a coward and a pup. I'll tell my big brother on you, and he can thrash you with his little finger, and I'll make him do it, too."

"What do I care for your big brother? I've got a brother that's bigger than he is—and what's more, he can throw him over that fence, too." (Both brothers were imaginary.)

"That's a lie."

"*Your* saying so don't make it so."

Tom drew a line in the dust with his big toe, and said:

"I dare you to step over that, and I'll lick you till you can't stand up. Anybody that'll take a dare will steal sheep."

The new boy stepped over promptly, and said:

"Now you said you'd do it, now let's see you do it."

"Don't you crowd me now; you better look out."

"Well, you *said* you'd do it—why don't you do it?"

"By jingo! for two cents I *will* do it."

The new boy took two broad coppers out of his pocket and held them out with derision. Tom struck them to the ground. In an instant both boys were rolling and tumbling in the dirt, gripped together like cats; and for the space of a minute they tugged and tore at each other's hair and clothes, punched and scratched each other's noses, and covered themselves with dust and glory. Presently the confusion took form and through the fog of battle Tom appeared, seated astride the new boy, and pounding him with his fists.

"Holler 'nuff!" said he.

The boy only struggled to free himself. He was crying—mainly from rage.

"Holler 'nuff!"—and the pounding went on.

At last the stranger got out a smothered " 'Nuff!" and Tom let him up and said:

"Now that'll learn you. Better look out who you're fooling with next time."

The new boy went off brushing the dust from his clothes, sobbing, snuffling, and occasionally looking back and shaking his head and threatening what he would do to Tom the "next time he caught him out." To which Tom responded with jeers, and started off in high feather, and as soon as his back was turned the new boy snatched up a stone, threw it and hit him between the shoulders and then turned tail and ran like an antelope. Tom chased the traitor home, and thus found out where he lived. He then held a position at the gate for some time, daring the enemy to come outside, but the enemy only made faces at him through the window and declined. At last the enemy's mother appeared, and called Tom a bad, vicious, vulgar child, and ordered him away. So he went away; but he said he " 'lowed" to "lay" for that boy.

He got home pretty late, that night, and when he climbed cautiously in at the window, he uncovered an ambuscade, in the person of his aunt; and when she saw the state his clothes were in her resolution to turn his Saturday holiday into captivity at hard labor became adamantine in its firmness.

2 *Strong Temptations—Strategic Movements—The Innocents Beguiled*

Saturday morning was come, and all the summer world was bright and fresh, and brimming with life. There was a song in every heart; and if the heart was young the music issued at the lips. There was cheer in every face and a spring in every step. The locust trees were in bloom and the fragrance of the blossoms filled the air. Cardiff Hill, beyond the village and above it, was green with vegetation, and it lay just far enough away to seem a Delectable Land, dreamy, reposeful, and inviting.

Tom appeared on the sidewalk with a bucket of whitewash and a long-handled brush. He surveyed the fence, and all the gladness left him and a deep melancholy settled down upon his spirit. Thirty yards of board fence nine feet high. Life to him seemed hollow, and existence but a burden. Sighing he dipped his brush and passed it along the topmost plank; repeated the operation; did it again; compared the insignificant whitewashed streak with the far-reaching continent of unwhitewashed fence, and sat down on a tree-box discouraged. Jim came skipping out at the gate with a tin pail, and singing "Buffalo Gals." Bringing water from the town pump had always been hateful work in Tom's eyes, before, but now it did not strike him so. He remembered that there was company at the pump. White, mulatto, and Negro boys and girls were always there waiting their turns, resting, trading playthings, quarreling, fighting, skylarking. And he remembered that although the pump was only a hundred and fifty yards off, Jim never got back with a bucket of water under an hour—and even then somebody generally had to go after him. Tom said:

"Say, Jim, I'll fetch the water if you'll whitewash some."

Jim shook his head and said:

"Can't, Mars Tom. Ole missis, she tole me I got to go an' git dis water an' not stop foolin' roun' wid anybody. She say she spec' Mars Tom gwine to ax me to whitewash, an' so she tole me go 'long an' 'tend to my own business—she 'lowed *she'd* 'tend to de whitewashin'."

"Oh, never you mind what she said, Jim. That's the way she always talks. Gimme the bucket—I won't be gone only a minute. *She* won't ever know."

"Oh, I dasn't, Mars Tom. Ole missis she'd take an' tar de head off'n me. 'Deed she would."

"*She!* She never licks anybody—whacks 'em over the head with her thimble—and who cares for that, I'd like to know. She talks awful, but talk don't hurt—anyways it don't if she don't cry. Jim, I'll give you a marvel. I'll give you a white alley!"

Jim began to waver.

"White alley, Jim! And it's a bully taw."

"My! Dat's a mighty gay marvel, *I* tell you! But Mars Tom I's powerful, 'fraid ole missis——"

"And besides, if you will I'll show you my sore toe."

Jim was only human—this attraction was too much for him. He put down his pail, took the white alley, and bent over the toe with absorbing interest while the bandage was being unwound. In another moment he was flying down the street with his pail and a tingling rear, Tom was whitewashing with vigor, and Aunt Polly was retiring from the field with a slipper in her hand and triumph in her eye.

But Tom's energy did not last. He began to think of the fun he had planned for this day, and his sorrows multiplied. Soon the free boys would come tripping along on all sorts of delicious expeditions, and they would make a world of fun of him for having to work—the very thought of it burnt him like fire. He got out his worldly wealth and examined it —bits of toys, marbles, and trash; enough to buy an exchange of *work,* maybe, but not half enough to buy so much as half an hour of pure freedom. So he returned his straitened means to his pocket, and gave up the idea of trying to buy the boys. At this dark and hopeless moment an inspiration burst upon him! Nothing less than a great, magnificent inspiration.

He took up his brush and went tranquilly to work. Ben Rogers hove in sight presently—the very boy, of all boys, whose ridicule he had been dreading. Ben's gait was the hop-skip-and-jump—proof enough that his heart was light and his anticipations high. He was eating an apple, and giving a long, melodious whoop, at intervals, followed by a deep-toned ding-dong-dong, ding-dong-dong, for he was personating a steamboat. As he drew near, he slackened speed, took the middle of the street, leaned far over to starboard and rounded to ponderously and with laborious pomp and circumstance—for he was personating the *Big Missouri,* and considered himself to be drawing nine feet of water. He was boat and captain and engine bells combined, so he had to imagine himself standing on his own hurricane deck giving the orders and executing them:

"Stop her, sir! Ting-a-ling-ling!" The headway ran almost out and he drew up slowly toward the sidewalk.

"Ship up to back! Ting-a-ling-ling!" His arms straightened and stiffened down his sides.

"Set her back on the stabboard! Ting-a-ling-ling! Chow! ch-chow-wow! Chow!" His right hand, meantime, describing stately circles, for it was representing a forty-foot wheel.

"Let her go back on the labboard! Ting-a-ling-ling! Chow-ch-chow-chow!" The left hand began to describe circles.

"Stop the stabboard! Ting-a-ling-ling! Stop the labboard! Come ahead on the stabboard! Stop her! Let your outside turn over slow! Ting-a-ling-ling! Chow-ow-ow! Get out that headline! *Lively* now! Come—out with your spring-line—what're you about there! Take a turn round that stump with the bight of it! Stand by that stage, now—let her go! Done with the engines, sir! Ting-a-ling-ling! *Sh't! s'h't! Sh't!*" (trying the gauge cocks).

Tom went on whitewashing—paid no attention to the steamboat. Ben stared a moment and then said:

"Hi-*yi! You're* up a stump, ain't you!"

No answer. Tom surveyed his last touch with the eye of an artist, then he gave his brush another gentle sweep and surveyed the result, as before. Ben ranged up alongside of him. Tom's mouth watered for the apple, but he stuck to his work. Ben said:

"Hello, old chap, you got to work, hey?"

Tom wheeled suddenly and said:

"Why, it's you, Ben! I warn't noticing."

"Say—*I*'m going in a-swimming, *I* am. Don't you wish you could? But of course you'd druther *work*—wouldn't you? Course you would!"

Tom contemplated the boy a bit, and said:

"What do you call work?"

"Why, ain't *that* work?"

Tom resumed his whitewashing, and answered carelessly:

"Well, maybe it is, and maybe it ain't. All I know, is, it suits Tom Sawyer."

"Oh come, now, you don't mean to let on that you *like* it?"

The brush continued to move.

"Like it? Well, I don't see why I oughtn't to like it. Does a boy get a chance to whitewash a fence every day?"

That put the thing in a new light. Ben stopped nibbling his apple. Tom swept his brush daintily back and forth—stepped back to note the effect—added a touch here and there—criticized the effect again—Ben watching every move and getting more and more interested, more and more absorbed. Presently he said:

"Say, Tom, let *me* whitewash a little."

Tom considered, was about to consent; but he altered his mind:

"No—no—I reckon it wouldn't hardly do, Ben. You see, Aunt Polly's awful particular about this fence—right here on the street, you know—but if it was the back fence I wouldn't mind and *she* wouldn't. Yes, she's awful particular about this fence; it's got to be done very careful; I reckon there ain't one boy in a thousand, maybe two thousand, that can do it the way it's got to be done."

"No—is that so? Oh come, now—lemme just try. Only just a little—I'd let *you*, if you was me, Tom."

"Ben, I'd like to, honest injun; but Aunt Polly—well, Jim wanted to do it, but she wouldn't let him; Sid wanted to do it, and she wouldn't let Sid. Now don't you see how I'm fixed? If you was to tackle this fence and anything was to happen to it——"

"Oh, shucks, I'll be just as careful. Now lemme try. Say—I'll give you the core of my apple."

"Well, here— No, Ben, now don't. I'm afeard——"

"I'll give you *all* of it!"

Tom gave up the brush with reluctance in his face, but alacrity in his heart. And while the late steamer *Big Missouri* worked and sweated in the sun, the retired artist sat on a barrel in the shade close by, dangled his legs, munched his apple, and planned the slaughter of more innocents. There was no lack of material; boys happened along every little while; they came to jeer, but remained to whitewash. By the time Ben was fagged out, Tom had traded the next chance to Billy Fisher for a kite, in good repair; and when *he* played out, Johnny Miller bought in for a dead rat and a string to swing it with—and so on, and so on, hour after hour. And when the middle of the afternoon came, from being a poor poverty-stricken boy in the morning, Tom was literally rolling in wealth. He had beside the things before mentioned, twelve marbles, part of a jew's-harp, a piece of blue bottle glass to look through, a spool cannon, a key that wouldn't unlock anything, a fragment of chalk, a glass stopper of a decanter, a tin soldier, a couple of tadpoles, six firecrackers, a kitten with only one eye, a brass doorknob, a dog collar—but no dog—the handle of a knife, four pieces of orange peel, and a dilapidated old window sash.

He had had a nice, good, idle time all the while—plenty of company—and the fence had three coats of whitewash on it! If he hadn't run out of whitewash, he would have bankrupted every boy in the village.

Tom said to himself that it was not such a hollow world, after all. He had discovered a great law of human action, without knowing it—namely, that in order to make a man or a boy covet a thing, it is only necessary to make the thing difficult to attain. If he had been a great and wise philosopher, like the writer of this book, he would now have comprehended that Work consists of whatever a body is *obliged* to do, and that Play consists of whatever a body is not obliged to do. And this would help him to understand why constructing artificial flowers or performing on a tread-mill is work, while rolling tenpens or climbing Mont Blanc is only amusement. There are wealthy gentlemen in England who drive four-horse passenger coaches twenty or thirty miles on a daily line, in the summer, because the privilege costs them considerable money; but if they were offered wages for the service, that would turn it into work and then they would resign.

The boy mused a while over the substantial change which had taken place in his worldly circumstances, and then wended toward headquarters to report.

3 *Tom as a General—Triumph and Reward—Dismal Felicity—Commission and Omission*

Tom presented himself before Aunt Polly, who was sitting by an open window in a pleasant rearward apartment, which was bedroom, breakfast room, dining room, and library, combined. The balmy summer air, the restful quiet, the odor of the flowers, and the drowsing murmur of the bees had had their effect, and she was nodding over her knitting—for she had no company but the cat, and it was asleep in her lap. Her spectacles were propped up on her gray head for safety. She had thought that of course Tom had deserted long ago, and she wondered at seeing him place himself in her power again in this intrepid way. He said: "Mayn't I go and play now, aunt?"

"What, a'ready? How much have you done?"

"It's all done, aunt."

"Tom, don't lie to me—I can't bear it."

"I ain't, aunt; it *is* all done."

Aunt Polly placed small trust in such evidence. She went out to see for herself; and she would have been content to find twenty per cent of Tom's statement true. When she found the entire fence whitewashed, and not only whitewashed but elaborately coated and recoated, and even a streak added to the ground, her astonishment was almost unspeakable. She said:

"Well, I never! There's no getting round it, you *can* work when you're a mind to, Tom." And then she diluted the compliment by adding, "But it's powerful seldom you're a mind to, I'm bound to say. Well, go 'long and play; but mind you get back some time in a week, or I'll tan you."

She was so overcome by the splendor of his achievement that she took him into the closet and selected a choice apple and delivered it to him, along with an improving lecture upon the added value and flavor a treat took to itself when it came without sin through virtuous effort. And while she closed with a happy Scriptural flourish, he "hooked" a doughnut.

Then he skipped out, and saw Sid just starting up the outside stairway that led to the back rooms on the second floor. Clods were handy and the air was full of them in a twinkling. They raged around Sid like a hailstorm; and before Aunt Polly could collect her surprised faculties and sally to the rescue, six or seven clods had taken personal effect, and Tom was over the fence and gone. There was a gate, but as a general thing he was too crowded for time to make use of it. His soul was at peace, now that he had settled with Sid for calling attention to his black thread and getting him into trouble.

Tom skirted the block, and came round into a muddy alley that led by the back of his aunt's cow stable. He presently got safely beyond the reach of capture and punishment, and hastened toward the public square of the village, where two "military" companies of boys had met for conflict, according to previous appointment. Tom was General of one of these armies, Joe Harper (a bosom friend) General of the other. These two great commanders did not condescend to fight in person—that being better suited to the still smaller fry—but sat together on an eminence and conducted the field operations by orders delivered through aides-de-camp. Tom's army won a great victory, after a long and hard-fought battle. Then the dead were counted, prisoners exchanged, the terms of the next disagreement agreed upon, and the day for the necessary battle appointed; after which the armies fell into line and marched away, and Tom turned homeward alone.

As he was passing by the house where Jeff Thatcher lived, he saw a new girl in the garden—a lovely little blue-eyed creature with yellow hair plaited into two long tails, white summer frock and embroidered pantalettes. The fresh-crowned hero fell without firing a shot. A certain Amy Lawrence vanished out of his heart and left not even a memory of herself behind. He had thought he loved her to distraction, he had regarded his passion as adoration; and behold it was only a poor little evanescent partiality. He had been months winning her; she had confessed hardly a week ago; he had been the happiest and the proudest boy in the world only seven short days, and here in one instant of time she had gone out of his heart like a casual stranger whose visit is done.

He worshipped this new angel with furtive eye, till he saw that she had discovered him; then he pretended he did not know she was present, and began to "show off" in all sorts of absurd boyish ways, in order to win her admiration. He kept up this grotesque foolishness for some time; but by and by, while he was in the midst of some dangerous gymnastic performances, he glanced aside and saw that the little girl was wending her way toward the house. Tom came up to the fence and leaned on it, grieving, and hoping she would tarry yet a while longer. She halted a moment on the steps and then moved toward the door. Tom heaved a great sigh as she put her foot on the threshold. But his face lit up, right away, for she tossed a pansy over the fence a moment before she disappeared.

The boy ran around and stopped within a foot or two of the flower, and then shaded his eyes with his hand and began to look down street as if he had discovered something of interest going on in that direction. Presently he picked up a straw and began trying to balance it on his nose, with his head tilted far back; and as he moved from side to side, in his efforts, he edged nearer and nearer toward the pansy; finally his bare foot rested upon it, his pliant toes closed upon it, and he hopped away with the treasure and disappeared round the corner. But only for a minute—only while he could button the flower inside his jacket, next to his heart—or next his stomach, possibly, for he was not much posted in anatomy, and not hypercritical, anyway.

He returned, now, and hung about the fence till nightfall, "showing off," as before, but the girl never exhibited herself again, though Tom comforted himself a little with the hope that she had been near some window, meantime, and been aware of his attentions. Finally he rode home reluctantly, with his poor head full of visions.

All through supper his spirits were so high that his aunt wondered "what had got into the child." He took a good scolding about clodding Sid, and did not seem to mind it in the least. He tried to steal sugar under his aunt's very nose, and got his knuckles rapped for it. He said:

"Aunt, you don't whack Sid when he takes it."

"Well, Sid don't torment a body the way you do. You'd be always into that sugar if I warn't watching you."

Presently she stepped into the kitchen, and Sid, happy in his immunity, reached for the sugar bowl—a sort of glorying over Tom which was well-nigh unbearable. But Sid's fingers slipped and the bowl dropped and broke. Tom was in ecstasies. In such ecstasies that he even controlled his tongue and was silent. He said to himself that he would not speak a word, even when his aunt came in, but would sit perfectly still till she asked who did the mischief; and then he would tell, and there would be nothing so good in the world as to see that pet model "catch it." He was so brim full of exultation that he could hardly hold himself when the old lady came back and stood above the wreck discharging lightnings of wrath from over her spectacles. He said to himself, "Now it's coming!" And the next instant he was sprawling on the floor! The potent palm was uplifted to strike again when Tom cried out:

"Hold on, now, what 'er you belting *me* for?—Sid broke it!"

Aunt Polly paused, perplexed, and Tom looked for healing pity. But when she got her tongue again, she only said:

"Umf! Well, you didn't get a lick amiss, I reckon. You been into some other audacious mischief when I wasn't around, like enough."

Then her conscience reproached her, and she yearned to say something kind and loving; but she judged that this would be construed into a confession that she had been in the wrong, and discipline forbade that. So she kept silence, and went about her affairs with a troubled heart. Tom sulked in a corner and exalted his woes. He knew that in her heart his aunt was on her knees to him, and he was morosely gratified by the consciousness of it. He would hang out no signals, he would take notice of none. He knew that a yearning glance fell upon him, now and then, through a film of tears, but he refused recognition of it. He pictured himself lying sick unto death and his aunt bending over him beseeching one little forgiving word, but he would turn his face to the wall, and die with that word unsaid. Ah, how would she feel then? And he pictured himself brought home from the river, dead, with his curls all wet, and his sore heart at rest. How she would throw herself upon him, and how her tears would fall like rain, and her lips pray God to give her back her boy and she would never, never abuse him any more! But he would lie there cold and white and make no sign—a poor little sufferer, whose griefs were at an end. He so worked upon his feelings with the pathos of these dreams, that he had to keep swallowing, he was so like to choke; and his eyes swam in a blur of water, which overflowed when he winked, and ran down and trickled from the end of his nose. And such a luxury to him was this petting of his sorrows, that he could not bear to have any worldly cheeriness or any grating delight intrude upon it; it was too sacred for such contact; and so, presently, when his cousin Mary danced in, all alive with the joy of seeing home again after an agelong visit of one week to the country, he got up and moved in clouds and darkness out at one door as she brought song and sunshine in at the other.

He wandered far from the accustomed haunts of boys, and sought desolate places that were in harmony with his spirit. A log raft in the river invited him, and he seated himself on its outer edge and contemplated the dreary vastness of the stream, wishing, the while, that he could only be drowned, all at once and unconsciously, without undergoing the uncomfortable routine devised by nature. Then he thought of his flower. He got it out, rumpled and wilted, and it mightily increased his dismal felicity. He wondered if *she* would pity him if she knew? Would she cry, and wish that she had a right to put her arms around his neck and comfort him? Or would she turn coldly away like all the hollow world? This picture brought such an agony of pleasurable suffering that he worked it over and over again in his mind and set it up in new and varied lights, till he wore it threadbare. At last he rose up sighing and departed in the darkness.

About half past nine or ten o'clock he came along the deserted street to where the Adored Unknown lived; he paused a moment; no sound fell upon his listening ear; a candle was casting a dull glow upon the curtain of a second story window. Was the sacred presence there? He climbed the fence, threaded his stealthy way through the plants, till he stood under that window; he looked up at it long, and with emotion; then he laid him down on the ground under it, disposing himself upon his back, with his hands clasped upon his breast and holding his poor wilted flower. And thus he would die—out in the cold world, with no shelter over his homeless head, no friendly hand to wipe the death-damps from his brow, no loving face to bend pityingly over him when the great agony came. And thus *she* would see him when she looked out upon the glad morning, and oh! would she drop one little tear upon his poor, lifeless form, would she heave one little sigh to see a bright young life so rudely blighted, so untimely cut down?

The window went up, a maidservant's discordant voice profaned the holy calm, and a deluge of water drenched the prone martyr's remains!

The strangling hero sprang up with a relieving snort. There was a whiz as of a missile in the air, mingled with the murmur of a curse, a sound as of shivering glass followed, and a small, vague form went over the fence and shot away in the gloom.

Not long after, as Tom, all undressed for bed, was surveying his drenched garments by the light of a tallow dip, Sid woke up; but if he had any dim idea of making any "references to allusions," he thought better of it and held his peace, for there was danger in Tom's eye.

Tom turned in without the added vexation of prayers, and Sid made mental note of the omission.

4 *Mental Acrobatics—Attending Sunday School—The Superintendent—"Showing Off"—Tom Lionized*

The sun rose upon a tranquil world, and beamed down upon the peaceful village like a benediction. Breakfast over, Aunt Polly had family worship: it began with a prayer built from the ground up of solid courses of Scriptural quotations, welded together with a thin mortar of originality; and from the summit of this she delivered a grim chapter of the Mosaic Law, as from Sinai.

Then Tom girded up his loins, so to speak, and went to work to "get his verses." Sid had learned his lesson days before. Tom bent all his energies to the memorizing of five verses, and he chose part of the Sermon on the Mount, because he could find no verses that were shorter. At the end of half an hour Tom had a vague general idea of his lesson, but no more, for his mind was traversing the whole field of human thought, and his hands were busy with distracting recreations. Mary took his book to hear him recite, and he tried to find his way through the fog:

"Blessed are the—a—a—"

"Poor—"

"Yes—poor; blessed are the poor—a—a—"

"In spirit—"

"In spirit; blessed are the poor in spirit, for they—they—"

"Theirs—"

"For *theirs*. Blessed are the poor in spirit, for *theirs* is the kingdom of heaven. Blessed are they that mourn, for they—they—"

"Sh—"

"For they—a—"

"S, H, A—"

"For they S, H—Oh, I don't know what it is!"

"Shall!"

"Oh, *shall!* for they shall—for they shall—a—a—shall mourn—a—a—blessed are they that shall—they that—a—they that shall mourn, for they shall—a—shall *what?* Why don't you tell me, Mary?—what do you want to be so mean for?"

"Oh, Tom, you poor thickheaded thing, I'm not teasing you. I wouldn't do that. You must go and learn it again. Don't you be discouraged, Tom, you'll manage it—and if you do, I'll give you something ever so nice. There, now, that's a good boy."

"All right! What is it, Mary, tell me what it is."

"Never you mind, Tom. You know if I say it's nice, it *is* nice."

"You bet you that's so, Mary. All right, I'll tackle it again."

And he did "tackle it again"—and under the double pressure of curiosity and prospective gain, he did it with such spirit that he accomplished a shining success. Mary gave him a brand-new "Barlow" knife worth twelve and a half cents; and the convulsion of delight that swept his system shook him to his foundations. True, the knife would not cut anything, but it was a "sure-enough" Barlow, and there was inconceivable grandeur in that—though where the Western boys ever got the idea that such a weapon could possibly be counterfeited to its injury, is an imposing mystery and will always remain so, perhaps. Tom contrived to scarify the cupboard with it, and was arranging to begin on the bureau, when he was called off to dress for Sunday school.

Mary gave him a tin basin of water and a piece of soap, and he went outside the door and set the basin on a little bench there; then he dipped the soap in the water and laid it down; turned up his sleeves; poured out the water on the ground, gently, and then entered the kitchen and began to wipe his face diligently on the towel behind the door. But Mary removed the towel and said:

"Now ain't you ashamed, Tom. You mustn't be so bad. Water won't hurt you."

Tom was a trifle disconcerted. The basin was refilled, and this time he stood over it a little while, gathering resolution; took in a big breath and began. When he entered the kitchen presently, with both eyes shut and groping for the towel with his hands, an honorable testimony of suds and water was dripping from his face. But when he emerged from the towel, he was not yet satisfactory, for the clean territory stopped short at his chin and his jaws, like a mask; below and beyond this line there was a dark expanse of unirrigated soil that spread downward in front and backward around his neck. Mary took him in hand, and when she was done with him he was a man and a brother, without distinction of color, and his saturated hair was neatly brushed, and its short curls wrought into a dainty and symmetrical general effect. (He privately smoothed out the curls, with labor and difficulty, and plastered his hair close down to his head; for he held curls to be effeminate, and his own filled his life with bitterness.) Then Mary got out a suit of his clothing that had been used only on Sundays during two years—they were simply called his "other clothes"—and so by that we know the size of his wardrobe. The girl "put him to rights" after he had dressed himself; she buttoned his neat roundabout up to his chin, turned his vast shirt collar down over his shoulders, brushed him off and crowned him with his speckled straw hat. He now looked exceedingly improved and uncomfortable. He was fully as uncomfortable as he looked; for there was a restraint about whole clothes and cleanliness that galled him. He hoped that Mary would forget his shoes, but the hope was blighted; she coated them thoroughly with tallow, as was the custom, and brought them out. He lost his temper and said he was always being made to do everything he didn't want to do. But Mary said, persuasively:

"Please, Tom—that's a good boy."

So he got into the shoes snarling. Mary was soon ready, and the three children set out for Sunday school—a place that Tom hated with his whole heart; but Sid and Mary were fond of it.

Sabbath-school hours were from nine to half past ten; and then church service. Two of the children always remained for the sermon voluntarily, and the other always remained too—for stronger reasons. The church's high-backed, uncushioned pews would seat about three hundred persons; the edifice was but a small, plain affair, with a sort of pine board tree-box on top of it for a steeple. At the door Tom dropped back a step and accosted a Sunday-dressed comrade.

"Say, Billy, got a yaller ticket?"

"Yes."

"What'll you take for her?"

"What'll you give?"

"Piece of lickrish and a fishhook."

"Less see 'em."

Tom exhibited. They were satisfactory, and the property changed hands. Then Tom traded a couple of white alleys for three red tickets, and some small trifle or other for a couple of blue ones. He waylaid other boys as they came, and went on buying tickets of various colors ten or fifteen minutes longer. He entered the church, now, with a swarm of clean and noisy boys and girls, proceeded to his seat and started a quarrel with the first boy that came handy. The teacher, a grave, elderly man, interfered; then turned his back a moment and Tom pulled a boy's hair in the next bench, and was absorbed in his book when the boy turned around; stuck a pin in another boy, presently, in order to hear him say "Ouch!" and got a new reprimand from his teacher. Tom's whole class were of a pattern—restless, noisy, and troublesome. When they came to recite their lessons, not one of them knew his verses perfectly, but had to be prompted all along. However, they worried through, and each got his reward—in small blue tickets, each with a passage of Scripture on it; each blue ticket was pay for two verses of the recitation. Ten blue tickets equaled a red one, and could be exchanged for it; ten red tickets equaled a yellow one; for ten yellow tickets the superintendent gave a very plainly bound Bible (worth forty cents in those easy times) to the pupil. How many of my readers would have the industry and application to memorize two thousand verses, even for a Doré Bible? And yet Mary had acquired two Bibles in this way—it was the patient work of two years—and a boy of German parentage had won four or five. He once recited three thousand verses without stopping; but the strain upon his mental faculties was too great, and he was little better than an idiot from that day forth—a grievous misfortune for the school, for on great occasions, before company, the superintendent (as Tom expressed it) had always made this boy come out and "spread himself." Only the older pupils managed to keep their tickets and stick to their tedious work long enough to get a Bible, and so the delivery of one of these prizes was a rare and noteworthy circumstance; the successful pupil was so great and conspicuous for that day that on the spot every scholar's heart was fired with a fresh ambition that often lasted a couple of weeks. It is possible that Tom's mental stomach had never really hungered for one of those prizes, but unquestionably his entire being had for many a day longed for the glory and the éclat that came with it.

In due course the superintendent stood up in front of the pulpit, with a closed hymnbook in his hand and his forefinger inserted between its leaves, and commanded attention. When a Sunday-school superintendent makes his customary little speech, a hymnbook in the hand is as necessary as is the inevitable sheet of music in the hand of a singer who stands forward on the platform and sings a solo at a concert—though why, is a mystery: for neither the hymnbook nor the sheet of music is ever referred to by the sufferer. This superintendent was a slim creature of thirty-five, with a sandy goatee and short sandy hair; he wore a stiff standing collar whose upper edge almost reached his ears and whose sharp points curved forward abreast the corners of his mouth—a fence that compelled a straight lookout ahead, and a turning of the whole body when a side view was required; his chin was propped on a spreading cravat which was as broad and as long as a banknote, and had fringed ends; his boot toes were turned sharply up, in the fashion of the day, like sleigh runners—an effect patiently and laboriously produced by the young men by sitting with their toes pressed against a wall for hours together. Mr. Walters was very earnest of mien, and very sincere and honest at heart; and he held sacred things and places in such reverence, and so separated them from worldly matters, that unconsciously to himself his Sunday-school voice had acquired a peculiar intonation which was wholly absent on weekdays. He began after this fashion:

"Now, children, I want you all to sit up just as straight and pretty as you can and give me all your attention for a minute or two. There—that is it. That is the way good little boys and girls should do. I see one little girl who is looking out of the window—I am afraid she thinks I am out there somewhere—perhaps up in one of the trees making a speech to the little birds. (Applausive titter.) I want to tell you how good it makes me feel to see so many bright, clean little faces assembled in a place like this, learning to do right and be good." And so forth and so on. It is not necessary to set down the rest of the oration. It was of a pattern which does not vary, and so it is familiar to us all.

The latter third of the speech was marred by the resumption of fights and other recreations among certain of the bad boys, and by fidgetings and whisperings that extended far and wide, washing even to the bases of isolated and incorruptible rocks like Sid and Mary. But now every sound ceased suddenly, with the subsidence of Mr. Walters' voice, and the conclusion of the speech was received with a burst of silent gratitude.

A good part of the whispering had been occasioned by an event which was more or less rare—the entrance of visitors: lawyer Thatcher, accompanied by a very feeble and aged man; a fine, portly, middle-aged gentleman with iron-gray hair; and a dignified lady who was doubtless the latter's wife. The lady was leading a child. Tom had been restless and full of chafings and repinings; conscience-smitten, too —he could not meet Amy Lawrence's eye, he could not brook her loving gaze. But when he saw this small newcomer his soul was all ablaze with bliss in a moment. The next moment he was "showing off" with all his might—cuffing boys, pulling hair, making faces—in a word, using every art that seemed likely to fascinate a girl and win her applause. His exaltation had but one alloy—the memory of his humiliation in this angel's garden—and that record in sand was fast washing out, under the waves of happiness that were sweeping over it now.

The visitors were given the highest seat of honor, and as soon as Mr. Walters' speech was finished, he introduced them to the school. The middle-aged man turned out to be a prodigious personage—no less a one than the county judge —altogether the most august creation these children had ever looked upon—and they wondered what kind of material he was made of—and they half wanted to hear him roar, and were half afraid he might, too. He was from Constantinople, twelve miles away—so he had traveled, and seen the world—these very eyes had looked upon the county courthouse—which was said to have a tin roof. The awe which these reflections inspired was attested by the impressive silence and the ranks of staring eyes. This was the great Judge Thatcher, brother of their own lawyer. Jeff Thatcher immediately went forward, to be familiar with the great man and be envied by the school. It would have been music to his soul to hear the whisperings:

"Look at him, Jim! He's a-going up there. Say—look! he's a-going to shake hands with him—he *is* shaking hands with him! By jings, don't you wish you was Jeff?"

Mr. Walters fell to "showing off," with all sorts of official bustlings and activities, giving orders, delivering judgments, discharging directions here, there, everywhere that he could find a target. The librarian "showed off"—running hither and thither with his arms full of books and making a deal of the splutter and fuss that insect authority delights in. The young lady teachers "showed off"—bending sweetly over pupils that were lately being boxed, lifting pretty warning fingers at bad little boys and patting good ones lovingly. The young gentlemen teachers "showed off" with small scoldings and other little displays of authority and fine attention to discipline—and most of the teachers, of both sexes, found business up at the library, by the pulpit; and it was business that frequently had to be done over again two or three times (with much seeming vexation). The little girls "showed off" in various ways, and the little boys "showed off" with such diligence that the air was thick with paper wads and the murmur of scufflings. And above it all the great man sat and beamed a majestic judicial smile upon all the house, and warmed himself in the sun of his own grandeur—for he was "showing off," too.

There was only one thing wanting, to make Mr. Walters' ecstasy complete, and that was a chance to deliver a Bible prize and exhibit a prodigy. Several pupils had a few yellow tickets, but none had enough—he had been around among the star pupils inquiring. He would have given worlds, now, to have that German lad back again with a sound mind.

And now at this moment, when hope was dead, Tom Sawyer came forward with nine yellow tickets, nine red tickets, and ten blue ones, and demanded a Bible. This was a thunderbolt out of a clear sky. Walters was not expecting an application from this source for the next ten years. But there was no getting around it—here were the certified checks, and they were good for their face. Tom was therefore elevated to a place with the Judge and the other elect, and the great news was announced from headquarters. It was the most stunning surprise of the decade, and so profound was the sensation that it lifted the new hero up to the judicial one's altitude, and the school had two marvels to gaze upon in place of one. The boys were all eaten up with envy—but those that suffered the bitterest pangs were those who perceived too late that they themselves had contributed to this hated splendor by trading tickets to Tom for the wealth he had amassed in selling whitewashing privileges. These despised themselves, as being the dupes of a wily fraud, a guileful snake in the grass.

The prize was delivered to Tom with as much effusion as the superintendent could pump up under the circumstances; but it lacked somewhat of the true gush, for the poor fellow's instinct taught him that there was a mystery here that could not well bear the light, perhaps; it was simply preposterous that *this* boy had warehoused two thousand sheaves of Scriptural wisdom on his premises—a dozen would strain his capacity, without a doubt.

Amy Lawrence was proud and glad, and she tried to make Tom see it in her face—but he wouldn't look. She wondered; then she was just a grain troubled; next a dim suspicion came and went—came again; she watched; a furtive glance told her worlds—and then her heart broke, and she was jealous, and angry, and the tears came and she hated everybody. Tom most of all (she thought).

Tom was introduced to the Judge; but his tongue was

tied, his breath would hardly come, his heart quaked—partly because of the awful greatness of the man, but mainly because he was *her* parent. He would have liked to fall down and worship him, if it were in the dark. The Judge put his hand on Tom's head and called him a fine little man, and asked him what his name was. The boy stammered, gasped, and got it out:

"Tom."

"Oh, no, not Tom—it is—"

"Thomas."

"Ah, that's it. I thought there was more to it, maybe. That's very well. But you've another one I daresay, and you'll tell it to me, won't you?"

"Tell the gentleman your other name, Thomas," said Walters, "and say *sir*. You mustn't forget your manners."

"Thomas Sawyer—sir."

"That's it! That's a good boy. Fine boy. Fine, manly little fellow. Two thousand verses is a great many—very, very great many. And you never can be sorry for the trouble you took to learn them; for knowledge is worth more than anything there is in the world; it's what makes great men and good men; you'll be a great man and a good man yourself, some day, Thomas, and then you'll look back and say, It's all owing to the precious Sunday-school privileges of my boyhood—it's all owing to my dear teachers that taught me to learn—it's all owing to the good superintendent, who encouraged me, and watched over me, and gave me a beautiful Bible—a splendid elegant Bible—to keep and have it all for my own, always—it's all owing to right bringing up! That is what you will say, Thomas—and you wouldn't take any money for those two thousand verses—no indeed you wouldn't. And now you wouldn't mind telling me and this lady some of the things you've learned—no, I know you wouldn't—for we are proud of little boys that learn. Now, no doubt you know the names of all the twelve disciples. Won't you tell us the names of the first two that were appointed?"

Tom was tugging at a buttonhole and looking sheepish.

He blushed, now, and his eyes fell. Mr. Walters' heart sank within him. He said to himself, it is not possible that the boy can answer the simplest question—why *did* the Judge ask him? Yet he felt obliged to speak up and say:

"Answer the gentleman, Thomas—don't be afraid."

Tom still hung fire.

"Now I know you'll tell *me*," said the lady. "The names of the first two disciples were—"

"DAVID AND GOLIATH!"

Let us draw the curtain of charity over the rest of the scene.

5 *A Useful Minister—In Church—The Climax*

About half past ten the cracked bell of the small church began to ring, and presently the people began to gather for the morning sermon. The Sunday-school children distributed themselves about the house and occupied pews with their parents, so as to be under supervision. Aunt Polly came, and Tom and Sid and Mary sat with her—Tom being placed next the aisle, in order that he might be as far away from the open window and the seductive outside summer scenes as possible. The crowd filed up the aisles: the aged and needy postmaster, who had seen better days; the mayor and his wife—for they had a mayor there, among other unnecessaries; the justice of the peace; the widow Douglas, fair, smart, and forty, a generous, good-hearted soul and well-to-do, her hill mansion the only palace in the town, and the most hospitable and much the most lavish in the matter of festivities that St. Petersburg could boast; the bent and venerable Major and Mrs. Ward; lawyer Riverson, the new notable from a distance; next the belle of the village, followed by a troop of lawn-clad and ribbon-decked young heartbreakers; then all the young clerks in town in a body —for they had stood in the vestibule sucking their cane heads, a circling wall of oiled and simpering admirers, till the last girl had run their gauntlet; and last of all came the Model Boy, Willie Mufferson, taking as heedful care of his mother as if she were cut glass. He always brought his mother to church, and was the pride of all the matrons. The boys all hated him, he was so good. And besides, he had been "thrown up to them" so much. His white handkerchief was hanging out of his pocket behind, as usual on Sundays—accidentally. Tom had no handkerchief, and he looked upon boys who had, as snobs.

The congregation being fully assembled, now, the bell rang once more, to warn laggards and stragglers, and then a solemn hush fell upon the church which was only broken by the tittering and whispering of the choir in the gallery. The choir always tittered and whispered all through service. There was once a church choir that was not ill-bred, but I have forgotten where it was, now. It was a great many years ago, and I can scarcely remember anything about it, but I think it was in some foreign country.

The minister gave out the hymn, and read it through with a relish, in a peculiar style which was much admired in that part of the country. His voice began on a medium key and climbed steadily up till it reached a certain point, where it bore with strong emphasis upon the topmost word and then plunged down as if from a springboard:

Shall I be car-ri-ed toe the skies, on flow'ry beds *of ease,*
Whilst others fight to win the prize, and sail thro' blood-*y seas?*

He was regarded as a wonderful reader. At church "sociables" he was always called upon to read poetry; and when he was through, the ladies would lift up their hands and let them fall helplessly in their laps, and "wall" their eyes, and shake their heads, as much as to say, "Words cannot express it; it is too beautiful, *too* beautiful for this mortal earth."

After the hymn had been sung, the Rev. Mr. Sprague turned himself into a bulletin board, and read off "notices" of meetings and societies and things till it seemed that the list would stretch out to the crack of doom—a queer custom which is still kept up in America, even in cities, away here in this age of abundant newspapers. Often, the less there is to justify a traditional custom, the harder it is to get rid of it.

And now the minister prayed. A good, generous prayer it was, and went into details: it pleaded for the church, and the little children of the church; for the other churches of the village; for the village itself; for the county; for the State; for the State officers; for the United States; for the churches of the United States; for Congress; for the President; for the officers of the Government; for poor sailors, tossed by stormy seas; for the oppressed millions groaning under the heel of European monarchies and Oriental despotisms; for such as have the light and the good tidings, and yet have not eyes to see nor ears to hear withal; for the heathen in the far islands of the sea; and closed with a supplication that the words he was about to speak might find grace and favor, and be as seed sown in fertile ground, yielding in time a grateful harvest of good. Amen.

There was a rustling of dresses, and the standing congregation sat down. The boy whose history this book relates did not enjoy the prayer, he only endured it—if he even did that much. He was restive all through it; he kept tally of the details of the prayer, unconsciously—for he was not listening, but he knew the ground of old, and the clergyman's regular route over it—and when a little trifle of new matter was interlarded, his ear detected it and his whole nature resented it; he considered additions unfair, and scoundrelly. In the midst of the prayer a fly had lit on the back of the pew in front of him and tortured his spirit by calmly rubbing its hands together, embracing its head with its arms, and polishing it so vigorously that it seemed to almost part company with the body, and the slender thread of a neck was exposed to view; scraping its wings with its hind legs and smoothing them to its body as if they had been coattails, going through its whole toilet as tranquilly as if it knew it was perfectly safe. As indeed it was; for as sorely as Tom's hands itched to grab for it they did not dare—he believed his soul would be instantly destroyed if he did such a thing while the prayer was going on. But with the closing sentence his hand began to curve and steal forward; and the instant the "Amen" was out the fly was a prisoner of war. His aunt detected the act and made him let it go.

The minister gave out his text and droned along monotonously through an argument that was so prosy that many a head by and by began to nod—and yet it was an argument that dealt in limitless fire and brimstone and thinned the predestined elect down to a company so small as to be hardly worth the saving. Tom counted the pages of the sermon; after church he always knew how many pages there had been, but he seldom knew anything else about the discourse. However, this time he was really interested for a little while. The minister made a grand and moving picture of the assembling together of the world's hosts at the millennium when the lion and the lamb should lie down together and a little child should lead them. But the pathos, the lesson, the moral of the great spectacle were lost upon the boy; he only thought of the conspicuousness of the principal character before the onlooking nations; his face lit with the thought, and he said to himself that he wished he could be that child, if it was a tame lion.

Now he lapsed into suffering again, as the dry argument was resumed. Presently he bethought him of a treasure he had and got it out. It was a large black beetle with formidable jaws—a "pinch bug," he called it. It was in a percussion-cap box. The first thing the beetle did was to take him by the finger. A natural fillip followed, the beetle went floundering into the aisle and lit on its back, and the hurt finger went into the boy's mouth. The beetle lay there working its helpless legs, unable to turn over. Tom eyed it, and longed for it; but it was safe out of his reach. Other people uninterested in the sermon, found relief in the beetle, and they eyed it too. Presently a vagrant poodle dog came idling along, sad at heart, lazy with the summer softness and the quiet, weary of captivity, sighing for change. He spied the beetle; the drooping tail lifted and wagged. He surveyed the prize; walked around it; smelt at it from a safe distance; walked around it again; grew bolder, and took a closer smell; then lifted his lip and made a gingerly snatch at it, just missing it; made another, and another; began to enjoy the diversion; subsided to his stomach with the beetle between his paws, and continued his experiments; grew weary at last, and then indifferent and absent-minded. His head nodded, and little by little his chin descended and touched the enemy, who seized it. There was a sharp yelp, a flirt of the poodle's head, and the beetle fell a couple of yards away, and lit on its back once more. The neighboring spectators shook with a gentle inward joy, several faces went behind fans and handkerchiefs, and Tom was entirely happy. The dog looked foolish, and probably felt so; but there was resentment in his heart, too, and a craving for revenge. So he went to the beetle and began a wary attack on it again; jumping at it from every point of a circle, lighting with his fore paws within an inch of the creature, making even closer snatches at it with his teeth, and jerking his head till his ears flapped again. But he grew tired once more, after a while; tried to amuse himself with a fly but found no relief; followed an ant around, with his nose close to the floor, and quickly wearied of that; yawned, sighed, forgot the beetle entirely, and sat down on it. Then there was a wild yelp of agony and the poodle went sailing up the aisle; the yelps continued, and so did the dog; he crossed the house in front of the altar; he flew down the other aisle; he crossed before the doors; he clamored up the homestretch; his anguish grew with his progress, till presently he was but a woolly comet moving in its orbit with the gleam and the speed of light. At last the frantic sufferer sheered from its course, and sprang into its master's lap; he flung it out of the window, and the voice of distress quickly thinned away and died in the distance.

By this time the whole church was red-faced and suffocating with suppressed laughter, and the sermon had come to a dead standstill. The discourse was resumed presently, but it went lame and halting, all possibility of impressiveness being at an end; for even the gravest sentiments were constantly being received with a smothered burst of unholy mirth, under cover of some remote pew back, as if the poor parson had said a rarely facetious thing. It was a genuine relief to the whole congregation when the ordeal was over and the benediction pronounced.

Tom Sawyer went home quite cheerful, thinking to himself that there was some satisfaction about divine service when there was a bit of variety in it. He had but one marring thought; he was willing that the dog should play with his pinch bug, but he did not think it was upright in him to carry it off.

6 *Self-Examination—Dentistry—The Midnight Charm—Witches and Devils—Cautious Approaches—Happy Hours*

Monday morning found Tom Sawyer miserable. Monday morning always found him so—because it began another week's slow suffering in school. He generally began that day with wishing he had had no intervening holiday, it made the going into captivity and fetters again so much more odious.

Tom lay thinking. Presently it occurred to him that he wished he was sick; then he could stay home from school. Here was a vague possibility. He canvassed his system. No ailment was found, and he investigated again. This time he thought he could detect colicky symptoms, and he began to encourage them with considerable hope. But they soon grew feeble, and presently died wholly away. He reflected further. Suddenly he discovered something. One of his upper front teeth was loose. This was lucky; he was about to begin to groan, as a "starter," as he called it, when it occurred to him that if he came into court with that argument, his aunt would pull it out, and that would hurt. So he thought he would hold the tooth in reserve for the present, and seek further. Nothing offered for some little time, and then he remembered hearing the doctor tell about a certain thing that laid up a patient for two or three weeks and threatened to make him lose a finger. So the boy eagerly drew his sore toe from under the sheet and held it up for inspection. But now he did not know the necessary symptoms. However, it seemed well worth while to chance it, so he fell to groaning with considerable spirit.

But Sid slept on unconscious.

Tom groaned louder, and fancied that he began to feel pain in the toe.

No result from Sid.

Tom was panting with his exertions by this time. He took a rest and then swelled himself up and fetched a succession of admirable groans.

Sid snored on.

Tom was aggravated. He said, "Sid, Sid!" and shook him. This course worked well, and Tom began to groan again. Sid yawned, stretched, then brought himself up on his elbow with a snort, and began to stare at Tom. Tom went on groaning. Sid said:

"Tom! Say, Tom!" (No response.) "Here, Tom! *Tom!* What is the matter, Tom?" And he shook him and looked in his face anxiously.

Tom moaned out:

"Oh, don't, Sid. Don't joggle me."

"Why, what's the matter, Tom? I must call auntie."

"No—never mind. It'll be over by and by, maybe. Don't call anybody."

"But I must! *Don't* groan so, Tom, it's awful. How long have you been this way?"

"Hours. Ouch! Oh, don't stir so, Sid, you'll kill me."

"Tom, why didn't you wake me sooner? Oh, Tom, *don't!* It makes my flesh crawl to hear you. Tom, what *is* the matter?"

"I forgive you everything, Sid. (Groan.) Everything you've ever done to me. When I'm gone——"

"Oh, Tom, you ain't dying, are you? Don't, Tom—oh, don't. Maybe——"

"I forgive everybody, Sid. (Groan.) Tell 'em so, Sid. And Sid, you give my window sash and my cat with one eye to that new girl that's come to town, and tell her——"

But Sid had snatched his clothes and gone. Tom was suffering in reality, now, so handsomely was his imagination working, and so his groans had gathered quite a genuine tone.

Sid flew downstairs and said:

"Oh, Aunt Polly, come! Tom's dying!"

"Dying!"

"Yes'm. Don't wait—come quick!"

"Rubbage! I don't believe it!"

But she fled upstairs, nevertheless, with Sid and Mary at her heels. And her face grew white, too, and her lip trembled. When she reached the bedside she gasped out:

"You, Tom! Tom, what's the matter with you?"

"Oh, auntie, I'm——"

"What's the matter with you—what *is* the matter with you, child?"

"Oh, auntie, my sore toe's mortified!"

The old lady sank down into a chair and laughed a little, then cried a little, then did both together. This restored her and she said:

"Tom, what a turn you did give me. Now you shut up that nonsense and climb out of this."

The groans ceased and the pain vanished from the toe. The boy felt a little foolish, and he said:

"Aunt Polly, it *seemed* mortified, and it hurt so I never minded my tooth at all."

"Your tooth, indeed! What's the matter with your tooth?"

"One of them's loose, and it aches perfectly awful."

"There, there, now, don't begin that groaning again. Open your mouth. Well—your tooth *is* loose, but you're not going to die about that. Mary, get me a silk thread, and a chunk of fire out of the kitchen."

Tom said:

"Oh, please auntie, don't pull it out. It don't hurt any more. I wish I may never stir if it does. Please don't, auntie. *I* don't want to stay home from school."

"Oh, you don't, don't you? So all this row was because you thought you'd get to stay home from school and go a-fishing? Tom, Tom, I love you so, and you seem to try every way you can to break my old heart with your outrageousness." By this time the dental instruments were ready. The old lady made one end of the silk thread fast to Tom's tooth with a loop and tied the other to the bedpost. Then she seized the chunk of fire and suddenly thrust it almost into the boy's face. The tooth hung dangling by the bedpost, now.

But all trials bring their compensations. As Tom wended to school after breakfast, he was the envy of every boy he met because the gap in his upper row of teeth enabled him to expectorate in a new and admirable way. He gathered quite a following of lads interested in the exhibition; and one that had cut his finger and had been a center of fascination and homage up to this time, now found himself suddenly without an adherent, and shorn of his glory. His heart was heavy, and he said with a disdain which he did not feel, that it wasn't anything to spit like Tom Sawyer; but another boy said "Sour grapes!" and he wandered away a dismantled hero.

Shortly Tom came upon the juvenile pariah of the village, Huckleberry Finn, son of the town drunkard. Huckleberry was cordially hated and dreaded by all the mothers of the town, because he was idle and lawless and vulgar and bad—and because all their children admired him so, and delighted in his forbidden society, and wished they dared to be like him. Tom was like the rest of the respectable boys, in that he envied Huckleberry his gaudy outcast condition, and was under strict orders not to play with him. So he played with him every time he got a chance. Huckleberry was always dressed in the castoff clothes of full-grown men, and they were in perennial bloom and fluttering with rags. His hat was a vast ruin with a wide crescent lopped out of its brim; his coat, when he wore one, hung nearly to his heels and had the rearward buttons far down the back; but one suspender supported his trousers; the seat of the trousers bagged low and contained nothing; the fringed legs dragged in the dirt when not rolled up.

Huckleberry came and went, at his own free will. He slept on doorsteps in fine weather and in empty hogsheads in wet; he did not have to go to school or to church, or call any being master or obey anybody; he could go fishing or swimming when and where he chose, and stay as long as it suited him; nobody forbade him to fight; he could sit up as late as he pleased; he was always the first boy that went barefoot in the spring and the last to resume leather in the fall; he never had to wash, nor put on clean clothes; he could swear wonderfully. In a word, everything that goes to make life precious, that boy had. So thought every harassed, hampered, respectable boy in St. Petersburg.

Tom hailed the romantic outcast:

"Hello, Huckleberry!"

"Hello yourself, and see how you like it."

"What's that you got?"

"Dead cat."

"Lemme see him, Huck. My, he's pretty stiff. Where'd you get him?"

"Bought him off'n a boy."

"What did you give?"

"I give a blue ticket and a bladder that I got at the slaughterhouse."

"Where'd you get the blue ticket?"

"Bought it off'n Ben Rogers two weeks ago for a hoop-stick."

"Say—what is dead cats good for, Huck?"

"Good for. Cure warts with."

"No! Is that so? I know something that's better."

"I bet you don't. What is it?"

"Why, spunk-water."

"Spunk-water! I wouldn't give a dern for spunk-water."

"You wouldn't, wouldn't you? D'you ever try it?"

"No, I hain't. But Bob Tanner did."

"Who told you so?"

"Why, he told Jeff Thatcher, and Jeff told Johnny Baker, and Johnny told Jim Hollis, and Jim told Ben Rogers, and Ben told a nigger, and the nigger told me. There now!"

"Well, what of it? They'll all lie. Leastways all but the nigger. I don't know *him*. But I never see a nigger that *wouldn't* lie. Shucks! Now you tell me how Bob Tanner done it, Huck."

"Why, he took and dipped his hand in a rotten stump where the rain water was."

"In the daytime?"

"Certainly."

"With his face to the stump?"

"Yes. Least I reckon so."

"Did he *say* anything?"

"I don't reckon he did. I don't know."

"Aha! Talk about trying to cure warts with spunk-water such a blame fool way as that! Why, that ain't a-going to do any good. You got to go all by yourself, to the middle of the woods, where you know there's a spunk-water stump, and just as it's midnight you back up against the stump and jam your hand in and say:

> Barley-corn, Barley-corn, injun-meal shorts,
> Spunk-water, spunk-water, swaller these warts,

and then walk away quick, eleven steps, with your eyes

shut, and then turn around three times and walk home without speaking to anybody. Because if you speak the charm's busted."

"Well, that sounds like a good way; but that ain't the way Bob Tanner done."

"No, sir, you can bet he didn't, becuz he's the wartiest boy in this town; and he wouldn't have a wart on him if he'd knowed how to work spunk-water. I've took off thousands of warts off of my hands that way, Huck. I play with frogs so much that I've always got considerable many warts. Sometimes I take 'em off with a bean."

"Yes, bean's good. I've done that."

"Have you? What's your way?"

"You take and split the bean, and cut the wart so as to get some blood, and then you put the blood on one piece of the bean and take and dig a hole and bury it 'bout midnight at the crossroads in the dark of the moon, and then you burn up the rest of the bean. You see that piece that's got the blood on it will keep drawing and drawing, trying to fetch the other piece to it, and so that helps the blood to draw the wart, and pretty soon off she comes."

"Yes, that's it, Huck—that's it; though when you're burying it if you say 'Down bean; off wart; come no more to bother me!' it's better. That's the way Joe Harper does, and he's been nearly to Coonville and most everywheres. But say—how do you cure 'em with dead cats?"

"Why, you take your cat and go and get in the graveyard 'long about midnight when somebody that was wicked has been buried; and when it's midnight a devil will come, or maybe two or three, but you can't see 'em, you can only hear something like the wind, or maybe hear 'em talk; and when they're taking that feller away, you heave your cat after 'em and say, 'Devil follow corpse, cat follow devil, warts follow cat, *I*'m done with ye!' That'll fetch *any* wart."

"Sounds right. D'you ever try it, Huck?"

"No, but old Mother Hopkins told me."

"Well, I reckon it's so, then. Becuz they say she's a witch."

"Say! Why, Tom, I *know* she is. She witched pap. Pap says so his own self. He come along one day, and he sees she was a-witching him, so he took up a rock, and if she hadn't dodged, he'd a got her. Well, that very night he rolled off'n a shed wher' he was a-layin' drunk, and broke his arm."

"Why, that's awful. How did he know she was a-witching him?"

"Lord, pap can tell, easy. Pap says when they keep looking at you right stiddy, they're a-witching you. Specially if they mumble. Becuz when they mumble they're saying the Lord's Prayer backards."

"Say, Hucky, when you going to try the cat?"

"Tonight. I reckon they'll come after old Hoss Williams tonight."

"But they buried him Saturday. Didn't they get him Saturday night?"

"Why, how you talk! How could their charms work till midnight?—and *then* it's Sunday. Devils don't slosh around much of a Sunday, I don't reckon."

"I never thought of that. That's so. Lemme go with you?"

"Of course—if you ain't afeard."

"Afeard! 'Tain't likely .Will you meow?"

"Yes—and you meow back, if you get a chance. Last time, you kep' me a-meowing around till old Hays went to throwing rocks at me and says 'Dern that cat!' and so I hove a brick through his window—but don't you tell."

"I won't. I couldn't meow that night, becuz auntie was watching me, but I'll meow this time. Say—what's that?"

"Nothing but a tick."

"Where'd you get him?"

"Out in the woods."

"What'll you take for him?"

"I don't know. I don't want to sell him."

"All right. It's a mighty small tick, anyway."

"Oh, anybody can run a tick down that don't belong to them. I'm satisfied with it. It's a good enough tick for me."

"Sho, there's ticks a-plenty. I could have a thousand of 'em if I wanted to."

"Well, why don't you? Becuz you know mighty well you can't. This is a pretty early tick, I reckon. It's the first one I've seen this year."

"Say, Huck—I'll give you my tooth for him."

"Less see it."

Tom got out a bit of paper and carefully unrolled it. Huckleberry viewed it wistfully. The temptation was very strong. At last he said:

"Is it genuwyne?"

Tom lifted his lip and showed the vacancy.

"Well, all right," said Huckleberry, "it's a trade."

Tom enclosed the tick in the percussion-cap box that had lately been the pinch bug's prison, and the boys separated, each feeling wealthier than before.

When Tom reached the little isolated frame schoolhouse, he strode in briskly, with the manner of one who had come with all honest speed. He hung his hat on a peg and flung himself into his seat with businesslike alacrity. The master, throned on high in his great splint-bottom armchair, was dozing, lulled by the drowsy hum of study. The interruption roused him.

"Thomas Sawyer!"

Tom knew that when his name was pronounced in full, it meant trouble.

"Sir!"

"Come up here. Now, sir, why are you late again, as usual?"

Tom was about to take refuge in a lie, when he saw two long tails of yellow hair hanging down a back that he recognized by the electric sympathy of love; and by that form was *the only vacant place* on the girls' side of the schoolhouse. He instantly said:

"I STOPPED TO TALK WITH HUCKLEBERRY FINN!"

The master's pulse stood still, and he stared helplessly. The buzz of study ceased. The pupils wondered if this foolhardy boy had lost his mind. The master said:

"You—you did what?"

"Stopped to talk with Huckleberry Finn."

There was no mistaking the words.

"Thomas Sawyer, this is the most astounding confession I have ever listened to. No mere ferule will answer for this offense. Take off your jacket."

The master's arm performed until it was tired and the stock of switches notably diminished. Then the order followed:

"Now, sir, go and sit with the *girls*. And let this be a warning to you."

The titter that rippled around the room appeared to abash the boy, but in reality that result was caused rather more by his worshipful awe of his unknown idol and the dread pleasure that lay in his high good fortune. He sat down upon the end of the pine bench and the girl hitched herself away from him with a toss of her head. Nudges and winks and whispers traversed the room, but Tom sat still, with his arms upon the long, low desk before him, and seemed to study his book.

By and by attention ceased from him, and the accustomed school murmur rose upon the dull air once more. Presently the boy began to steal furtive glances at the girl. She observed it, "made a mouth" at him and gave him the back of her head for the space of a minute. When she cautiously faced around again, a peach lay before her. She thrust it away. Tom gently put it back. She thrust it away again, but with less animosity. Tom patiently returned it to its place. Then she let it remain. Tom scrawled on his slate, "Please take it—I got more." The girl glanced at the words, but made no sign. Now the boy began to draw something on the slate, hiding his work with his left hand. For a time the girl refused to notice; but her human curiosity presently began to manifest itself by hardly perceptible signs. The boy worked on, apparently unconscious. The girl made a sort of noncommittal attempt to see, but the boy did not betray that he was aware of it. At last she gave in and hesitatingly whispered:

"Let me see it."

Tom partly uncovered a dismal caricature of a house with two gable ends to it and a corkscrew of smoke issuing from the chimney. Then the girl's interest began to fasten itself upon the work and she forgot everything else. When it was finished, she gazed a moment, then whispered:

"It's nice—make a man."

The artist erected a man in the front yard, that resembled a derrick. He could have stepped over the house; but the girl was not hypercritical; she was satisfied with the monster, and whispered:

"It's a beautiful man—now make me coming along."

Tom drew an hourglass with a full moon and straw limbs to it and armed the spreading fingers with a portentous fan. The girl said:

"It's ever so nice—I wish I could draw."

"It's easy," whispered Tom, "I'll learn you."

"Oh, will you? When?"

"At noon. Do you go home to dinner?"

"I'll stay if you will."

"Good—that's a whack. What's your name?"

"Becky Thatcher. What's yours? Oh, I know. It's Thomas Sawyer."

"That's the name they lick me by. I'm Tom when I'm good. You call me Tom, will you?"

"Yes."

Now Tom began to scrawl something on the slate, hiding the words from the girl. But she was not backward this time. She begged to see. Tom said:

"Oh, it ain't anything."

"Yes it is."

"No it ain't. You don't want to see."

"Yes I do, indeed I do. Please let me."

"You'll tell."

"No I won't—deed and deed and double deed I won't."

"You won't tell anybody at all? Ever, as long as you live?"

"No, I won't ever tell *any*body. Now let me."

"Oh, *you* don't want to see!"

"Now that you treat me so, I *will* see." And she put her small hand upon his and a little scuffle ensued, Tom pretending to resist in earnest but letting his hand slip by degrees till these words were revealed: *"I love you."*

"Oh, you bad thing!" And she hit his hand a smart rap, but reddened and looked pleased, nevertheless.

Just at this juncture the boy felt a slow, fateful grip closing on his ear, and a steady lifting impulse. In that vise he was borne across the house and deposited in his own seat, under a peppering fire of giggles from the whole school. Then the master stood over him during a few awful moments, and finally moved away to his throne without saying a word. But although Tom's ear tingled, his heart was jubilant.

As the school quieted down Tom made an honest effort to study, but the turmoil within him was too great. In turn he took his place in the reading class and made a botch of it; then in the geography class and turned lakes into mountains, mountains into rivers, and rivers into continents, till chaos was come again; then in the spelling class, and got "turned down," by a succession of mere baby words, till he brought up at the foot and yielded up the pewter medal which he had worn with ostentation for months.

7 *A Treaty Entered Into—Early Lessons—A Mistake Made*

The harder Tom tried to fasten his mind on his book, the more his ideas wandered. So at last, with a sigh and a yawn, he gave it up. It seemed to him that the noon recess would never come. The air was utterly dead. There was not a breath stirring. It was the sleepiest of sleepy days. The drowsing murmur of the five and twenty studying scholars soothed the soul like the spell that is in the murmur of bees. Away off in the flaming sunshine, Cardiff Hill lifted its soft green sides through a shimmering veil of heat, tinted with the purple of distance; a few birds floated on lazy wing high in the air; no other living thing visible but some cows, and they were asleep. Tom's heart ached to be free, or else to have something of interest to do to pass the dreary time. His hand wandered into his pocket and his face lit up with a glow of gratitude that was prayer, though he did not know it. Then furtively the percussion-cap box came out. He released the tick and put him on the long flat desk. The creature probably glowed with a gratitude that amounted to prayer, too, at this moment, but it was premature: for when he started thankfully to travel off, Tom turned him aside with a pin and made him take a new direction.

Tom's bosom friend sat next him, suffering just as Tom had been, and now he was deeply and gratefully interested in this entertainment in an instant. This bosom friend was Joe Harper. The two boys were sworn friends all the week, and embattled enemies on Saturdays. Joe took a pin out of his lapel and began to assist in exercising the prisoner. The sport grew in interest momently. Soon Tom said that they were interfering with each other, and neither getting the fullest benefit of the tick. So he put Joe's slate on the desk and drew a line down the middle of it from top to bottom.

"Now," said he, "as long as he is on your side you can stir him up and I'll let him alone; but if you let him get away and get on my side, you're to leave him alone as long as I can keep him from crossing over."

"All right, go ahead; start him up."

The tick escaped from Tom, presently, and crossed the equator. Joe harassed him a while, and then he got away and crossed back again. This change of base occurred often. While one boy was worrying the tick with absorbing interest, the other would look on with interest as strong, the two heads bowed together over the slate, and the two souls dead to all things else. At last luck seemed to settle and abide with Joe. The tick tried this, that, and the other course, and got as excited and as anxious as the boys themselves, but time and again just as he would have victory in his very grasp, so to speak, and Tom's fingers would be twitching to begin, Joe's pin would deftly head him off, and keep possession. At last Tom could stand it no longer. The temptation was too strong. So he reached out and lent a hand with his pin. Joe was angry in a moment. Said he:

"Tom, you let him alone."

"I only just want to stir him up a little, Joe."

"No, sir, it ain't fair; you just let him alone."

"Blame it, I ain't going to stir him much."

"Let him alone, I tell you."

"I won't!"

"You shall—he's on my side of the line."

"Look here, Joe Harper, whose is that tick?"

"*I* don't care whose tick he is—he's on my side of the line, and you shan't touch him."

"Well, I'll just bet I will, though. He's my tick and I'll do what I blame please with him, or die!"

A tremendous whack came down on Tom's shoulders, and its duplicate on Joe's; and for the space of two minutes the dust continued to fly from the two jackets and the whole school to enjoy it. The boys had been too absorbed to notice the hush that had stolen upon the school a while before when the master came tiptoeing down the room and stood over them. He had contemplated a good part of the performance before he contributed his bit of variety to it.

When school broke up at noon, Tom flew to Becky Thatcher, and whispered in her ear:

"Put on your bonnet and let on you're going home; and when you get to the corner, give the rest of 'em the slip, and turn down through the lane and come back. I'll go the other way and come it over 'em the same way."

So the one went off with one group of scholars, and the other with another. In a little while the two met at the bottom of the lane, and when they reached the school they had it all to themselves. Then they sat together, with a slate before them, and Tom gave Becky the pencil and held her hand in his, guiding it, and so created another surprising house. When the interest in art began to wane, the two fell to talking. Tom was swimming in bliss. He said:

"Do you love rats?"

"No! I hate them!"

"Well, I do, too—*live* ones. But I mean dead ones, to swing round your head with a string."

"No, I don't care for rats much, anyway. What *I* like is chewing gum."

"Oh, I should say so! I wish I had some now."

"Do you? I've got some. I'll let you chew it awhile, but you must give it back to me."

That was agreeable, so they chewed it turn about, and dangled their legs against the bench in excess of contentment.

"Was you ever at a circus?" said Tom.

"Yes, and my pa's going to take me again some time, if I'm good."

"I been to the circus three or four times—lots of times. Church ain't shucks to a circus. There's things going on at a circus all the time. I'm going to be a clown in a circus when I grow up."

"Oh, are you! That will be nice. They're so lovely, all spotted up."

"Yes, that's so. And they get slathers of money—most a dollar a day, Ben Rogers says. Say, Becky, was you ever engaged?"

"What's that?"

"Why, engaged to be married."

"No."

"Would you like to?"

"I reckon so. I don't know. What is it like?"

"Like? Why it ain't like anything. You only just tell a boy you won't ever have anybody but him, ever ever *ever,* and then you kiss and that's all. Anybody can do it."

"Kiss? What do you kiss for?"

"Why, that, you know, is to—well, they always do that."

"Everybody?"

"Why, yes, everybody that's in love with each other. Do you remember what I wrote on the slate?"

"Ye—yes."

"What was it?"

"I shan't tell you."

"Shall I tell *you?*"

"Ye—yes—but some other time."

"No, now."

"No, not now—tomorrow."

"Oh, no, *now*. Please, Becky—I'll whisper it, I'll whisper it ever so easy."

Becky hesitating, Tom took silence for consent, and passed his arm about her waist and whispered the tale ever so softly, with his mouth close to her ear. And then he added:

"Now you whisper it to me—just the same."

She resisted, for a while, and then said:

"You turn your face away so you can't see, and then I will. But you mustn't ever tell anybody—*will* you, Tom? Now you won't, *will* you?"

"No, indeed, indeed I won't. Now, Becky."

He turned his face away. She bent timidly around till her breath stirred his curls and whispered, "I—love—you!"

Then she sprang away and ran around and around the desks and benches, with Tom after her, and took refuge in a corner at last, with her little white apron to her face. Tom clasped her about her neck and pleaded:

"Now, Becky, it's all done—all over but the kiss. Don't you be afraid of that—it ain't anything at all. Please, Becky." And he tugged at her apron and the hands.

By and by she gave up, and let her hands drop; her face, all glowing with the struggle, came up and submitted. Tom kissed the red lips and said:

"Now it's all done, Becky. And always after this, you know, you ain't ever to love anybody but me, and you ain't ever to marry anybody but me, never never and forever. Will you?"

"No, I'll never love anybody but you, Tom, and I'll never marry anybody but you—and you ain't to ever marry anybody but me, either."

"Certainly. Of course. That's *part* of it. And always coming to school or when we're going home, you're to walk with me, when there ain't anybody looking—and you choose me and I choose you at parties, because that's the way you do when you're engaged."

"It's so nice. I never heard of it before."

"Oh, it's ever so gay! Why, me and Amy Lawrence——"

The big eyes told Tom his blunder and he stopped, confused.

"Oh, Tom! Then I ain't the first you've ever been engaged to!"

The child began to cry. Tom said:

"Oh, don't cry, Becky, I don't care for her any more."

"Yes, you do, Tom—you know you do."

Tom tried to put his arm about her neck, but she pushed him away and turned her face to the wall, and went on crying. Tom tried again, with soothing words in his mouth, and was repulsed again. Then his pride was up, and he strode away and went outside. He stood about, restless and uneasy, for a while, glancing at the door, every now and then, hoping she would repent and come to find him. But she did not. Then he began to feel badly and fear that he was in the wrong. It was a hard struggle with him to make new advances, now, but he nerved himself to it and entered. She was still standing back there in the corner, sobbing, with her face to the wall. Tom's heart smote him. He went to her and stood a moment, not knowing exactly how to proceed. Then he said hesitatingly:

"Becky, I—I don't care for anybody but you."

No reply—but sobs.

"Becky"—pleadingly. "Becky, won't you say something?"

More sobs.

Tom got out his chiefest jewel, a brass knob from the top

of an andiron, and passed it around her so that she could see it, and said:

"Please, Becky, won't you take it?"

She struck it to the floor. Then Tom marched out of the house and over the hills and far away, to return to school no more that day. Presently Becky began to suspect. She ran to the door; he was not in sight; she flew around to the play yard; he was not there. Then she called:

"Tom! Come back, Tom!"

She listened intently, but there was no answer. She had no companions but silence and loneliness. So she sat down to cry again and upbraid herself; and by this time the scholars began to gather again, and she had to hide her griefs and still her broken heart and take up the cross of a long, dreary, aching afternoon, with none among the strangers about her to exchange sorrows with.

8 *Tom Decides on His Course—Old Scenes Re-enacted*

Tom dodged hither and thither through lanes until he was well out of the track of returning scholars, and then fell into a moody jog. He crossed a small "branch" two or three times, because of a prevailing juvenile superstition that to cross water baffled pursuit. Half an hour later he was disappearing behind the Douglas mansion on the summit of Cardiff Hill, and the schoolhouse was hardly distinguishable away off in the valley behind him. He entered a dense wood, picked his pathless way to the center of it, and sat down on a mossy spot under a spreading oak. There was not even a zephyr stirring; the dead noonday heat had even stilled the songs of the birds; nature lay in a trance that was broken by no sound but the occasional far-off hammering of a woodpecker, and this seemed to render the pervading silence and sense of loneliness the more profound. The boy's soul was steeped in melancholy; his feelings were in happy accord with his surroundings. He sat long with his elbows on his knees and his chin in his hands, meditating. It seemed to him that life was but a trouble, at best, and he more than half envied Jimmy Hodges, so lately released; it must be very peaceful, he thought, to lie and slumber and dream forever and ever, with the wind whispering through the trees and caressing the grass and the flowers over the grave, and nothing to bother and grieve about, ever any more. If he only had a clean Sunday-school record he could be willing to go, and be done with it all. Now as to this girl. What had he done? Nothing. He had meant the best in the world, and been treated like a dog—like a very dog. She would be sorry some day—maybe when it was too late. Ah, if he could only die *temporarily!*

But the elastic heart of youth cannot be compressed into one constrained shape long at a time. Tom presently began to drift insensibly back into the concerns of this life again. What if he turned his back, now, and disappeared mysteriously? What if he went away—ever so far away, into unknown countries beyond the seas—and never came back any more! How would she feel then! The idea of being a clown recurred to him now, only to fill him with disgust. For frivolity and jokes and spotted tights were an offense, when they intruded themselves upon a spirit that was exalted into the vague august realm of the romantic. No, he would be a soldier, and return after long years, all warworn and illustrious. No—better still, he would join the Indians, and hunt buffaloes and go on the warpath in the mountain ranges and the trackless great plains of the Far West, and away in the future come back a great chief, bristling with feathers, hideous with paint, and prance into Sunday school, some drowsy summer morning, with a bloodcurdling war whoop, and sear the eyeballs of all his companions with unappeasable envy. But no, there was something gaudier even than this. He would be a pirate! That was it! *Now* his future lay plain before him, and glowing with unimaginable splendor. How his name would fill the world, and make people shudder! How gloriously he would go plowing the dancing seas, in his long, low, black-hulled racer, the *Spirit of the Storm,* with his grisly flag flying at the fore! And at the zenith of his fame, how he would suddenly appear at the old village and stalk into church, brown and weather-beaten, in his black velvet doublet and trunks, his great jackboots, his crimson sash, his belt bristling with horse pistols, his crime-rusted cutlass at his side, his slouch hat with waving plumes, his black flag unfurled, with the skull and crossbones on it, and hear with swelling ecstasy the whisperings, "It's Tom Sawyer the Pirate!—the Black Avenger of the Spanish Main!"

Yes, it was settled; his career was determined. He would run away from home and enter upon it. He would start the very next morning. Therefore he must now begin to get ready. He would collect his resources together. He went to a rotten log near at hand and began to dig under one end of it with his Barlow knife. He soon struck wood that sounded hollow. He put his hand there and uttered this incantation impressively:

"What hasn't come here, *come!* What's here, *stay* here!"

Then he scraped away the dirt, and exposed a pine shingle. He took it up and disclosed a shapely little treasure house whose bottom and sides were of shingles. In it lay a marble. Tom's astonishment was boundless! He scratched his head with a perplexed air, and said:

"Well, that beats anything!"

Then he tossed the marble away pettishly, and stood cogitating. The truth was, that a superstition of his had failed, here, which he and all his comrades had always looked upon as infallible. If you buried a marble with certain necessary incantations, and left it alone a fortnight, and then opened the place with the incantation he had just used, you would find that all the marbles you had ever lost had gathered themselves together there, meantime, no matter how widely they had been separated. But now, this thing had actually and unquestionably failed. Tom's whole structure of faith was shaken to its foundations. He had many a time heard of this thing succeeding, but never of its failing before. It did not occur to him that he had tried it several times before, himself, but could never find the hiding places afterward. He puzzled over the matter some time, and finally decided that some witch had interfered and broken the charm. He thought he would satisfy himself on that point; so he searched around till he found a small sandy spot with a little funnel-shaped depression in it. He laid himself down and put his mouth close to this depression and called:

"Doodlebug, doodlebug, tell me what I want to know! Doodlebug, doodlebug, tell me what I want to know!"

The sand began to work, and presently a small black bug appeared for a second and then darted under again in a fright.

"He dasn't tell! So it *was* a witch that done it. I just knowed it."

He well knew the futility of trying to contend against witches, so he gave up discouraged. But it occurred to him that he might as well have the marble he had just thrown away, and therefore he went and made a patient search for it. But he could not find it. Now he went back to his treasure house and carefully placed himself just as he had been standing when he tossed the marble away; then he took another marble from his pocket and tossed it in the same way, saying:

"Brother, go find your brother!"

He watched where it stopped, and went there and looked. But it must have fallen short or gone too far; so he tried twice more. The last repetition was successful. The two marbles lay within a foot of each other.

Just here the blast of a toy tin trumpet came faintly down the green aisles of the forest. Tom flung off his jacket and trousers, turned a suspender into a belt, raked away some brush behind the rotten log, disclosing a rude bow and arrow, a lath sword and a tin trumpet, and in a moment had seized these things and bounded away, barelegged, with fluttering shirt. He presently halted under a great elm, blew an answering blast, and then began to tiptoe and look warily out, this way and that. He said cautiously—to an imaginary company:

"Hold, my merry men! Keep hid till I blow."

Now appeared Joe Harper, as airily clad and elaborately armed as Tom. Tom called:

"Hold! Who comes here into Sherwood Forest without my pass?"

"Guy of Guisborne wants no man's pass. Who art thou that—that——"

"Dares to hold such language," said Tom, prompting—for they talked "by the book," from memory.

"Who art thou that dares to hold such language?"

"I, indeed! I am Robin Hood, as thy caitiff carcase soon shall know."

"Then art thou indeed that famous outlaw? Right gladly will I dispute with thee the passes of the merry wood. Have at thee!"

They took their lath swords, dumped their other traps on the ground, struck a fencing attitude, foot to foot, and began a grave, careful combat, "two up and two down." Presently Tom said:

"Now, if you've got the hang, go it lively!"

So they "went it lively," panting and perspiring with the work. By and by Tom shouted:

"Fall! fall! Why don't you fall?"

"I shan't! Why don't you fall yourself? You're getting the worst of it."

"Why, that ain't anything. *I* can't fall; that ain't the way it is in the book. The book says, 'Then with one back-handed stroke he slew poor Guy of Guisborne.' You're to turn around and let me hit you in the back."

There was no getting around the authorities, so Joe turned, received the whack and fell.

"Now," said Joe, getting up, "you got to let me kill *you*. That's fair."

"Why, I can't do that, it ain't in the book."

"Well, it's blamed mean—that's all."

"Well, say, Joe, you can be Friar Tuck or Much the miller's son, and lam me with a quarterstaff; or I'll be the Sheriff of Nottingham and you be Robin Hood a little while and kill me."

This was satisfactory, and so these adventures were carried out. Then Tom became Robin Hood again, and was allowed by the treacherous nun to bleed his strength away through his neglected wound. And at last Joe, representing a whole tribe of weeping outlaws, dragged him sadly forth, gave his bow into his feeble hands, and Tom said, "Where this arrow falls, there bury poor Robin Hood under the greenwood tree." Then he shot the arrow and fell back and would have died, but he lit on a nettle and sprang up too gaily for a corpse.

The boys dressed themselves, hid their accouterments, and went off grieving that there were no outlaws any more, and wondering what modern civilization could claim to have done to compensate for their loss. They said they would rather be outlaws a year in Sherwood Forest than President of the United States forever.

9 *A Solemn Situation—Grave Subjects Introduced—Injun Joe Explains*

At half past nine, that night, Tom and Sid were sent to bed, as usual. They said their prayers, and Sid was soon asleep. Tom lay awake and waited, in restless impatience. When it seemed to him that it must be nearly daylight, he heard the clock strike ten! This was despair. He would have tossed and fidgeted, as his nerves demanded, but he was afraid he might wake Sid. So he lay still, and stared up into the dark. Everything was dismally still. By and by, out of the stillness, little, scarcely perceptible noises began to emphasize themselves. The ticking of the clock began to bring itself into notice. Old beams began to crack mysteriously. The stairs creaked faintly. Evidently spirits were abroad. A measured, muffled snore issued from Aunt Polly's chamber. And now the tiresome chirping of a cricket that no human ingenuity could locate, began. Next the ghastly ticking of a deathwatch in the wall at the bed's head made Tom shudder—it meant that somebody's days were numbered. Then the howl of a far-off dog rose on the night air, and was answered by a fainter howl from a remoter distance. Tom was in an agony. At last he was satisfied that time had ceased and eternity begun; he began to doze, in spite of himself; the clock chimed eleven, but he did not hear it. And then there came, mingling with his half-formed dreams, a most melancholy caterwauling. The raising of a neighboring window disturbed him. A cry of "Scat! you devil!" and the crash of an empty bottle against the back of his aunt's woodshed brought him wide awake, and a single minute later he was dressed and out of the window and creeping along the roof of the "ell" on all fours. He "meow'd" with caution once or twice, as he went; then jumped to the roof of the woodshed and thence to the ground. Huckleberry Finn was there, with his dead cat. The boys moved off and disappeared in the gloom. At the end of half an hour they were wading through the tall grass of the graveyard.

It was a graveyard of the old-fashioned Western kind. It was on a hill, about a mile and a half from the village. It had a crazy board fence around it, which leaned inward in places, and outward the rest of the time, but stood upright nowhere. Grass and weeds grew rank over the whole cemetery. All the old graves were sunken in, there was not a tombstone on the place; round-topped, worm-eaten boards staggered over the graves, leaning for support and finding none. "Sacred to the memory of" So-and-So had been painted on them once, but it could no longer have been read, on the most of them, now, even if there had been light.

A faint wind moaned through the trees, and Tom feared it might be the spirits of the dead, complaining at being disturbed. The boys talked little, and only under their breath, for the time and the place and the pervading solemnity and silence oppressed their spirits. They found the sharp new heap they were seeking, and ensconced themselves within the protection of three great elms that grew in a bunch within a few feet of the grave.

Then they waited in silence for what seemed a long time. The hooting of a distant owl was all the sound that troubled the dead stillness. Tom's reflections grew oppressive. He must force some talk. So he said in a whisper:

"Hucky, do you believe the dead people like it for us to be here?"

Huckleberry whispered:

"I wisht I knowed. It's awful solemn like, *ain't* it?"

"I bet it is."

There was a considerable pause, while the boys canvassed this matter inwardly. Then Tom whispered:

"Say, Hucky—do you reckon Hoss Williams hears us talking?"

"O' course he does. Least his sperrit does."

Tom, after a pause:

"I wish I'd said *Mister* Williams. But I never meant any harm. Everybody calls him Hoss."

"A body can't be too partic'lar how they talk 'bout these-yer dead people, Tom."

This was a damper, and conversation died again.

Presently Tom seized his comrade's arm and said:

"Sh!"

"What is it, Tom?" And the two clung together with beating hearts.

"Sh! There 'tis again! Didn't you hear it?"

"I——"

"There! Now you hear it."

"Lord, Tom, they're coming! They're coming, sure. What'll we do?"

"I dono. Think they'll see us?"

"Oh, Tom, they can see in the dark, same as cats. I wisht I hadn't come."

"Oh, don't be afeard. *I* don't believe they'll bother us. We ain't doing any harm. If we keep perfectly still, maybe they won't notice us at all."

"I'll try to, Tom, but Lord, I'm all of a shiver."

"Listen!"

The boys bent their heads together and scarcely breathed. A muffled sound of voices floated up from the far end of the graveyard.

"Look! See there!" whispered Tom. "What is it?"

"It's a devil-fire. Oh, Tom, this is awful."

Some vague figures approached through the gloom, swinging an old-fashioned tin lantern that freckled the ground with innumerable little spangles of light. Presently Huckleberry whispered with a shudder:

"It's the devils sure enough. Three of 'em! Lordy, Tom, we're goners! Can you pray?"

"I'll try, but don't you be afeard. They ain't going to hurt us. Now I lay me down to sleep, I—"

"Sh!"

"What is it, Huck?"

"They're *humans!* One of 'em is, anyway. One of 'em's old Muff Potter's voice."

"No—'tain't so, is it?"

"I bet I know it. Don't you stir nor budge. *He* ain't sharp enough to notice us. Drunk, the same as usual, likely—blamed old rip!"

"All right, I'll keep still. Now they're stuck. Can't find it. Here they come again. Now they're hot. Cold again. Hot again. Red hot! They're p'inted right, this time. Say, Huck, I know another o' them voices; it's Injun Joe."

"That's so—that murderin' half-breed! I'd druther they was devils a dern sight. What kin they be up to?"

The whisper died wholly out, now, for the three men had

reached the grave and stood within a few feet of the boys' hiding place.

"Here it is," said the third voice; and the owner of it held the lantern up and revealed the face of young Dr. Robinson.

Potter and Injun Joe were carrying a handbarrow with a rope and a couple of shovels on it. They cast down their load and began to open the grave. The doctor put the lantern at the head of the grave and came and sat down with his back against one of the elm trees. He was so close the boys could have touched him.

"Hurry, men!" he said in a low voice; "the moon might come out at any moment."

They growled a response and went on digging. For some time there was no noise but the grating sound of the shovels discharging their freight of mould and gravel. It was very monotonous. Finally a spade struck upon the coffin with a dull woody accent, and within another minute or two the men had hoisted it out on the ground. They pried off the lid with their shovels, got out the body and dumped it rudely on the ground. The moon drifted from behind the clouds and exposed the pallid face. The barrow was got ready and the corpse placed on it, covered with a blanket, and bound to its place with the rope. Potter took out a large spring-knife and cut off the dangling end of the rope and then said:

"Now the cussed thing's ready, Sawbones, and you'll just out with another five, or here she stays."

"That's the talk!" said Injun Joe.

"Look here, what does this mean?" said the doctor. "You required your pay in advance, and I've paid you."

"Yes, and you done more than that," said Injun Joe, approaching the doctor, who was now standing. "Five years ago you drove me away from your father's kitchen one night, when I come to ask for something to eat, and you said I warn't there for any good; and when I swore I'd get even with you if it took a hundred years, your father had me jailed for a vagrant. Did you think I'd forget? The Injun blood ain't in me for nothing. And now I've *got* you, and you got to *settle*, you know!"

He was threatening the doctor, with his fist in his face, by this time. The doctor struck out suddenly and stretched the ruffian on the ground. Potter dropped his knife, and exclaimed:

"Here, now, don't you hit my pard!" and the next moment he had grappled with the doctor and the two were struggling with might and main, trampling the grass and tearing the ground with their heels. Injun Joe sprang to his feet, his eyes flaming with passion, snatched up Potter's knife, and went creeping, catlike and stooping, round and round about the combatants, seeking an opportunity. All at once the doctor flung himself free, seized the heavy headboard of Williams' grave and felled Potter to the earth with it—and in the same instant the half-breed saw his chance and drove the knife to the hilt in the young man's breast. He reeled and fell partly upon Potter, flooding him with his blood, and in the same moment the clouds blotted out the dreadful spectacle and the two frightened boys went speeding away in the dark.

Presently, when the moon emerged again, Injun Joe was standing over the two forms, contemplating them. The doctor murmured inarticulately, gave a long gasp or two and was still. The half-breed muttered:

"*That* score is settled—damn you."

Then he robbed the body. After which he put the fatal knife in Potter's open right hand, and sat down on the dismantled coffin. Three—four—five minutes passed, and then Potter began to stir and moan. His hand closed upon the knife; he raised it, glanced at it, and let it fall, with a shudder. Then he sat up, pushing the body from him, and gazed at it, and then around him, confusedly. His eyes met Joe's.

"Lord, how is this, Joe?" he said.

"It's a dirty business," said Joe, without moving. "What did you do it for?"

"I! I never done it!"

"Look here! That kind of talk won't wash."

Potter trembled and grew white.

"I thought I'd got sober. I'd no business to drink tonight. But it's in my head yet—worse'n when we started here. I'm all in a muddle; can't recollect anything of it, hardly. Tell me, Joe—*honest*, now, old feller—did I do it? Joe, I never meant to—'pon my soul and honor, I never meant to, Joe. Tell me how it was, Joe. Oh, it's awful—and him so young and promising."

"Why, you two was scuffling, and he fetched you one with the headboard and you fell flat; and then up you come, all reeling and staggering, like, and snatched the knife and jammed it into him, just as he fetched you another awful clip—and here you've laid, as dead as a wedge till now."

"Oh, I didn't know what I was a-doing. I wish I may die this minute if I did. It was all on account of the whisky; and the excitement, I reckon. I never used a weepon in my life before, Joe. I've fought, but never with weepons. They'll all say that. Joe, don't tell! Say you won't tell, Joe —that's a good feller. I always liked you, Joe, and stood up for you, too. Don't you remember? You *won't* tell, *will* you Joe?" And the poor creature dropped on his knees before the stolid murderer, and clasped his appealing hands.

"No, you've always been fair and square with me, Muff Potter, and I won't go back on you. There, now, that's as fair as a man can say."

"Oh, Joe, you're an angel. I'll bless you for this the longest day I live." And Potter began to cry.

"Come, now, that's enough of that. This ain't any time for blubbering. You be off yonder way and I'll go this. Move, now, and don't leave any tracks behind you."

Potter started on a trot that quickly increased to a run. The half-breed stood looking after him. He muttered:

"If he's as much stunned with the lick and fuddled with the rum as he had the look of being, he won't think of the knife till he's gone so far he'll be afraid to come back after it to such a place by himself—chicken heart!"

Two or three minutes later the murdered man, the blanketed corpse, the lidless coffin, and the open grave were under no inspection but the moon's. The stillness was complete again, too.

10 *A Solemn Oath—Terror Brings Repentance—Mental Punishment*

The two boys flew on and on, toward the village, speechless with horror. They glanced backward over their shoulders from time to time, apprehensively, as if they feared they might be followed. Every stump that started up in their path seemed a man and an enemy, and made them catch their breath; and as they sped by some outlying cottages that lay near the village, the barking of the aroused watchdogs seemed to give wings to their feet.

"If we can only get to the old tannery before we break down!" whispered Tom, in short catches between breaths, "I can't stand it much longer."

Huckleberry's hard pantings were his only reply, and the boys fixed their eyes on the goal of their hopes and bent to their work to win it. They gained steadily on it, and at last, breast to breast, they burst through the open door and fell grateful and exhausted in the sheltering shadows beyond. By and by their pulses slowed down, and Tom whispered:

"Huckleberry, what do you reckon 'll come of this?"

"If Dr. Robinson dies, I reckon hanging 'll come of it."

"Do you though?"

"Why, I *know* it, Tom."

Tom thought a while, then he said:

"Who'll tell? We?"

"What are you talking about? S'pose something happened and Injun Joe *didn't* hang? Why he'd kill us some time or other, just as dead sure as we're a-laying here."

"That's just what I was thinking to myself, Huck."

"If anybody tells, let Muff Potter do it, if he's fool enough. He's generally drunk enough."

Tom said nothing—went on thinking. Presently he whispered:

"Huck, Muff Potter don't *know* it. How can he tell?"

"What's the reason he don't know it?"

"Because he'd just got that whack when Injun Joe done it. D' you reckon he could see anything? D' you reckon he knowed anything?"

"By hokey, that's so, Tom!"

"And besides, look-a-here—maybe that whack done for *him!*"

"No, 'tain't likely, Tom. He had liquor in him; I could see that; and besides, he always has. Well, when pap's full, you might take and belt him over the head with a church and you couldn't faze him. He says so, his own self. So it's the same with Muff Potter, of course. But if a man was dead sober, I reckon maybe that whack might fetch him; I dono."

After another reflective silence, Tom said:

"Hucky, you sure you can keep mum?"

"Tom, we *got* to keep mum. *You* know that. That Injun devil wouldn't make any more of drownding us than a couple of cats, if we was to squeak 'bout this and they didn't hang him. Now, look-a-here, Tom, less take and swear to one another—that's what we got to do—swear to keep mum."

"I'm agreed. It's the best thing. Would you just hold hands and swear that we—"

"Oh, no, that wouldn't do for this. That's good enough for little rubbishy common things—specially with gals, cuz *they* go back on you anyway, and blab if they get in a huff—but there orter be writing 'bout a big thing like this. And blood."

Tom's whole being applauded this idea. It was deep, and dark, and awful; the hour, the circumstances, the surroundings, were in keeping with it. He picked up a clean pine shingle that lay in the moonlight, took a little fragment of "red keel" out of his pocket, got the moon on his work, and painfully scrawled these lines, emphasizing each slow down-stroke by clamping his tongue between his teeth, and letting up the pressure on the upstrokes.

"Huck Finn and
Tom Sawyer swears
they will keep mum
about This and They
wish They may Drop
down dead in Their
tracks if They ever
tell and Rot."

Huckleberry was filled with admiration of Tom's facility in writing, and the sublimity of his language. He at once took a pin from his lapel and was going to prick his flesh, but Tom said:

"Hold on! Don't do that. A pin's brass. It might have verdigrease on it."

"What's verdigrease?"

"It's p'ison. That's what it is. You just swaller some of it once—you'll see."

So Tom unwound the thread from one of his needles, and each boy pricked the ball of his thumb and squeezed out a drop of blood. In time, after many squeezes, Tom managed to sign his initials, using the ball of his little finger for a pen. Then he showed Huckleberry how to make an H and an F, and the oath was complete. They buried the shingle close to the wall, with some dismal ceremonies and incantations, and the fetters that bound their tongues were considered to be locked and the key thrown away.

A figure crept stealthily through a break in the other end of the ruined building, now, but they did not notice it.

"Tom," whispered Huckleberry, "does this keep us from *ever* telling—*always?*"

"Of course it does. It don't make any difference *what* happens, we got to keep mum. We'd drop down dead—don't *you* know that?"

"Yes, I reckon that's so."

They continued to whisper for some little time. Presently a dog set up a long, lugubrious howl just outside—within ten feet of them. The boys clasped each other suddenly, in an agony of fright.

"Which of us does he mean?" gasped Huckleberry.

"I duno—peep through the crack. Quick!"

"No, *you*, Tom!"

"I can't—I can't do it, Huck!"

"Please, Tom. There 'tis again!"

"Oh, lordy, I'm thankful!" whispered Tom. "I know his voice. It's Bull Harbison."[1]

"Oh, that's good—I tell you, Tom, I was most scared to death; I'd a bet anything it was a *stray* dog."

The dog howled again. The boys' hearts sank once more.

"Oh, my! that ain't no Bull Harbison!" whispered Huckleberry. "*Do*, Tom!"

Tom, quaking with fear, yielded, and put his eye to the crack. His whisper was hardly audible when he said: "Oh, Huck, IT'S A STRAY DOG!"

"Quick, Tom, quick! Who does he mean?"

[1] If Mr. Harbison had owned a slave named Bull, Tom would have spoken of him as "Harbison's Bull," but a son or a dog of that name was "Bull Harbison."

"Huck, he must mean us both—we're right together."

"Oh, Tom, I reckon we're goners. I reckon there ain't no mistake 'bout where *I'll* go to. I been so wicked."

"Dad fetch it! This comes of playing hooky and doing everything a feller's told *not* to do. I might a been good, like Sid, if I'd a tried—but no, I wouldn't, of course. But if ever I get off this time, I lay I'll just *waller* in Sunday schools!" And Tom began to snuffle a little.

"*You* bad!" and Huckleberry began to snuffle too. "Consound it, Tom Sawyer, you're just old pie, 'longside o'what *I* am. Oh, *lordy*, lordy, lordy, I wisht I only had half your chance."

Tom choked off and whispered:

"Look, Hucky, look! He's got his *back* to us!"

Hucky looked, with joy in his heart.

"Well, he has, by jingoes! Did he before?"

"Yes, he did. But I, like a fool, never thought. Oh, this is bully, you know. *Now* who can he mean?"

The howling stopped. Tom pricked up his ears.

"Sh! What's that?" he whispered.

"Sounds like—like hogs grunting. No—it's somebody snoring, Tom."

"That *is* it! Where 'bouts is it, Huck?"

"I bleeve it's down at 'tother end. Sounds so, anyway. Pap used to sleep there, sometimes, 'long with the hogs, but laws bless you, he just lifts things when *he* snores. Besides, I reckon he ain't ever coming back to this town any more."

The spirit of adventure rose in the boys' souls once more.

"Hucky, do you das't to go if I lead?"

"I don't like to, much. Tom, s'pose it's Injun Joe!"

Tom quailed. But presently the temptation rose up strong again and the boys agreed to try, with the understanding that they would take to their heels if the snoring stopped. So they went tiptoeing stealthily down, the one behind the other. When they had got to within five steps of the snorer, Tom stepped on a stick, and it broke with a sharp snap. The man moaned, writhed a little, and his face came into the moonlight. It was Muff Potter. The boys' hearts had stood still, and their hopes too, when the man moved, but their fears passed away now. They tiptoed out, through the broken weatherboarding, and stopped at a little distance to exchange a parting word. That long, lugubrious howl rose on the night air again! They turned and saw the strange dog standing within a few feet of where Potter was lying, and *facing* Potter, with his nose pointing heavenward.

"Oh, geeminy, it's *him!*" exclaimed both boys, in a breath.

"Say, Tom—they say a stray dog come howling around Johnny Miller's house, 'bout midnight, as much as two weeks ago; and a whippoorwill come in and lit on the banisters and sung, the very same evening; and there ain't anybody dead there yet."

"Well, I know that. And suppose there ain't. Didn't Gracie Miller fall in the kitchen fire and burn herself terrible the very next Saturday?"

"Yes, but she ain't *dead*. And what's more, she's getting better, too."

"All right, you wait and see. She's a goner, just as dead sure as Muff Potter's a goner. That's what the niggers say, and they know all about these kind of things, Huck."

Then they separated, cogitating. When Tom crept in at his bedroom window the night was almost spent. He undressed with excessive caution, and fell asleep congratulating himself that nobody knew of his escapade. He was not aware that the gently-snoring Sid was awake, and had been so for an hour.

When Tom awoke, Sid was dressed and gone. There was a late look in the light, a late sense in the atmosphere. He was startled. Why had he not been called—persecuted till he was up, as usual? The thought filled him with bodings. Within five minutes he was dressed and downstairs, feeling sore and drowsy. The family were still at table, but they had finished breakfast. There was no voice of rebuke; but there were averted eyes; there was a silence and an air of solemnity that struck a chill to the culprit's heart. He sat down and tried to seem gay, but it was uphill work; it roused no smile, no response, and he lapsed into silence and let his heart sink down to the depths.

After breakfast his aunt took him aside, and Tom almost brightened in the hope that he was going to be flogged; but it was not so. His aunt wept over him and asked him how he could go and break her old heart so; and finally told him to go on, and ruin himself and bring her gray hairs with sorrow to the grave, for it was no use for her to try any more. This was worse than a thousand whippings, and Tom's heart was sorer now than his body. He cried, he pleaded for forgiveness, promised to reform over and over again, and then received his dismissal, feeling that he had won but an imperfect forgiveness and established but a feeble confidence.

He left the presence too miserable to even feel revengeful toward Sid; and so the latter's prompt retreat through the back gate was unnecessary. He moped to school gloomy and sad, and took his flogging, along with Joe Harper, for playing hooky the day before, with the air of one whose heart was busy with heavier woes and wholly dead to trifles. Then he betook himself to his seat, rested his elbows on his desk and his jaws in his hands, and stared at the wall with the stony stare of suffering that has reached the limit and can no further go. His elbow was pressing against some hard substance. After a long time he slowly and sadly changed his position, and took up this object with a sigh. It was in a paper. He unrolled it. A long, lingering, colossal sigh followed, and his heart broke. It was his brass andiron knob!

This final feather broke the camel's back.

11 *Muff Potter Comes Himself—Tom's Conscience at Work*

Close upon the hour of noon the whole village was suddenly electrified with the ghastly news. No need of the as yet undreamed-of telegraph; the tale flew from man to man, from group to group, from house to house, with little less than telegraphic speed. Of course the schoolmaster gave holiday for that afternoon; the town would have thought strangely of him if he had not.

A gory knife had been found close to the murdered man, and it had been recognized by somebody as belonging to Muff Potter—so the story ran. And it was said that a belated citizen had come upon Potter washing himself in the "branch" about one or two o'clock in the morning, and that Potter had at once sneaked off—suspicious circumstances, especially the washing, which was not a habit with Potter. It was also said that the town had been ransacked for this "murderer" (the public are not slow in the matter of sifting evidence and arriving at a verdict), but that he could not be found. Horsemen had departed down all the roads in every direction, and the Sheriff "was confident" that he would be captured before night.

All the town was drifting toward the graveyard. Tom's heartbreak vanished and he joined the procession, not because he would not a thousand times rather go anywhere else, but because an awful, unaccountable fascination drew him on. Arrived at the dreadful place, he wormed his small body through the crowd and saw the dismal spectacle. It seemed to him an age since he was there before. Somebody pinched his arm. He turned, and his eyes met Huckleberry's. Then both looked elsewhere at once, and wondered if anybody had noticed anything in their mutual glance. But everybody was talking, and intent upon the grisly spectacle before them.

"Poor fellow!" "Poor young fellow!" "This ought to be a lesson to grave robbers!" "Muff Potter'll hang for this if they catch him!" This was the drift of remark; and the minister said, "It was a judgment; His hand is here."

Now Tom shivered from head to heel; for his eye fell upon the stolid face of Injun Joe. At this moment the crowd began to sway and struggle, and voices shouted, "It's him! it's him! he's coming himself!"

"Who? Who?" from twenty voices.

"Muff Potter!"

"Hallo, he's stopped!—Look out, he's turning! Don't let him get away!"

People in the branches of the trees over Tom's head said he wasn't trying to get away—he only looked doubtful and perplexed.

"Infernal impudence!" said a bystander; "wanted to come and take a quiet look at his work, I reckon—didn't expect any company."

The crowd fell apart, now, and the Sheriff came through, ostentatiously leading Potter by the arm. The poor fellow's face was haggard, and his eyes showed the fear that was upon him. When he stood before the murdered man, he shook as with a palsy, and he put his face in his hands and burst into tears.

"I didn't do it, friends," he sobbed; " 'pon my word and honor I never done it."

"Who's accused you?" shouted a voice.

This shot seemed to carry home. Potter lifted his face and looked around him with a pathetic hopelessness in his eyes. He saw Injun Joe, and exclaimed:

"Oh, Injun Joe, you promised me you'd never—"

"Is that your knife?" and it was thrust before him by the Sheriff.

Potter would have fallen if they had not caught him and eased him to the ground. Then he said:

"Something told me 't if I didn't come back and get—" He shuddered; then waved his nerveless hand with a vanquished gesture and said, "Tell 'em, Joe, tell 'em—it ain't any use any more."

Then Huckleberry and Tom stood dumb and staring, and heard the stonyhearted liar reel off his serene statement, they expecting every moment that the clear sky would deliver God's lightnings upon his head, and wondering to see how long the stroke was delayed. And when he had finished and still stood alive and whole, their wavering impulse to break their oath and save the poor betrayed prisoner's life faded and vanished away, for plainly this miscreant had sold himself to Satan and it would be fatal to meddle with the property of such a power as that.

"Why didn't you leave? What did you want to come here for?" somebody said.

"I couldn't help it—I couldn't help it," Potter moaned. "I wanted to run away, but I couldn't seem to come anywhere but here." And he fell to sobbing again.

Injun Joe repeated his statement, just as calmly, a few minutes afterward on the inquest, under oath; and the boys, seeing that the lightnings were still withheld, were confirmed in their belief that Joe had sold himself to the devil. He was now become, to them, the most balefully interesting object they had ever looked upon, and they could not take their fascinated eyes from his face.

They inwardly resolved to watch him, nights, when opportunity should offer, in the hope of getting a glimpse of his dread master.

Injun Joe helped to raise the body of the murdered man and put it in a wagon for removal; and it was whispered through the shuddering crowd that the wound bled a little! The boys thought that this happy circumstance would turn suspicion in the right direction; but they were disappointed, for more than one villager remarked:

"It was within three feet of Muff Potter when it done it."

Tom's fearful secret and gnawing conscience disturbed his sleep for as much as a week after this; and at breakfast one morning Sid said:

"Tom, you pitch around and talk in your sleep so much that you keep me awake half the time."

Tom blanched and dropped his eyes.

"It's a bad sign," said Aunt Polly, gravely. "What you got on your mind, Tom?"

"Nothing. Nothing 't I know of." But the boy's hand shook so that he spilled his coffee.

"And you do talk such stuff," Sid said. "Last night you said 'it's blood, it's blood, that's what it is!' You said that over and over. And you said, 'Don't torment me so—I'll tell!' Tell *what?* What is it you'll tell?"

Everything was swimming before Tom. There is no telling what might have happened, now, but luckily the concern passed out of Aunt Polly's face and she came to Tom's relief without knowing it. She said:

"Sho! It's that dreadful murder. I dream about it most every night myself. Sometimes I dream it's me that done it."

Mary said she had been affected much the same way. Sid seemed satisfied. Tom got out of the presence as quick as he plausibly could, and after that he complained of toothache for a week, and tied up his jaws every night. He never knew that Sid lay nightly watching, and frequently slipped the bandage free and then leaned on his elbow listening a good while at a time, and afterward slipped the bandage back to its place again. Tom's distress of mind wore off gradually and the toothache grew irksome and was discarded. If Sid really managed to make anything out of Tom's disjointed mutterings, he kept it to himself.

It seemed to Tom that his schoolmates never would get done holding inquests on dead cats, and thus keeping his trouble present to his mind. Sid noticed that Tom never was coroner at one of these inquiries, though it had been his habit to take the lead in all new enterprises; he noticed, too, that Tom never acted as a witness—and that was strange; and Sid did not overlook the fact that Tom even showed a marked aversion to these inquests, and always avoided them when he could. Sid marveled, but said nothing. However, even inquests went out of vogue at last, and ceased to torture Tom's conscience.

Every day or two, during this time of sorrow, Tom watched his opportunity and went to the little grated jail window and smuggled such small comforts through to the "murderer" as he could get hold of. The jail was a trifling little brick den that stood in a marsh at the edge of the village, and no guards were afforded for it; indeed it was seldom occupied. These offerings greatly helped to ease Tom's conscience.

The villagers had a strong desire to tar and feather Injun Joe and ride him on a rail, for body snatching, but so formidable was his character that nobody could be found who was willing to take the lead in the matter, so it was dropped. He had been careful to begin both of his inquest statements with the fight, without confessing the grave robbery that preceded it; therefore it was deemed wisest not to try the case in the courts at present.

12 *Tom Shows His Generosity—Aunt Polly Weakens*

One of the reasons why Tom's mind had drifted away from its secret troubles was, that it had found a new and weighty matter to interest itself about. Becky Thatcher had stopped coming to school. Tom had struggled with his pride a few days, and tried to "whistle her down the wind," but failed. He began to find himself hanging around her father's house, nights, and feeling very miserable. She was ill. What if she should die! There was distraction in the thought. He no longer took an interest in war, nor even in piracy. The charm of life was gone; there was nothing but dreariness left. He put his hoop away, and his bat; there was no joy in them any more. His aunt was concerned. She began to try all manner of remedies on him. She was one of those people who are infatuated with patent medicines and all newfangled methods of producing health or mending it. She was an inveterate experimenter in these things. When something fresh in this line came out she was in a fever, right away, to try it; not on herself, for she was never ailing, but on anybody else that came handy. She was a subscriber for all the "Health" periodicals and phrenological frauds; and the solemn ignorance they were inflated with was breath to her nostrils. All the "rot" they contained about ventilation, and how to go to bed, and how to get up, and what to eat, and what to drink, and how much exercise to take, and what frame of mind to keep one's self in, and what sort of clothing to wear, was all gospel to her, and she never observed that her health journals of the current month customarily upset everything they had recommended the month before. She was as simple-hearted and honest as the day was long, and so she was an easy victim. She gathered together her quack periodicals and her quack medicines, and thus armed with death, went about on her pale horse, metaphorically speaking, with "hell following after." But she never suspected that she was not an angel of healing and the balm of Gilead in disguise, to the suffering neighbors.

The water treatment was new, now, and Tom's low condition was a windfall to her. She had him out at daylight every morning, stood him up in the woodshed and drowned him with a deluge of cold water; then she scrubbed him down with a towel like a file, and so brought him to; then she rolled him up in a wet sheet and put him away under blankets till she sweated his soul clean and "the yellow stains of it came through his pores"—as Tom said.

Yet notwithstanding all this, the boy grew more and more melancholy and pale and dejected. She added hot baths, sitz baths, shower baths, and plunges. The boy remained as dismal as a hearse. She began to assist the water with a slim oatmeal diet and blister plasters. She calculated his capacity as she would a jug's, and filled him up every day with quack cure-alls.

Tom had become indifferent to persecution by this time. This phase filled the old lady's heart with consternation. This indifference must be broken up at any cost. Now she heard of Painkiller for the first time. She ordered a lot at once. She tasted it and was filled with gratitude. It was simply fire in a liquid form. She dropped the water treatment and everything else, and pinned her faith to Painkiller. She gave Tom a teaspoonful and watched with the deepest anxiety for the result. Her troubles were instantly at rest, her soul at peace again; for the "indifference" was broken up. The boy could not have shown a wilder, heartier interest, if she had built a fire under him.

Tom felt that it was time to wake up; this sort of life might be romantic enough, in his blighted condition, but it was getting to have too little sentiment and too much distracting variety about it. So he thought over various plans for relief, and finally hit upon that of professing to be fond of Painkiller. He asked for it so often that he became a nuisance, and his aunt ended by telling him to help himself and quit bothering her. If it had been Sid, she would have had no misgivings to alloy her delight; but since it was Tom, she watched the bottle clandestinely. She found that the medicine did really diminish, but it did not occur to her that the boy was mending the health of a crack in the sitting room floor with it.

One day Tom was in the act of dosing the crack when his aunt's yellow cat came along, purring, eyeing the teaspoon avariciously, and begging for a taste. Tom said:

"Don't ask for it unless you want it, Peter."

But Peter signified that he did want it.

"You better make sure."

Peter was sure.

"Now you've asked for it, and I'll give it to you, because there ain't anything mean about *me;* but if you find you don't like it, you mustn't blame anybody but your own self."

Peter was agreeable. So Tom pried his mouth open and poured down the Painkiller. Peter sprang a couple of yards in the air, and then delivered a war whoop and set off round and round the room, banging against furniture, upsetting flowerpots, and making general havoc. Next he rose on his hind feet and pranced around, in a frenzy of enjoyment, with his head over his shoulder and his voice proclaiming his unappeasable happiness. Then he went tearing around the house again spreading chaos and destruction in his path. Aunt Polly entered in time to see him throw a few double somersets, deliver a final mighty hurrah, and sail through the open window, carrying the rest of the flowerpots with him. The old lady stood petrified with astonishment, peering over her glasses; Tom lay on the floor expiring with laughter.

"Tom, what on earth ails that cat?"

"*I* don't know, aunt," gasped the boy.

"Why, I never see anything like it. What *did* make him act so?"

"Deed I don't know, Aunt Polly; cats always act so when they're having a good time."

"They do, do they?" There was something in the tone that made Tom apprehensive.

"Yes'm. That is, I believe they do."

"You *do?*"

"Yes'm."

The old lady was bending down, Tom watching, with interest emphasized by anxiety. Too late he divined her "drift." The handle of the telltale teaspoon was visible under the bed valance. Aunt Polly took it, held it up. Tom winced, and dropped his eyes. Aunt Polly raised him by the usual handle—his ear—and cracked his head soundly with her thimble.

"Now, sir, what did you want to treat that poor dumb beast so, for?"

"I done it out of pity for him—because he hadn't any aunt."

"Hadn't any aunt!—you numbskull. What has that got to do with it?"

"Heaps. Because if he'd a had one she'd a burnt him out herself! She'd a roasted his bowels out of him 'thout any more feeling than if he was a human!"

Aunt Polly felt a sudden pang of remorse. This was putting the thing in a new light; what was cruelty to a cat *might* be cruelty to a boy, too. She began to soften; she felt sorry. Her eyes watered a little, and she put her hand on Tom's head and said gently:

"I was meaning for the best, Tom. And Tom, it *did* do you good."

Tom looked up in her face with just a perceptible twinkle peeping through his gravity.

"I know you was meaning for the best, aunty, and so was I with Peter. It done *him* good, too. I never see him get around so since——"

"Oh, go 'long with you, Tom, before you aggravate me

again. And you try and see if you can't be a good boy, for once, and you needn't take any more medicine."

Tom reached school ahead of time. It was noticed that this strange thing had been occurring every day latterly. And now, as usual of late, he hung about the gate of the schoolyard instead of playing with his comrades. He was sick, he said, and he looked it. He tried to seem to be looking everywhere but whither he really was looking—down the road. Presently Jeff Thatcher hove in sight, and Tom's face lighted; he gazed a moment, and then turned sorrowfully away. When Jeff arrived, Tom accosted him, and "led up" warily to opportunities for remark about Becky, but the giddy lad never could see the bait. Tom watched and watched, hoping whenever a frisking frock came in sight, and hating the owner of it as soon as he saw she was not the right one. At last frocks ceased to appear, and he dropped hopelessly into the dumps; he entered the empty schoolhouse and sat down to suffer. Then one more frock passed in at the gate, and Tom's heart gave a great bound. The next instant he was out, and "going on" like an Indian; yelling, laughing, chasing boys, jumping over the fence at risk of life and limb, throwing handsprings, standing on his head—doing all the heroic things he could conceive of, and keeping a furtive eye out all the while, to see if Becky Thatcher was noticing. But she seemed to be unconscious of it all; she never looked. Could it be possible that she was not aware that he was there? He carried his exploits to her immediate vicinity; came war-whooping around, snatched a boy's cap, hurled it to the roof of the schoolhouse, broke through a group of boys, tumbling them in every direction, and fell sprawling, himself, under Becky's nose, almost upsetting her—and she turned, with her nose in the air, and he heard her say: "Mf! some people think they're mighty smart—always showing off!"

Tom's cheeks burned. He gathered himself up and sneaked off, crushed and crestfallen.

13 *The Young Pirates—Going to the Rendezvous—The Campfire Talk*

Tom's mind was made up now. He was gloomy and desperate. He was a forsaken, friendless boy, he said; nobody loved him; when they found out what they had driven him to, perhaps they would be sorry; he had tried to do right and get along, but they would not let him; since nothing would do them but to be rid of him, let it be so; and let them blame *him* for the consequences—why shouldn't they? What right had the friendless to complain? Yes, they had forced him to it at last: he would lead a life of crime. There was no choice.

By this time he was far down Meadow Lane, and the bell for school to "take up" tinkled faintly upon his ear. He sobbed, now, to think he should never, never hear that old familiar sound any more—it was very hard, but it was forced on him; since he was driven out into the cold world, he must submit—but he forgave them. Then the sobs came thick and fast.

Just at this point he met his soul's sworn comrade, Joe Harper—hard-eyed, and with evidently a great and dismal purpose in his heart. Plainly here were "two souls with but a single thought." Tom, wiping his eyes with his sleeve, began to blubber out something about a resolution to escape from hard usage and lack of sympathy at home by roaming abroad into the great world never to return; and ended by hoping that Joe would not forget him.

But it transpired that this was a request which Joe had just been going to make of Tom, and had come to hunt him up for that purpose. His mother had whipped him for drinking some cream which he had never tasted and knew nothing about; it was plain that she was tired of him and wished him to go; if she felt that way, there was nothing for him to do but succumb; he hoped she would be happy, and never regret having driven her poor boy out into the unfeeling world to suffer and die.

As the two boys walked sorrowing along, they made a new compact to stand by each other and be brothers and never separate till death relieved them of their troubles. Then they began to lay their plans. Joe was for being a hermit, and living on crusts in a remote cave, and dying, sometime, of cold and want and grief; but after listening to Tom, he conceded that there were some conspicuous advantages about a life of crime, and so he consented to be a pirate.

Three miles below St. Petersburg, at a point where the Mississippi River was a trifle over a mile wide, there was a long, narrow, wooded island, with a shallow bar at the head of it, and this offered well as a rendezvous. It was not inhabited; it lay far over toward the further shore, abreast a dense and almost wholly unpeopled forest. So Jackson's Island was chosen. Who were to be the subjects of their piracies, was a matter that did not occur to them. Then they hunted up Huckleberry Finn, and he joined them promptly, for all careers were one to him; he was indifferent. They presently separated to meet at a lonely spot on the riverbank two miles above the village at the favorite hour—which was midnight. There was a small log raft there which they meant to capture. Each would bring hooks and lines, and such provisions as he could steal in the most dark and mysterious way—as became outlaws. And before the afternoon was done, they had all managed to enjoy the sweet glory of spreading the fact that pretty soon the town would "hear something." All who got this vague hint were cautioned to "be mum and wait."

About midnight Tom arrived with a boiled ham and a few trifles, and stopped in a dense undergrowth on a small bluff overlooking the meeting place. It was starlight, and very still. The mighty river lay like an ocean at rest. Tom listened a moment, but no sound disturbed the quiet. Then he gave a low, distinct whistle. It was answered from under the bluff. Tom whistled twice more; these signals were answered in the same way. Then a guarded voice said:

"Who goes there?"

"Tom Sawyer, the Black Avenger of the Spanish Main. Name your names."

"Huck Finn the Red-Handed, and Joe Harper the Terror of the Seas." Tom had furnished these titles, from his favorite literature.

" 'Tis well. Give the countersign."

Two hoarse whispers delivered the same awful word simultaneously to the brooding night:

"BLOOD!"

Then Tom tumbled his ham over the bluff and let himself down after it, tearing both skin and clothes to some extent in the effort. There was an easy, comfortable path along the shore under the bluff, but it lacked the advantages of difficulty and danger so valued by a pirate.

The Terror of the Seas had brought a side of bacon, and had about worn himself out with getting it there. Finn the Red-Handed had stolen a skillet and a quantity of half-cured leaf tobacco, and had also brought a few corncobs to make pipes with. But none of the pirates smoked or "chewed" but himself. The Black Avenger of the Spanish Main said it would never do to start without some fire. That was a wise thought; matches were hardly known there in that day. They saw a fire smouldering upon a great raft a hundred yards above, and they went stealthily thither and helped themselves to a chunk. They made an imposing adventure of it, saying, "Hist!" every now and then, and suddenly halting with finger on lip; moving with hands on imaginary dagger hilts; and giving orders in dismal whispers that if "the foe" stirred, to "let him have it to the hilt," because "dead men tell no tales." They knew well enough that the raftsmen were all down at the village laying in stores or having a spree, but still that was no excuse for their conducting this thing in an unpiratical way.

They shoved off, presently, Tom in command, Huck at the after oar and Joe at the forward. Tom stood amidships, gloomy-browed, and with folded arms, and gave his orders in a low, stern whisper:

"Luff, and bring her to the wind!"

"Aye-aye, sir!"

"Steady, steady-y-y-y!"

"Steady it is, sir!"

"Let her go off a point!"

"Point it is, sir!"

As the boys steadily and monotonously drove the raft toward midstream it was no doubt understood that these orders were given only for "style," and were not intended to mean anything in particular.

"What sail's she carrying?"

"Courses, tops'ls, and flying jib, sir."

"Send the r'yals up! Lay out aloft, there, half a dozen of ye—foretopmaststuns'l! Lively, now!"

"Aye-aye, sir!"

"Shake out that maintogalans'l! Sheets and braces! *Now*, my hearties!"

"Aye-aye, sir!"

"Hellum-a-lee—hard aport! Stand by to meet her when she comes! Port, port! *Now*, men! With a will! Stead-y-y-y!"

"Steady it is, sir!"

The raft drew beyond the middle of the river; the boys pointed her head right, and then lay on their oars. The river was not high, so there was not more than a two- or three-mile current. Hardly a word was said during the next three-quarters of an hour. Now the raft was passing before the distant town. Two or three glimmering lights showed where it lay, peacefully sleeping, beyond the vague vast sweep of star-gemmed water, unconscious of the tremendous event that was happening. The Black Avenger stood still with folded arms, "looking his last" upon the scene of his former joys and his later sufferings, and wishing "she" could see him now, abroad on the wild sea, facing peril and death with dauntless heart, going to his doom with a grim smile on his lips. It was but a small strain on his imagination to remove Jackson's Island beyond eyeshot of the village, and so he "looked his last" with a broken and satisfied heart. The other pirates were looking their last, too; and they all looked so long that they came near letting the current drift them out of the range of the island. But they discovered the danger in time, and made shift to avert it. About two o'clock in the morning the raft grounded on the bar two hundred yards above the head of the island, and they waded back and forth until they had landed their freight. Part of the little raft's belongings consisted of an old sail, and this they spread over a nook in the bushes for a tent to shelter their provisions; but they themselves would sleep in the open air in good weather, as became outlaws.

They built a fire against the side of a great log twenty or thirty steps within the somber depths of the forest, and then cooked some bacon in the frying pan for supper, and used up half of the corn "pone" stock they had brought. It seemed glorious sport to be feasting in that wild free way in the virgin forest of an unexplored and uninhabited island, far from the haunts of men, and they said they never would return to civilization. The climbing fire lit up their faces and threw its ruddy glare upon the pillared tree trunks of their forest temple, and upon the varnished foliage and festooning vines.

When the last crisp slice of bacon was gone, and the last allowance of corn pone devoured, the boys stretched themselves out on the grass, filled with contentment. They could have found a cooler place, but they would not deny themselves such a romantic feature as the roasting campfire.

"*Ain't* it gay?" said Joe.

"It's *nuts!*" said Tom. "What would the boys say if they could see us?"

"Say? Well, they'd just die to be here—hey, Hucky!"

"I reckon so," said Huckleberry; "anyways *I*'m suited. I don't want nothing better'n this. I don't ever get enough to eat, gen'ally—and here they can't come and pick at a feller and bullyrag him so."

"It's just the life for me," said Tom. "You don't have to get up, mornings, and you don't have to go to school, and wash, and all that blame foolishness. You see a pirate don't have to do *anything,* Joe, when he's ashore, but a hermit *he* has to be praying considerable, and then he don't have any fun, anyway, all by himself that way."

"Oh, yes, that's so," said Joe, "but I hadn't thought

much about it, you know. I'd a good deal rather be a pirate, now that I've tried it."

"You see," said Tom, "people don't go much on hermits, nowadays, like they used to in old times, but a pirate's always respected. And a hermit's got to sleep on the hardest place he can find, and put sackcloth and ashes on his head, and stand out in the rain, and——"

"What does he put sackcloth and ashes on his head for?" inquired Huck.

"*I* dono. But they've *got* to do it. Hermits always do. You'd have to do that if you was a hermit."

"Dern'd if I would," said Huck.

"Well, what would you do?"

"I dono. But I wouldn't do that."

"Why, Huck, you'd *have* to. How'd you get around it?"

"Why, I just wouldn't stand it. I'd run away."

"Run away! Well, you *would* be a nice old slouch of a hermit. You'd be a disgrace."

The Red-Handed made no response, being better employed. He had finished gouging out a cob, and now he fitted a weed stem to it, loaded it with tobacco, and was pressing a coal to the charge and blowing a cloud of fragrant smoke—he was in the full bloom of luxurious contentment. The other pirates envied him this majestic vice, and secretly resolved to acquire it shortly. Presently Huck said:

"What does pirates have to do?"

Tom said:

"Oh, they have just a bully time—take ships and burn them, and get the money and bury it in awful places in their island where there's ghosts and things to watch it, and kill everybody in the ships—make 'em walk a plank."

"And they carry the women to the island," said Joe; "they don't kill the women."

"No," assented Tom, "they don't kill the women—they're too noble. And the women's always beautiful, too."

"And don't they wear the bulliest clothes! Oh, no! All gold and silver and di'monds," said Joe, with enthusiasm.

"Who?" said Huck.

"Why, the pirates."

Huck scanned his own clothing forlornly.

"I reckon I ain't dressed fitten for a pirate," said he, with a regretful pathos in his voice; "but I ain't got none but these."

But the other boys told him the fine clothes would come fast enough, after they should have begun their adventures. They made him understand that his poor rags would do to begin with, though it was customary for wealthy pirates to start with a proper wardrobe.

Gradually their talk died out and drowsiness began to steal upon the eyelids of the little waifs. The pipe dropped from the fingers of the Red-Handed, and he slept the sleep of the conscience-free and the weary. The Terror of the Seas and the Black Avenger of the Spanish Main had more difficulty in getting to sleep. They said their prayers inwardly, and lying down, since there was nobody there with authority to make them kneel and recite aloud; in truth, they had a mind not to say them at all, but they were afraid to proceed to such lengths as that, less they might call down a sudden and special thunderbolt from Heaven. Then at once they reached and hovered upon the imminent verge of sleep—but an intruder came, now, that would not "down." It was conscience. They began to feel a vague fear that they had been doing wrong to run away; and next they thought of the stolen meat, and then the real torture came. They tried to argue it away by reminding conscience that they had purloined sweetmeats and apples scores of times; but the conscience was not to be appeased by such thin plausibilities; it seemed to them, in the end, that there was no getting around the stubborn fact that taking sweetmeats was only "hooking," while taking bacon and hams and such valuables was plain simple *stealing*—and there was a command against that in the Bible. So they inwardly resolved that so long as they remained in the business, their piracies should not again be sullied with the crime of stealing. Then conscience granted a truce, and these curiously inconsistent pirates fell peacefully to sleep.

14 *Camp Life—A Sensation—Tom Steals Away from Camp*

When Tom awoke in the morning, he wondered where he was. He sat up and rubbed his eyes and looked around. Then he comprehended. It was the cool gray dawn, and there was a delicious sense of repose and peace in the deep pervading calm and silence of the woods. Not a leaf stirred; not a sound obtruded upon great Nature's meditation. Beaded dewdrops stood upon the leaves and grasses. A white layer of ashes covered the fire, and a thin blue breath of smoke rose straight into the air. Joe and Huck still slept.

Now, far away in the woods a bird called; another answered; presently the hammering of a woodpecker was heard. Gradually the cool dim gray of the morning whitened, and as gradually sounds multiplied and life manifested itself. The marvel of Nature shaking off sleep and going to work unfolded itself to the musing boy. A little green worm came crawling over a dewy leaf, lifting two-thirds of his body into the air from time to time and "sniffing around," then proceeding again—for he was measuring, Tom said; and when the worm approached him, of its own accord, he sat as still as a stone, with his hopes rising and falling, by turns, as the creature still came toward him or seemed inclined to go elsewhere; and when at last it considered a painful moment with its curved body in the air and then came decisively down upon Tom's leg and began a journey over him, his whole heart was glad—for that meant that he was going to have a new suit of clothes—without the shadow of a doubt a gaudy piratical uniform. Now a procession of ants appeared, from nowhere in particular, and went about their labors; one struggled manfully by with a dead spider five times as big as itself in its arms, and lugged it straight up a tree trunk. A brown-spotted ladybug climbed the dizzy height of a grass blade, and Tom bent down close to it and said, "Ladybug, ladybug, fly away home, your house is on fire, your children's alone," and she took wing and went off to see about it—which did not surprise the boy, for he knew of old that this insect was credulous about conflagrations, and he had practiced upon its simplicity more than once. A tumblebug came next, heaving sturdily at its ball, and Tom touched the creature, to see it shut its legs against its body and pretend to be dead. The birds were fairly rioting by this time. A catbird, the northern mocker, lit in a tree over Tom's head, and trilled out her imitations of her neighbors in a rapture of enjoyment; then a shrill jay swept down, a flash of blue flame, and stopped on a twig almost within the boy's reach, cocked his head to one side and eyed the strangers with a consuming curiosity; a gray squirrel and a big fellow of the "fox" kind came scurrying along, sitting up at intervals to inspect and chatter at the boys, for the wild things had probably never seen a human being before and scarcely knew whether to be afraid or not. All Nature was wide awake and stirring, now; long lances of sunlight pierced down through the dense foliage far and near, and a few butterflies came fluttering upon the scene.

Tom stirred up the other pirates and they all clattered away with a shout, and in a minute or two were stripped and chasing after and tumbling over each other in the shallow limpid water of the white sandbar. They felt no longing for the little village sleeping in the distance beyond the majestic waste of water. A vagrant current or a slight rise in the river had carried off their raft, but this only gratified them, since its going was something like burning the bridge between them and civilization.

They came back to camp wonderfully refreshed, gladhearted, and ravenous; and they soon had the campfire blazing up again. Huck found a spring of clear cold water close by, and the boys made cups of broad oak or hickory leaves, and felt that water, sweetened with such a wildwood charm as that, would be a good enough substitute for coffee. While Joe was slicing bacon for breakfast, Tom and Huck asked him to hold on a minute; they stepped to a promising nook in the riverbank and threw in their lines; almost immediately they had reward. Joe had not had time to get impatient before they were back again with some handsome bass, a couple of sun perch and a small catfish—provisions enough for quite a family. They fried the fish with the bacon and were astonished; for no fish had ever seemed so delicious before. They did not know that the quicker a fresh-water fish is on the fire after he is caught the better he is; and they reflected little upon what a sauce open-air sleeping, open-air exercise, bathing, and a large ingredient of hunger makes, too.

They lay around in the shade, after breakfast, while Huck had a smoke, and then went off through the woods on an exploring expedition. They tramped gaily along, over decaying logs, through tangled underbrush, among solemn monarchs of the forest, hung from their crowns to the ground with a drooping regalia of grapevines. Now and then they came upon snug nooks carpeted with grass and jeweled with flowers.

They found plenty of things to be delighted with, but nothing to be astonished at. They discovered that the island was about three miles long and a quarter of a mile wide, and that the shore it lay closest to was only separated from it by a narrow channel hardly two hundred yards wide. They took a swim about every hour, so it was close upon the middle of the afternoon when they got back to camp. They were too hungry to stop to fish, but they fared sumptuously upon cold ham, and then threw themselves down in the shade to talk. But the talk soon began to drag, and then died. The stillness, the solemnity that brooded in the woods, and the sense of loneliness, began to tell upon the spirits of the boys. They fell to thinking. A sort of undefined longing crept upon them. This took dim shape, presently—it was budding homesickness. Even Finn the Red-Handed was dreaming of his doorsteps and empty hogsheads. But they were all ashamed of their weakness, and none was brave enough to speak his thought.

For some time, now, the boys had been dully conscious of a peculiar sound in the distance, just as one sometimes is of the ticking of a clock which he takes no distinct note of. But now this mysterious sound became more pronounced, and forced a recognition. The boys started, glanced at each other, and then each assumed a listening attitude. There was a long silence, profound and unbroken; then a deep, sullen boom came floating down out of the distance.

"What is it!" exclaimed Joe, under his breath.

"I wonder," said Tom in a whisper.

"'Tain't thunder," said Huckleberry, in an awed tone, "becuz thunder——"

"Hark!" said Tom. "Listen—don't talk."

They waited a time that seemed an age, and then the same muffled boom troubled the solemn hush.

"Let's go and see."

They sprang to their feet and hurried to the shore toward the town. They parted the bushes on the bank and peered out over the water. The little steam ferryboat was about a mile below the village, drifting with the current. Her broad deck seemed crowded with people. There were a great many skiffs rowing about or floating with the stream in the neighborhood of the ferryboat, but the boys could not determine what the men in them were doing. Presently a great jet of white smoke burst from the ferryboat's side, and as it expanded and rose in a lazy cloud, that same dull throb of sound was borne to the listeners again.

"I know now!" exclaimed Tom; "somebody's drownded!"

"That's it!" said Huck; "they done that last summer, when Bill Turner got drownded; they shoot a cannon over the water, and that makes him come up to the top. Yes, and they take loaves of bread and put quicksilver in 'em and set 'em afloat, and wherever there's anybody that's drownded, they'll float right there and stop."

"Yes, I've heard about that," said Joe. "I wonder what makes the bread do that."

"Oh, it ain't the bread, so much," said Tom; "I reckon it's mostly what they *say* over it before they start it out."

"But they don't say anything over it," said Huck. "I've seen 'em and they don't."

"Well, that's funny," said Tom. "But maybe they say it to themselves. Of *course* they do. Anybody might know that."

The other boys agreed that there was reason in what Tom said, because an ignorant lump of bread, uninstructed by an incantation, could not be expected to act very intelligently when sent upon an errand of such gravity.

"By jings, I wish I was over there, now," said Joe.

"I do too," said Huck. "I'd give heaps to know who it is."

The boys still listened and watched. Presently a revealing thought flashed through Tom's mind, and he exclaimed:

"Boys, I know who's drownded—it's us!"

They felt like heroes in an instant. Here was a gorgeous triumph; they were missed; they were mourned; hearts were breaking on their account; tears were being shed; accusing memories of unkindnesses to these poor lost lads were rising up, and unavailing regrets and remorse were being indulged; and best of all, the departed were the talk of the whole town, and the envy of all the boys, as far as this dazzling notoriety was concerned. This was fine. It was worth while to be a pirate, after all.

As twilight drew on, the ferryboat went back to her accustomed business and the skiffs disappeared. The pirates returned to camp. They were jubilant with vanity over their new grandeur and the illustrious trouble they were making. They caught fish, cooked supper and ate it, and then fell to guessing at what the village was thinking and saying about them; and the pictures they drew of the public distress on their account were gratifying to look upon—from their point of view. But when the shadows of night closed them in, they gradually ceased to talk, and sat gazing into the fire, with their minds evidently wandering elsewhere. The excitement was gone, now, and Tom and Joe could not keep back thoughts of certain persons at home who were not enjoying this fine frolic as much as they were. Misgivings came; they grew troubled and unhappy; a sigh or two escaped, unawares. By and by Joe timidly ventured upon a roundabout "feeler" as to how the others might look upon a return to civilization—not right now, but——

Tom withered him with derision! Huck, being uncommitted as yet, joined in with Tom, and the waverer quickly "explained," and was glad to get out of the scrape with as little taint of chicken-hearted homesickness clinging to his garments as he could. Mutiny was effectually laid to rest for the moment.

As the night deepened, Huck began to nod, and presently to snore. Joe followed next. Tom lay upon his elbow motionless, for some time, watching the two intently. At last he got up cautiously, on his knees, and went searching among the grass and the flickering reflections flung by the campfire. He picked up and inspected several large semicylinders of the thin white bark of a sycamore, and finally chose two which seemed to suit him. Then he knelt by the fire and painfully wrote something upon each of these with his "red keel"; one he rolled up and put in his jacket pocket, and the other he put in Joe's hat and removed it to a little distance from the owner. And he also put into the hat certain schoolboy treasures of almost inestimable value—among them a lump of chalk, an India-rubber ball, three fishhooks, and one of that kind of marbles known as a "sure-'nough crystal." Then he tiptoed his way cautiously among the trees till he felt that he was out of hearing, and straightway broke into a keen run in the direction of the sandbar.

15 *Tom Reconnoiters—Learns the Situation—Reports at Camp*

A few minutes later Tom was in the shoal water of the bar, wading toward the Illinois shore. Before the depth reached his middle he was halfway over; the current would permit no more wading, now, so he struck out confidently to swim the remaining hundred yards. He swam quartering upstream, but still was swept downward rather faster than he had expected. However, he reached the shore finally, and drifted along till he found a low place and drew himself out. He put his hand on his jacket pocket, found his piece of bark safe, and then struck through the woods, following the shore, with streaming garments. Shortly before ten o'clock he came out into an open place opposite the village, and saw the ferryboat lying in the shadow of the trees and the high bank. Everything was quiet under the blinking stars. He crept down the bank, watching with all his eyes, slipped into the water, swam three or four strokes and climbed into the skiff that did "yawl" duty at the boat's stern. He laid himself down under the thwarts and waited, panting.

Presently the cracked bell tapped and a voice gave the order to "cast off." A minute or two later the skiff's head was standing high up, against the boat's swell, and the voyage was begun. Tom felt happy in his success, for he knew it was the boat's last trip for the night. At the end of a long twelve or fifteen minutes the wheels stopped, and Tom slipped overboard and swam ashore in the dusk, landing fifty yards downstream, out of danger of possible stragglers.

He flew along unfrequented alleys, and shortly found himself at his aunt's back fence. He climbed over, approached the "ell" and looked in at the sitting room window, for a light was burning there. There sat Aunt Polly, Sid, Mary, and Joe Harper's mother, grouped together, talking. They were by the bed, and the bed was between them and the door. Tom went to the door and began to softly lift the latch; then he pressed gently and the door yielded a crack; he continued pushing cautiously, and quaking every time it creaked, till he judged he might squeeze through on his knees; so he put his head through and began, warily.

"What makes the candle blow so?" said Aunt Polly. Tom hurried up. "Why that door's open, I believe. Why of course it is. No end of strange things now. Go 'long and shut it, Sid."

Tom disappeared under the bed just in time. He lay and "breathed" himself for a time, and then crept to where he could almost touch his aunt's foot.

"But as I was saying," said Aunt Polly, "he warn't *bad*, so to say—only mische*e*vous. Only just giddy, and harum-scarum, you know. He warn't any more responsible than a colt. *He* never meant any harm, and he was the best-hearted boy that ever was"—and she began to cry.

"It was just so with my Joe—always full of his devilment, and up to every kind of mischief, but he was just as unselfish and kind as he could be—and laws bless me, to think I went and whipped him for taking that cream, never once recollecting that I throwed it out myself because it was sour, and I never to see him again in this world, never, never, never, poor abused boy!" And Mrs. Harper sobbed as if her heart would break.

"I hope Tom's better off where he is," said Sid, "but if he'd been better in some ways——"

"Sid!" Tom felt the glare of the old lady's eye, though he could not see it. "Not a word against my Tom, now that he's gone! God'll take care of *him*—never you trouble *your*self, sir! Oh, Mrs. Harper, I don't know how to give him up! I don't know how to give him up! He was such a comfort to me, although he tormented my old heart out of me, 'most."

"The Lord giveth and the Lord hath taken away— Blessed be the name of the Lord! But it's *so* hard— Oh, it's so hard!

Only last Saturday my Joe busted a firecracker right under my nose and I knocked him sprawling. Little did I know then, how soon— Oh, if it was to do over again I'd hug him and bless him for it."

"Yes, yes, yes, I know just how you feel, Mrs. Harper, I know just exactly how you feel. No longer ago than yesterday noon, my Tom took and filled the cat full of Painkiller, and I did think the cretur would tear the house down. And God forgive me, I cracked Tom's head with my thimble, poor boy, poor dead boy. But he's out of all his troubles now. And the last words I ever heard him say was to reproach——"

But this memory was too much for the old lady, and she broke entirely down. Tom was snuffling, now, himself—and more in pity of himself than anybody else. He could hear Mary crying, and putting in a kindly word for him from time to time. He began to have a nobler opinion of himself than ever before. Still, he was sufficiently touched by his aunt's grief to long to rush out from under the bed and overwhelm her with joy—and the theatrical gorgeousness of the thing appealed strongly to his nature, too, but he resisted and lay still.

He went on listening, and gathered by odds and ends that it was conjectured at first that the boys had got drowned while taking a swim; then the small raft had been missed; next, certain boys said the missing lads had promised that the village should "hear something" soon; the wiseheads had "put this and that together" and decided that the lads had gone off on that raft and would turn up at the next town below, presently; but toward noon the raft had been found, lodged against the Missouri shore some five or six miles below the village—and then hope perished; they must be drowned, else hunger would have driven them home by nightfall if not sooner. It was believed that the search for the bodies had been a fruitless effort merely because the drowning must have occurred in midchannel, since the boys, being good swimmers, would otherwise have escaped to shore. This was Wednesday night. If the bodies continued missing until Sunday, all hope would be given over, and the funerals would be preached on that morning. Tom shuddered.

Mrs. Harper gave a sobbing good night and turned to go. Then with a mutual impulse the two bereaved women flung themselves into each other's arms and had a good, consoling cry, and then parted. Aunt Polly was tender far beyond her wont, in her good night to Sid and Mary. Sid snuffled a bit and Mary went off crying with all her heart.

Aunt Polly knelt down and prayed for Tom so touchingly, so appealingly, and with such measureless love in her words and her old trembling voice, that he was weltering in tears again, long before she was through.

He had to keep still long after she went to bed, for she kept making brokenhearted ejaculations from time to time, tossing unrestfully, and turning over. But at last she was still, only moaning a little in her sleep. Now the boy stole out, rose gradually by the bedside, shaded the candlelight with his hand, and stood regarding her. His heart was full of pity for her. He took out his sycamore scroll and placed it by the candle. But something occurred to him, and he lingered considering. His face lighted with a happy solution of his thought; he put the bark hastily in his pocket. Then he bent over and kissed the faded lips, and straightway made his stealthy exit, latching the door behind him.

He threaded his way back to the ferry landing, found nobody at large there, and walked boldly on board the boat, for he knew she was tenantless except that there was a watchman, who always turned in and slept like a graven image. He untied the skiff at the stern, slipped into it, and was soon rowing cautiously upstream. When he had pulled a mile above the village, he started quartering across and bent himself stoutly to his work. He hit the landing on the other side neatly, for this was a familiar bit of work to him. He was moved to capture the skiff, arguing that it might be considered a ship and therefore legitimate prey for a pirate, but he knew a thorough search would be made for it and that might end in revelations. So he stepped ashore and entered the wood.

He sat down and took a long rest, torturing himself meantime to keep awake, and then started warily down the homestretch. The night was far spent. It was broad daylight before he found himself fairly abreast the island bar. He rested again until the sun was well up and gilding the great river with its splendor, and then he plunged into the stream. A little later he paused, dripping, upon the threshold of the camp, and heard Joe say:

"No, Tom's true-blue, Huck, and he'll come back. He won't desert. He knows that would be a disgrace to a pirate, and Tom's too proud for that sort of thing. He's up to something or other. Now I wonder what?"

"Well, the things is ours, anyway, ain't they?"

"Pretty near, but not yet, Huck. The writing says they are if he ain't back here to breakfast."

"Which he is!" exclaimed Tom, with fine dramatic effect, stepping grandly into camp.

A sumptuous breakfast of bacon and fish was shortly provided, and as the boys set to work upon it, Tom recounted (and adorned) his adventures. They were a vain and boastful company of heroes when the tale was done. Then Tom hid himself away in a shady nook to sleep till noon, and the the other pirates got ready to fish and explore.

16 *A Day's Amusements—Tom Reveals a Secret—The Pirates Take a Lesson—A Night Surprise—An Indian War*

After dinner all the gang turned out to hunt for turtle eggs on the bar. They went about poking sticks into the sand, and when they found a soft place they went down on their knees and dug with their hands. Sometimes they would take fifty or sixty eggs out of one hole. They were perfectly round white things a trifle smaller than an English walnut. They had a famous fried egg feast that night, and another on Friday morning.

After breakfast they went whooping and prancing out on the bar, and chased each other round and round, shedding clothes as they went, until they were naked, and then continued the frolic far away up the shoal water of the bar, against the stiff current which later tripped their legs from under them from time to time and greatly increased the fun. And now and then they stooped in a group and splashed water in each other's faces with their palms, gradually approaching each other, with averted faces to avoid the strangling sprays, and finally gripping and struggling till the best man ducked his neighbor, and then they all went under in a tangle of white legs and arms and came up blowing, sputtering, laughing, and gasping for breath at one and the same time.

When they were well exhausted, they would run out and sprawl on the dry, hot sand, and lie there and cover themselves up with it, and by and by break for the water again and go through the original performance once more. Finally it occurred to them that their naked skin represented flesh-colored "tights" very fairly; so they drew a ring in the sand and had a circus—with three clowns in it, for none would yield this proudest post to his neighbor.

Next they got their marbles and played "knucks" and "ringtaw" and "keeps" till that amusement grew stale. Then Joe and Huck had another swim, but Tom would not venture, because he found that in kicking off his trousers he had kicked his string of rattlesnake rattles off his ankle, and he wondered how he had escaped cramp so long without the protection of this mysterious charm. He did not venture again until he had found it, and by that time the other boys were tired and ready to rest. They gradually wandered apart, dropped into the "dumps," and fell to gazing longingly across the wide river to where the village lay drowsing in the sun.

Tom found himself writing "BECKY" in the sand with his big toe; he scratched it out, and was angry with himself for his weakness. But he wrote it again, nevertheless; he could not help it. He erased it once more and then took himself out of temptation by driving the other boys together and joining them.

But Joe's spirits had gone down almost beyond resurrection. He was so homesick that he could hardly endure the misery of it. The tears lay very near the surface. Huck was melancholy, too. Tom was downhearted, but tried hard not to show it. He had a secret which he was not ready to tell, yet, but if this mutinous depression was not broken up soon, he would have to bring it out. He said, with a great show of cheerfulness:

"I bet there's been pirates on this island before, boys. We'll explore it again. They've hid treasures here somewhere. How'd you feel to light on a rotten chest full of gold and silver—hey?"

But it roused only a faint enthusiasm, which faded out, with no reply. Tom tried one or two other seductions; but they failed, too. It was discouraging work. Joe sat poking up the sand with a stick and looking very gloomy. Finally he said:

"Oh, boys, let's give it up. I want to go home. It's so lonesome."

"Oh, no, Joe, you'll feel better by and by," said Tom. "Just think of the fishing that's here."

"I don't care for fishing. I want to go home."

"But, Joe, there ain't such another swimming place anywhere."

"Swimming's no good. I don't seem to care for it, somehow, when there ain't anybody to say I shan't go in. I mean to go home."

"Oh, shucks! Baby! You want to see your mother, I reckon."

"Yes, I *do* want to see my mother—and you would, too, if you had one. I ain't any more baby than you are." And Joe snuffled a little.

"Well, we'll let the crybaby go home to his mother, *won't* we, Huck? Poor thing—does it want to see its mother? And so it shall. *You* like it here, *don't* you, Huck? We'll stay, won't we?"

Huck said "Y-e-s"—without any heart in it.

"I'll never speak to you again as long as I live," said Joe, rising. "There now!" And he moved moodily away and began to dress himself.

"Who cares!" said Tom. "Nobody wants you to. Go 'long home and get laughed at. Oh, you're a nice pirate. Huck and me ain't crybabies. We'll stay, won't we, Huck? Let him go if he wants to. I reckon we can get along without him, per'aps."

But Tom was uneasy, nevertheless, and was alarmed to see Joe go sullenly on with his dressing. And then it was discomforting to see Huck eyeing Joe's preparations so wistfully, and keeping up such an ominous silence. Presently, without a parting word, Joe began to wade off toward the Illinois shore. Tom's heart began to sink. He glanced at Huck. Huck could not bear the look, and dropped his eyes. Then he said:

"I want to go, too, Tom. It was getting so lonesome anyway, and now it'll be worse. Let's us go, too, Tom."

"I won't! You can all go, if you want to. I mean to stay."

"Tom, I better go."

"Well, go 'long—who's hendering you."

Huck began to pick up his scattered clothes. He said:

"Tom, I wisht you'd come, too. Now you think it over. We'll wait for you when we get to shore."

"Well, you'll wait a blame long time, that's all."

Huck started sorrowfully away, and Tom stood looking after him, with a strong desire tugging at his heart to yield his pride and go along too. He hoped the boys would stop, but they still waded slowly on. It suddenly dawned on Tom that it was become very lonely and still. He made one final struggle with his pride, and then darted after his comrades, yelling:

"Wait! Wait! I want to tell you something!"

They presently stopped and turned around. When he got to where they were, he began unfolding his secret, and they listened moodily till at last they saw the "point" he was driving at, and then they set up a war whoop of applause and said it was "splendid!" and said if he had told them at first, they wouldn't have started away. He made a plausible excuse; but his real reason had been the fear that not even the secret would keep them with him any very great length of time, and so he had meant to hold it in reserve as a last seduction.

The lads came gaily back and went at their sports again with a will, chattering all the time about Tom's stupendous plan and admiring the genius of it. After a dainty egg and fish dinner, Tom said he wanted to learn to smoke, now. Joe caught at the idea and said he would like to try, too. So Huck made pipes and filled them. These novices had never smoked anything before but cigars made of grapevine, and they "bit" the tongue, and were not considered manly anyway.

Now they stretched themselves out on their elbows and began to puff, charily, and with slender confidence. The smoke had an unpleasant taste, and they gagged a little, but Tom said:

"Why, it's just as easy! If I'd a knowed *this* was all, I'd a learnt long ago."

"So would I," said Joe. "It's just nothing."

"Why, many a time I've looked at people smoking, and thought well I wish I could do that; but I never thought I could," said Tom.

"That's just the way with me, hain't it, Huck? You've heard me talk just that way—haven't you, Huck? I'll leave it to Huck if I haven't."

"Yes—heaps of times," said Huck.

"Well, I have too," said Tom; "oh, hundreds of times. Once down by the slaughterhouse. Don't you remember, Huck? Bob Tanner was there, and Johnny Miller, and Jeff Thatcher, when I said it. Don't you remember, Huck, 'bout me saying that?"

"Yes, that's so," said Huck. "That was the day after I lost a white alley. No, 'twas the day before."

"There—I told you so," said Tom. "Huck recollects it."

"I bleeve I could smoke this pipe all day," said Joe. "*I* don't feel sick."

"Neither do I," said Tom. "*I* could smoke it all day. But I bet you Jeff Thatcher couldn't."

"Jeff Thatcher! Why he'd keel over just with two draws. Just let him try it once. *He'd* see!"

"I bet he would. And Johnny Miller—I wish I could see Johnny Miller tackle it once."

"Oh, don't *I!*" said Joe. "Why, I bet you Johnny Miller couldn't any more do this than nothing. Just one little snifter would fetch *him*."

" 'Deed it would, Joe. Say—I wish the boys could see us now."

"So do I."

"Say—boys, don't say anything about it, and some time when they're around, I'll come up to you and say 'Joe, got a pipe? I want a smoke.' And you'll say, kind of careless like, as if it warn't anything, you'll say, 'Yes, I got my *old* pipe, and another one, but my tobacker ain't very good.' And I'll say, 'Oh, that's all right, if it's *strong* enough.' And then you'll out with the pipes, and we'll light up just as ca'm, and then just see 'em look!"

"By jings, that'll be gay, Tom! I wish it was *now!*"

"So do I! And when we tell 'em we learned when we was off pirating, won't they wish they'd been along?"

"Oh, I reckon not! I'll just *bet* they will!"

So the talk ran on. But presently it began to flag a trifle, and grow disjointed. The silences widened; the expectoration marvelously increased. Every pore inside the boys' cheeks became a spouting fountain; they could scarcely bail out the cellars under their tongues fast enough to prevent an inundation; little overflowings down their throats occurred in spite of all they could do, and sudden retchings followed every time. Both boys were looking very pale and miserable, now. Joe's pipe dropped from his nerveless fingers. Tom's followed. Both fountains were going furiously and both pumps bailing with might and main. Joe said feebly:

"I've lost my knife. I reckon I better go and find it."

Tom said, with quivering lips and halting utterance:

"I'll help you. You go over that way and I'll hunt around by the spring. No, you needn't come, Huck—we can find it."

So Huck sat down again, and waited an hour. Then he found it lonesome, and went to find his comrades. They were wide apart in the woods, both very pale, both fast asleep. But something informed him that if they had had any trouble they had got rid of it.

They were not talkative at supper that night. They had a humble look, and when Huck prepared his pipe after the meal and was going to prepare theirs, they said no, they were not feeling very well—something they ate at dinner had disagreed with them.

About midnight Joe awoke, and called the boys. There was a brooding oppressiveness in the air that seemed to bode something. The boys huddled themselves together and sought the friendly companionship of the fire, though the dull dead heat of the breathless atmosphere was stifling. They sat still, intent and waiting. The solemn hush continued. Beyond the light of the fire everything was swallowed up in the blackness of darkness. Presently there came a quivering glow that vaguely revealed the foliage for a moment and then vanished. By and by another came, a little stronger. Then another. Then a faint moan came sighing through the branches of the forest and the boys felt a fleeting breath upon their cheeks, and shuddered with the fancy that the Spirit of the Night had gone by. There was a pause. Now a weird flash turned night into day and showed every little grass blade, separate and distinct, that grew about their feet. And it showed three white, startled faces, too. A deep peal of thunder went rolling and tumbling down the heavens and lost itself in sullen rumblings in the distance. A sweep of chilly air passed by, rustling all the leaves and snowing the flaky ashes broadcast about the fire. Another fierce glare lit up the forest and an instant crash followed that seemed to rend the treetops right over the boys' heads. They clung together in terror, in the thick gloom that followed. A few big raindrops fell pattering upon the leaves.

"Quick! boys, go for the tent!" exclaimed Tom.

They sprang away, stumbling over roots and among vines in the dark, no two plunging in the same direction. A furious blast roared through the trees, making everything sing as it went. One blinding flash after another came, and peal on peal of deafening thunder. And now a drenching rain poured down and the rising hurricane drove it in sheets along the ground. The boys cried out to each other, but the roaring wind and the booming thunderblasts drowned their voices utterly. However, one by one they straggled in at last and took shelter under the tent, cold, scared, and streaming with water; but to have company in misery seemed something to be grateful for. They could not talk, the old sail flapped so furiously, even if the other noises would have allowed them. The tempest rose higher and higher, and presently the sail tore loose from its fastenings and went winging away on the blast. The boys seized each others' hands and fled, with many tumblings and bruises, to the shelter of a great oak that stood upon the riverbank. Now the battle was at its highest. Under the ceaseless conflagration of lightning that flamed in the skies, everything below stood out in clean-cut and shadowless distinctness: the bending trees, the billowy river, white with foam, the driving spray of spume flakes, the dim outlines of the high bluffs on the other side, glimpsed through the drifting cloud rack and the slanting veil of rain. Every little while some giant tree yielded the fight and fell crashing through the younger growth; and the unflagging thunderpeals came now in earsplitting explosive bursts, keen and sharp, and unspeakably appalling. The storm culminated in one matchless effort that seemed likely to tear the island to pieces, burn it up, drown it to the treetops, blow it away, and deafen every creature on it, all at one and the same moment. It was a wild night for homeless young heads to be out in.

But at last the battle was done, and the forces retired with weaker and weaker threatenings and grumblings, and peace resumed her sway. The boys went back to camp, a good deal awed; but they found there was still something to be thankful for, because the great sycamore, the shelter of their beds, was a ruin, now, blasted by the lightnings, and they were not under it when the catastrophe happened.

Everything in camp was drenched, the campfire as well; for they were but heedless lads, like their generation, and had made no provision against rain. Here was matter for dismay, for they were soaked through and chilled. They were eloquent in their distress; but they presently discovered that the fire had eaten so far up under the great log it had been built against (where it curved upward and separated itself from the ground), that a handbreadth or so of it had escaped wetting; so they patiently wrought until, with shreds and bark gathered from the under sides of sheltered logs, they coaxed the fire to burn again. Then they piled on great dead boughs till they had a roaring furnace, and were glad-hearted once more. They dried their boiled ham and had a feast, and after that they sat by the fire and expanded and glorified their midnight adventure until morning, for there was not a dry spot to sleep on anywhere around.

As the sun began to steal in upon the boys, drowsiness came over them and they went out on the sandbar and lay down to sleep. They got scorched out by and by, and drearily set about getting breakfast. After the meal they felt rusty, and stiff-jointed, and a little homesick once more. Tom saw the signs, and fell to cheering up the pirates as well as he could. But they cared nothing for marbles, or circus, or swimming, or anything. He reminded them of the imposing secret, and raised a ray of cheer. While it lasted, he got them interested in a new device. This was to knock off being pirates, for a while, and be Indians for a change. They were attracted by this idea; so it was not long before they were stripped, and striped from head to heel with black mud, like so many zebras—all of them chiefs, of course—and then they went tearing through the woods to attack an English settlement.

By and by they separated into three hostile tribes and darted upon each other from ambush with dreadful war whoops, and killed and scalped each other by thousands. It was a gory day. Consequently it was an extremely satisfactory one.

They assembled in camp toward supper time, hungry and happy; but now a difficulty arose—hostile Indians could not break the bread of hospitality together without first making peace, and this was a simple impossibility without smoking a pipe of peace. There was no other process that ever they had heard of. Two of the savages almost wished they had remained pirates. However, there was no other way; so with such show of cheerfulness as they could muster they called for the pipe and took their whiff as it passed, in due form.

And behold, they were glad they had gone into savagery, for they had gained something; they found that they could now smoke a little without having to go and hunt for a lost knife; they did not get sick enough to be seriously uncomfortable. They were not likely to fool away this high promise for lack of effort. No, they practiced cautiously, after supper, with right fair success, and so they spent a jubilant evening. They were prouder and happier in their new acquirement than they would have been in the scalping and skimming of the Six Nations. We will leave them to smoke and chatter and brag, since we have no further use for them at present.

17 *Memories of the Lost Heroes—The Point in Tom's Secret*

But there was no hilarity in the little town that same tranquil Saturday afternoon. The Harpers, and Aunt Polly's family, were being put into mourning, with great grief and many tears. An unusual quiet possessed the village, although it was ordinarily quiet enough, in all conscience. The villagers conducted their concerns with an absent air, and talked little; but they sighed often. The Saturday holiday seemed a burden to the children. They had no heart in their sports, and gradually gave them up.

In the afternoon Becky Thatcher found herself moping about the deserted schoolhouse yard, and feeling very melancholy. But she found nothing there to comfort her. She soliloquized:

"Oh, if I only had a brass andiron knob again! But I haven't got anything now to remember him by." And she choked back a little sob.

Presently she stopped, and said to herself:

"It was right here. Oh, if it was to do over again, I wouldn't say that—I wouldn't say it for the whole world. But he's gone now; I'll never never never see him any more."

This thought broke her down and she wandered away, with the tears rolling down her cheeks. Then quite a group of boys and girls—playmates of Tom's and Joe's—came by, and stood looking over the paling fence and talking in reverent tones of how Tom did so-and-so, the last time they saw him, and how Joe said this and that small trifle (pregnant with awful prophecy, as they could easily see now!) —and each speaker pointed out the exact spot where the lost lads stood at the time, and then added something like "and I was a-standing just so—just as I am now, and as if you was him—I was as close as that—and he smiled, just this way—and then something seemed to go all over me, like—awful, you know—and I never thought what it meant, of course, but I can see now!"

Then there was a dispute about who saw the dead boys last in life, and many claimed that dismal distinction, and offered evidences, more or less tampered with by the witness; and when it was ultimately decided who *did* see the departed last, and exchanged the last words with them, the lucky parties took upon themselves a sort of sacred importance, and were gaped at and envied by all the rest. One poor chap, who had no other grandeur to offer, said with tolerably manifest pride in the remembrance:

"Well, Tom Sawyer he licked me once."

But that bid for glory was a failure. Most of the boys could say that, and so that cheapened the distinction too much. The group loitered away, still recalling memories of the lost heroes, in awed voices.

When the Sunday-school hour was finished, the next morning, the bell began to toll, instead of ringing in the usual way. It was a very still Sabbath, and the mournful sound seemed in keeping with the musing hush that lay upon nature. The villagers began to gather, loitering a moment in the vestibule to converse in whispers about the sad event. But there was no whispering in the house; only the funereal rustling of dresses as the women gathered to their seats, disturbed the silence there. None could remember when the little church had been so full before. There was finally a waiting pause, an expectant dumbness, and then Aunt Polly entered, followed by Sid and Mary, and they by the Harper family, all in deep black, and the whole congregation, the old minister as well, rose reverently and stood, until the mourners were seated in the front pew. There was another communing silence, broken at intervals by muffled sobs, and then the minister spread his hands abroad and prayed. A moving hymn was sung, and the text followed: "I am the Resurrection and the Life."

As the service proceeded, the clergyman drew such pictures of the graces, the winning ways, and the rare promise of the lost lads, that every soul there, thinking he recognized these pictures, felt a pang in remembering that he had persistently blinded himself to them, always before, and had as persistently seen only faults and flaws in the poor boys. The minister related many a touching incident in the lives of the departed, too, which illustrated their sweet, generous natures, and the people could easily see, now, how noble and beautiful those episodes were, and remembered with grief that at the time they occurred they had seemed rank rascalities, well deserving of the cowhide. The congregation became more and more moved, as the pathetic tale went on, till at last the whole company broke down and joined the weeping mourners in a chorus of anguished sobs, the preacher himself giving way to his feelings, and crying in the pulpit.

There was a rustle in the gallery, which nobody noticed; a moment later the church door creaked; the minister raised his streaming eyes above his handkerchief, and stood transfixed! First one and then another pair of eyes followed the minister's, and then almost with one impulse the congregation rose and stared while the three dead boys came marching up the aisle, Tom in the lead, Joe next, and Huck, a ruin of drooping rags, sneaking sheepishly in the rear! They had been hid in the unused gallery listening to their own funeral sermon!

Aunt Polly, Mary, and the Harpers threw themselves upon their restored ones, smothered them with kisses and poured out thanksgivings, while poor Huck stood abashed and uncomfortable, not knowing exactly what to do or where to hide from so many unwelcoming eyes. He wavered, and started to slink away, but Tom seized him and said:

"Aunt Polly, it ain't fair. Somebody's got to be glad to see Huck."

"And so they shall. *I*'m glad to see him, poor motherless thing!" And the loving attentions Aunt Polly lavished upon him were the one thing capable of making him more uncomfortable than he was before.

Suddenly the minister shouted at the top of his voice: "Praise God from whom all blessings flow—SING!—and put your hearts in it!"

And they did. Old Hundred swelled up with a triumphant burst, and while it shook the rafters Tom Sawyer the Pirate looked around upon the envying juveniles about him and confessed in his heart that this was the proudest moment of his life.

As the "sold" congregation trooped out they said they would almost be willing to be made ridiculous again to hear Old Hundred sung like that once more.

Tom got more cuffs and kisses that day—according to Aunt Polly's varying moods—than he had earned before in a year; and he hardly knew which expressed the most gratefulness to God and affection for himself.

18 *Tom's Feelings Investigated—Wonderful Dreams —Becky Thatcher Overshadowed—Tom Becomes Jealous—Black Revenge*

That was Tom's great secret—the scheme to return home with his brother pirates and attend their own funerals. They had paddled over to the Missouri shore on a log, at dusk on Saturday, landing five or six miles below the village; they had slept in the woods at the edge of the town till nearly daylight, and had then crept through back lanes and alleys and finished their sleep in the gallery of the church among a chaos of invalided benches.

At breakfast, Monday morning, Aunt Polly and Mary were very loving to Tom, and very attentive to his wants. There was an unusual amount of talk. In the course of it Aunt Polly said:

"Well, I don't say it wasn't a fine joke, Tom, to keep everybody suffering 'most a week so you boys had a good time, but it is a pity you could be so hardhearted as to let *me* suffer so. If you could have come over on a log to go to your funeral, you could have come over and give me a hint some way that you warn't *dead,* but only run off."

"Yes, you could have done that, Tom," said Mary; "and I believe you would if you had thought of it."

"Would you, Tom?" said Aunt Polly, her face lighting wistfully. "Say, now, would you, if you'd thought of it?"

"I—well, I don't know. 'Twould a spoiled everything."

"Tom, I hoped you loved me that much," said Aunt Polly, with a grieved tone that discomforted the boy. "It would have been something if you'd cared enough to *think* of it, even if you didn't *do* it."

"Now auntie, that ain't any harm," pleaded Mary; "it's only Tom's giddy way—he is always in such a rush that he never thinks of anything."

"More's the pity. Sid would have thought. And Sid would have come and *done* it, too. Tom, you'll look back, some day, when it's too late, and wish you'd cared a little more for me when it would have cost you so little."

"Now auntie, you know I do care for you," said Tom.

"I'd know it better if you acted more like it."

"I wish now I'd thought," said Tom, with a repentant tone; "but I dreamed about you, anyway. That's something, ain't it?"

"It ain't much—a cat does that much—but it's better than nothing. What did you dream?"

"Why, Wednesday night I dreamt that you was sitting over there by the bed, and Sid was sitting by the woodbox, and Mary next to him."

"Well, so we did. So we always do. I'm glad your dreams could take even that much trouble about us."

"And I dreamt that Joe Harper's mother was here."

"Why, she *was* here! Did you dream any more?"

"Oh, lots. But it's so dim, now."

"Well, *try* to recollect—can't you?"

"Somehow it seems to me that the wind—the wind blowed the—the—"

"Try harder, Tom! The wind did blow something. Come!"

Tom pressed his fingers on his forehead an anxious minute, and then said:

"I've got it now! I've got it now! It blowed the candle!"

"Mercy on us! Go on, Tom—go on!"

"And it seems to me that you said, 'Why, I believe that that door—' "

"Go *on,* Tom!"

"Just let me study a moment—just a moment. Oh, yes—you said you believed the door was open."

"As I'm sitting here, I did! Didn't I, Mary! Go on!"

"And then—and then—well I won't be certain, but it seems like as if you made Sid go and—and—"

"Well? Well? What did I make him do, Tom? What did I make him do?"

"You made him—you— Oh, you made him shut it."

"Well, for the land's sake! I never heard the beat of that in all my days! Don't tell *me* there ain't anything in dreams, any more. Sereny Harper shall know of this before I'm an hour older. I'd like to see her get around *this* with her rubbage 'bout superstition. Go on, Tom!"

"Oh, it's all getting just as bright as day, now. Next you said I warn't *bad,* only mischeevous and harum-scarum, and not any more responsible than—than—I think it was a colt, or something."

"And so it was! Well, goodness gracious! Go on, Tom!"

"And then you began to cry."

"So I did. So I did. Not the first time, neither. And then—"

"Then Mrs. Harper she began to cry, and said Joe was just the same, and she wished she hadn't whipped him for taking cream when she'd throwed it out her own self—"

"Tom! The sperrit was upon you! You was a-prophesying—that's what you was doing! Land alive, go on, Tom!"

"Then Sid he said—he said—"

"I don't think I said anything," said Sid.

"Yes you did, Sid," said Mary.

"Shut your heads and let Tom go on! What did he say, Tom?"

"He said—I *think* he said he hoped I was better off where I was gone to, but if I'd been better sometimes—"

"*There,* d'you hear that! It was his very words!"

"And you shut him up sharp."

"I lay I did! There must a been an angel there. There *was* an angel there, somewheres!"

"And Mrs. Harper told about Joe scaring her with a firecracker, and you told about Peter and the Painkiller—"

"Just as true as I live!"

"And then there was a whole lot of talk 'bout dragging the river for us, and 'bout having the funeral Sunday, and then you and old Miss Harper hugged and cried, and she went."

"It happened just so! It happened just so, as sure as I'm a-sitting in these very tracks. Tom, you couldn't told it more like, if you'd a-seen it! And *then* what? Go on, Tom."

"Then I thought you prayed for me—and I could see you and hear every word you said. And you went to bed, and I was so sorry, that I took and wrote on a piece of sycamore bark, *'We ain't dead—we are only off being pirates,'* and put it on the table by the candle; and then you looked so good, laying there asleep, that I thought I went and leaned over and kissed you on the lips."

"Did you, Tom, *did* you! I just forgive you everything for that!" And she seized the boy in a crushing embrace that made him feel like the guiltiest of villains.

"It was very kind, even though it was only a—dream," Sid soliloquized just audibly.

"Shut up, Sid! A body does just the same in a dream as he'd do if he was awake. Here's a big Milum apple I've been saving for you, Tom, if you was ever found again—now go 'long to school. I'm thankful to the good God and Father of us all I've got you back, that's long-suffering and merciful to them that believe on Him and keep His word, though goodness knows I'm unworthy of it, but if only the worthy ones got His blessings and had His hand to help them over the rough places, there's few enough would smile here or ever enter into His rest when the long night comes. Go 'long, Sid, Mary, Tom—take yourselves off—you've hendered me long enough."

The children left for school, and the old lady to call on Mrs. Harper and vanquish her realism with Tom's marvelous dream. Sid had better judgment than to utter the thought that was in his mind as he left the house. It was this: "Pretty thin—as long a dream as that, without any mistakes in it!"

What a hero Tom was become, now! He did not go skipping and prancing, but moved with a dignified swagger as became a pirate who felt that the public eye was on him. And indeed it was; he tried not to seem to see the looks or hear the remarks as he passed along, but they were food and drink to him. Smaller boys than himself flocked at his heels, as proud to be seen with him, and tolerated by him, as if he had been the drummer at the head of a procession or the elephant leading a menagerie into town. Boys of his own size pretended not to know he had been away at all; but they were consuming with envy, nevertheless. They would have given anything to have that swarthy sun-tanned skin of his, and his glittering notoriety; and Tom would not have parted with either for a circus.

At school the children made so much of him and of Joe, and delivered such eloquent admiration from their eyes, that the two heroes were not long in becoming insufferably "stuck-up." They began to tell their adventures to hungry listeners—but they only began; it was not a thing likely to have an end, with imaginations like theirs to furnish material. And finally, when they got out their pipes and went serenely puffing around, the very summit of glory was reached.

Tom decided that he could be independent of Becky Thatcher now. Glory was sufficient. He would live for glory. Now that he was distinguished, maybe she would be wanting to "make up." Well, let her—she should see that he could be as indifferent as some other people. Presently she arrived. Tom pretended not to see her. He moved away and joined a group of boys and girls and began to talk. Soon he observed that she was tripping gaily back and forth with flushed face and dancing eyes, pretending to be busy chasing schoolmates, and screaming with laughter when she made a capture; but he noticed that she always made her captures in his vicinity, and that she seemed to cast a conscious eye in his direction at such times, too. It gratified all the vicious vanity that was in him; and so, instead of winning him it only "set him up" the more and made him the more diligent to avoid betraying that he knew she was about. Presently she gave over skylarking, and moved irresolutely about, sighing once or twice and glancing furtively and wistfully toward Tom. Then she observed that now Tom was talking more particularly to Amy Lawrence than to any one else. She felt a sharp pang and grew disturbed and uneasy at once. She tried to go away, but her feet were treacherous, and carried her to the group instead. She said to a girl almost at Tom's elbow—with sham vivacity:

"Why, Mary Austin! you bad girl, why didn't you come to Sunday school?"

"I did come—didn't you see me?"

"Why, no! Did you? Where did you sit?"

"I was in Miss Peters' class, where I always go. I saw *you*."

"Did you? Why, it's funny I didn't see you. I wanted to tell you about the picnic."

"Oh, that's jolly. Who's going to give it?"

"My ma's going to let me have one."

"Oh, goody; I hope she'll let *me* come."

"Well, she will. The picnic's for me. She'll let anybody come that I want, and I want you."

"That's ever so nice. When is it going to be?"

"By and by. Maybe about vacation."

"Oh, won't it be fun! You going to have all the girls and boys?"

"Yes, every one that's friends to me—or wants to be"; and she glanced ever so furtively at Tom, but he talked right along to Amy Lawrence about the terrible storm on the island, and how the lightning tore the great sycamore tree "all to flinders" while he was "standing within three feet of it."

"Oh, may I come?" said Gracie Miller.

"Yes."

"And me?" said Sally Rogers.

"Yes."

"And me, too?" said Susy Harper. "And Joe?"

"Yes."

And so on, with clapping of joyful hands till all the group had begged for invitations but Tom and Amy. Then Tom turned coolly away, still talking, and took Amy with him. Becky's legs trembled and the tears came to her eyes; she hid these signs with a forced gaiety and went on chattering, but the life had gone out of the picnic, now, and out of everything else; she got away as soon as she could and hid herself and had what her sex call "a good cry." Then she sat moody, with wounded pride, till the bell rang. She roused up, now, with a vindictive cast in her eye, and gave her plaited tails a shake and said she knew what *she'd* do.

At recess Tom continued his flirtation with Amy with jubilant self-satisfaction. And he kept drifting about to find Becky and lacerate her with the performance. At last he spied her, but there was a sudden falling of his mercury. She was sitting cozily on a little bench behind the schoolhouse looking at a picture book with Alfred Temple—and so absorbed were they, and their heads so close together over the book, that they did not seem to be conscious of anything in the world besides. Jealousy ran red-hot through Tom's veins. He began to hate himself for throwing away the chance Becky had offered for a reconciliation. He called himself a fool, and all the hard names he could think of. He wanted to cry with vexation. Amy chatted happily along, as they walked, for her heart was singing, but Tom's tongue had lost its function. He did not hear what Amy was saying, and whenever she paused expectantly he could only stammer an awkward assent, which was as often misplaced as otherwise. He kept drifting to the rear of the schoolhouse, again and again, to sear his eyeballs with the hateful spectacle there. He could not help it. And it maddened him to see, as he thought he saw, that Becky Thatcher never once suspected that he was even in the land of the living. But she did see, nevertheless; and she knew she was winning her fight, too, and was glad to see him suffer as she had suffered.

Amy's happy prattle became intolerable. Tom hinted at things he had to attend to; things that must be done; and time was fleeting. But in vain—the girl chirped on. Tom thought, "Oh, hang her, ain't I ever going to get rid of her?" At last he *must* be attending to those things—and she said artlessly that she would be "around" when school let out. And he hastened away, hating her for it.

"Any other boy!" Tom thought, grating his teeth. "Any boy in the whole town but that St. Louis smarty that thinks he dresses so fine and is aristocracy! Oh, all right, I licked you the first day you ever saw this town, mister, and I'll lick you again! You just wait till I catch you out! I'll just take and—"

And he went through the motions of thrashing an imaginary boy—pummeling the air, and kicking and gouging. "Oh, you do, do you? You holler 'nough, do you? Now, then, let that learn you!" And so the imaginary flogging was finished to his satisfaction.

Tom fled home at noon. His conscience could not endure any more of Amy's grateful happiness, and his jealousy could bear no more of the other distress. Becky resumed her picture inspections with Alfred, but as the minutes dragged along and no Tom came to suffer, her triumph began to cloud and she lost interest; gravity and absent-mindedness followed, and then melancholy; two or three times she pricked up her ear at a footstep, but it was a false hope; no Tom came. At last she grew entirely miserable and wished she hadn't carried it so far. When poor Alfred, seeing that he was losing her, he did not know how, kept exclaiming: "Oh, here's a jolly one! look at this!" she lost patience at last, and said, "Oh, don't bother me! I don't care for them!" and burst into tears, and got up and walked away.

Alfred dropped alongside and was going to try to comfort her, but she said:

"Go away and leave me alone, can't you! I hate you!"

So the boy halted, wondering what he could have done—for she had said she would look at pictures all through the nooning—and she walked on, crying. Then Alfred went musing into the deserted schoolhouse. He was humiliated and angry. He easily guessed his way to the truth—the girl had simply made a convenience of him to vent her spite upon Tom Sawyer. He was far from hating Tom the less when this thought occurred to him. He wished there was some way to get that boy into trouble without much risk to himself. Tom's spelling book fell under his eye. Here was his opportunity. He gratefully opened to the lesson for the afternoon and poured ink upon the page.

Becky, glancing in at a window behind him at the moment, saw the act, and moved on, without discovering herself. She started homeward, now, intending to find Tom and tell him; Tom would be thankful and their troubles would be healed. Before she was halfway home, however, she had changed her mind. The thought of Tom's treatment of her when she was talking about her picnic came scorching back and filled her with shame. She resolved to let him get whipped on the damaged spelling book's account, and to hate him forever, into the bargain.

19 *Tom Tells the Truth*

Tom arrived at home in a dreary mood, and the first thing his aunt said to him showed him that he had brought his sorrows to an unpromising market:

"Tom, I've a notion to skin you alive!"

"Auntie, what have I done?"

"Well, you've done enough. Here I go over to Sereny Harper, like an old softy, expecting I'm going to make her believe all that rubbage about that dream, when lo and behold you she'd found out from Joe that you was over here and heard all the talk we had that night. Tom, I don't know what is to become of a boy that will act like that. It makes me feel so bad to think you could let me go to Sereny Harper and make such a fool of myself and never say a word."

This was a new aspect of the thing. His smartness of the morning had seemed to Tom a good joke before, and very ingenious. It merely looked mean and shabby now. He hung his head and could not think of anything to say for a moment. Then he said:

"Auntie, I wish I hadn't done it—but I didn't think."

"Oh, child, you never think. You never think of anything but your own selfishness. You could think to come all the way over here from Jackson's Island in the night to laugh at our troubles, and you could think to fool me with a lie about a dream; but you couldn't ever think to pity us and save us from sorrow."

"Auntie, I know now it was mean, but I didn't mean to be mean. I didn't, honest. And besides, I didn't come over here to laugh at you that night."

"What did you come for, then?"

"It was to tell you not to be uneasy about us, because we hadn't got drowned."

"Tom, Tom, I would be the thankfullest soul in this world if I could believe you ever had as good a thought as that, but you know you never did—and *I* know it, Tom."

"Indeed, and 'deed I did, auntie—I wish I may never stir if I didn't."

"Oh, Tom, don't lie—don't do it. It only makes things a hundred times worse."

"It ain't a lie, auntie, it's the truth. I wanted to keep you from grieving—that was all that made me come."

"I'd give the whole world to believe that—it would cover up a power of sins, Tom. I'd 'most be glad you'd run off and acted so bad. But it ain't reasonable; because, why didn't you tell me, child?"

"Why, you see, when you got to talking about the funeral, I just got all full of the idea of our coming and hiding in the church, and I couldn't somehow bear to spoil it. So I just put the bark back in my pocket and kept mum."

"What bark?"

"The bark I had wrote on to tell you we'd gone pirating. I wish, now, you'd waked up when I kissed you—I do, honest."

The hard lines in his aunt's face relaxed and a sudden tenderness dawned in her eyes.

"*Did* you kiss me, Tom?"

"Why, yes, I did."

"Are you sure you did, Tom?"

"Why, yes, I did, auntie—certain sure."

"What did you kiss me for, Tom?"

"Because I loved you so, and you laid there moaning and I was so sorry."

The words sounded like truth. The old lady could not hide a tremor in her voice when she said:

"Kiss me again, Tom!—and be off with you to school, now, and don't bother me any more."

The moment he was gone, she ran to a closet and got out the ruin of a jacket which Tom had gone pirating in. Then she stopped, with it in her hand, and said to herself:

"No, I don't dare. Poor boy, I reckon he's lied about it—but it's a blessed, blessed lie, there's such a comfort come from it. I hope the Lord—I *know* the Lord will forgive him, because it was such goodheartedness in him to tell it. But I don't want to find out it's a lie. I won't look."

She put the jacket away, and stood by musing a minute. Twice she put out her hand to take the garment again, and twice she refrained. Once more she ventured, and this time she fortified herself with the thought: "It's a good lie—it's a good lie—I won't let it grieve me." So she sought the jacket pocket. A moment later she was reading Tom's piece of bark through flowing tears and saying: "I could forgive the boy, now, if he'd committed a million sins!"

20 *Becky in a Dilemma—Tom's Nobility Asserts Itself*

There was something about Aunt Polly's manner, when she kissed Tom, that swept away his low spirits and made him lighthearted and happy again. He started to school and had the luck of coming upon Becky Thatcher at the head of Meadow Lane. His mood always determined his manner. Without a moment's hesitation he ran to her and said:

"I acted mighty mean today, Becky, and I'm so sorry. I won't ever, ever do that way again, as long as ever I live —please make up, won't you?"

The girl stopped and looked him scornfully in the face:

"I'll thank you to keep yourself *to* yourself, Mr. Thomas Sawyer. I'll never speak to you again."

She tossed her head and passed on. Tom was so stunned that he had not even presence of mind enough to say "Who cares, Miss Smarty?" until the right time to say it had gone by. So he said nothing. But he was in a fine rage, nevertheless. He moped into the schoolyard wishing she were a boy, and imagining how he would trounce her if she were. He presently encountered her and delivered a stinging remark as he passed. She hurled one in return, and the angry breach was complete. It seemed to Becky, in her hot resentment, that she could hardly wait for school to "take in," she was so impatient to see Tom flogged for the injured spelling book. If she had had any lingering notion of exposing Alfred Temple, Tom's offensive fling had driven it entirely away.

Poor girl, she did not know how fast she was nearing trouble herself. The master, Mr. Dobbins, had reached middle age with an unsatisfied ambition. The darling of his desires was to be a doctor, but poverty had decreed that he should be nothing higher than a village schoolmaster. Every day he took a mysterious book out of his desk and absorbed himself in it at times when no classes were reciting. He kept that book under lock and key. There was not an urchin in school but was perishing to have a glimpse of it, but the chance never came. Every boy and girl had a theory about the nature of that book; but no two theories were alike, and there was no way of getting at the facts in the case. Now, as Becky was passing by the desk, which stood near the door, she noticed that the key was in the lock! It was a precious moment. She glanced around; found herself alone, and the next instant she had the book in her hands. The title page—Professor Somebody's *Anatomy*—carried no information to her mind; so she began to turn the leaves. She came at once upon a handsomely engraved and colored frontispiece—a human figure, stark naked. At that moment a shadow fell on the page and Tom Sawyer stepped in at the door, and caught a glimpse of the picture. Becky snatched at the book to close it, and had the hard luck to tear the pictured page half down the middle. She thrust the volume into the desk, turned the key, and burst out crying with shame and vexation.

"Tom Sawyer, you are just as mean as you can be, to sneak up on a person and look at what they're looking at."

"How could *I* know you was looking at anything?"

"You ought to be ashamed of yourself, Tom Sawyer; you know you're going to tell on me, and oh, what shall I do, what shall I do! I'll be whipped, and I never was whipped in school."

Then she stamped her little foot and said:

"*Be* so mean if you want to! *I* know something that's going to happen. You just wait and you'll see! Hateful, hateful, hateful!"—and she flung out of the house with a new explosion of crying.

Tom stood still, rather flustered by this onslaught. Presently he said to himself:

"What a curious kind of a fool a girl is. Never been

licked in school! Shucks. What's a licking! That's just like a girl—they're so thin-skinned and chicken-hearted. Well, of course *I* ain't going to tell old Dobbins on this little fool, because there's other ways of getting even on her, that ain't so mean; but what of it? Old Dobbins will ask who it was tore his book. Nobody'll answer. Then he'll do just the way he always does—ask first one and then t'other, and when he comes to the right girl he'll know it, without any telling. Girls' faces always tell on them. They ain't got any backbone. She'll get licked. Well, it's a kind of a tight place for Becky Thatcher, because there ain't any way out of it." Tom conned the thing a moment longer and then added: "All right, though; she'd like to see me in just such a fix—let her sweat it out!"

Tom joined the mob of skylarking scholars outside. In a few moments the master arrived and school "took in." Tom did not feel a strong interest in his studies. Every time he stole a glance at the girls' side of the room Becky's face troubled him. Considering all things, he did not want to pity her, and yet it was all he could do to help it. He could get up no exultation that was really worthy the name. Presently the spelling book discovery was made, and Tom's mind was entirely full of his own matters for a while after that. Becky roused up from her lethargy of distress and showed good interest in the proceedings. She did not expect that Tom could get out of his trouble by denying that he spilt the ink on the book himself; and she was right. The denial only seemed to make the thing worse for Tom. Becky supposed she would be glad of that, and she tried to believe she was glad of it, but she found she was not certain. When the worst came to the worst, she had an impulse to get up and tell on Alfred Temple, but she made an effort and forced herself to keep still—because, said she to herself, "he'll tell about me tearing the picture sure. I wouldn't say a word, not to save his life!"

Tom took his whipping and went back to his seat not at all brokenhearted, for he thought it was possible that he had unknowingly upset the ink on the spelling book himself, in some skylarking bout—he had denied it for form's sake and because it was custom, and had stuck to the denial from principle.

A whole hour drifted by, the master sat nodding on his throne, the air was drowsy with the hum of study. By and by, Mr. Dobbins straightened himself up, yawned, then unlocked his desk, and reached for his book, but seemed undecided whether to take it out or leave it. Most of the pupils glanced up languidly, but there were two among them that watched his movements with intent eyes. Mr. Dobbins fingered his book absently for a while, then took it out and settled himself in his chair to read! Tom shot a glance at Becky. He had seen a hunted and helpless rabbit look as she did, with a gun leveled at its head. Instantly he forgot his quarrel with her. Quick—something must be done! done in a flash, too! But the very imminence of the emergency paralyzed his invention. Good!—he had an inspiration! He would run and snatch the book, spring through the door and fly. But his resolution shook for one little instant, and the chance was lost—the master opened the volume. If Tom only had the wasted opportunity back again! Too late. There was no help for Becky now, he saw. The next moment the master faced the school. Every eye sunk under his gaze. There was that in it which smote even the innocent with fear. There was silence while one might count ten; the master was gathering his wrath. Then he spoke:

"Who tore this book?"

There was not a sound. One could have heard a pin drop. The stillness continued; the master searched face after face for signs of guilt.

"Benjamin Rogers, did you tear this book?"

A denial. Another pause.

"Joseph Harper, did you?"

Another denial. Tom's uneasiness grew more and more intense under the slow torture of these proceedings. The master scanned the ranks of the boys—considered a while, then turned to the girls:

"Amy Lawrence?"

A shake of the head.

"Gracie Miller?"

The same sign.

"Susan Harper, did you do this?"

Another negative. The next girl was Becky Thatcher. Tom was trembling from head to foot with excitement and a sense of the hopelessness of the situation.

"Rebecca Thatcher" (Tom glanced at her face—it was white with terror)—"did you tear—no, look me in the face" (her hands rose in appeal)—"did you tear this book?"

A thought shot like lightning through Tom's brain. He sprang to his feet and shouted—"*I* done it!"

The school stared in perplexity at this incredible folly. Tom stood a moment, to gather his dismembered faculties; and when he stepped forward to go to his punishment the surprise, the gratitude, the adoration that shone upon him out of poor Becky's eyes seemed pay enough for a hundred floggings. Inspired by the splendor of his own act, he took without an outcry the most merciless flaying that even Mr. Dobbins had ever administered; and also received with indifference the added cruelty of a command to remain two hours after school should be dismissed—for he knew who would wait for him outside till his captivity was done, and not count the tedious time as loss, either.

Tom went to bed that night planning vengeance against Alfred Temple; for with shame and repentance Becky had told him all, not forgetting her own treachery; but even the longing for vengeance had to give way, soon, to pleasanter musings, and he fell asleep at last, with Becky's latest words lingering dreamily in his ear—

"Tom, how *could* you be so noble!"

21 *Youthful Eloquence—Compositions by the Young Ladies—A Lengthy Vision—The Boy's Vengeance Satisfied*

Vacation was approaching. The schoolmaster, always severe, grew severer and more exacting than ever, for he wanted the school to make a good showing on "Examination" day. His rod and his ferule were seldom idle now—at least among the smaller pupils. Only the biggest boys, and young ladies of eighteen and twenty, escaped lashing. Mr. Dobbins' lashings were very vigorous ones, too; for although he carried, under his wig, a perfectly bald and shiny head, he had only reached middle age and there was no sign of feebleness in his muscle. As the great day approached, all the tyranny that was in him came to the surface; he seemed to take a vindictive pleasure in punishing the least shortcomings. The consequence was, that the smaller boys spent their days in terror and suffering and their nights in plotting revenge. They threw away no opportunity to do the master a mischief. But he kept ahead all the time. The retribution that followed every vengeful success was so sweeping and majestic that the boys always retired from the field badly worsted. At last they conspired together and hit upon a plan that promised a dazzling victory. They swore in the sign painter's boy, told him the scheme, and asked his help. He had his own reasons for being delighted, for the master boarded in his father's family and had given the boy ample cause to hate him. The master's wife would go on a visit to the country in a few days, and there would be nothing to interfere with the plan; the master always prepared himself for great occasions by getting pretty well fuddled, and the sign painter's boy said that when the dominie had reached the proper condition on Examination Evening he would "manage the thing" while he napped in his chair; then he would have him awakened at the right time and hurried away to school.

In the fullness of time the interesting occasion arrived. At eight in the evening the schoolhouse was brilliantly lighted, and adorned with wreaths and festoons of foliage and flowers. The master sat throned in his great chair upon a raised platform, with his blackboard behind him. He was looking tolerably mellow. Three rows of benches on each side and six rows in front of him were occupied by the dignitaries of the town and by the parents of the pupils. To his left, back of the rows of citizens, was a spacious temporary platform upon which were seated the scholars who were to take part in the exercises of the evening; rows of small boys, washed and dressed to an intolerable state of discomfort; rows of gawky big boys; snowbanks of girls and young ladies clad in lawn and muslin and conspicuously conscious of their bare arms, their grandmothers' ancient trinkets, their bits of pink and blue ribbon and the flowers in their hair. All the rest of the house was filled with nonparticipating scholars.

The exercises began. A very little boy stood up and sheepishly recited, "You'd scarce expect one of my age to speak in public on the stage," etc.—accompanying himself with the painfully exact and spasmodic gestures which a machine might have used—supposing the machine to be a trifle out of order. But he got through safely, though cruelly scared, and got a fine round of applause when he made his manufactured bow and retired.

A little shamefaced girl lisped "Mary had a little lamb," etc., performed a compassion-inspiring curtsy, got her meed of applause, and sat down flushed and happy.

Tom Sawyer stepped forward with conceited confidence and soared into the unquenchable and indestructible "Give me liberty or give me death" speech, with fine fury and frantic gesticulation, and broke down in the middle of it. A ghastly stage fright seized him, his legs quaked under him and he was like to choke. True, he had the manifest sympathy of the house—but he had the house's silence, too, which was even worse than its sympathy. The master frowned, and this completed the disaster. Tom struggled a while and then retired, utterly defeated. There was a weak attempt at applause, but it died early.

"The Boy Stood on the Burning Deck" followed; also "The Assyrian Came Down," and other declamatory gems. Then there were reading exercises, and a spelling fight. The meager Latin class recited with honor. The prime feature of the evening was in order, now—original "compositions" by the young ladies. Each in her turn stepped forward to the edge of the platform, cleared her throat, held up her manuscript (tied with dainty ribbon), and proceeded to read, with labored attention to "expression" and punctuation. The themes were the same that had been illuminated upon similar occasions by their mothers before them, their grandmothers, and doubtless all their ancestors in the female line clear back to the Crusades. "Friendship" was one; "Memories of Other Days"; "Religion in History"; "Dream Land"; "The Advantages of Culture"; "Forms of Political Government Compared and Contrasted"; "Melancholy"; "Filial Love"; "Heart Longings," etc., etc.

A prevalent feature in these compositions was a nursed and petted melancholy; another was a wasteful and opulent gush of "fine language"; another was a tendency to lug in by the ears particularly prized words and phrases until they were worn entirely out; and a peculiarity that conspicuously marked and marred them was the inveterate and intolerable sermon that wagged its crippled tail at the end of each and every one of them. No matter what the subject might be, a brain-racking effort was made to squirm it into some aspect or other that the moral and religious mind could contemplate with edification. The glaring insincerity of these sermons was not sufficient to compass the banishment of the fashion from the schools, and it is not sufficient today; it never will be sufficient while the world stands, perhaps. There is no school in all our land where the young ladies do not feel obliged to close their compositions with a sermon; and you will find that the sermon of the most frivolous and the least religious girl in the school is always the longest and the most relentlessly pious. But enough of this. Homely truth is unpalatable.

Let us return to the "Examination." The first composition that was read was one entitled "Is this, then, Life?" Perhaps the reader can endure an extract from it:

In the common walks of life, with what delightful emotions does the youthful mind look forward to some anticipated scene of festivity! Imagination is busy sketching rose-tinted pictures of joy. In fancy, the voluptuous votary of fashion sees herself amid the festive throng, "the observed of all observers." Her graceful form, arrayed in snowy robes, is whirling through the mazes of the joyous dance; her eye is brightest, her step is lightest in the gay assembly.

In such delicious fancies time quickly glides by, and the welcome hour arrives for her entrance into the Elysian world, of which she has had such bright dreams. How fairy-like does everything appear to her enchanted vision! Each new scene is more charming than the last. But after a while she finds that beneath this goodly exterior, all is vanity: the flattery which once charmed her soul, now grates harshly upon her ear; the ballroom has lost its charms; and with wasted health and embittered heart, she turns away with the conviction that earthly pleasures cannot satisfy the longing of the soul!

And so forth and so on. There was a buzz of gratification from time to time during the reading, accompanied by whispered ejaculations of "How sweet!" "How eloquent!" "So true!" etc., and after the thing had closed with a peculiarly afflicting sermon the applause was enthusiastic.

Then arose a slim, melancholy girl, whose face had the "interesting" paleness that comes of pills and indigestion, and read a "poem." Two stanzas of it will do:

A MISSOURI MAIDEN'S FAREWELL TO ALABAMA

Alabama, good-by! I love thee well!
  But yet for awhile do I leave thee now!
Sad, yes, sad thoughts of thee my heart doth swell,
  And burning recollections throng my brow!
For I have wandered through thy flowery woods;
  Have roamed and read near Tallapoosa's stream;
Have listened to Tallassee's warring floods,
  And wooed on Coosa's side Aurora's beam.
Yet shame I not to bear an o'er-full heart,
  Nor blush to turn behind my tearful eyes;
'Tis from no stranger land I now must part,
  'Tis to no strangers left I yield these sighs.
Welcome and home were mine within this State,
  Whose vales I leave—whose spires fade fast from me;
And cold must be mine eyes, and heart, and tête,
  When, dear Alabama! they turn cold on thee!

There were very few there who knew what *"tête"* meant, but the poem was very satisfactory, nevertheless.

Next appeared a dark-complexioned, black-eyed, black-haired young lady, who paused an impressive moment, assumed a tragic expression, and began to read in a measured, solemn tone.

A VISION

Dark and tempestuous was night. Around the throne on high not a single star quivered; but the deep intonations of the heavy thunder constantly vibrated upon the ear; whilst the terrific lightning revelled in angry mood through the cloudy chambers of heaven, seeming to scorn the power exerted over its terror by the illustrious Franklin! Even the boisterous winds unanimously came forth from their mystic homes, and blustered about as if to enhance by their aid the wildness of the scene.

At such a time, so dark, so dreary, for human sympathy my very spirit sighed; but instead thereof,

"My dearest friend, my counsellor, my comforter and guide—
My joy in grief, my second bliss in joy," came to my side.

She moved like one of those bright beings pictured in the sunny walks of fancy's Eden by the romantic and young, a queen of beauty unadorned save by her own transcendent loveliness. So soft was her step, it failed to make even a sound, and but for the magical thrill imparted by her genial touch, as other unobtrusive beauties, she would have glided away unperceived—unsought. A strange sadness rested upon her features, like icy tears upon the robe of December, as she pointed to the contending elements without, and bade me contemplate the two beings presented.

This nightmare occupied some ten pages of manuscript and wound up with a sermon so destructive of all hope to non-Presbyterians that it took the first prize. This composition was considered to be the very finest effort of the evening. The mayor of the village, in delivering the prize to the author of it, made a warm speech in which he said that it was by far the most "eloquent" thing he had ever listened to, and that Daniel Webster himself might well be proud of it.

It may be remarked, in passing, that the number of compositions in which the word "beauteous" was overfondled, and human experience referred to as "life's page," was up to the usual average.

Now the master, mellow almost to the verge of geniality, put his chair aside, turned his back to the audience, and began to draw a map of America on the blackboard, to exercise the geography class upon. But he made a sad business of it with his unsteady hand, and a smothered titter rippled over the house. He knew what the matter was and set himself to right it. He sponged out lines and remade them; but he only distorted them more than ever, and the tittering was more pronounced. He threw his entire attention upon his work, now, as if determined not to be put down by the mirth. He felt that all eyes were fastened upon him; he imagined he was succeeding, and yet the tittering continued; it even manifestly increased. And well it might. There was a garret above, pierced with a scuttle over his head; and down through this scuttle came a cat, suspended around the haunches by a string; she had a rag tied about her head and jaws to keep her from mewing; as she slowly descended she curved upward and clawed at the string, she swung downward and clawed at the intangible air. The tittering rose higher and higher—the cat was within six inches of the absorbed teacher's head—down, down, a little lower, and she grabbed his wig with her desperate claws, clung to it, and was snatched up into the garret in an instant with her trophy still in her possession! And how the light did blaze abroad from the master's bald pate—for the sign painter's boy had *gilded* it!

That broke up the meeting. The boys were avenged. Vacation had come.

NOTE.—The pretended "compositions" quoted in this chapter are taken without alteration from a volume entitled *Prose and Poetry, by a Western Lady*—but they are exactly and precisely after the schoolgirl pattern, and hence are much happier than any mere imitations could be.

22 *Tom's Confidence Betrayed—Expects Signal Punishment*

Tom joined the new order of Cadets of Temperance, being attracted by the showy character of their "regalia." He promised to abstain from smoking, chewing, and profanity as long as he remained a member. Now he found out a new thing—namely, that to promise not to do a thing is the surest way in the world to make a body want to go and do that very thing. Tom soon found himself tormented with a desire to drink and swear; the desire grew to be so intense that nothing but the hope of a chance to display himself in his red sash kept him from withdrawing from the order. Fourth of July was coming; but he soon gave that up—gave it up before he had worn his shackles over forty-eight hours—and fixed his hopes upon old Judge Frazer, justice of the peace, who was apparently on his deathbed and would have a big public funeral, since he was so high an official. During three days Tom was deeply concerned about the Judge's condition and hungry for news of it. Sometimes his hopes ran high—so high that he would venture to get out his regalia and practice before the looking glass. But the Judge had a most discouraging way of fluctuating. At last he was pronounced upon the mend—and then convalescent. Tom was disgusted; and felt a sense of injury, too. He handed in his resignation at once—and that night the Judge suffered a relapse and died. Tom resolved that he would never trust a man like that again.

The funeral was a fine thing. The Cadets paraded in a style calculated to kill the late member with envy. Tom was a free boy again, however—there was something in that. He could drink and swear, now—but found to his surprise that he did not want to. The simple fact that he could, took the desire away, and the charm of it.

Tom presently wondered to find that his coveted vacation was beginning to hang a little heavily on his hands.

He attempted a diary—but nothing happened during three days, and so he abandoned it.

The first of all the Negro minstrel shows came to town, and made a sensation. Tom and Joe Harper got up a band of performers and were happy for two days.

Even the Glorious Fourth was in some sense a failure, for it rained hard, there was no procession in consequence, and the greatest man in the world (as Tom supposed) Mr. Benton, an actual United States Senator, proved an overwhelming disappointment—for he was not twenty-five feet high, nor even anywhere in the neighborhood of it.

A circus came. The boys played circus for three days afterward in tents made of rag carpeting—admission, three pins for boys, two for girls—and then circusing was abandoned.

A phrenologist and a mesmerizer came—and went again and left the village duller and drearier than ever.

There were some boys-and-girls' parties, but they were so few and so delightful that they only made the aching voids between ache the harder.

Becky Thatcher was gone to her Constantinople home to stay with her parents during vacation—so there was no bright side to life anywhere.

The dreadful secret of the murder was a chronic misery. It was a very cancer for permanency and pain.

Then came the measles.

During two long weeks Tom lay a prisoner dead to the world and its happenings. He was very ill, he was interested in nothing. When he got upon his feet at last and moved feebly down town, a melancholy change had come over everything and every creature. There had been a "revival," and everybody had "got religion," not only the adults, but even the boys and girls. Tom went about, hoping against hope for the sight of one blessed sinful face, but disappointment crossed him everywhere. He found Joe Harper studying a Testament, and turned sadly away from the depressing spectacle. He sought Ben Rogers, and found him visiting the poor with a basket of tracts. He hunted up Jim Hollis, who called his attention to the precious blessing of his late measles as a warning. Every boy he encountered added another ton to his depression; and when, in desperation, he flew for refuge at last to the bosom of Huckleberry Finn and was received with a Scriptural quotation, his heart broke and he crept home and to bed realizing that he alone of all the town was lost, forever and forever.

And that night there came on a terrific storm, with driving rain, awful claps of thunder and blinding sheets of lightning. He covered his head with the bedclothes and waited in a horror of suspense for his doom; for he had not the shadow of a doubt that all this hubbub was about him. He believed he had taxed the forbearance of the powers above to the extremity of endurance and that this was the result. It might have seemed to him a waste of pomp and ammunition to kill a bug with a battery of artillery, but there seemed nothing incongruous about the getting up such an expensive thunderstorm as this to knock the turf from under an insect like himself.

By and by the tempest spent itself and died without accomplishing its object. The boy's first impulse was to be grateful, and reform. His second was to wait—for there might not be any more storms.

The next day the doctors were back; Tom had relapsed. The three weeks he spent on his back this time seemed an entire age. When he got abroad at last he was hardly grateful that he had been spared, remembering how lonely was his estate, how companionless and forlorn he was. He drifted listlessly down the street and found Jim Hollis acting as a judge in a juvenile court that was trying a cat for murder, in the presence of her victim, a bird. He found Joe Harper and Huck Finn up an alley eating a stolen melon. Poor lads! they—like Tom—had suffered a relapse.

23 *Old Muff's Friends—Muff Potter in Court—Muff Potter Saved*

At last the sleepy atmosphere was stirred—and vigorously: the murder trial came on in the court. It became the absorbing topic of village talk immediately. Tom could not get away from it. Every reference to the murder sent a shudder to his heart, for his troubled conscience and fears almost persuaded him that these remarks were put forth in his hearing as "feelers"; he did not see how he could be suspected of knowing anything about the murder, but still he could not be comfortable in the midst of this gossip. It kept him in a cold shiver all the time. He took Huck to a lonely place to have a talk with him. It would be some relief to unseal his tongue for a little while; to divide his burden of distress with another sufferer. Moreover, he wanted to assure himself that Huck had remained discreet.

"Huck, have you ever told anybody about—that?"

" 'Bout what?"

"You know what."

"Oh—'course I haven't."

"Never a word?"

"Never a solitary word, so help me. What makes you ask?"

"Well, I was afeard."

"Why, Tom Sawyer, we wouldn't be alive two days if that got found out. *You* know that."

Tom felt more comfortable. After a pause:

"Huck, they couldn't anybody get you to tell, could they?"

"Get me to tell? Why, if I wanted that half-breed devil to drownd me they could get me to tell. They ain't no different way."

"Well, that's all right, then. I reckon we're safe as long as we keep mum. But let's swear again, anyway. It's more surer."

"I'm agreed."

So they swore again with dread solemnities.

"What is the talk around, Huck? I've heard a power of it."

"Talk? Well, it's just Muff Potter, Muff Potter, Muff Potter all the time. It keeps me in a sweat, constant, so's I want to hide som'ers."

"That's just the same way they go on round me. I reckon he's a goner. Don't you feel sorry for him, sometimes?"

"Most always—most always. He ain't no account; but then he hain't ever done anything to hurt anybody. Just fishes a little, to get money to get drunk on—and loafs around considerable; but lord, we all do that—leastways most of us—preachers and suchlike. But he's kind of good—he give me half a fish, once, when there warn't enough for two; and lots of times he's kind of stood by me when I was out of luck."

"Well, he's mended kites for me, Huck, and knitted hooks on to my line. I wish we could get him out of there."

"My! we couldn't get him out, Tom. And besides, 'twouldn't do any good; they'd ketch him again."

"Yes—so they would. But I hate to hear 'em abuse him so like the dickens when he never done—that."

"I do too, Tom. Lord, I hear 'em say he's the bloodiest-looking villain in this country, and they wonder he wasn't ever hung before."

"Yes, they talk like that, all the time. I've heard 'em say that if he was to get free they'd lynch him."

"And they'd do it, too."

The boys had a long talk, but it brought them little comfort. As the twilight drew on, they found themselves hanging about the neighborhood of the little isolated jail, perhaps with an undefined hope that something would happen that might clear away their difficulties. But nothing happened; there seemed to be no angels or fairies interested in this luckless captive.

The boys did as they had often done before—went to the cell grating and gave Potter some tobacco and matches. He was on the ground floor and there were no guards.

His gratitude for their gifts had always smote their consciences before—it cut deeper than ever, this time. They felt cowardly and treacherous to the last degree when Potter said:

"You've been mighty good to me, boys—better'n anybody else in this town. And I don't forget it, I don't. Often I says to myself, says I, 'I used to mend all the boys' kites and things, and show 'em where the good fishin' places was, and befriend 'em what I could, and now they've all forgot old Muff when he's in trouble; but Tom don't, and Huck don't—*they* don't forget him,' says I, 'and I don't forget them.' Well, boys, I done an awful thing—drunk and crazy at the time—that's the only way I account for it—and now I got to swing for it, and it's right. Right, and *best,* too, I reckon—hope so, anyway. Well, we won't talk about that. I don't want to make *you* feel bad; you've befriended me. But what I want to say, is, don't *you* ever get drunk—then you won't ever get here. Stand a litter furder west—so—that's it; it's a prime comfort to see faces that's friendly when a body's in such a muck of trouble, and there don't none come here but yourn. Good friendly faces—good friendly faces. Git up on one another's backs and let me touch 'em. That's it. Shake hands—yourn'll come through the bars, but mine's too big. Little hands, and weak—but they've helped Muff Potter a power, and they'd help him more if they could."

Tom went home miserable, and his dreams that night were full of horrors. The next day and the day after, he hung about the courtroom, drawn by an almost irresistible impulse to go in, but forcing himself to stay out. Huck was having the same experience. They studiously avoided each other. Each wandered away, from time to time, but the same dismal fascination always brought them back presently. Tom kept his ears open when idlers sauntered out of the courtroom, but invariably heard distressing news—the toils were closing more and more relentlessly around poor Potter. At the end of the second day the village talk was to the effect that Injun Joe's evidence stood firm and unshaken, and that there was not the slightest question as to what the jury's verdict would be.

Tom was out late, that night, and came to bed through the window. He was in a tremendous state of excitement. It was hours before he got to sleep. All the village flocked to the courthouse the next morning, for this was to be the great day. Both sexes were about equally represented in the packed audience. After a long wait the jury filed in and took their places; shortly afterward, Potter, pale and haggard, timid and hopeless, was brought in, with chains upon him, and seated where all the curious eyes could stare at him; no less conspicuous was Injun Joe, stolid as ever. There was another pause, and then the judge arrived and the sheriff proclaimed the opening of the court. The usual whisperings among the lawyers and gathering together of papers followed. These details and accompanying delays worked up an atmosphere of preparation that was as impressive as it was fascinating.

Now a witness was called who testified that he found Muff Potter washing in the brook, at an early hour of the morning that the murder was discovered, and that he immediately sneaked away. After some further questioning, counsel for the prosecution said:

"Take the witness."

The prisoner raised his eyes for a moment, but dropped them again when his own counsel said:

"I have no questions to ask him."

The next witness proved the finding of the knife near the corpse. Counsel for the prosecution said:

"Take the witness."

"I have no questions to ask him," Potter's lawyer replied.

A third witness swore he had often seen the knife in Potter's possession.

"Take the witness."

Counsel for Potter declined to question him. The faces of the audience began to betray annoyance. Did this attorney mean to throw away his client's life without an effort?

Several witnesses deposed concerning Potter's guilty behavior when brought to the scene of the murder. They were allowed to leave the stand without being cross-questioned.

Every detail of the damaging circumstances that occurred in the graveyard upon that morning which all present remembered so well, was brought out by credible witnesses, but none of them was cross-examined by Potter's lawyer. The perplexity and dissatisfaction of the house expressed itself in murmurs and provoked a reproof from the bench. Counsel for the prosecution now said:

"By the oaths of citizens whose simple word is above suspicion, we have fastened this awful crime, beyond all possibility of question, upon the unhappy prisoner at the bar. We rest our case here."

A groan escaped from poor Potter, and he put his face in his hands and rocked his body softly to and fro, while a painful silence reigned in the courtroom. Many men were moved, and many women's compassion testified itself in tears. Counsel for the defense rose and said:

"Your honor, in our remarks at the opening of this trial, we foreshadowed our purpose to prove that our client did this fearful deed while under the influence of a blind and irresponsible delirium produced by drink. We have changed our mind. We shall not offer that plea." (Then to the clerk): "Call Thomas Sawyer!"

A puzzled amazement awoke in every face in the house, not even excepting Potter's. Every eye fastened itself with wondering interest upon Tom as he rose and took his place upon the stand. The boy looked wild enough, for he was badly scared. The oath was administered.

"Thomas Sawyer, where were you on the seventeenth of June, about the hour of midnight?"

Tom glanced at Injun Joe's iron face and his tongue

failed him. The audience listened breathless, but the words refused to come. After a few moments, however, the boy got a little of his strength back, and managed to put enough of it into his voice to make part of the house hear:

"In the graveyard!"

"A little bit louder, please. Don't be afraid. You were——"

"In the graveyard."

A contemptuous smile flitted across Injun Joe's face.

"Were you anywhere near Horse Williams' grave?"

"Yes, sir."

"Speak up—just a trifle louder. How near were you?"

"Near as I am to you."

"Were you hidden, or not?"

"I was hid."

"Where?"

"Behind the elms that's on the edge of the grave."

Injun Joe gave a barely perceptible start.

"Anyone with you?"

"Yes, sir. I went there with——"

"Wait—wait a moment. Never mind mentioning your companion's name. We will produce him at the proper time. Did you carry anything there with you?"

Tom hesitated and looked confused.

"Speak out, my boy—don't be diffident. The truth is always respectable. What did you take there?"

"Only a—a—dead cat."

There was a ripple of mirth, which the court checked.

"We will produce the skeleton of that cat. Now, my boy, tell us everything that occurred—tell it in your own way—don't skip anything, and don't be afraid."

Tom began—hesitatingly at first, but as he warmed up to his subject, his words flowed more and more easily; in a little while every sound ceased but his own voice; every eye fixed itself upon him; with parted lips and bated breath the audience hung upon his words, taking no note of time, rapt in the ghastly fascinations of the tale. The strain upon pent emotion reached its climax when the boy said:

"—and as the doctor fetched the board around and Muff Potter fell, Injun Joe jumped with the knife and——"

Crash! Quick as lightning the half-breed sprang for a window, tore his way through all opposers, and was gone!

24 *Tom as the Village Hero—Days of Splendor and Nights of Horror—Pursuit of Injun Joe*

Tom was a glittering hero once more—the pet of the old, the envy of the young. His name even went into immortal print, for the village paper magnified him. There were some that believed he would be President, yet, if he escaped hanging.

As usual, the fickle, unreasoning world took Muff Potter to its bosom and fondled him as lavishly as it had abused him before. But that sort of conduct is to the world's credit; therefore it is not well to find fault with it.

Tom's days were days of splendor and exultation to him, but his nights were seasons of horror. Injun Joe infested all his dreams, and always with doom in his eye. Hardly any temptation could persuade the boy to stir abroad after nightfall. Poor Huck was in the same state of wretchedness and terror, for Tom had told the whole story to the lawyer the night before the great day of the trial, and Huck was sore afraid that his share in the business might leak out yet, notwithstanding Injun Joe's flight had saved him the suffering of testifying in court. The poor fellow had got the attorney to promise secrecy, but what of that? Since Tom's harassed conscience had managed to drive him to the lawyer's house by night and wring a dread tale from lips that had been sealed with the dismalest and most formidable of oaths, Huck's confidence in the human race was well-nigh obliterated.

Daily Muff Potter's gratitude made Tom glad he had spoken; but nightly he wished he had sealed up his tongue.

Half the time Tom was afraid Injun Joe would never be captured; the other half he was afraid he would be. He felt sure he never could draw a safe breath again until that man was dead and he had seen the corpse.

Rewards had been offered, the country had been scoured, but no Injun Joe was found. One of those omniscient and awe-inspiring marvels, a detective, came up from Saint Louis, moused around, shook his head, looked wise, and made that sort of astounding success which members of that craft usually achieve. That is to say, he "found a clew." But you can't hang a "clew" for murder, and so after that detective had got through and gone home, Tom felt just as insecure as he was before.

The slow days drifted on, and each left behind it a slightly lightened weight of apprehension.

25 *About Kings and Diamonds—Search for the Treasure—Dead People and Ghosts*

There comes a time in every rightly constructed boy's life when he has a raging desire to go somewhere and dig for hidden treasure. This desire suddenly came upon Tom one day. He sallied out to find Joe Harper, but failed of success. Next he sought Ben Rogers; he had gone fishing. Presently he stumbled upon Huck Finn the Red-Handed. Huck would answer. Tom took him to a private place and opened the matter to him confidentially. Huck was willing. Huck was always willing to take a hand in any enterprise that offered entertainment and required no capital, for he had a troublesome superabundance of that sort of time which is *not* money. "Where'll we dig?" said Huck.

"Oh, most anywhere."

"Why, is it hid all around?"

"No indeed it ain't. It's hid in mighty particular places, Huck—sometimes on islands, sometimes in rotten chests under the end of a limb of an old dead tree, just where the shadow falls at midnight; but mostly under the floor in ha'nted houses."

"Who hides it?"

"Why, robbers, of course—who'd you reckon? Sunday-school sup'rintendents?"

"I don't know. If 'twas mine I wouldn't hide it; I'd spend it and have a good time."

"So would I. But robbers don't do that way. They always hide it and leave it there."

"Don't they come after it any more?"

"No, they think they will, but they generally forget the marks, or else they die. Anyway, it lays there a long time and gets rusty; and by and by somebody finds an old yellow paper that tells how to find the marks—a paper that's got to be ciphered over about a week because it's mostly signs and hy'roglyphics."

"Hyro—which?"

"Hy'roglyphics—pictures and things, you know, that don't seem to mean anything."

"Have you got one of them papers, Tom?"

"No."

"Well, then, how you going to find the marks?"

"I don't want any marks. They always bury it under a ha'nted house or on an island, or under a dead tree that's got one limb sticking out. Well, we've tried Jackson's Island a little, and we can try it again some time; and there's the old ha'nted house up the Still-House branch, and there's lots of dead-limb trees—dead loads of 'em."

"Is it under all of them?"

"How you talk! No!"

"Then how you going to know which one to go for?"

"Go for all of 'em!"

"Why, Tom, it'll take all summer."

"Well, what of that? Suppose you find a brass pot with a hundred dollars in it, all rusty and gay, or a rotten chest full of di'monds. How's that?"

Huck's eyes glowed.

"That's bully. Plenty bully enough for me. Just you gimme the hundred dollars and I don't want no di'monds."

"All right. But I bet you *I* ain't going to throw off on di'monds. Some of 'em's worth twenty dollars apiece—there ain't any, hardly, but's worth six bits or a dollar."

"No! Is that so?"

"Cert'nly—anybody'll tell you so. Hain't you ever seen one, Huck?"

"Not as I remember."

"Oh, kings have slathers of them."

"Well, I don't know no kings, Tom."

"I reckon you don't. But if you was to go to Europe you'd see a raft of 'em hopping around."

"Do they hop?"

"Hop?—your granny! No!"

"Well, what did you say they did for?"

"Shucks, I only meant you'd *see* 'em—not hopping of course—what do they want to hop for?—but I mean you'd just see 'em—scattered around, you know, in a kind of a general way. Like that old humpbacked Richard."

"Richard? What's his other name?"

"He didn't have any other name. Kings don't have any but a given name."

"No?"

"But they don't."

"Well, if they like it, Tom, all right; but I don't want to be a king and have only just a given name, like a nigger. But say—where you going to dig first?"

"Well, I don't know. S'pose we tackle that old dead-limb tree on the hill t'other side of Still-House branch?"

"I'm agreed."

So they got a crippled pick and a shovel, and set out on

their three-mile tramp. They arrived hot and panting, and threw themselves down in the shade of a neighboring elm to rest and have a smoke.

"I like this," said Tom.

"So do I."

"Say, Huck, if we find a treasure here, what you going to do with your share?"

"Well, I'll have pie and a glass of soda every day, and I'll go to every circus that comes along. I bet I'll have a gay time."

"Well, ain't you going to save any of it?"

"Save it? What for?"

"Why, so as to have something to live on, by and by."

"Oh, that ain't any use. Pap would come back to thish-yer town some day and get his claws on it if I didn't hurry up, and I tell you he'd clean it out pretty quick. What you going to do with yourn, Tom?"

"I'm going to buy a new drum, and a sure-'nough sword, and a red necktie and a bull pup, and get married."

"Married!"

"That's it."

"Tom, you—why, you ain't in your right mind."

"Wait—you'll see."

"Well, that's the foolishest thing you could do. Look at pap and my mother. Fight! Why, they used to fight all the time. I remember, mighty well."

"That ain't anything. The girl I'm going to marry won't fight."

"Tom, I reckon they're all alike. They'll all comb a body. Now you better think 'bout this awhile. I tell you you better. What's the name of the gal?"

"It ain't a gal at all—it's a girl."

"It's all the same, I reckon; some says gal, some says girl —both's right, like enough. Anyway, what's her name, Tom?"

"I'll tell you sometime—not now."

"All right—that'll do. Only if you get married I'll be more lonesomer than ever."

"No you won't. You'll come and live with me. Now stir out of this and we'll go to digging."

They worked and sweated for half an hour. No result. They toiled another half hour. Still no result. Huck said:

"Do they always bury it as deep as this?"

"Sometimes—not always. Not generally. I reckon we haven't got the right place."

So they chose a new spot and began again. The labor dragged a little, but still they made progress. They pegged away in silence for some time. Finally Huck leaned on his shovel, swabbed the beaded drops from his brow with his sleeve, and said:

"Where you going to dig next, after we get this one?"

"I reckon maybe we'll tackle the old tree that's over yonder on Cardiff Hill back of the widow's."

"I reckon that'll be a good one. But won't the widow take it away from us, Tom? It's on her land."

"*She* take it away! Maybe she'd like to try it once. Whoever finds one of these hid treasures, it belongs to him. It don't make any difference whose land it's on."

That was satsfactory. The work went on. By and by Huck said:

"Blame it, we must be in the wrong place again. What do you think?"

"It *is* mighty curious, Huck. I don't understand it. Sometimes witches interfere. I reckon maybe that's what's the trouble now."

"Shucks, witches ain't got no power in the daytime."

"Well, that's so. I didn't think of that. Oh, *I* know what the matter is! What a blamed lot of fools we are! You got to find out where the shadow of the limb falls at midnight, and that's where you dig!"

"Then consound it, we've fooled away all this work for nothing. Now hang it all, we got to come back in the night. It's an awful long way. Can you get out?"

"I bet I will. We've got to do it tonight, too, because if somebody sees these holes they'll know in a minute what's here and they'll go for it."

"Well, I'll come around and meow tonight."

"All right. Let's hide the tools in the bushes."

The boys were there that night, about the appointed time. They sat in the shadow waiting. It was a lonely place, and an hour made solemn by old traditions. Spirits whispered in the rustling leaves, ghosts lurked in the murky nooks, the deep baying of a hound floated up out of the distance, an owl answered with his sepulchral note. The boys were subdued by these solemnities, and talked little. By and by they judged that twelve had come; they marked where the shadow fell, and began to dig. Their hopes commenced to rise. Their interest grew stronger, and their industry kept pace with it. The hole deepened and still deepened, but every time their hearts jumped to hear the pick strike upon something, they only suffered a new disappointment. It was only a stone or a chunk. At last Tom said:

"It ain't any use, Huck, we're wrong again."

"Well, but we *can't* be wrong. We spotted the shadder to a dot."

"I know it, but then there's another thing."

"What's that?"

"Why, we only guessed at the time. Like enough it was too late or too early."

Huck dropped his shovel.

"That's it," said he. "That's the very trouble. We got to give this one up. We can't ever tell the right time, and besides this kind of thing's too awful, here this time of night with witches and ghosts a-fluttering around so. I feel as if something's behind me all the time; and I'm afeard to turn around, becuz maybe there's others in front a-waiting for a chance. I been creeping all over, ever since I got here."

"Well, I've been pretty much so too, Huck. They most always put in a dead man when they bury a treasure under a tree, to look out for it."

"Lordy!"

"Yes, they do. I've always heard that."

"Tom, I don't like to fool around much where there's

dead people. A body's bound to get into trouble with 'em, sure."

"I don't like to stir 'em up, either. S'pose this one here was to stick his skull out and say something!"

"Don't, Tom! It's awful."

"Well, it just is. Huck, I don't feel comfortable a bit."

"Say, Tom, let's give this place up, and try somewheres else."

"All right, I reckon we better."

"What'll it be?"

Tom considered a while; and then said:

"The ha'nted house. That's it!"

"Blame it, I don't like ha'nted houses, Tom. Why, they're a dern sight wors'n dead people. Dead people might talk, maybe, but they don't come sliding around in a shroud, when you ain't noticing, and peep over your shoulder all of a sudden and grit their teeth, the way a ghost does. I couldn't stand such a thing as that, Tom—nobody could."

"Yes, but Huck, ghosts don't travel around only at night. They won't hender us from digging there in the daytime."

"Well, that's so. But you know mighty well people don't go about that ha'nted house in the day nor the night."

"Well, that's mostly because they don't like to go where a man's been murdered, anyway—but nothing's ever been seen around that house except in the night—just some blue lights slipping by the windows—no regular ghosts."

"Well, where you see one of them blue lights flickering around, Tom, you can bet there's a ghost mighty close behind it. It stands to reason. Becuz *you* know that they don't anybody but ghosts use 'em."

"Yes, that's so. But anyway they don't come around in the daytime, so what's the use of our being afeard?"

"Well, all right. We'll tackle the ha'nted house if you say so—but I reckon it's taking chances."

They had started down the hill by this time. There in the middle of the moonlit valley below them stood the "ha'nted" house, utterly isolated, its fences gone long ago, rank weeds smothering the very doorsteps, the chimney crumbled to ruin, the window sashes vacant, a corner of the roof caved in. The boys gazed a while, half expecting to see a blue light flit past a window; then talking in a low tone, as befitted the time and the circumstances, they struck far off to the right, to give the haunted house a wide berth, and took their way homeward through the woods that adorned the rearward side of Cardiff Hill.

26 *The Haunted House—Sleepy Ghosts—A Box of Gold—Bitter Luck*

About noon the next day the boys arrived at the dead tree; they had come for their tools. Tom was impatient to go to the haunted house; Huck was measurably so, also—but suddenly said:

"Looky-here, Tom, do you know what day it is?"

Tom mentally ran over the days of the week, and then quickly lifted his eyes with a startled look in them—

"My! I never once thought of it, Huck!"

"Well, I didn't neither, but all at once it popped onto me that it was Friday."

"Blame it, a body can't be too careful, Huck. We might a got into an awful scrape, tackling such a thing on a Friday."

"*Might!* Better say we *would!* There's some lucky days, maybe, but Friday ain't."

"Any fool knows that. I don't reckon *you* was the first that found it out, Huck."

"Well, I never said I was, did I? And Friday ain't all, neither. I had a rotten bad dream last night—dreampt about rats."

"No! Sure sign of trouble. Did they fight?"

"No."

"Well, that's good, Huck. When they don't fight it's only a sign that there's trouble around, you know. All we got to do is to look mighty sharp and keep out of it. We'll drop this thing for today, and play. Do you know Robin Hood, Huck?"

"No. Who's Robin Hood?"

"Why, he was one of the greatest men that was ever in England—and the best. He was a robber."

"Cracky, I wisht I was. Who did he rob?"

"Only sheriffs and bishops and rich people and kings, and such like. But he never bothered the poor. He loved 'em. He always divided up with 'em perfectly square."

"Well, he must 'a' been a brick."

"I bet you he was, Huck. Oh, he was the noblest man that ever was. They ain't any such men now, I can tell you. He could lick any man in England, with one hand tied behind him; and he could take his yew bow and plug a ten-cent piece every time, a mile and a half."

"What's a *yew* bow?"

"*I* don't know. It's some kind of a bow, of course. And if he hit that dime only on the edge he would set down and cry —and curse. But we'll play Robin Hood—it's nobby fun. I'll learn you."

"I'm agreed."

So they played Robin Hood all the afternoon, now and then casting a yearning eye down upon the haunted house and passing a remark about the morrow's prospects and possibilities there. As the sun began to sink into the west they took their way homeward athwart the long shadows of the trees and soon were buried from sight in the forests of Cardiff Hill.

On Saturday, shortly after noon, the boys were at the dead tree again. They had a smoke and a chat in the shade, and then dug a little in their last hole, not with great hope, but merely because Tom said there were so many cases where people had given up a treasure after getting down within six inches of it, and then somebody else had come along and turned it up with a single thrust of a shovel. The thing failed this time, however, so the boys shouldered their tools and went away feeling that they had not trifled with fortune, but had fulfilled all the requirements that belong to the business of treasure hunting.

When they reached the haunted house there was something so weird and grisly about the dead silence that reigned there under the baking sun, and something so depressing about the loneliness and desolation of the place, that they were afraid, for a moment, to venture in. Then they crept to the door and took a trembling peep. They saw a weed-grown, floorless room, unplastered, an ancient fireplace, vacant windows, a ruinous staircase; and here, there, and everywhere, hung ragged and abandoned cobwebs. They presently entered, softly, with quickened pulses, talking in whispers, ears alert to catch the slightest sound, and muscles tense and ready for instant retreat.

In a little while familiarity modified their fears and they gave the place a critical and interested examination, rather admiring their own boldness, and wondering at it, too. Next they wanted to look upstairs. This was something like cutting off retreat, but they got to daring each other, and of course there could be but one result—they threw their tools into a corner and made the ascent. Up there were the same signs of decay. In one corner they found a closet that promised mystery, but the promise was a fraud—there was nothing in it. Their courage was up now and well in hand. They were about to go down and begin work when—

"Sh!" said Tom.

"What is it?" whispered Huck, blanching with fright.

"Sh! . . . There! . . . Hear it?"

"Yes! . . . Oh, my! Let's run!"

"Keep still! Don't you budge! They're coming right toward the door."

The boys stretched themselves upon the floor with their eyes to knotholes in the planking, and lay waiting, in a misery of fear.

"They've stopped. . . . No—coming. . . . Here they

are. Don't whisper another word, Huck. My goodness, I wish I was out of this!"

Two men entered. Each boy said to himself: "There's the old deaf-and-dumb Spaniard that's been about town once or twice lately—never saw t'other man before."

"T'other" was a ragged, unkempt creature, with nothing very pleasant in his face. The Spaniard was wrapped in a serape; he had bushy white whiskers; long white hair flowed from under his sombrero, and he wore green goggles. When they came in, "t'other" was talking in a low voice; they sat down on the ground, facing the door, with their backs to the wall, and the speaker continued his remarks. His manner became less guarded and his words more distinct as he proceeded: "No," said he, "I've thought it all over, and I don't like it. It's dangerous."

"Dangerous!" grunted the "deaf-and-dumb" Spaniard—to the vast surprise of the boys. "Milksop!"

This voice made the boys gasp and quake. It was Injun Joe's! There was silence for some time. Then Joe said:

"What's any more dangerous than that job up yonder—but nothing's come of it."

"That's different. Away up the river so, and not another house about. 'Twon't ever be known that we tried, anyway, long as we didn't succeed."

"Well, what's more dangerous than coming here in the daytime!—anybody would suspicion us that saw us."

"*I* know that. But there warn't any other place as handy after that fool of a job. I want to quit this shanty. I wanted to yesterday, only it warn't any use trying to stir out of here, with those infernal boys playing over there on the hill right in full view."

"Those infernal boys" quaked again under the inspiration of this remark, and thought how lucky it was that they remembered it was Friday and concluded to wait a day. They wished in their hearts they had waited a year.

The two men got out some food and made a luncheon. After a long and thoughtful silence, Injun Joe said:

"Look here, lad—you go back up the river where you

belong. Wait there till you hear from me. I'll take the chances on dropping into this town just once more, for a look. We'll do that 'dangerous' job after I've spied around a little and think things look well for it. Then for Texas! We'll leg it together!"

This was satisfactory. Both men presently fell to yawning, and Injun Joe said: "I'm dead for sleep! It's your turn to watch."

He curled down in the weeds and soon began to snore. His comrade stirred him once or twice and he became quiet. Presently the watcher began to nod, his head drooped lower and lower, both men began to snore now.

The boys drew a long, grateful breath. Tom whispered: "Now's our chance—come!"

Huck said: "I can't—I'd die if they was to wake."

Tom urged—Huck held back. At last Tom rose slowly and softly, and started alone. But the first step he made wrung such a hideous creak from the crazy floor that he sank down almost dead with fright. He never made a second attempt. The boys lay there counting the dragging moments till it seemed to them that time must be done and eternity growing gray; and then they were grateful to note that at last the sun was setting.

Now one snore ceased. Injun Joe sat up, stared around—smiled grimly upon his comrade, whose head was drooping upon his knees—stirred him up with his foot and said:

"Here! *You're* a watchman, ain't you! All right, though—nothing's happened."

"My! have I been asleep?"

"Oh, partly, partly. Nearly time for us to be moving, pard. What'll we do with what little swag we've got left?"

"I don't know—leave it here as we've always done, I reckon. No use to take it away till we start south. Six hundred and fifty in silver's something to carry."

"Well—all right—it won't matter to come here once more."

"No—but I'd say come in the night as we used to do—it's better."

"Yes: but look here; it may be a good while before I get

the right chance at that job; accidents might happen; 'tain't in such a very good place; we'll just regularly bury it—and bury it deep."

"Good idea," said the comrade, who walked across the room, knelt down, raised one of the rearward hearthstones and took out a bag that jingled pleasantly. He subtracted from it twenty or thirty dollars for himself and as much for Injun Joe and passed the bag to the latter, who was on his knees in the corner, now, digging with his bowie knife.

The boys forgot all their fears, all their miseries in an instant. With gloating eyes they watched every movement. Luck!—the splendor of it was beyond all imagination! Six hundred dollars was money enough to make half a dozen boys rich! Here was treasure hunting under the happiest auspices—there would not be any bothersome uncertainty as to where to dig. They nudged each other every moment—eloquent nudges and easily understood, for they simply meant—"Oh, but ain't you glad *now* we're here!"

Joe's knife struck upon something. "Hello!" said he.

"What is it?" said his comrade.

"Half-rotten plank—no, it's a box, I believe. Here—bear a hand and we'll see what it's here for. Never mind, I've broke a hole." He reached his hand in and drew it out—"Man, it's money!"

The two men examined the handful of coins. They were gold. The boys above were as excited as themselves, and as delighted. Joe's comrade said:

"We'll make quick work of this. There's an old rusty pick over amongst the weeds in the corner the other side of the fireplace—I saw it a minute ago."

He ran and brought the boys' pick and shovel. Injun Joe took the pick, looked it over critically, shook his head, muttered something to himself, and then began to use it. The box was soon unearthed. It was not very large; it was iron bound and had been very strong before the slow years had injured it. The men contemplated the treasure a while in blissful silence.

"Pard, there's thousands of dollars here," said Injun Joe.

" 'Twas always said that Murrel's gang used to be around here one summer," the stranger observed.

"I know it," said Injun Joe; "and this looks like it, I should say."

"*Now* you won't need to do that job."

The half-breed frowned. Said he:

"You don't know me. Least you don't know all about that thing. 'Tain't robbery altogether—it's *revenge!*" and a wicked light flamed in his eyes. "I'll need your help in it. When it's finished—then Texas. Go home to your Nance and your kids, and stand by till you hear from me."

"Well—if you say so, what'll we do with this—bury it again?"

"Yes. (Ravishing delight overhead.) *No!* by the great Sachem, no! (Profound distress overhead.) I'd nearly forgot. That pick had fresh earth on it! (The boys were sick with terror in a moment.) What business has a pick and a shovel here? What business with fresh earth on them? Who brought them here—and where are they gone? Have you heard anybody?—seen anybody? What! bury it again and leave them to come and see the ground disturbed? Not exactly—not exactly. We'll take it to my den."

"Why, of course! Might have thought of that before. You mean Number One?"

"No— Number Two—under the cross. The other place is bad—too common."

"All right. It's nearly dark enough to start."

Injun Joe got up and went about from window to window cautiously peeping out. Presently he said:

"Who could have brought those tools here? Do you reckon they can be upstairs?"

The boys' breath forsook them. Injun Joe put his hand on his knife, halted a moment, undecided, and then turned toward the stairway. The boys thought of the closet, but their strength was gone. The steps came creaking up the stairs—the intolerable distress of the situation woke the stricken resolution of the lads—they were about to spring for the closet, when there was a crash of rotten timbers and

Injun Joe landed on the ground amid the debris of the ruined stairway. He gathered himself up cursing, and his comrade said:

"Now what's the use of all that? If it's anybody, and they're up there, let them *stay* there—who cares? If they want to jump down, now, and get into trouble, who objects? It will be dark in fifteen minutes—and then let them follow us if they want to. I'm willing. In my opinion, whoever hove those things in here caught a sight of us and took us for ghosts or devils or something. I'll bet they're running yet."

Joe grumbled a while; then he agreed with his friend that what daylight was left ought to be economized in getting things ready for leaving. Shortly afterward they slipped out of the house in the deepening twilight, and moved toward the river with their precious box.

Tom and Huck rose up, weak but vastly relieved, and stared after them through the chinks between the logs of the house. Follow? Not they. They were content to reach ground again without broken necks, and take the townward track over the hill. They did not talk much. They were too much absorbed in hating themselves—hating the ill luck that made them take the spade and the pick there. But for that, Injun Joe never would have suspected. He would have hidden the silver with the gold to wait there till his "revenge" was satisfied, and then he would have had the misfortune to find that money turn up missing. Bitter, bitter luck that the tools were ever brought there!

They resolved to keep a lookout for that Spaniard when he should come to town spying out for chances to do his revengeful job, and follow him to "Number Two," wherever that might be. Then a ghastly thought occurred to Tom:

"Revenge? What if he means *us* Huck!"

"Oh, don't!" said Huck, nearly fainting.

They talked it all over, and as they entered town they agreed to believe that he might possibly mean somebody else —at least that he might at least mean nobody but Tom, since only Tom had testified.

Very, very small comfort it was to Tom to be alone in danger! Company would be a palpable improvement, he thought.

27 *Doubts to Be Settled—The Young Detectives*

The adventure of the day mightily tormented Tom's dreams that night. Four times he had his hands on that rich treasure and four times it wasted to nothingness in his fingers as sleep forsook him and wakefulness brought back the hard reality of his misfortune. As he lay in the early morning recalling the incidents of his great adventure, he noticed that they seemed curiously subdued and far away—somewhat as if they had happened in another world, or in a time long gone by. Then it occurred to him that the great adventure itself must be a dream! There was one very strong argument in favor of this idea—namely, that the quantity of coin he had seen was too vast to be real. He had never seen as much as fifty dollars in one mass before, and he was like all boys of his age and station in life, in that he imagined that all references to "hundreds" and "thousands" were mere fanciful forms of speech, and that no such sums really existed in the world. He never had supposed for a moment that so large a sum as a hundred dollars was to be found in actual money in anyone's possession. If his notions of hidden treasure had been analyzed, they would have been found to consist of a handful of real dimes and a bushel of vague, splendid, ungraspable dollars.

But the incidents of his adventure grew sensibly sharper and clearer under the attrition of thinking them over, and so he presently found himself leaning to the impression that the thing might not have been a dream, after all. This uncertainty must be swept away. He would snatch a hurried breakfast and go and find Huck.

Huck was sitting on the gunwale of a flatboat, listlessly dangling his feet in the water and looking very melancholy. Tom concluded to let Huck lead up to the subject. If he did not do it, then the adventure would be proved to have been only a dream.

"Hello, Huck!"

"Hello, yourself."

Silence, for a minute.

"Tom, if we'd 'a' left the blame tools at the dead tree, we'd 'a' got the money. Oh, ain't it awful!"

" 'Tain't a dream, then, 'tain't a dream! Somehow I most wish it was. Dog'd if I don't, Huck."

"What ain't a dream?"

"Oh, that thing yesterday. I been half thinking it was."

"Dream! If them stairs hadn't broke down you'd 'a' seen how much dream it was! I've had dreams enough all night—with that patch-eyed Spanish devil going for me all through 'em—rot him!"

"No, not rot him. *Find* him! Track the money!"

"Tom, we'll never find him. A feller don't have only one chance for such a pile—and that one's lost. I'd feel mighty shaky if I was to see him, anyway."

"Well, so'd I; but I'd like to see him, anyway—and track him out—to his Number Two."

"Number Two—yes, that's it. I been thinking 'bout that. But I can't make nothing out of it. What do you reckon it is?"

"I dono. It's too deep. Say, Huck—maybe it's the number of a house!"

"Goody! . . . No, Tom, that ain't it. If it is, it ain't in this one-horse town. They ain't no numbers here."

"Well, that's so. Lemme think a minute. Here—it's the number of a room—in a tavern, you know!"

"Oh, that's the trick! They ain't only two taverns. We can find out quick."

"You stay here, Huck, till I come."

Tom was off at once. He did not care to have Huck's company in public places. He was gone half an hour. He found that in the best tavern, No. 2 had long been occupied by a young lawyer, and was still so occupied. In the less ostentatious house No. 2 was a mystery. The tavernkeeper's young son said it was kept locked all the time, and he never saw anybody go into it or come out of it except at night; he did not know any particular reason for this state of things; had had some little curiosity, but it was rather feeble; had made the most of the mystery by entertaining himself with the idea that that room was "ha'nted"; had noticed that there was a light in there the night before.

"That's what I've found out, Huck. I reckon that's the very No. 2 we're after."

"I reckon it is, Tom. Now what you going to do?"

"Lemme think."

Tom thought a long time. Then he said:

"I'll tell you. The back door of that No. 2 is the door that comes out into that little close alley between the tavern and the old rattletrap of a brick store. Now you get hold of all the doorkeys you can find, and I'll nip all of Auntie's, and the first dark night we'll go there and try 'em. And mind you, keep a lookout for Injun Joe, because he said he was going to drop into town and spy around once more for a chance to get his revenge. If you see him, you just follow him; and if he don't go to that No. 2, that ain't the place."

"Lordy, I don't want to foller him by myself!"

"Why, it'll be night, sure. He mightn't ever see you—and if he did, maybe he'd never think anything."

"Well, if it's pretty dark I reckon I'll track him. I dono—I dono. I'll try."

"You bet *I'll* follow him, if it's dark, Huck. Why, he might 'a' found out he couldn't get his revenge, and be going right after that money."

"It's so, Tom, it's so. I'll foller him; I will, by jingoes!"

"Now you're *talking!* Don't you ever weaken, Huck, and I won't."

28 *An Attempt at Number Two— Huck Mounts Guard*

That night Tom and Huck were ready for their adventure. They hung about the neighborhood of the tavern until after nine, one watching the alley at a distance and the other the tavern door. Nobody entered the alley or left it; nobody resembling the Spaniard entered or left the tavern door. The night promised to be a fair one; so Tom went home with the understanding that if a considerable degree of darkness came on, Huck was to come and "meow," whereupon he would slip out and try the keys. But the night remained clear, and Huck closed his watch and retired to bed in an empty sugar hogshead about twelve.

Tuesday the boys had the same ill luck. Also Wednesday. But Thursday night promised better. Tom slipped out in good season with his aunt's old tin lantern, and a large towel to blindfold it with. He hid the lantern in Huck's sugar hogshead and the watch began. An hour before midnight the tavern closed up and its lights (the only ones thereabouts) were put out. No Spaniard had been seen. Nobody had entered or left the alley. Everything was auspicious. The blackness of darkness reigned, and the perfect stillness was interrupted only by occasional mutterings of distant thunder.

Tom got his lantern, lit it in the hogshead, wrapped it closely in the towel, and the two adventurers crept in the gloom toward the tavern. Huck stood sentry and Tom felt his way into the alley. Then there was a season of waiting anxiety that weighed upon Huck's spirits like a mountain. He began to wish he could see a flash from the lantern—it would frighten him, but it would at least tell him that Tom was alive yet. It seemed hours since Tom had disappeared.

Surely he must have fainted; maybe he was dead; maybe his heart had burst under terror and excitement. In his uneasiness Huck found himself drawing closer and closer to the alley; fearing all sorts of dreadful things, and momentarily expecting some catastrophe to happen that would take away his breath. There was not much to take away, for he seemed only able to inhale it by thimblefuls, and his heart would soon wear itself out, the way it was beating. Suddenly there was a flash of light and Tom came tearing by him:

"Run!" said he; "run, for your life!"

He needn't have repeated it; once was enough; Huck was making thirty or forty miles an hour before the repetition was uttered. The boys never stopped till they reached the shed of a deserted slaughterhouse at the lower end of the village. Just as they got within its shelter the storm and the rain poured down. As soon as Tom got his breath he said:

"Huck, it was awful! I tried two of the keys, just as soft as I could! but they seemed to make such a power of racket that I couldn't hardly get my breath I was so scared. They wouldn't turn in the lock, either. Well, without noticing what I was doing, I took hold of the knob, and open comes the door! It warn't locked. I hopped in, and shook off the towel, and, *great Caesar's ghost!*"

"What!—what'd you see, Tom!"

"Huck, I most stepped onto Injun Joe's hand!"

"No!"

"Yes! He was laying there, sound asleep on the floor, with his old patch on his eye and his arms spread out."

"Lordy, what did you do? Did he wake up?"

"No, never budged. Drunk, I reckon. I just grabbed that towel and started!"

"I'd never 'a' thought of the towel, I bet!"

"Well, *I* would. My aunt would make me mighty sick if I lost it."

"Say, Tom, did you see that box?"

"Huck, I didn't wait to look around. I didn't see the box, I didn't see the cross. I didn't see anything but a bottle and a tin cup on the floor by Injun Joe; yes, and I saw two barrels and lots more bottles in the room. Don't you see, now, what's the matter with that ha'nted room?"

"How?"

"Why, it's ha'nted with whisky! Maybe *all* the Temperance Taverns have got a ha'nted room, hey, Huck?"

"Well, I reckon maybe that's so. Who'd 'a' thought such a thing? But say, Tom, now's a mighty good time to get that box, if Injun Joe's drunk."

"It is, that! You try it!"

Huck shuddered.

"Well, no—I reckon not."

"And *I* reckon not, Huck. Only one bottle alongside of Injun Joe ain't enough. If there'd been three, he'd be drunk enough and I'd do it."

There was a long pause for reflection, and then Tom said:

"Looky-here, Huck, less not try that thing any more till we know Unjun Joe's not in there. It's too scary. Now, if we watch every night, we'll be dead sure to see him go out, some time or other, and then we'll snatch that box quicker'n lightning."

"Well, I'm agreed. I'll watch the whole night long, and I'll do it every night, too, if you'll do the other part of the job."

"All right, I will. All you got to do is to trot up Hooper Street a block and meow—and if I'm asleep, you throw some gravel at the window and that'll fetch me."

"Agreed, and good as wheat!"

"Now, Huck, the storm's over, and I'll go home. It'll begin to be daylight in a couple of hours. You go back and watch that long, will you?"

"I said I would, Tom, and I will. I'll ha'nt that tavern every night for a year! I'll sleep all day and I'll stand watch at night."

"That's all right. Now, where you going to sleep?"

"In Ben Rogers' hayloft. He lets me, and so does his pap's niggerman, Uncle Jake. I tote water for Uncle Jake whenever he wants me to, and any time I ask him he gives me a little something to eat if he can spare it. That's a mighty good nigger, Tom. He likes me, becuz I don't ever act as if

I was above him. Sometimes, I've set right down and eat *with* him. But you needn't tell that. A body's got to do things when he's awful hungry he wouldn't want to do as a steady thing."

"Well, if I don't want you in the daytime, I'll let you sleep. I won't come bothering around. Any time you see something's up, in the night, just skip right around and meow."

29 *The Picnic—Huck on Injun Joe's Track—The "Revenge" Job—Aid for the Widow*

The first thing Tom heard on Friday morning was a glad piece of news—Judge Thatcher's family had come back to town the night before. Both Injun Joe and the treasure sank into secondary importance for a moment, and Becky took the chief place in the boy's interest. He saw her and they had an exhausting good time playing "hi-spy" and "gully-keeper" with a crowd of their schoolmates. The day was completed and crowned in a peculiarly satisfactory way: Becky teased her mother to appoint the next day for the long-promised and long-delayed picnic, and she consented. The child's delight was boundless; and Tom's not more moderate. The invitations were sent out before sunset, and straightway the young folks of the village were thrown into a fever of preparation and pleasurable anticipation. Tom's excitement enabled him to keep awake until a pretty late hour, and he had good hopes of hearing Huck's "meow," and of having his treasure to astonish Becky and the picnickers with, next day; but he was disappointed. No signal came that night.

Morning came, eventually, and by ten or eleven o'clock a giddy and rollicking company were gathered at Judge Thatcher's, and everything was ready for a start. It was not the custom for elderly people to mar picnics with their presence. The children were considered safe enough under the wings of a few young ladies of eighteen and a few young gentlemen of twenty-three or thereabouts. The old steam ferryboat was chartered for the occasion; presently the gay throng filed up the main street laden with provision baskets. Sid was sick and had to miss the fun; Mary remained at home to entertain him. The last thing Mrs. Thatcher said to Becky, was:

"You'll not get back till late. Perhaps you'd better stay all night with some of the girls that live near the ferry landing, child."

"Then I'll stay with Susy Harper, mamma."

"Very well. And mind and behave yourself and don't be any trouble."

Presently, as they tripped along, Tom said to Becky:

"Say—I'll tell you what we'll do. 'Stead of going to Joe Harper's we'll climb right up the hill and stop at the Widow Douglas'. She'll have ice cream! She has it most every day—dead loads of it. And she'll be awful glad to have us."

"Oh, that will be fun!"

Then Becky reflected a moment and said:

"But what will mamma say?"

"How'll she ever know?"

The girl turned the idea over in her mind, and said reluctantly:

"I reckon it's wrong—but——"

"But shucks! Your mother won't know, and so what's the harm? All she wants is that you'll be safe; and I bet you she'd 'a' said go there if she'd 'a' thought of it. I know she would!"

The Widow Douglas' splendid hospitality was a tempting bait. It and Tom's persuasions presently carried the day. So it was decided to say nothing to anybody about the night's program. Presently it occurred to Tom that maybe Huck might come this very night and give the signal. The thought took a deal of the spirit out of his anticipations. Still he could not bear to give up the fun at Widow Douglas'. And why should he give it up, he reasoned—the signal did not come the night before, so why should it be any more likely to come tonight? The sure fun of the evening outweighed the uncertain treasure; and boylike, he determined to yield to the stronger inclination and not allow himself to think of the box of money another time that day.

Three miles below town the ferryboat stopped at the mouth of a woody hollow and tied up. The crowd swarmed ashore and soon the forest distances and craggy heights echoed far and near with shoutings and laughter. All the different ways of getting hot and tired were gone through with, and by and by the rovers straggled back to camp fortified with responsible appetites, and then the destruction of the good things began. After the feast there was a refreshing season of rest and chat in the shade of spreading oaks. By and by somebody shouted:

"Who's ready for the cave?"

Everybody was. Bundles of candles were procured, and straightway there was a general scamper up the hill. The mouth of the cave was up the hillside—an opening shaped like a letter A. Its massive oaken door stood unbarred. Within was a small chamber, chilly as an icehouse, and walled by Nature with solid limestone that was dewy with a cold sweat. It was romantic and mysterious to stand here in the deep gloom and look out upon the green valley shining in the sun. But the impressiveness of the situation quickly wore off, and the romping began again. The moment a candle was lighted there was a general rush upon the owner of it; a struggle and a gallant defense followed, but the candle was soon knocked down or blown out, and then there was a glad clamor of laughter and a new chase. But all things have to end. By and by the procession went filing down the steep descent of the main avenue, the flickering rank of lights dimly revealing the lofty walls of rock almost to their point of junction sixty feet overhead. This main avenue was not more than eight or ten feet wide. Every few steps other lofty and still narrower crevices branched from it on either hand —for McDougal's cave was but a vast labyrinth of crooked aisles that ran into each other and out again and led nowhere. It was said that one might wander days and nights together through its intricate tangle of rifts and chasms, and never find the end of the cave; and that he might go down, and down, and still down, into the earth, and it was just the same—labyrinth underneath labyrinth, and no end to any of them. No man "knew" the cave. That was an impossible thing. Most of the young men knew a portion of it, and it was not customary to venture much beyond this known portion. Tom Sawyer knew as much of the cave as any one.

The procession moved along the main avenue some three-quarters of a mile, and then groups and couples began to slip aside into branch avenues, fly along the dismal corridors, and take each other by surprise at points where the corridors joined again. Parties were able to elude each other for the space of half an hour without going beyond the "known" ground.

By and by, one group after another came straggling back to the mouth of the cave, panting, hilarious, smeared from head to foot with tallow drippings, daubed with clay, and entirely delighted with the success of the day. Then they were astonished to find that they had been taking no note of time and that night was about at hand. The clanging bell had been calling for half an hour. However, this sort of close to the day's adventures was romantic and therefore satisfactory. When the ferryboat with her wild freight pushed into the stream, nobody cared sixpence for the wasted time but the captain of the craft.

Huck was already upon his watch when the ferryboat's lights went glinting past the wharf. He heard no noise on board, for the young people were as subdued and still as people usually are who are nearly tired to death. He wondered what boat it was, and why she did not stop at the wharf—and then he dropped her out of his mind and put his attention upon his business. The night was growing cloudy and dark. Ten o'clock came, and the noise of vehicles ceased, scattered lights began to wink out, all straggling foot passengers disappeared, the village betook itself to its slumbers and left the small watcher alone with the silence and the ghosts. Eleven o'clock came, and the tavern lights were put out; darkness everywhere, now. Huck waited what seemed a weary long time, but nothing happened. His faith was weakening. Was there any use? Was there really any use? Why not give it up and turn in?

A noise fell upon his ear. He was all attention in an instant. The alley door closed softly. He sprang to the corner of the brick store. The next moment two men brushed by him, and one seemed to have something under his arm. It must be that box! So they were going to remove the treasure. Why call Tom now? It would be absurd—the men would get away with the box and never be found again. No, he would stick to their wake and follow them; he would trust to the darkness for security from discovery. So communing with himself, Huck stepped out and glided along behind the men, catlike, with bare feet, allowing them to keep just far enough ahead not to be invisible.

They moved up the river street three blocks, then turned to the left up a cross street. They went straight ahead, then, until they came to the path that led up Cardiff Hill; this they took. They passed by the old Welshman's house, half way up the hill without hesitating, and still climbed upward. Good, thought Huck, they will bury it in the old quarry. But they never stopped at the quarry. They passed on, up the summit. They plunged into the narrow path between the tall sumac bushes, and were at once hidden in the gloom. Huck closed up and shortened his distance, now, for they would never be able to see him. He trotted along a while; then slackened his pace, fearing he was gaining too fast; moved on a piece, then stopped altogether; listened; no sound; none, save that he seemed to hear the beating of his own heart. The hooting of an owl came from over the hill —ominous sound! But no footsteps. Heavens, was everything lost! He was about to spring with winged feet, when a man cleared his throat not four feet from him! Huck's heart shot into his throat, but he swallowed it again; and then he stood there shaking as if a dozen agues had taken charge of him at once, and so weak that he thought he must surely fall to the ground. He knew where he was. He knew he was within five steps of the stile leading into Widow Douglas' grounds. Very well, he thought, let them bury it there; it won't be hard to find.

Now there was a voice—a very low voice—Injun Joe's:

"Damn her, maybe she's got company—there's lights, late as it is."

"I can't see any."

This was that stranger's voice—the stranger of the haunted house. A deadly chill went to Huck's heart—this, then, was the "revenge" job! His thought was to fly. Then he remembered that the Widow Douglas had been kind to him more than once, and maybe these men were going to murder her. He wished he dared venture to warn her; but he knew he didn't dare—they might come and catch him. He thought all this and more in the moment that elapsed between the stranger's remark and Injun Joe's next—which was—

"Because the bush is in your way. Now—this way—now you see, don't you?"

"Yes. Well, there *is* company there, I reckon. Better give it up."

"Give it up, and I just leaving this country forever! Give it up and maybe never have another chance. I tell you again, as I've told you before, I don't care for her swag—you may have it. But her husband was rough on me—many times he was rough on me—and mainly he was the justice of the peace that jugged me for a vagrant. And that ain't all. It ain't a millionth part of it! He had me *horsewhipped!*—horsewhipped in front of the jail, like a nigger!—with all the town looking on! HORSEWHIPPED!—do you understand? He took advantage of me and died. But I'll take it out on *her*."

"Oh, don't kill her. Don't do that!"

"Kill? Who said anything about killing? I would kill *him* if he was here; but not her. When you want to get revenge on a woman you don't kill her—bosh! you go for her looks. You slit her nostrils—you notch her ears like a sow!"

"By God, that'——"

"Keep your opinion to yourself! It will be safest for you. I'll tie her to the bed. If she bleeds to death, is that my fault? I'll not cry, if she does. My friend, you'll help in this thing—for *my* sake—that's why you're here—I mightn't be able alone. If you flinch, I'll kill you. Do you understand that? And if I have to kill you, I'll kill her—and then I reckon nobody'll ever know much about who done this business."

"Well, if it's got to be done, let's get at it. The quicker the better—I'm all in a shiver."

"Do it *now?* And company there? Look here—I'll get suspicious of you, first thing you know. No—we'll wait till the lights are out—there's no hurry."

Huck felt that a silence was going to ensue—a thing still more awful than any amount of murderous talk; so he held his breath and stepped gingerly back; planted his foot carefully and firmly, after balancing, one-legged, in a precarious way and almost toppling over, first on one side and then on the other. He took another step back, with the same elaboration and the same risks; then another and another, and—a twig snapped under his foot! His breath stopped and he listened. There was no sound—the stillness was perfect. His gratitude was measureless. Now he turned in his tracks, between the walls of sumac bushes—turned himself as carefully as if he were a ship—and then stepped quickly but cautiously along. When he emerged at the quarry he felt secure, and so he picked up his nimble heels and flew. Down, down he sped, till he reached the Welshman's. He banged at the door, and presently the heads of the old man and his two stalwart sons were thrust from windows.

"What's the row there? Who's banging? What do you want?"

"Let me in—quick! I'll tell everything."

"Why, who are you?"

"Huckleberry Finn—quick, let me in!"

"Huckleberry Finn, indeed! It ain't a name to open many doors, I judge! But let him in, lads, and let's see what's the trouble."

"Please don't ever tell *I* told you," were Huck's first words when he got in. "Please don't—I'd be killed, sure—but the widow's been good friends to me sometimes, and I want to tell—I *will* tell if you'll promise you won't ever say it was me."

"By George, he *has* got something to tell, or he wouldn't act so!" exclaimed the old man. "Out with it and nobody here'll ever tell, lad."

Three minutes later the old man and his sons, well armed, were up the hill, and just entering the sumac path on tiptoe, their weapons in their hands. Huck accompanied them no further. He hid behind a great boulder and fell to listening. There was a lagging, anxious silence, and then all of a sudden there was an explosion of firearms and a cry.

Huck waited for no particulars. He sprang away and sped down the hill as fast as his legs could carry him.

30 *The Welshman Reports—Huck Under Fire—The Story Circulated—A New Sensation—Hope Giving Way to Despair*

As the earliest suspicion of dawn appeared on Sunday morning, Huck came groping up the hill and rapped gently at the old Welshman's door. The inmates were asleep, but it was a sleep that was set on a hair trigger, on account of the exciting episode of the night. A call came from a window:

"Who's there?"

Huck's scared voice answered in a low tone:

"Please let me in! It's only Huck Finn!"

"It's a name that can open this door night or day, lad!—and welcome!"

These were strange words to the vagabond boy's ears, and the pleasantest he had ever heard. He could not recollect that the closing word had ever been applied in his case before. The door was quickly unlocked, and he entered. Huck was given a seat and the old man and his brace of tall sons speedily dressed themselves.

"Now, my boy, I hope you're good and hungry, because breakfast will be ready as soon as the sun's up, and we'll have a piping hot one, too—make yourself easy about that! I and the boys hoped you'd turn up and stop here last night."

"I was awful scared," said Huck, "and I run. I took out when the pistols went off, and I didn't stop for three mile. I've come now becuz I wanted to know about it, you know; and I come before daylight becuz I didn't want to run acrost them devils, even if they was dead."

"Well, poor chap, you do look as if you'd had a hard night of it—but there's a bed here for you when you've had your breakfast. No, they ain't dead, lad—we are sorry enough for that. You see we knew right where to put our hands on them, by your description; so we crept along on tiptoe till we got within fifteen feet of them—dark as a cellar that sumac path was—and just then I found I was going to sneeze. It was the meanest kind of luck! I tried to keep it back, but no use—'twas bound to come, and it did come! I was in the lead with my pistol raised, and when the sneeze started those scoundrels a-rustling to get out of the path, I sung out, 'Fire, boys!' and blazed away at the place where the rustling was. So did the boys. But they were off in a jiffy, those villains, and we after them, down through the woods. I judge we never touched them. They fired a shot apiece as they started, but their bullets whizzed by and didn't do us any harm. As soon as we lost the sound of their feet we quit chasing, and went down and stirred up the constables. They got a posse together, and went off to guard the riverbank, and as soon as it is light the sheriff and a gang are going to beat up the woods. My boys will be with them presently. I wish we had some sort of description of those rascals—'twould help a good deal. But you couldn't see what they were like, in the dark, lad, I suppose?"

"Oh, yes, I saw them downtown and follered them."

"Splendid! Describe them—describe them, my boy!"

"One's the old deaf-and-dumb Spaniard that's been around here once or twice, and t'other's a mean-looking, ragged——"

"That's enough, lad, we know the men! Happened on them in the woods back of the widow's one day, and they slunk away. Off with you, boys, and tell the sheriff—get your breakfast tomorrow morning!"

The Welshman's sons departed at once. As they were leaving the room Huck sprang up and exclaimed:

"Oh, please don't tell *any*body it was me that blowed on them! Oh, please!"

"All right if you say it, Huck, but you ought to have the credit of what you did."

"Oh, no, no! Please don't tell!"

When the young men were gone, the old Welshman said:

"They won't tell—and I won't. But why don't you want it known?"

Huck would not explain, further than to say that he already knew too much about one of those men and would not have the man know that he knew anything against him for the whole world—he would be killed for knowing it, sure.

The old man promised secrecy once more, and said:

"How did you come to follow these fellows, lad? Were they looking suspicious?"

Huck was silent while he framed a duly cautious reply. Then he said:

"Well, you see, I'm a kind of a hard lot—least everybody says so, and I don't see nothing agin it—and sometimes I can't sleep much, on accounts of thinking about it and sort of trying to strike out a new way of doing. That was the way of it last night. I couldn't sleep, and so I come along up street 'bout midnight, a-turning it all over, and when I got to that old shackly brick store by the Temperance Tavern, I backed up agin the wall to have another think. Well, just then along comes these two chaps slipping along close by me, with something under their arm and I reckoned they'd stole it. One was a-smoking, and t'other one wanted a light; so they stopped right before me and the cigars lit up their faces and I see that the big one was the deaf-and-dumb Spaniard, by his white whiskers and the patch on his eye, and t'other one was a rusty, ragged-looking devil."

"Could you see the rags by the light of the cigars?"

This staggered Huck for a moment. Then he said:

"Well, I don't know—but somehow it seems as if I did."

"Then they went on, and you——"

"Followed 'em—yes. That was it. I wanted to see what was up—they sneaked along so. I dogged 'em to the widder's stile, and stood in the dark and heard the ragged one beg for the widder, and the Spaniard swear he'd spile her looks just as I told you and your two——"

"What! The *deaf-and-dumb* man said all that!"

Huck had made another terrible mistake! He was trying his best to keep the old man from getting the faintest hint of who the Spaniard might be, and yet his tongue seemed determined to get him into trouble in spite of all he could do. He made several efforts to creep out of his scrape, but the old man's eye was upon him and he made blunder after blunder. Presently the Welshman said:

"My boy, don't be afraid of me. I wouldn't hurt a hair of your head for all the world. No—I'd protect you—I'd protect you. This Spaniard is not deaf and dumb; you've let that slip without intending it; you can't cover that up now. You know something about that Spaniard that you want to keep dark. Now trust me—tell me what it is, and trust me—I won't betray you."

Huck looked into the old man's honest eyes a moment, then bent over and whispered in his ear:

" 'Tain't a Spaniard—it's Injun Joe!"

The Welshman almost jumped out of his chair. In a moment he said:

"It's all plain enough, now. When you talked about notching ears and slitting noses I judged that that was your own embellishment, because white men don't take that sort of revenge. But an Injun! That's a different matter altogether."

During breakfast the talk went on, and in the course of it the old man said that the last thing which he and his sons had done, before going to bed, was to get a lantern and examine the stile and its vicinity for marks of blood. They found none, but captured a bulky bundle of—

"Of WHAT?"

If the words had been lightning they could not have leaped with a more stunning suddenness from Huck's blanched lips. His eyes were staring wide, now, and his breath suspended —waiting for the answer. The Welshman started—stared in return—three seconds—five seconds—ten—then replied:

"Of burglar's tools. Why, what's the *matter* with you?"

Huck sank back, panting gently, but deeply, unutterably grateful. The Welshman eyed him gravely, curiously—and presently said:

"Yes, burglar's tools. That appears to relieve you a good deal. But what did give you that turn? What were *you* expecting we'd found?"

Huck was in a close place—the inquiring eye was upon him—he would have given anything for material for a plausible answer—nothing suggested itself—the inquiring eye was boring deeper and deeper—a senseless reply offered —there was no time to weigh it, so at a venture he uttered it —feebly:

"Sunday-school books, maybe."

Poor Huck was too distressed to smile, but the old man laughed loudly and joyously, shook up the details of his anatomy from head to foot, and ended by saying that such a laugh was money in a man's pocket, because it cut down the doctor's bills like everything. Then he added:

"Poor old chap, you're white and jaded—you ain't well a bit—no wonder you're a little flighty and off your balance. But you'll come out of it. Rest and sleep will fetch you out all right, I hope."

Huck was irritated to think he had been such a goose and betrayed such a suspicious excitement, for he had dropped the idea that the parcel brought from the tavern was the treasure, as soon as he had heard the talk at the widow's stile. He had only *thought* it was not the treasure, however —he had not known that it wasn't—and so the suggestion of a captured bundle was too much for his self-possession. But on the whole he felt glad the little episode had happened, for now he knew beyond all question that that bundle was not *the* bundle, and so his mind was at rest and exceedingly comfortable. In fact, everything seemed to be drifting just in the right direction, now; the treasure must be still in No. 2, the men would be captured and jailed that day, and he and Tom could seize the gold that night without any trouble or any fear of interruption.

Just as breakfast was completed there was a knock at the door. Huck jumped for a hiding place, for he had no mind to be connected even remotely with the late event. The Welshman admitted several ladies and gentlemen, among them the Widow Douglas, and noticed that groups of citizens were climbing up the hill—to stare at the stile. So the news had spread.

The Welshman had to tell the story of the night to the visitors. The widow's gratitude for her preservation was outspoken.

"Don't say a word about it, madam. There's another that you're more beholden to than you are to me and my boys, maybe, but he don't allow me to tell his name. We wouldn't have been there but for him."

Of course this excited a curiosity so vast that it almost belittled the main matter—but the Welshman allowed it to eat into the vitals of his visitors, and through them be transmitted to the whole town, for he refused to part with his secret. When all else had been learned, the widow said:

"I went to sleep reading in bed and slept straight through all that noise. Why didn't you come and wake me?"

"We judged it warn't worth while. Those fellows warn't likely to come again—they hadn't any tools left to work with, and what was the use of waking you up and scaring you to death? My three Negro men stood guard at your house all the rest of the night. They've just come back."

More visitors came, and the story had to be told and retold for a couple of hours more.

There was no Sabbath school during day-school vacation, but everybody was early at church. The stirring event was well canvassed. News came that not a sign of the two villains had been yet discovered. When the sermon was finished, Judge Thatcher's wife dropped alongside of Mrs. Harper as she moved down the aisle with the crowd and said:

"Is my Becky going to sleep all day? I just expected she would be tired to death."

"Your Becky?"

"Yes," with a startled look—"didn't she stay with you last night?"

"Why, no."

Mrs. Thatcher turned pale, and sank into a pew, just as Aunt Polly, talking briskly with a friend, passsed by. Aunt Polly said:

"Good morning, Mrs. Thatcher. Good morning, Mrs. Harper. I've got a boy that's turned up missing. I reckon my Tom stayed at your house last night—one of you. And now he's afraid to come to church. I've got to settle with him."

Mrs. Thatcher shook her head feebly and turned paler than ever.

"He didn't stay with us," said Mrs. Harper, beginning to look uneasy. A marked anxiety came into Aunt Polly's face.

"Joe Harper, have you seen my Tom this morning?"

"No'm."

"When did you see him last?"

Joe tried to remember, but was not sure he could say. The people had stopped moving out of church. Whispers passed along, and a boding uneasiness took possession of every countenance. Children were anxiously questioned, and young teachers. They all said they had not noticed whether Tom and Becky were on board the ferryboat on the homeward trip; it was dark; no one thought of inquiring if anyone was missing. One young man finally blurted out his fear that they were still in the cave! Mrs. Thatcher swooned away. Aunt Polly fell to crying and wringing her hands.

The alarm swept from lip to lip, from group to group, from street to street, and within five minutes the bells were wildly clanging and the whole town was up! The Cardiff Hill episode sank into instant insignificance, the burglars were forgotten, horses were saddled, skiffs were manned, the ferryboat ordered out, and before the horror was half an hour old, two hundred men were pouring down highroad and river toward the cave.

All the long afternoon the village seemed empty and dead. Many women visited Aunt Polly and Mrs. Thatcher and tried to comfort them. They cried with them, too, and that was still better than words. All the tedious night the town waited for news; but when the morning dawned at last, all the word that came was, "Send more candles—and send food." Mrs. Thatcher was almost crazed; and Aunt Polly, also. Judge Thatcher sent messages of hope and encouragement from the cave, but they conveyed no real cheer.

The old Welshman came home toward daylight, spattered with candle grease, smeared with clay, and almost worn out. He found Huck still in the bed that had been provided for him, and delirious with fever. The physicians were all at the cave, so the Widow Douglas came and took charge of the patient. She said she would do her best by him, because, whether he was good, bad, or indifferent, he was the Lord's, and nothing that was the Lord's was a thing to be neglected. The Welshman said Huck had good spots in him, and the widow said:

"You can depend on it. That's the Lord's mark. He don't leave it off. He never does. Puts it somewhere on every creature that comes from His hands."

Early in the forenoon parties of jaded men began to straggle into the village, but the strongest of the citizens continued searching. All the news that could be gained was that remotenesses of the cavern were being ransacked that had never been visited before; that every corner and crevice was going to be thoroughly searched; that wherever one wandered through the maze of passages, lights were to be seen flitting hither and thither in the distance, and shoutings and pistol shots sent their hollow reverberations to the ear down the somber aisles. In one place, far from the section usually traversed by tourists, the names "BECKY & TOM" had been found traced upon the rocky wall with candle smoke, and near at hand a grease-soiled bit of ribbon. Mrs. Thatcher recognized the ribbon and cried over it. She said it was the last relic she should ever have of her child; and that no other memorial of her could ever be so precious, because this one parted latest from the living body before the awful death came. Some said that now and then, in the cave, a faraway speck of light would glimmer, and then a glorious shout would burst forth and a score of men go trooping down the echoing aisle—and then a sickening disappointment always followed; the children were not there; it was only a searcher's light.

Three dreadful days and nights dragged their tedious hours along, and the village sank into a hopeless stupor. No one had heart for anything. The accidental discovery, just made, that the proprietor of the Temperance Tavern kept liquor on his premises, scarcely fluttered the public pulse, tremendous as the fact was. In a lucid interval, Huck feebly led up to the subject of taverns, and finally asked—dimly dreading the worst—if anything had been discovered at the Temperance Tavern since he had been ill.

"Yes," said the widow.

Huck started up in bed, wild-eyed:

"What! What was it?"

"Liquor!—and the place has been shut up. Lie down, child—what a turn you did give me!"

"Only tell me just one thing—only just one—please! Was it Tom Sawyer that found it?"

The widow burst into tears. "Hush, hush, child, hush! I've told you before, you must *not* talk. You are very, very sick!"

Then nothing but liquor had been found; there would have been a great powwow if it had been the gold. So the treasure was gone forever—gone forever! But what could she be crying about? Curious that she should cry.

These thoughts worked their dim way through Huck's mind, and under the weariness they gave him he fell asleep. The widow said to herself:

"There—he's asleep, poor wreck. Tom Sawyer find it! Pity but somebody could find Tom Sawyer! Ah, there ain't many left, now, that's got hope enough, or strength enough, either, to go on searching."

31 *An Exploring Expedition—Trouble Commences—Lost in the Cave—Total Darkness—Found but Not Saved*

Now to return to Tom and Becky's share in the picnic. They tripped along the murky aisles with the rest of the company, visiting the familiar wonders of the cave—wonders dubbed with rather overdescriptive names, such as "The Drawing Room," "The Cathedral," "Aladdin's Palace," and so on. Presently the hide-and-seek frolicking began, and Tom and Becky engaged in it with zeal until the exertion began to grow a trifle wearisome; then they wandered down a sinuous avenue holding their candles aloft and reading the tangled webwork of names, dates, post-office addresses, and mottoes with which the rocky walls had been frescoed (in candle smoke). Still drifting along and talking, they scarcely noticed that they were now in a part of the cave whose walls were not frescoed. They smoked their own names under an overhanging shelf and moved on. Presently they came to a place where a little stream of water, trickling over a ledge and carrying a limestone sediment with it, had, in the slow-dragging ages, formed a laced and ruffled Niagara in gleaming and imperishable stone. Tom squeezed his small body behind it in order to illuminate it for Becky's gratification. He found that it curtained a sort of steep natural stairway which was enclosed between narrow walls, and at once the ambition to be a discoverer seized him. Becky responded to his call, and they made a smoke mark for future guidance, and started upon their quest. They wound this way and that, far down into the secret depths of the cave, made another mark, and branched off in search of novelties to tell the upper world about. In one place they found a spacious cavern, from whose ceiling depended a multitude of shining stalactites of the length and circumference of a man's leg; they walked all about it, wondering and admiring, and presently left it by one of the numerous passages that opened into it. This shortly brought them to a bewitching spring, whose basin was encrusted with a frostwork of glittering crystals; it was in the midst of a cavern whose walls were supported by many fantastic pillars which had been formed by the joining of great stalactites and stalagmites together, the result of the ceaseless water-drip of centuries. Under the roof vast knots of bats had packed themselves together, thousands in a bunch; the lights disturbed the creatures and they came flocking down by hundreds, squeaking and darting furiously at the candles. Tom knew their ways and the danger of this sort of conduct. He seized Becky's hand and hurried her into the first corridor that offered: and none too soon, for a bat struck Becky's light out with its wing while she was passing out of the cavern. The bats chased the children a good distance; but the fugitives plunged into every new passage that offered, and at last got rid of the perilous things. Tom found a subterranean lake, shortly, which stretched its dim length away until its shape was lost in the shadows. He wanted to explore its borders, but concluded that it would be best to sit down and rest a while, first. Now, for the first time, the deep stillness of the place laid a clammy hand upon the spirits of the children. Becky said:

"Why, I didn't notice, but it seems ever so long since I heard any of the others."

"Come to think, Becky, we are away down below them—and I don't know how far away north, or south, or east, or whichever it is. We couldn't hear them here."

Becky grew apprehensive.

"I wonder how long we've been down here, Tom. We better start back."

"Yes, I reckon we better. P'raps we better."

"Can you find the way, Tom? It's all a mixed-up crookedness to me."

"I reckon I could find it—but then the bats. If they put both our candles out it will be an awful fix. Let's try some other way, so as not to go through there."

"Well. But I hope we won't get lost. It would be so awful!" and the girl shuddered at the thought of the dreadful possibilities.

They started through a corridor, and traversed it in silence a long way, glancing at each new opening, to see if there was anything familiar about the look of it; but they were all strange. Every time Tom made an examination, Becky would watch his face for an enocuraging sign, and he would say cheerily:

"Oh, it's all right. This ain't the one, but we'll come to it right away!"

But he felt less and less hopeful with each failure, and presently began to turn off into diverging avenues at sheer random, in desperate hope of finding the one that was wanted. He still said it was "all right," but there was such a leaden dread at his heart, that the words had lost their ring and sounded just as if he had said, "All is lost!" Becky clung to his side in an anguish of fear, and tried hard to keep back the tears, but they would come. At last she said:

"Oh, Tom, never mind the bats, let's go back that way! We seem to get worse and worse off all the time."

Tom stopped.

"Listen!" said he.

Profound silence; silence so deep that even their breathings were conspicuous in the hush. Tom shouted. The call went echoing down the empty aisles and died out in the distance in a faint sound that resembled a ripple of mocking laughter.

"Oh, don't do it again, Tom, it is too horrid," said Becky.

"It is horrid, but I better, Becky; they *might* hear us, you know," and he shouted again.

The "might" was even a chillier horror than the ghostly laughter, it so confessed a perishing hope. The children stood still and listened; but there was no result. Tom turned upon the back track at once, and hurried his steps. It was but a little while before a certain indecision in his manner revealed another fearful fact to Becky—he could not find his way back!

"Oh, Tom, you didn't make any marks!"

"Becky, I was such a fool! Such a fool! I never thought we might want to come back! No—I can't find the way. It's all mixed up."

"Tom, Tom, we're lost! we're lost! We never can get out of this awful place! Oh, why *did* we ever leave the others!"

She sank to the ground and burst into such a frenzy of crying that Tom was appalled with the idea that she might die, or lose her reason. He sat down by her and put his arms around her; she buried her face in his bosom, she clung to him, she poured out her terrors, her unavailing regrets, and the far echoes turned them all to jeering laughter. Tom begged her to pluck up hope again, and she said she could not. He fell to blaming and abusing himself for getting her into this miserable situation; this had a better effect. She said she would try to hope again, she would get up and follow wherever he might lead if only he would not talk like that any more. For he was no more to blame than she, she said.

So they moved on, again—aimlessly—simply at random—all they could do was to move, keep moving. For a little while, hope made a show of reviving—not with any reason to back it, but only because it is its nature to revive when the spring has not been taken out of it by age and familiarity with failure.

By and by Tom took Becky's candle and blew it out. This economy meant so much! Words were not needed. Becky understood, and her hope died again. She knew that Tom had a whole candle and three or four pieces in his pockets—yet he must economize.

By and by, fatigue began to assert its claims; the children tried to pay no attention, for it was dreadful to think of sitting down when time was grown to be so precious; moving, in some direction, in any direction, was at least progress and might bear fruit; but to sit down was to invite death and shorten its pursuit.

At last Becky's frail limbs refused to carry her farther. She sat down. Tom rested with her, and they talked of home, and the friends there, and the comfortable beds and, above all, the light! Becky cried, and Tom tried to think of some way of comforting her, but all his encouragements were grown threadbare with use, and sounded like sarcasms. Fatigue bore so heavily upon Becky that she drowsed off to sleep. Tom was grateful. He sat looking into her drawn face and saw it grow smooth and natural under the influence of pleasant dreams; and by and by a smile dawned and rested there. The peaceful face reflected somewhat of peace and healing into his own spirit, and his thoughts wandered away to bygone times and dreamy memories. While he was deep in his musings, Becky woke up with a breezy little laugh—but it was stricken dead upon her lips, and a groan followed it.

"Oh, how *could* I sleep! I wish I never, never had waked! No! No, I don't, Tom! Don't look so! I won't say it again."

"I'm glad you've slept, Becky; you'll feel rested, now, and we'll find the way out."

"We can try, Tom; but I've seen such a beautiful country in my dream. I reckon we are going there."

"Maybe not, maybe not. Cheer up, Becky, and let's go on trying."

They rose up and wandered along, hand in hand and hopeless. They tried to estimate how long they had been in the cave, but all they knew was that it seemed days and weeks, and yet it was plain that this could not be, for their candles were not gone yet. A long time after this—they could not tell how long—Tom said they must go softly and listen for dripping water—they must find a spring. They found one presently, and Tom said it was time to rest again. Both were cruelly tired, yet Becky said she thought she could go on a little farther. She was surprised to hear Tom dissent. She could not understand it. They sat down, and Tom fastened his candle to the wall in front of them with some clay. Thought was soon busy; nothing was said for some time. Then Becky broke the silence:

"Tom, I am so hungry!"

Tom took something out of his pocket.

"Do you remember this?" said he.

Becky almost smiled.

"It's our wedding cake, Tom."

"Yes—I wish it was as big as a barrel, for it's all we've got."

"I saved it from the picnic for us to dream on, Tom, the way grown-up people do with wedding cake—but it'll be our——"

She dropped the sentence where it was. Tom divided the cake and Becky ate with good appetite, while Tom nibbled at his moiety. There was abundance of cold water to finish the feast with. By and by Becky suggested that they move on again. Tom was silent a moment. Then he said:

"Becky, can you bear it if I tell you something?"

Becky's face paled, but she thought she could.

"Well, then, Becky, we must stay here, where there's water to drink. That little piece is our last candle!"

Becky gave loose to tears and wailings. Tom did what he could to comfort her, but with little effect. At length Becky said:

"Tom!"

"Well, Becky?"

"They'll miss us and hunt for us!"

"Yes, they will! Certainly they will!"

"Maybe they're hunting for us now, Tom."

"Why, I reckon maybe they are. I hope they are."

"When would they miss us, Tom?"

"When they get back to the boat, I reckon."

"Tom, it might be dark then—would they notice we hadn't come?"

"I don't know. But anyway, your mother would miss you as soon as they got home."

A frightened look in Becky's face brought Tom to his senses and he saw that he had made a blunder. Becky was not to have gone home that night! The children became silent and thoughtful. In a moment a new burst of grief from Becky showed Tom that the thing in his mind had struck hers also—that the Sabbath morning might be half spent before Mrs. Thatcher discovered that Becky was not at Mrs. Harper's.

The children fastened their eyes upon their bit of candle and watched it melt slowly and pitilessly away; saw the half inch of wick stand alone at last; saw the feeble flame rise and fall, climb the thin column of smoke, linger at its top a moment, and then—the horror of utter darkness reigned.

How long afterward it was that Becky came to a slow consciousness that she was crying in Tom's arms, neither could tell. All that they knew was, that after what seemed a mighty stretch of time, both awoke out of a dead stupor of sleep and resumed their miseries once more. Tom said it might be Sunday, now—maybe Monday. He tried to get Becky to talk, but her sorrows were too oppressive, all her hopes were gone. Tom said that they must have been missed long ago, and no doubt the search was going on. He would shout and maybe someone would come. He tried it; but in the darkness the distant echoes sounded so hideously that he tried it no more.

The hours wasted away, and hunger came to torment the captives again. A portion of Tom's half of the cake was left; they divided and ate it. But they seemed hungrier than before. The poor morsel of food only whetted desire.

By and by Tom said:

"*Sh!* Did you hear that?"

Both held their breath and listened. There was a sound like the faintest, far-off shout. Instantly Tom answered it, and leading Becky by the hand, started groping down the corridor in its direction. Presently he listened again; again the sound was heard, and apparently a little nearer.

"It's them!" said Tom; "they're coming! Come along, Becky—we're all right now!"

The joy of the prisoners was almost overwhelming. Their speed was slow, however, because pitfalls were somewhat common, and had to be guarded against. They shortly came to one and had to stop. It might be three feet deep, it might be a hundred—there was no passing it at any rate. Tom got down on his breast and reached as far down as he could. No bottom. They must stay there and wait until the searchers came. They listened; evidently the distant shoutings were growing more distant! a moment or two more and they had gone altogether. The heart-sinking misery of it! Tom whooped until he was hoarse, but it was of no use. He talked hopefully to Becky; but an age of anxious waiting passed and no sounds came again.

The children groped their way back to the spring. The weary time dragged on; they slept again, and awoke famished and woe-stricken. Tom believed it must be Tuesday by this time.

Now an idea struck him. There were some side passages near at hand. It would be better to explore some of these than bear the weight of the heavy time in idleness. He took a kite line from his pocket, tied it to a projection, and he and Becky started, Tom in the lead, unwinding the line as he groped along. At the end of twenty steps the corridor ended in a "jumping-off place." Tom got down on his knees and felt below, and then as far around the corner as he could reach with his hands conveniently; he made an effort to stretch yet a little further to the right, and at that moment, not twenty yards away, a human hand, holding a candle, appeared from behind a rock! Tom lifted up a glorious shout, and instantly that hand was followed by the body it belonged to—Injun Joe's! Tom was paralyzed; he could not move. He was vastly gratified the next moment, to see the "Spaniard" take to his heels and get himself out of sight.

Tom wondered that Joe had not recognized his voice and come over and killed him for testifying in court. But the echoes must have disguised the voice. Without doubt, that was it, he reasoned. Tom's fright weakened every muscle in his body. He said to himself that if he had strength enough to get back to the spring he would stay there, and nothing should tempt him to run the risk of meeting Injun Joe again. He was careful to keep from Becky what it was he had seen. He told her he had only shouted "for luck."

But hunger and wretchedness rise superior to fears in the long run. Another tedious wait at the spring and another long sleep brought changes. The children awoke tortured with a raging hunger. Tom believed that it must be Wednesday or Thursday or even Friday or Saturday, now, and that the search had been given over. He proposed to explore another passage. He felt willing to risk Injun Joe and all other terrors. But Becky was very weak. She had sunk into a dreary apathy and would not be roused. She said she would wait, now, where she was, and die—it would not be long. She told Tom to go with the kite line and explore if he chose; but she implored him to come back every little while and speak to her; and she made him promise that when the awful time came, he would stay by her and hold her hand until all was over.

Tom kissed her, with a choking sensation in his throat, and made a show of being confident of finding the searchers or an escape from the cave; then he took the kite line in his hand and went groping down one of the passages on his hands and knees, distressed with hunger and sick with bodings of coming doom.

32 *Tom Tells the Story of Their Escape—Tom's Enemy in Safe Quarters*

Tuesday afternoon came, and waned to the twilight. The village of St. Petersburg still mourned. The lost children had not been found. Public prayers had been offered up for them, and many and many a private prayer that had the petitioner's whole heart in it; but still no good news came from the cave. The majority of the searchers had given up the quest and gone back to their daily avocations, saying that it was plain the children could never be found. Mrs. Thatcher was very ill, and a great part of the time delirious. People said it was heartbreaking to hear her call her child, and raise her head and listen a whole minute at a time, then lay it wearily down again with a moan. Aunt Polly had drooped into a settled melancholy, and her gray hair had grown almost white. The village went to its rest on Tuesday night, sad and forlorn.

Away in the middle of the night a wild peal burst from the village bells, and in a moment the streets were swarming with frantic half-clad people, who shouted, "Turn out! turn out! they're found! they're found!" Tin pans and horns were added to the din, the population massed itself and moved toward the river, met the children coming in an open carriage drawn by shouting citizens, thronged around it, joined its homeward march, and swept magnificently up the main street roaring huzzah after huzzah!

The village was illuminated; nobody went to bed again; it was the greatest night the little town had ever seen. During the first half hour a procession of villagers filed through Judge Thatcher's house, seized the saved ones and kissed them, squeezed Mrs. Thatcher's hand, tried to speak but couldn't—and drifted out raining tears all over the place.

Aunt Polly's happiness was complete, and Mrs. Thatcher's nearly so. It would be complete, however, as soon as the messenger dispatched with the great news to the cave should get the word to her husband. Tom lay upon a sofa with an eager auditory about him and told the history of the wonderful adventure, putting in many striking additions to adorn it withal; and closed with a description of how he left Becky and went on an exploring expedition; how he followed two avenues as far as his kite line would reach; how he followed a third to the fullest stretch of the kite line, and was about to turn back when he glimpsed a far-off speck that looked like daylight; dropped the line and groped toward it, pushed his head and shoulders through a small hole and saw the broad Mississippi rolling by! And if it had only happened to be night he would not have seen that speck of daylight and would not have explored that passage any more! He told how he went back for Becky and broke the good news and she told him not to fret her with such stuff, for she was tired, and knew she was going to die, and wanted to. He described how he labored with her and convinced her; and how she almost died for joy when she had groped to where she actually saw the blue speck of daylight; how he pushed his way out at the hole and then helped her out; how they sat there and cried for gladness; how some men came along in a skiff and Tom hailed them and told them their situation and their famished condition; how the men didn't believe the wild tale at first, "because," said they, "you are five miles down the river below the valley the cave is in"—then took them aboard, rowed to a house, gave them supper, made them rest till two or three hours after dark and then brought them home.

Before day dawn, Judge Thatcher and the handful of searchers with him were tracked out, in the cave, by the twine clews they had strung behind them, and informed of the great news.

Three days and nights of toil and hunger in the cave were not to be shaken off at once, as Tom and Becky soon discovered. They were bedridden all of Wednesday and Thursday, and seemed to grow more and more tired and worn, all the time. Tom got about, a little, on Thursday, was downtown Friday, and nearly as whole as ever Saturday; but Becky did not leave her room until Sunday, and then she looked as if she had passed through a wasting illness.

Tom learned of Huck's sickness and went to see him on Friday, but could not be admitted to the bedroom; neither could he on Saturday or Sunday. He was admitted daily after that, but was warned to keep still about his adventure and introduce no exciting topic. The Widow Douglas stayed by to see that he obeyed. At home Tom learned of the Cardiff Hill event; also that the "ragged man's" body had eventually been found in the river near the ferry landing; he had been drowned while trying to escape, perhaps.

About a fortnight after Tom's rescue from the cave, he started off to visit Huck, who had grown plenty strong enough, now, to hear exciting talk, and Tom had some that would interest him, he thought. Judge Thatcher's house was on Tom's way, and he stopped to see Becky. The Judge and some friends set Tom to talking, and someone asked him ironically if he wouldn't like to go to the cave again. Tom said he thought he wouldn't mind it. The Judge said:

"Well, there are others just like you, Tom, I've not the least doubt. But we have taken care of that. Nobody will get lost in that cave any more."

"Why?"

"Because I had its big door sheathed with boiler iron two weeks ago, and triple-locked—and I've got the keys."

Tom turned as white as a sheet.

"What's the matter, boy! Here, run, somebody! Fetch a glass of water!"

The water was brought and thrown into Tom's face.

"Ah, now you're all right. What was the matter with you, Tom?"

"Oh, Judge, Injun Joe's in the cave!"

33 *The Fate of Injun Joe—Huck and Tom Compare Notes—An Expedition to the Cave—Protection Against Ghosts—"An Awful Snug Place"—A Reception at Widow Douglas'*

Within a few minutes the news had spread, and a dozen skiff-loads of men were on their way to McDougal's cave, and the ferryboat, well filled with passengers, soon followed. Tom Sawyer was in the skiff that bore Judge Thatcher.

When the cave door was unlocked, a sorrowful sight presented itself in the dim twilight of the place. Injun Joe lay stretched upon the ground, dead, with his face close to the crack of the door, as if his longing eyes had been fixed, to the latest moment, upon the light and the cheer of the free world outside. Tom was touched, for he knew by his own experience how this wretch had suffered. His pity was moved, but nevertheless he felt an abounding sense of relief and security, now, which revealed to him in a degree which he had not fully appreciated before how vast a weight of dread had been lying upon him since the day he lifted his voice against this bloody-minded outcast.

Injun Joe's bowie knife lay close by, its blade broken in two. The great foundation beam of the door had been chipped and hacked through, with tedious labor; useless labor, too, it was, for the native rock formed a sill outside it, and upon that stubborn material the knife had wrought no effect; the only damage done was to the knife itself. But if there had been no stony obstruction there the labor would have been useless still, for if the beam had been wholly cut away Injun Joe could not have squeezed his body under the door, and he knew it. So he had only hacked that place in order to be doing something—in order to pass the weary time

—in order to employ his tortured faculties. Ordinarily one could find half a dozen bits of candle stuck around in the crevices of this vestibule, left there by tourists; but there were none now. The prisoner had searched them out and eaten them. He had also contrived to catch a few bats, and these, also, he had eaten, leaving only their claws. The poor unfortunate had starved to death. In one place near at hand, a stalagmite had been slowly growing up from the ground for ages, builded by the water-drip from a stalactite overhead. The captive had broken off the stalagmite, and upon the stump had placed a stone, wherein he had scooped a shallow hollow to catch the precious drop that fell once every three minutes with the dreary regularity of a clock tick—a dessert spoonful once in four and twenty hours. That drop was falling when the Pyramids were new; when Troy fell; when the foundations of Rome were laid; when Christ was crucified; when the Conqueror created the British empire; when Columbus sailed; when the massacre at Lexington was "news." It is falling now; it will still be falling when all these things shall have sunk down the afternoon of history, and the twilight of tradition, and been swallowed up in the thick night of oblivion. Has everything a purpose and a mission? Did this drop fall patiently during five thousand years to be ready for this flitting human insect's need? and has it another important object to accomplish ten thousand years to come? No matter. It is many and many a year since the hapless half-breed scooped out the stone to catch the priceless drops, but to this day the tourist stares longest at that pathetic stone and that slow-dropping water when he comes to see the wonders of McDougal's cave. Injun Joe's cup stands first in the list of the cavern's marvels; even "Aladdin's Palace" cannot rival it.

Injun Joe was buried near the mouth of the cave; and people flocked there in boats and wagons from the towns and from all the farms and hamlets for seven miles around; they brought their children, and all sorts of provisions, and confessed that they had had almost as satisfactory a time at the funeral as they could have had at the hanging.

This funeral stopped the further growth of one thing—the petition to the Governor for Injun Joe's pardon. The petition had been largely signed; many tearful and eloquent meetings had been held, and a committee of sappy women been appointed to go in deep mourning and wail around the governor, and implore him to be a merciful ass and trample his duty under foot. Injun Joe was believed to have killed five citizens of the village, but what of that? If he had been Satan himself there would have been plenty of weaklings ready to scribble their names to a pardon petition, and drip a tear on it from their permanently impaired and leaky waterworks.

The morning after the funeral Tom took Huck to a private place to have an important talk. Huck had learned all about Tom's adventure from the Welshman and the Widow Douglas, by this time, but Tom said he reckoned there was one thing they had not told him; that thing was what he wanted to talk about now. Huck's face saddened. He said:

"I know what it is. You got into No. 2 and never found anything but whisky. Nobody told me it was you; but I just knowed it must 'a' been you, soon as I heard 'bout that whisky business; and I knowed you hadn't got the money becuz you'd a got at me some way or other and told me even if you was mum to everybody else. Tom, something's always told me we'd never get holt of that swag."

"Why, Huck, *I* never told on that tavernkeeper. *You* know his tavern was all right the Saturday I went to the picnic. Don't you remember you was to watch there that night?"

"Oh, yes! Why, it seems 'bout a year ago. It was that very night that I follered Injun Joe to the widder's."

"*You* followed him?"

"Yes—but you keep mum. I reckon Injun Joe's left friends behind him, and I don't want 'em souring on me and doing me mean tricks. If it hadn't been for me he'd be down in Texas now, all right."

Then Huck told his entire adventure in confidence to

Tom, who had only heard of the Welshmen's part of it before.

"Well," said Huck, presently, coming back to the main question, "whoever nipped the whisky in No. 2, nipped the money, too, I reckon—anyways it's a goner for us, Tom."

"Huck, that money wasn't ever in No. 2!"

"What!" Huck searched his comrade's face keenly. "Tom, have you got on the track of that money again?"

"Huck, it's in the cave!"

Huck's eyes blazed.

"Say it again, Tom."

"The money's in the cave!"

"Tom—honest injun, now—is it fun, or earnest?"

"Earnest, Huck—just as earnest as ever I was in my life. Will you go in there with me and help get it out?"

"I bet I will! I will if it's where we can blaze our way to it and not get lost."

"Huck, we can do that without the least little bit of trouble in the world."

"Good as wheat! What makes you think the money's——"

"Huck, you just wait till we get in there. If we don't find it I'll agree to give you my drum and everything I've got in the world. I will, by jings."

"All right—it's a whiz. When do you say?"

"Right now, if you say it. Are you strong enough?"

"Is it far in the cave? I ben on my pins a little, three or four days, now, but I can't walk more'n a mile, Tom—least I don't think I could."

"It's about five mile into there the way anybody but me would go, Huck, but there's a mighty short cut that they don't anybody but me know about. Huck, I'll take you right to it in a skiff. I'll float the skiff down there, and I'll pull it back again all by myself. You needn't ever turn your hand over."

"Less start right off, Tom."

"All right. We want some bread and meat, and our pipes, and a little bag or two, and two or three kite strings, and some of these newfangled things they call lucifer matches. I tell you, many's the time I wished I had some when I was in there before."

A trifle after noon the boys borrowed a small skiff from a citizen who was absent, and got under way at once. When they were several miles below "Cave Hollow," Tom said:

"Now you see this bluff here looks all alike all the way down from the cave hollow—no houses, no woodyards, bushes all alike. But do you see that white place up yonder where there's been a landslide? Well, that's one of my marks. We'll get ashore, now."

They landed.

"Now, Huck, where we're a-standing you could touch that hole I got out of with a fishing pole. See if you can find it."

Huck searched all the place about, and found nothing. Tom proudly marched into a thick clump of sumac bushes and said:

"Here you are! Look at it, Huck; it's the snuggest hole in this country. You just keep mum about it. All along I've been wanting to be a robber, but I knew I'd got to have a thing like this, and where to run across it was the bother. We've got it now, and we'll keep it quiet, only we'll let Joe Harper and Ben Rogers in—because of course there's got to be a Gang, or else there wouldn't be any style about it. Tom Sawyer's Gang—it sounds splendid, don't it, Huck?"

"Well, it just does, Tom. And who'll we rob?"

"Oh, most anybody. Waylay people—that's mostly the way."

"And kill them?"

"No, not always. Hide them in the cave till they raise a ransom."

"What's a ransom?"

"Money. You make them raise all they can, off'n their friends; and after you've kept them a year, if it ain't raised then you kill them. That's the general way. Only you don't kill the women. You shut up the women, but you don't kill them. They're always beautiful and rich, and awfully scared. You take their watches and things, but you always take your hat off and talk polite. They ain't anybody as polite as robbers—you'll see that in any book. Well, the women get to loving you, and after they've been in the cave a week or two weeks they stop crying and after that you couldn't get them to leave. If you drove them out they'd turn right around and come back. It's so in all the books."

"Why, it's real bully, Tom. I b'lieve it's better'n to be a pirate."

"Yes, it's better in some ways, because it's close to home and circuses and all that."

By this time everything was ready and the boys entered the hole, Tom in the lead. They toiled their way to the farther end of the tunnel, then made their spliced kite strings fast and moved on. A few steps brought them to the spring, and Tom felt a shudder quiver all through him. He showed Huck the fragment of candlewick perched on a lump of clay against the wall, and described how he and Becky had watched the flame struggle and expire.

The boys began to quiet down to whispers, now, for the stillness and gloom of the place oppressed their spirits. They went on, and presently entered and followed Tom's other corridor until they reached the "jumping-off place." The candles revealed the fact that it was not really a precipice, but only a steep clay hill twenty or thirty feet high. Tom whispered:

"Now I'll show you something, Huck."

He held his candle aloft and said:

"Look as far around the corner as you can. Do you see that? There—on the big rock over yonder—done with candle smoke."

"Tom, it's a *cross!*"

"*Now* where's your Number Two? *'Under the cross,'* hey? Right yonder's where I saw Injun Joe poke up his candle, Huck!"

Huck stared at the mystic sign a while, and then said with a shaky voice:

"Tom, less git out of here!"

"What! and leave the treasure?"

"Yes—leave it. Injun Joe's ghost is round about there, certain."

"No it ain't, Huck, no it ain't. It would ha'nt the place where he died—away out at the mouth of the cave—five mile from here."

"No, Tom, it wouldn't. It would hang round the money. I know the ways of ghosts, and so do you."

Tom began to fear that Huck was right. Misgivings gathered in his mind. But presently an idea occurred to him—

"Looky-here, Huck, what fools we're making of ourselves! Injun Joe's ghost ain't a-going to come around where there's a cross!"

The point was well taken. It had its effect.

"Tom, I didn't think of that. But that's so. It's luck for us, that cross is. I reckon we'll climb down there and have a hunt for that box."

Tom went first, cutting rude steps in the clay hill as he descended. Huck followed. Four avenues opened out of the small cavern which the great rock stood in. The boys examined three of them with no result. They found a small recess in the one nearest the base of the rock, with a pallet of blankets spread down in it; also an old suspender, some bacon rind, and the well-gnawed bones of two or three fowls. But there was no money box. The lads searched and re-searched this place, but in vain. Tom said:

"He said *under* the cross. Well, this comes nearest to being under the cross. It can't be under the rock itself, because that sets solid on the ground."

They searched everywhere once more, and then sat down discouraged. Huck could suggest nothing. By and by Tom said:

"Looky-here, Huck, there's footprints and some candle grease on the clay about one side of this rock, but not on the other sides. Now, what's that for? I bet you the money *is* under the rock. I'm going to dig in the clay."

"That ain't no bad notion, Tom!" said Huck with animation.

Tom's "real Barlow" was out at once, and he had not dug four inches before he struck wood.

"Hey, Huck!—you hear that?"

Huck began to dig and scratch now. Some boards were soon uncovered and removed. They had concealed a natural chasm which led under the rock. Tom got into this and held his candle as far under the rock as he could, but said he could not see to the end of the rift. He proposed to explore. He stooped and passed under; the narrow way descended gradually. He followed its winding course, first to the right, then to the left, Huck at his heels. Tom turned a short curve, by and by, and exclaimed:

"My goodness, Huck, looky here!"

It was the treasure box, sure enough, occupying a snug little cavern, along with an empty powder keg, a couple of guns in leather cases, two or three pairs of old moccasins, a leather belt, and some other rubbish well soaked with water-drip.

"Got it at last!" said Huck, plowing among the tarnished coins with his hand. "My, but we're rich, Tom!"

"Huck, I always reckoned we'd get it. It's just too good to believe, but we *have* got it, sure! Say—let's not fool around here. Let's snake it out. Lemme see if I can lift the box."

It weighed about fifty pounds. Tom could lift it, after an awkward fashion, but could not carry it conveniently.

"I thought so," he said; "*they* carried it like it was heavy, that day at the ha'nted house. I noticed that. I reckon I was right to think of fetching the little bags along."

The money was soon in the bags and the boys took it up to the cross rock.

"Now less fetch the guns and things," said Huck.

"No, Huck—leave them there. They're just the tricks to have when we go to robbing. We'll keep them there all the time, and we'll hold our orgies there, too. It's an awful snug place for orgies."

"What's orgies?"

"*I* dono. But robbers always have orgies, and of course we've got to have them, too. Come along, Huck, we've been in here a long time. It's getting late, I reckon. I'm hungry, too. We'll eat and smoke when we get to the skiff."

They presently emerged into the clump of sumac bushes, looked warily out, found the coast clear, and were soon lunching and smoking in the skiff. As the sun dipped toward the horizon they pushed out and got under way. Tom skimmed up the shore through the long twilight, chatting cheerily with Huck, and landed shortly after dark.

"Now, Huck," said Tom, "we'll hide the money in the loft of the widow's woodshed, and I'll come up in the morning and we'll count it and divide, and then we'll hunt up a place out in the woods for it where it will be safe. Just you lay quiet here and watch the stuff till I run and hook Benny Taylor's little wagon; I won't be gone a minute."

He disappeared, and presently returned with the wagon, put the two small sacks into it, threw some old rags on top of them, and started off, dragging his cargo behind him. When the boys reached the Welshman's house, they stopped to rest. Just as they were about to move on, the Welshman stepped out and said:

"Hallo, who's that?"

"Huck and Tom Sawyer."

"Good! Come along with me, boys, you are keeping everybody waiting. Here—hurry up, trot ahead—I'll haul the wagon for you. Why, it's not as light as it might be. Got bricks in it?—or old metal?"

"Old metal," said Tom.

"I judged so; the boys in this town will take more trouble and fool away more time, hunting up six bits' worth of old iron to sell to the foundry than they would to make twice the money at regular work. But that's human nature —hurry along, hurry along!"

The boys wanted to know what the hurry was about.

"Never mind; you'll see, when we get to the Widow Douglas'."

Huck said with some apprehension—for he was long used to being falsely accused:

"Mr. Jones, *we* haven't been doing nothing."

The Welshman laughed.

"Well, I don't know, Huck, my boy. I don't know about that. Ain't you and the widow good friends?"

"Yes. Well, she's ben good friends to me, anyways."

"All right, then. What do you want to be afraid for?"

This question was not entirely answered in Huck's slow mind before he found himself pushed, along with Tom, into Mrs. Douglas' drawing room. Mr. Jones left the wagon near the door and followed.

The place was grandly lighted, and everybody that was of any consequence in the village was there. The Thatchers were there, the Harpers, the Rogerses, Aunt Polly, Sid, Mary, the minister, the editor, and a great many more, and all dressed in their best. The widow received the boys as heartily as anyone could well receive two such looking beings. They were covered with clay and candle grease. Aunt Polly blushed crimson with humiliation, and frowned and shook her head at Tom. Nobody suffered half as much as the two boys did, however. Mr. Jones said:

"Tom wasn't at home, yet, so I gave him up; but I stumbled on him and Huck right at my door, and so I just brought them along in a hurry."

"And you did just right," said the widow. "Come with me, boys."

She took them to a bedchamber and said:

"Now wash and dress yourselves. Here are two new suits of clothes—shirts, socks, everything complete. They're Huck's—no, no thanks, Huck—Mr. Jones bought one and I the other. But they'll fit both of you. Get into them. We'll wait—come down when you are slicked up enough."

Then she left.

34 *Springing a Secret—Mr Jones' Surprise a Failure*

Huck said: "Tom, we can slope, if we can find a rope. The window ain't high from the ground."

"Shucks, what do you want to slope for?"

"Well, I ain't used to that kind of a crowd. I can't stand it. I ain't going down there, Tom."

"Oh, bother! It ain't anything. I don't mind it a bit. I'll take care of you."

Sid appeared.

"Tom," said he, "Auntie has been waiting for you all the afternoon. Mary got your Sunday clothes ready, and everybody's been fretting about you. Say—ain't this grease and clay, on your clothes?"

"Now, Mr. Siddy, you jist 'tend to your own business. What's all this blowout about, anyway?"

"It's one of the widow's parties that she's always having. This time it's for the Welshman and his sons, on account of that scrape they helped her out of the other night. And say—I can tell you something, if you want to know."

"Well, what?"

"Why, old Mr. Jones is going to try to spring something on the people here tonight, but I overheard him tell auntie today about it, as a secret, but I reckon it's not much of a secret *now*. Everybody knows—the widow, too, for all she tries to let on she don't. Mr. Jones was bound Huck should be here—couldn't get along with his grand secret without Huck, you know!"

"Secret about what, Sid?"

"About Huck tracking the robbers to the widow's. I reckon Mr. Jones was going to make a grand time over his surprise, but I bet you it will drop pretty flat."

Sid chuckled in a very contented and satisfied way.

"Sid, was it you that told?"

"Oh, never mind who it was. *Somebody* told—that's enough."

"Sid, there's only one person in this town mean enough to do that, and that's you. If you had been in Huck's place you'd 'a' sneaked down the hill and never told anybody on the robbers. You can't do any but mean things, and you can't bear to see anybody praised for doing good ones. There—no thanks, as the widow says"—and Tom cuffed Sid's ears and helped him to the door with several kicks. "Now go and tell auntie if you dare—and tomorrow you'll catch it!"

Some minutes later the widow's guests were at the supper table, and a dozen children were propped up at little side tables in the same room, after the fashion of that country and that day. At the proper time Mr. Jones made his little speech, in which he thanked the widow for the honor she was doing himself and his sons, but said that there was another person whose modesty—

And so forth and so on. He sprung his secret about Huck's share in the adventure in the finest dramatic manner he was master of, but the surprise it occasioned was largely counterfeit and not as clamorous and effusive as it might have been under happier circumstances. However, the widow made a pretty fair show of astonishment, and heaped so many compliments and so much gratitude upon Huck that he almost forgot the nearly intolerable discomfort of his new clothes in the entirely intolerable discomfort of being set up as a target for everybody's gaze and everybody's laudations.

The widow said she meant to give Huck a home under her roof and have him educated; and that when she could spare the money she would start him in business in a modest way. Tom's chance was to come. He said:

"Huck don't need it. Huck's rich."

Nothing but a heavy strain upon the good manners of the company kept back the due and proper complimentary laugh at this pleasant joke. But the silence was a little awkward. Tom broke it:

"Huck's got money. Maybe you don't believe it, but he's gots lots of it. Oh, you needn't smile—I reckon I can show you. You just wait a minute."

Tom ran out of doors. The company looked at each other with a perplexed interest—and inquiringly at Huck, who was tongue-tied.

"Sid, what ails Tom?" said Aunt Polly. "He—well, there ain't ever any making of that boy out. I never——"

Tom entered, struggling with the weight of his sacks, and Aunt Polly did not finish her sentence. Tom poured the mass of yellow coin upon the table and said:

"There—what did I tell you? Half of it's Huck's and half of it's mine!"

The spectacle took the general breath away. All gazed, nobody spoke for a moment. Then there was a unanimous call for an explanation. Tom said he could furnish it, and he did. The tale was long, but brimful of interest. There was scarcely an interruption from anyone to break the charm of its flow. When he had finished, Mr. Jones said:

"I thought I had fixed up a little surprise for this occasion, but it don't amount to anything now. This one makes it sing mighty small, I'm willing to allow."

The money was counted. The sum amounted to a little over twelve thousand dollars. It was more than anyone present had ever seen at one time before, though several persons were there who were worth considerably more than that in property.

35 *A New Order of Things—Poor Huck—New Adventures Planned*

The reader may rest satisfied that Tom's and Huck's windfall made a mighty stir in the poor little village of St. Petersburg. So vast a sum, all in actual cash, seemed next to incredible. It was talked about, gloated over, glorified, until the reason of many of the citizens tottered under the strain of the unhealthy excitement. Every "haunted" house in St. Petersburg and the neighboring villages was dissected, plank by plank, and its foundations dug up and ransacked for hidden treasure—and not by boys, but men—pretty grave, unromantic men, too, some of them. Wherever Tom and Huck appeared they were courted, admired, stared at. The boys were not able to remember that their remarks had possessed weight before; but now their sayings were treasured and repeated; everything they did seemed somehow to be regarded as remarkable; they had evidently lost the power of doing and saying commonplace things; moreover, their past history was raked up and discovered to bear marks of conspicuous originality. The village paper published biographical sketches of the boys.

The Widow Douglas put Huck's money out at six per cent, and Judge Thatcher did the same with Tom's at Aunt Polly's request. Each lad had an income, now, that was simply prodigious—a dollar for every weekday in the year and half of the Sundays. It was just what the minister got—no, it was what he was promised—he generally couldn't collect it. A dollar and a quarter a week would board, lodge, and school a boy in those old simple days—and clothe him and wash him, too, for that matter.

Judge Thatcher had conceived a great opinion of Tom.

He said that no commonplace boy would ever have got his daughter out of the cave. When Becky told her father, in strict confidence, how Tom had taken her whipping at school, the Judge was visibly moved; and when she pleaded grace for the mighty lie which Tom had told in order to shift that whipping from her shoulders to his own, the Judge said with a fine outburst that it was a noble, a generous, a magnanimous lie—a lie that was worthy to hold up its head and march down through history breast to breast with George Washington's lauded Truth about the hatchet! Becky thought her father had never looked so tall and so superb as when he walked the floor and stamped his foot and said that. She went straight off and told Tom about it.

Judge Thatcher hoped to see Tom a great lawyer or a great soldier some day. He said he meant to look to it that Tom should be admitted to the National Military Academy and afterward trained in the best law school in the country, in order that he might be ready for either career or both.

Huck Finn's wealth and the fact that he was now under the Widow Douglas' protection introduced him into society —no, dragged him into it, hurled him into it—and his sufferings were almost more than he could bear. The widow's servants kept him clean and neat, combed and brushed, and they bedded him nightly in unsympathetic sheets that had not one little spot or stain which he could press to his heart and know for a friend. He had to eat with knife and fork; he had to use napkin, cup, and plate; he had to learn his book, he had to go to church; he had to talk so properly that speech was become insipid in his mouth; whithersoever he turned, the bars and shackles of civilization shut him in and bound him hand and foot.

He bravely bore his miseries three weeks, and then one day turned up missing. For forty-eight hours the widow hunted for him everywhere in great distress. The public were profoundly concerned; they searched high and low, they dragged the river for his body. Early the third morning Tom Sawyer wisely went poking among some old empty hogsheads down behind the abandoned slaughterhouse, and in one of them he found the refugee. Huck had slept there; he had just breakfasted upon some stolen odds and ends of food, and was lying off, now, in comfort, with his pipe. He was unkempt, uncombed, and clad in the same old ruin of rags that had made him picturesque in the days when he was free and happy. Tom routed him out, told him the trouble he had been causing, and urged him to go home. Huck's face lost its tranquil content, and took a melancholy cast. He said:

"Don't talk about it, Tom. I've tried it, and it don't work; it don't work, Tom. It ain't for me; I ain't used to it. The widder's good to me, and friendly; but I can't stand them ways. She makes me git up just at the same time every morning; she makes me wash, they comb me all to thunder; she won't let me sleep in the woodshed; I got to wear them blamed clothes that just smothers me, Tom; they don't seem to any air git through 'em, somehow; and they're so rotten nice that I can't set down, nor lay down, nor roll around anywhere's; I hain't slid on a cellar door for —well, it 'pears to be years; I got to go to church and sweat and sweat—I hate them ornery sermons! I can't ketch a fly in there, I can't chaw. I got to wear shoes all Sunday. The widder eats by a bell; she goes to bed by a bell; she gits up by a bell—everything's so awful reg'lar a body can't stand it."

"Well, everybody does that way, Huck."

"Tom, it don't make no difference. I ain't everybody, and I can't *stand* it. It's awful to be tied up so. And grub comes too easy—I don't take no interest in vittles, that way. I got to ask to go a-fishing; I got to ask to go in a-swimming— dern'd if I hain't got to ask to do everything. Well, I'd got to talk so nice it wasn't no comfort—I'd got to go up in the attic and rip out awhile, every day, to git a taste in my mouth, or I'd a died, Tom. The widder wouldn't let me smoke; she wouldn't let me yell, she wouldn't let me gape, nor stretch, nor scratch, before folks—" (Then with a spasm of special irritation and injury)—"And dad fetch it, she prayed all the time! I never *see* such a woman! I *had* to shove, Tom—I just had to. And besides, that school's going to open, and I'd a had to go to it—well, I wouldn't stand *that,* Tom. Looky-here, Tom, being rich ain't what it's cracked up to be. It's just worry and worry, and sweat and sweat, and a-wishing you was dead all the time. Now these clothes suits me, and this bar'l suits me, and I ain't ever going to shake 'em any more. Tom, I wouldn't ever got into all this trouble if it hadn't 'a' been for that money; now you just take my sheer of it along with your'n, and gimme a ten-center sometimes—not many times, becuz I don't give a dern for a thing 'thout it's tollable hard to git—and you go and beg off for me with the widder."

"Oh, Huck, you know I can't do that. 'Tain't fair; and besides if you'll try this thing just a while longer you'll come to like it."

"Like it! Yes—the way I'd like a hot stove if I was to set on it long enough. No, Tom, I won't be rich, and I won't live in them cussed smothery houses. I like the woods, and the river, and hogsheads, and I'll stick to 'em, too. Blame it all! just as we'd got guns, and a cave, and all just fixed to rob, here this dern foolishness has got to come up and spile it all!"

Tom saw his opportunity—

"Looky-here, Huck, being rich ain't going to keep me back from turning robber."

"No! Oh, good-licks, are you in real deadwood earnest, Tom?"

"Just as dead earnest as I'm a-sitting here. But Huck, we can't let you into the gang if you ain't respectable, you know."

Huck's joy was quenched.

"Can't let me in, Tom? Didn't you let me go for a pirate?"

"Yes, but that's different. A robber is more high-toned than what a pirate is—as a general thing. In most countries they're awful high up in the nobility—dukes and such."

"Now, Tom, hain't you always ben friendly to me? You

wouldn't shet me out, would you, Tom? You wouldn't do that, now, *would* you, Tom?"

"Huck, I wouldn't want to, and I *don't* want to—but what would people say? Why, they'd say, 'Mph! Tom Sawyer's Gang! pretty low characters in it!' They'd mean you, Huck. You wouldn't like that, and I wouldn't."

Huck was silent for some time, engaged in a mental struggle. Finally he said:

"Well, I'll go back to the widder for a month and tackle it and see if I can come to stand it, if you'll let me b'long to the gang, Tom."

"All right, Huck, it's a whiz! Come along, old chap, and I'll ask the widow to let up on you a little, Huck."

"Will you, Tom—now will you? That's good. If she'll let up on some of the roughest things, I'll smoke private and cuss private, and crowd through or bust. When you going to start the gang and turn robbers?"

"Oh, right off. We'll get the boys together and have the initiation tonight, maybe."

"Have the which?"

"Have the initiation."

"What's that?"

"It's to swear to stand by one another, and never tell the gang's secrets, even if you're chopped all to flinders, and kill anybody and all his family that hurts one of the gang."

"That's gay—that's mighty gay, Tom, I tell you."

"Well, I bet it is. And all that swearing's got to be done at midnight, in the lonesomest, awfulest place you can find—a ha'nted house is the best, but they're all ripped up now."

"Well, midnight's good, anyway, Tom."

"Yes, so it is. And you've got to swear on a coffin, and sign it with blood."

"Now, that's something *like!* Why, it's a million times bullier than pirating. I'll stick to the widder till I rot, Tom; and if I git to be a reg'lar ripper of a robber, and everybody talking 'bout it, I reckon she'll be proud she snaked me in out of the wet."

CONCLUSION

So endeth this chronicle. It being strictly a history of a *boy,* it must stop here; the story could not go much further without becoming the history of a *man.* When one writes a novel about grown people, he knows exactly where to stop—that is, with a marriage; but when he writes of juveniles, he must stop where he best can.

Most of the characters that perform in this book still live, and are prosperous and happy. Some day it may seem worth while to take up the story of the younger ones again and see what sort of men and women they turned out to be; therefore it will be wisest not to reveal any of that part of their lives at present.

6—76

OTHER AIRMONT CLASSICS

Complete and Unabridged with Introductions

CL60 A JOURNEY TO THE CENTER OF THE EARTH, *Verne*
CL61 THE AGE OF CHIVALRY, *Thomas Bulfinch*
CL62 THE HOUND OF THE BASKERVILLES, *Doyle*
CL63 THE MAYOR OF CASTERBRIDGE, *Thomas Hardy*
CL64 THE SEA WOLF, *Jack London*
CL65 DAVID COPPERFIELD, *Charles Dickens*
CL66 TWICE-TOLD TALES, *Nathaniel Hawthorne*
CL67 ROBIN HOOD
CL68 GREAT EXPECTATIONS, *Charles Dickens*
CL69 THE WIZARD OF OZ, *L. Frank Baum*
CL70 THE STORY OF MY LIFE, *Helen Keller*
CL71 THE AUTOBIOGRAPHY OF BENJAMIN FRANKLIN
CL72 DRACULA, *Bram Stoker*
CL73 MASTER OF THE WORLD, *Jules Verne*
CL74 BEN HUR, *Lew Wallace*
CL75 KIM, *Rudyard Kipling*
CL76 THE MOONSTONE, *William Wilkie Collins*
CL77 THE MYSTERIOUS ISLAND, *Jules Verne*
CL78 THE FIRST MEN IN THE MOON, *H. G. Wells*
CL79 ALICE'S ADVENTURES IN WONDERLAND, *L. Carroll*
CL80 THE AGE OF FABLE, *Thomas Bulfinch*
CL81 AESOP'S FABLES
CL82 TESS OF THE D'URBERVILLES, *Thomas Hardy*
CL83 WALDEN—ESSAY ON CIVIL DISOBEDIENCE, *Thoreau*
CL84 PÈRE GORIOT, *Honoré de Balzac*
CL85 TWO YEARS BEFORE THE MAST, *Charles Henry Dana*
CL86 THE JUNGLE, *Upton Sinclair*
CL87 GREEN MANSIONS, *W. H. Hudson*
CL88 THE MUTINY ON BOARD H.M.S. BOUNTY, *Wm. Bligh*
CL89 MADAME BOVARY, *Gustave Flaubert*
CL90 THE WAY OF ALL FLESH, *Samuel Butler*
CL91 LEAVES OF GRASS, *Walt Whitman*
CL92 MASTER SKYLARK, *John Bennett*
CL93 MEN OF IRON, *Howard Pyle*
CL94 EVANGELINE and other poems, *Henry W. Longfellow*
CL95 THE AMBASSADORS, *Henry James*
CL96 MAN AND SUPERMAN, *George Bernard Shaw*
CL97 THE ADVENTURES OF SHERLOCK HOLMES, *Doyle*
CL98 THE PORTRAIT OF A LADY, *Henry James*
CL99 HANS BRINKER; OR, THE SILVER SKATES, *Mary Mapes Dodge*
CL100 AT THE BACK OF THE NORTH WIND, *George Macdonald*
CL101 THE ADVENTURES OF PINOCCHIO, *Carlo Collodi*
CL102 EMMA, *Jane Austen*
CL103 ADAM BEDE, *George Eliot*
CL104 THE MARBLE FAUN, *Nathaniel Hawthorne*
CL105 THE WIND IN THE WILLOWS, *Kenneth Grahame*
CL106 LITTLE WOMEN, *Louisa May Alcott*
CL107 PERSUASION, *Jane Austen*
CL108 JUDE THE OBSCURE, *Thomas Hardy*
CL109 THE JUNGLE BOOKS, *Rudyard Kipling*
CL110 THE ISLAND OF DR. MOREAU, *H. G. Wells*
CL111 IN THE DAYS OF THE COMET, *H. G. Wells*
CL112 HEART OF DARKNESS and THE END OF THE TETHER, *Joseph Conrad*
CL113 AN OUTCAST OF THE ISLANDS, *Joseph Conrad*
CL114 THE MYSTERY OF EDWIN DROOD, *Charles Dickens*
CL115 THE ILLIAD, *Homer*
CL116 BILLY BUDD AND THE ENCANTADAS, *H. Melville*
CL117 CANDIDE AND ZADIG, *Voltaire*
CL118 A WONDER BOOK, *Nathaniel Hawthorne*
CL119 CAESAR AND CLEOPATRA, *George Bernard Shaw*